THE BLACK ELITE

SECOND EDITION

THE BLACK ELITE

SECOND EDITION

Still Facing the Color Line in the Twenty-First Century

Lois Benjamin

ROWMAN & LITTLEFIELD PUBLISHERS, INC.

Lanham • Boulder • New York • Toronto • Oxford

ROWMAN & LITTLEFIELD PUBLISHERS, INC.

Published in the United States of America
by Rowman & Littlefield Publishers, Inc.
A wholly owned subsidiary of The Rowman & Littlefield Publishing Group, Inc.
4501 Forbes Boulevard, Suite 200, Lanham, Maryland 20706
www.rowmanlittlefield.com

PO Box 317
Oxford
OX2 9RU, UK

British Library Cataloguing in Publication Information Available

Library of Congress Cataloging-in-Publication Data

Benjamin, Lois, 1944-
 The black elite : still facing the color line in the twenty-first century / Lois Benjamin.—
2nd ed.
    p. cm.
Includes bibliographical references and index.
 ISBN 10: 0-7425-4184-3 (cloth : alk. paper) —
 ISBN 13: 978-0-7425-4184-9
 ISBN 10: 0-7425-4185-1 (pbk. : alk. paper)
 ISBN 978-0-7425-4185-6
1. African Americans—Social conditions—1975- 2. African Americans—Race identity.
3. United States—Race relations. 4. Race awareness—United States. 5. Racism—United
States. 6. Elite (Social sciences)—United States. 7. African Americans—Interviews.
8. Successful people—United States—Interviews. I. Title. E185.86.B379 2005
 305.896'073'0090511—dc22

                                                              2005006197

Printed in the United States of America

∞ ™ The paper used in this publication meets the minimum requirements of American
National Standard for Information Sciences—Permanence of Paper
for Printed Library Materials, ANSI/NISO Z39.48-1992.

This book is dedicated to Frances H. Hawkins

CONTENTS

FOREWORD

The effect of racism on Afro Americans has been the subject of numerous writers, each of whom had a unique story to tell. However, in focusing primarily on the black underclass, each of these stories engages an age-old story and so threatens to diminish the complexity of the black experience. In this volume, Lois Benjamin adds her voice to those of others who have dared to offer a fresh perspective on the dynamics of black experiences by explicating the racial experiences of the Talented One Hundred.

In this original approach to the study of black professionals, the author challenges the widespread notion that the black elite, by virtue of their achievements, transcend the barriers of racism. She argues very forcefully that racism, as both an individualized and institutionalized phenomenon, permeates the lives of all Afro Americans, regardless of social strata. In identifying the subjects of her study, she has utilized the traditional objective measures of success. What sets her work apart, however, is that she analyzes the effects of the subjective components of racism on objective success.

As a departure from the usual sociological treatises on racism in America, Lois Benjamin's book is a major contribution to sociological scholarship. As a documentation of the individual experiences and the collective experience shared by the black elite, this work helps to complete the history of the Afro American experience in this country. As a delineation of successful strategies for coping with racial oppression, the book is a source of inspiration for all Afro Americans in our arduous journey toward self-realization, freedom, and equality in a racist society.

Finally, for those of us who, like Lois Benjamin's Rev. Ross, have found that our stories are too much to tell and that there is not enough time to tell them, through Lois Benjamin, the voices of the Talented One Hundred have told them for us. Lois Benjamin, bearer of the flame, keeper of the charge, has related these stories with extraordinary insight, exceptional intensity, and uncompromising clarity.

William R. Harvey, *President*
HAMPTON UNIVERSITY
HAMPTON, VIRGINIA

ACKNOWLEDGMENTS

First and foremost, I would like to express appreciation to the members of the Talented Thirty for their cooperation and participation as interviewees for this new edition. Since the present is a link to the past and future, this edition would not have been possible without the previous contributions of members of the Talented One Hundred and the input of all those who made it possible to produce the first edition of *The Black Elite: Facing the Color Line in the Twilight of the Twentieth Century*.

I would also like to thank the following people, who offered their support and assistance during this project: Bernice Fortson, Janet Adeyiga, JoAnn Obie, Debra White, and Adrienna Davis. I am indebted to Jeffery Fortson and Zina McGee for taking the time to read drafts of this manuscript. Their constructive and helpful comments improved the work. I thank Jeffery Fortson also for his assistance in identifying talented individuals for this edition. I owe a special debt of gratitude to John Sibley Butler and Delores P. Aldridge for their helpful suggestions for revising this manuscript.

I am especially indebted to Brooke Obie, my undergraduate research assistant, who went beyond the call of duty to lend her support to this project. She spent countless hours of her time and energy providing editing and typing services. Likewise, I am particularly thankful to Frances Hawkins for her assistance in transcribing the interviews and for her guidance and support for this work. She read several drafts of this manuscript and made valuable suggestions for reorganization. She was always critical, yet extremely supportive, and her ideas improved the manuscript. I consider our friendship invaluable.

Finally, I would like to thank my family members for their support and encouragement throughout this project.

PROLOGUE

Rudy's calm exterior did not mask the pain in his eyes when he spoke in disparagement, "Somebody ought to tell the story of what it is like for a black professional in this society." Earlier that week, Rudy, a highly respected therapist in the Tampa community, appeared as an expert witness in court to testify on the state of a client's mental health. The judge ignored him, dismissing his testimony. Rudy is black. The judge is white. His remarks struck a resonant chord, echoing my own experience as the only black professor in the history of the University of Tampa. As we parted from a luncheon engagement on that hot and hazy summer day of 1978 in Tampa, I wondered if there was a tale to tell of two black experiences.

In 1978, William Julius Wilson published *The Declining Significance of Race*, telling another tale. In the opening chapter of this award-winning book from the American Sociological Association, he claimed, "Race relations in America have undergone fundamental changes in recent years, so much so that now the life chances of individual Blacks have more to do with their economic class position than with their day-to-day encounters with Whites."

A plethora of academic studies seemed to support Wilson's claim, telling the tale of the objective successes and strides of the black elite. There has been a dearth of studies, however, telling the tale of the subjective aspect of their successes. One tale was of the objective economic and educational gains made by blacks; but there was another tale pleading, like Rudy's, for a listening post and asking questions like, What does it mean to be a marginal black elite poised between two social worlds of class and race? What psychological roadblocks do blacks have to overcome to "make it" in this society? What are

the sociopsychological costs of mainstreaming for successful blacks? Are
there achievement-related stresses that are caused by the marginality of
blacks in society, and if so, how do they manifest themselves? What are the
mechanisms adopted by marginals in handling stress? How do styles of adaptation shape values, attitudes, and behaviors toward personal, class, and racial
identity? Do high-achieving blacks experience race relations differently from
those from the working class or the poor? How do high-achieving blacks cope
with racism?[1]

Rudy's comment sparked questions about the subjective component of
blacks' success, adding a racial dimension to my own evolving interest in objective success. The pain in his eyes was indelibly etched in my consciousness,
leaving no doubt that there was another tale to tell. I promised myself that day
in 1978 that I would tell the collective Rudys' story of "what it is like for a black
professional in this society."

It seems a perpetual interest of mine to understand why some individuals
overcame economic and psychological barriers to achieve objective success and
others did not. The seed of this intellectual odyssey had been sown many seasons ago; however, the racial dimension was not primary. My late friend and
colleague Josie King remembered the idea fermenting during the early spring
of my graduate days at the University of California, Berkeley, in the late sixties.
Another colleague and friend, Elizabeth Morgan, saw some seeds sprouting in
my dissertation's chapter "Isolation and the Professional Black Woman" and
concluded it was unfinished.

By 1980, race emerged as an important subjective variable in understanding
the success of the black elite. My own visceral and wrenching encounter with
racism at the University of Tampa validated this interest. I wanted to tell the story
of black achievers in higher education. I shared my interest with James B. Stewart, a colleague and friend, whom I met in 1981. We considered a collaborative
effort, and we scattered a few seminal grains; however, they never germinated.

During the holiday season of 1984–1985 while I was visiting my family in Atlanta, the course of my long mental journey changed. I was connecting with
friends to extend greetings, and I wanted particularly to greet an old college
chum's mother and to inquire about Sheba (a pseudonym). During our undergraduate days at Clark College, Sheba and I spent many hours searching for answers to life's complex questions in the philosophies of Martin Buber, Albert
Camus, Martin Heidegger, Søren Kierkegaard, Plato, Bertrand Russell, and
Jean-Paul Sartre, and in the writings of James Baldwin, W. E. B. Du Bois, Malcolm X, Betty Friedan, and Simone de Beauvoir. We were pioneer feminists.
We were freethinkers, the gadflies of the campus. Sheba was more radical than
I was in her philosophical search. She explored the Eastern philosophy of Zen
Buddhism, hoping one day to reach Nirvana, a peaceful state of existence. I,
sticking more with the collective consciousness of the day, read Emile
Durkheim, the father of scientific sociology.

We "floated" on ideas, as we often said. But we dreamed also about academic success and "making it" in this society. We wanted to get our PhDs by twenty-five and write books. Though Sheba and I dreamed about success, she frequently expressed a haunting and lurking fear that she would return as a catatonic schizophrenic to the then neatly kept housing project near campus in which she had grown up. I brushed off her fear as another one of Sheba's numerous anxiety antics. I knew Sheba would be the brighter star.

After college, Sheba went to graduate school in Canada, feeling race relations there would be more tolerable. I chose Berkeley. We kept in touch frequently by long letters and occasional visits. She liked Canada during her first year. But she did not fare as well during her second year in the PhD program in experimental psychology. Sheba reported racial incidents, and she grew angrier and more bitter in each letter. Finally, she flunked out of graduate school, blaming her white professors for her failure. She left Canada and entered another PhD program in the same field at a university in the Northeast. Interestingly, she had chosen experimental psychology over developmental psychology; Sheba thought that dealing with rats rather than humans would lessen her encounters with racism. She was singing in harmony with her new university, the professors regarding Sheba as a promising student. But soon her happy harmony with the university was disrupted. When a professor discovered she had been a PhD candidate at another university, Sheba was dismissed from the program. She had misinformed the university about her previous studies in Canada. She returned to Canada, an embittered young woman, singing a sad refrain. In a final letter before leaving North America, she wrote, "Another racial blow I've suffered. I am so paranoid of whites, I can't bear to see their frozen faces." The soil of North America had produced another bitter fruit. She married and left for Nigeria, hoping that the Motherland would extend an embracing arm and offer protection from racial strife in her womb. Eventually, she obtained a PhD in experimental psychology at a university in England, returning to Nigeria as a college professor.

Although our friendship grew more distant over the years, occasionally I contacted Sheba's mother while in Atlanta. One joyous Christmas Eve, I dialed her phone and a distant, abrupt, and barely audible voice answered. I asked to speak with Mrs. Martha, Sheba's mother. The stranger mumbled, "She's not here." There was a slight hint of familiarity in the voice. "Is this Sheba?" I asked. "No, no." The phone clicked, a song of silence. I was baffled. Later that evening, I called again. Mrs. Martha answered the phone. I reported the strange scenario. She said Sheba had suffered a mental breakdown in Africa and had returned to the United States four months earlier. She asked if I could come by to see them. I agreed.

With my sister Pat, I approached Mrs. Martha's apartment, recalling fond memories of the daily lunchtime debates and discussions Sheba and I had there. I remembered the neatly painted housing project of the sixties with its well-manicured lawns and flowers lacing the borders. They had disappeared, replaced now by debris and barren earth, as if swarms of locusts had descended upon the green. I wanted to avoid becoming mired in this murky Georgia clay. We entered the small apartment.

My visit with Mrs. Martha was warm. I was unable, however, to connect with Sheba. How prophetic her fear! She sat in a catatonic stupor on a well-worn sofa. Her eyes were glazed. Where had the gleam in her eyes gone? Was this the Nirvana she sought? Other times, Sheba would pace the floor and mumble incoherently. Between snatches in our conversation, Mrs. Martha would shake her head. When our eyes met, hers pleaded for my help. I looked away, feeling helpless at seeing this brilliant mind lying wasted in a barren housing project, wondering if it was here many seasons ago, when the earth was green and fertile, that the seeds of my long intellectual odyssey were sown.

Pat and I left, driving in silence against the backdrop of "Silent Night," the Christmas carol playing softly on the radio. I went to bed knowing, "There, but for the grace of God, go I."

I paused mentally in my long journey to ponder this milestone and to search for my next guidepost. It read, "Let Sheba be the motivation and charge for your mission to tell the story. Learn the lessons of how the marginal black elite have succeeded in the face of racial adversities and have continued to move forward—keeping their eyes on the prize and remaining active keepers and fanners of the flame. Each generation must be flame keepers of these race lessons and stories, passing on the flaming torch."

I was still musing over this mysterious guidepost when my eyes caught a glimpse of another signpost by the roadside marked "DO NOT ENTER! Dangerous Cliff." Had Sheba not heeded the warning sign? She had skated on the cliff of marginality all her life across the three social worlds of class, race, and culture and across the three continents of North America, Europe, and Africa. But she had always "kept her eyes on the prize," remaining the dreamer.

What, then, betrayed the dream and the dreamer? I searched for the key to this mystery. Was it the lack of a supportive bridge? There were long years of separation from family, friends, and culture. Had not Mother Africa nurtured her by extending her arms across the waters, forming the bridge? Was it the bitter fruit produced from the racial soil of North America to which she had finally succumbed? Was it the scars from her childhood that took her beyond the cliff? She was born "out of wedlock" and had grown up in a housing project in Atlanta with her mother, a hardworking domestic. Sheba had been a brilliant young woman with a gleam in her eyes. She was dark-skinned with naturally curly, short hair. Her coming of age in America was before "Black is beautiful," a time when she was devalued by the black community as well as by herself.

Finally, I asked, was it her lack of faith in a higher being? Sheba and I had challenged and overthrown, while at Clark College, our old childhood God of Abraham, Isaac, and Jacob, both claiming we would never set foot in a church again. Though we challenged the form of God and religion, could she not have been comforted by the content and substance that nourished her during childhood and our forebears during slavery and "freedom"?

I had balanced on the edge of the cliff many times. But I hypocritically drew strength from the very genre and source I rejected. If I felt isolation in the belly of the whale, I sang the old spirituals of my mother as she prepared the daily bread—"Through many dangers, toils, and snares, I have already come. 'Tis grace that brought me safe thus far and grace will lead me home," and "A charge to keep I have." It was my way of escaping the whale. I also played church. I preached my father's sermons and the sermons of other ministers whom I had heard each Sunday, as a child, to my closest friends.

I was particularly fond of making mockery of one of Rev. E. A. Ross's sermons, "I Got a Story to Tell," that I heard when I would occasionally steal away to Antioch Baptist, a little brick, steepled church nestled deep in the wooded clay mines of Dry Branch, Georgia. I was inspired by the stories he told during his sermon and the warm communalism of the annual homecomings. But on that August homecoming in 1978, Rev. Ross was unable to tell his story. The words did not flow from his lips. They seemed choked in his throat. He would punctuate his chokes with a repeated clear calling refrain, "I got a story to tell." For many years, I jokingly laughed at this sermon, not understanding what he was trying to tell that August of 1978. It took me nearly a decade to get the message. Yet, the members heard his choked voice and understood his story—the choir, the deacon board, the deaconess board, the missionary board, the trustee board, the usher board, and the congregation. They responded resoundingly, "Preach on." "Preach, Reverend Ross." "Tell the story." They sang and shouted.

When the unfinished story stopped, and the singing and shouting ceased, Mama Mattie Calhoun and the womenfolk spread the tables near the ancestral burial ground with food taken from their brown cardboard boxes. Perhaps they were symbolically offering their greens, fried chicken, biscuits, potato salad, potato pies, and cakes to their ancestors, knowing it was their nourishment that had sustained them through the vicissitudes of life. For me, this homecoming was as distant as the miles from the more austere A.M.E. church in Atlanta. Yet, it was the spiritual bridge that carried me across until the next homecoming.

Had Sheba not heard the voices of black women, who were ripped from the soil of the Motherland and who had borne the racial crudities in America, rising from the ancestral burial ground? Had she not heard their voices singing, "Nobody Knows the Troubles I've Seen" and "Sometimes I Feel Like a Motherless Child a Long Way from Home" and rocked her weary soul in the "bosom of Abraham"?

I took a final look at the signpost. In my anger and quiet desperation, I turned to the lore of the Motherland of Africa, asking, "Did some African fetish god cast a spell over Sheba?" There was no answer, only the warning, DO NOT ENTER! Dangerous Cliff. I turned to the flashing message of the guidepost, "You have a charge to keep."

I have kept the charge to learn the lessons of how the black elite have succeeded in the face of racial adversities and why others, like Sheba, have not.

Though Sheba's family background and psychological constitution might also
have been underlying factors that contributed to her emotional collapse, it appears that her preoccupation with racial oppression and her lack of coping skills
pushed her over the cliff. With Sheba as the motivating catalyst for telling the
stories of the black elite, I traversed this country for two and one-half years, not
only spending many hours being a listening post for the stories of the psychic
pain of the Talented One Hundred, but also hearing the stories of how they
have coped creatively with the duality of their blackness.

This mission produced a rich harvest of stories from the best of the brightest
in the race; from the best of the brightest in the nation; and from the best of
the brightest in the world. I had promised to tell the collective Rudys' story that
summer of 1978 in Tampa. A decade later, in the simmering summer of 1988,
and nearly a thousand miles from Tampa, I kept my promise. No grant or farm
subsidy helped produce and support this mission crop, only the sustaining of
the guidepost's charge and the richness of the harvest.

Ten summer seasons have also passed since that August homecoming in 1978
in Dry Branch, Georgia, when Rev. Ross preached "I Got a Story to Tell." I finally heard his story. Now that I have grown a bit wiser with life's seasons, I understand that there was too much to tell and not enough time to tell it. There
were many people who wanted to tell their stories, too, for this study, but there
is not enough time to tell them. If somehow I missed your story, perhaps you
will hear it from the collective voices of the Talented One Hundred and the Talented Thirty.[2]

At the dawn of the twentieth century, W. E. B. Du Bois declared, "The problem of the twentieth century is the problem of the color-line." Clearly, race still
matters in the twenty-first century, thus explaining the derivation of this volume's subtitle.

METHOD OF DATA COLLECTION

In collecting the stories of the Talented One Hundred,[3] I have employed, in the
tradition of Max Weber, the German sociologist, the hermeneutic approach, an
interpretive understanding of social behavior and social history of individuals.
I interviewed one hundred highly successful blacks, using a purposive population. By any objective measures of success—education, income, occupation,
and reputation—the Talented One Hundred stand at the apex of the upper
middle class. I chose this population because, first, I wanted a population of
blacks at the highest strata of society in order to test the widespread hypothesis that racism declines as blacks move upward in North American society. Second, I wanted to avoid the theoretical debate over the definition of middle class

and the number of blacks in the middle class. Third, this population of blacks would have the broadest contact with a diversity of individuals, groups, and experiences and with the movers and shakers of power in this society and in the international arena. Everett Stonequist, in *The Marginal Man,* believed also that "the life histories of marginal men offer the most significant material for the analysis of the cultural process as it springs from the context of social groups."[4] Though he was referring to Jews, I feel his statement is appropriate to the marginal black elite in North America.

Although I consulted *Who's Who in Black America* and other references, I relied mostly on personal resources to find distinguished blacks through professional societies and meetings, on personal contacts, and on strategically placed individuals. With some exceptions, the choice of the population was based on practical and sociological grounds—practical because of its accessibility to me and sociological because of its large representation of middle-class blacks. The selected population included blacks who had obtained success by traditional avenues—having obtained at least a college degree and being gainfully employed and renowned in their professional or managerial specialty or their public service. I also included those who followed nontraditional avenues of success—people who achieved local, national, or international distinction in spite of their lack of educational background or income, and those persons who achieved a relatively obscure but "special feat" in society. Most of the Talented One Hundred, however, had achieved objective success—educationally, economically, and occupationally.

In general, the black elite of this study had achieved educationally: 32 percent held doctoral degrees; 27 percent held master's degrees; 11 percent held medical degrees; 6 percent held law degrees; 13 percent held bachelor's degrees; 7 percent attended college; and only 4 percent had only a high school diploma or less.

The average median personal income of the black elite was above $50,000: 64 percent earned over $50,000; 18 percent earned between $35,000 and $50,000; 12 percent earned between $20,000 and $34,999; and 6 percent earned less than $20,000.[5]

The population represents prominent blacks in a cross section of occupations—artists, performers, brokers, financial analysts, doctors, educators, entrepreneurs, journalists, managers, administrators, ministers, lawyers, politicians, public officials, scientists, engineers, and social activists. Although athletes are absent from this population, it is not by choice. Some individuals permitted me to use their names: Jeraldyne Blunden, artistic director and founder of the Dayton Contemporary Dance Company; Dorothy Bolden, president and founder of the National Domestic Workers of America, Inc.; William Holmes Borders Sr., pastor of Wheat Street Baptist Church in Atlanta, Georgia; Vernon E. Jordan Jr., partner in the law firm of Akin, Gump, Strauss, Hauer, and Feld and former president of the National Urban League, Inc.; Michael L. Lomax, chairman of the board of the

Fulton County Commission; Joseph E. Lowery, president of the Southern Christian Leadership Conference; James Paschal, executive vice president of Dobbs-
Paschal Midfield Corporation; Joshua I. Smith, chairman and CEO of Maxima
Corporation and chairman of the Commission on Minority Business Development; Bernice Sumlin, educator and past national president of Alpha Kappa Alpha sorority; Yvonne Walker-Taylor, first woman president of Wilberforce University; Vangie Watkins, social activist and community organizer in Atlanta, Georgia;
the late Booty Wood, former musician with the Duke Ellington, Count Basie, and
Lionel Hampton bands; and Robert L. Woodson, president of the National Center for Neighborhood Enterprise and chairman of the Council for a Black Economic Agenda.

Perhaps the age composition of the population reflects the cohort of individuals who benefited most from the gains made during the civil rights movement.
Thirty-five percent of the Talented One Hundred ranged in age from thirty-five
to forty-four; 33 percent were forty-five to fifty-four; 18 percent were fifty-five
to sixty-four; 8 percent were sixty-five and over; and only 6 percent were under
thirty-five.

Males are more heavily represented in my population, reflecting the social
reality that males, black or white, are more likely to be represented at the top
of the social stratum. Of the Talented One Hundred, 63 percent are males, and
37 percent, females. I recognize, of course, that recent trends in college attendance are producing larger numbers of black women with college degrees than
black men. Thus, in the future, we may see a shift in the gender composition of
the black elite.

The population includes individuals from diverse regional and socioeconomic backgrounds. The largest number, 38 percent, came of age in the South;
32 percent grew up in the North Central region; 12 percent grew up in the
Northeast; 6 percent grew up in the West; 6 percent came from outside
the United States; and 6 percent were highly mobile, living in many sections of
the country.

Though some individuals came from privileged backgrounds, most descended from the various strata of the working class; many were very poor. I
agree with Sheridan Williams, professor of English at a major university, who
expressed it best when she stated, "To discuss poverty is not even interesting
when you are talking about the backgrounds of middle-class blacks."

There is a widespread notion that the upward mobility of blacks affects class
identity. The new black elite, unlike the old bourgeoisie, which Frazier criticized as "status seekers in a world of make believe," is interested in acquiring
power and the "social, professional, and political attitudes that are more class-
linked than race-linked."[6] Traditionally, people in the higher strata of society
identify with the Republican Party; however, blacks have been heavily represented in the Democratic Party since Roosevelt's New Deal. In my population,
this pattern prevailed. Most individuals, 67 percent, were registered Demo-

crats, and only 5 percent were Republicans. Twenty-six percent declared themselves as independent, yet they voted overwhelmingly for Jesse Jackson in the 1988 presidential primary and for the Democratic candidate in the 1984 presidential race. Two persons were members of a third party. In a survey of nine hundred blacks, the Joint Center for Political Studies found that 54 percent were strong Democrats in 1984, but only 41 percent in 1987. Young blacks between eighteen and twenty-nine were more likely to vote Republican.

In collecting the data, I used an in-depth, open-ended, structured interview schedule. Because of the sensitive nature of the information I sought, a questionnaire was most inappropriate for obtaining the desired responses. I took advantage of the pilot survey approach because it affords the researcher the opportunity and the flexibility to reformulate and redirect the research as new information is obtained. The formal interviews lasted an average of two and one-half to three hours, often longer. They were taped. But for some individuals, the informal interviews continued for many hours, yielding more fruitful insights.

I interviewed the Talented One Hundred in a variety of settings: their offices and my office; their homes and my home; and their hotel rooms and my hotel room. I interviewed one person in a car, while he was making his rounds of business appointments, and another at a recreational park, while we were walking along a railroad track. Although the individuals lived in many parts of the country, I conducted the interviews in California, Georgia, Kentucky, Ohio, Maryland, Virginia, and the District of Columbia. I conducted all the interviews with the exception of three. Two were done by colleagues of mine whom the interviewees trusted, and one was a taped self-interview. I promised the Talented One Hundred that their interviews would be confidential and that I would protect their anonymity. Consequently, I personally transcribed nearly two hundred 90-minute tapes. The real names of people are not used in this book, except for those who gave their permission.

I must point out the limitations and strengths of my purposive population. First, the population should not be considered representative of all professional blacks. However, it does contain a cross section of professional blacks, and thus their experiences are valid for that category. I agree with Glaser and Strauss that it is not necessary to "know the whole field" or to have all the facts "from a careful random sample" to discover phenomena of importance.[7] Representative survey studies of the black middle class, like that produced by Bart Landry, offer a skeletal portrait of their objective achievements and a statistical portrait of their encounters with discrimination.[8] But those studies do not tell us much about the subjective side of how success is achieved and maintained in a racist society. While such studies focus on the structural effects of racism, they neglect its psychological impact. This psychological emphasis would require in-depth interviews, which differentiates my approach from those of scholars like Landry. Hence, my study is designed to contribute to understanding the psychological impact of racism on the black elite by adding flesh and blood to the skeletal bones of survey studies.

Second, my population may be inherently biased because it includes only those persons willing to share their feelings, thus differentiating in some way those who are unwilling or unavailable to be interviewed. Third, the literature clearly points out the inherent limitations of self-reporting. The interview subject may distort reality, giving the interviewer answers that he or she wants to hear.

I attempted to circumvent these limitations by using check questions to probe into the Talented One Hundred's privately expressed attitudes and behaviors on the one hand and their publicly expressed ones on the other.

Despite these limitations, I hope that this study will serve as a catalyst for further investigation of the microdynamics of marginality and the psychological impact of racism using a more scientific random population.

The process of the interviews, which took place between December 1985 and April 1988, in itself was revealing and thus merits comment. The cooperation from the Talented One Hundred was ideal, or as was appropriately expressed by a colleague, a "researcher's dream." Having been ensured anonymity and confidentiality, they very willingly discussed candidly and openly their marginal statuses, their encounters with racism, and their feelings and responses to it.

I got beyond the mask. I know this because 35 to 40 percent of the Talented One Hundred cried, their voices quavered or changed emotional octaves, and their eyes filled with tears. They took long pauses to reflect. They laughed. I laughed, cried, and paused with them. They entrusted their emotions to me. I accepted them as sacred trusts. The Talented One Hundred described the interview as therapeutic, most indicating they had never had an interview like this one, nor ever told anyone before about a particular behavior, emotion, or event. Many recommended colleagues and acquaintances for participation in this study. When I had a four-hour interview with a well-known sociologist, I mentioned that I saw a social pattern emerging and felt I could stop at seventy-five people. He responded, "Don't deprive twenty-five people of this experience." He also expressed amazement that I had made contact with people in such high-ranking positions, feeling that this project could have been undertaken only by an ambassador's daughter, a well-known person's daughter, or an eminent social scientist. I responded, "Like yourself?" He smiled and nodded affirmatively.

Initially, when I started the interviews, I was surprised when individuals cancelled important appointments or extended the initial time given, thinking it was an idiosyncratic occurrence. By the end of the interview process, it was the norm. I wrote letters thanking them for their participation. Again, I was surprised when I received responses. One public official wrote, "I thoroughly enjoyed being interviewed by you last week. I have concluded the interview process was at least as much an educational experience for me as it was a source of research for you."

For many, the interview was a process of self-discovery and self-validation. Numerous individuals apologized for or seemed embarrassed about their feelings and beliefs toward racial attitudes and experiences. Often they wanted to know if others among the Talented One Hundred shared them. I validated their experiences, encouraging them to continue their story.

Many individuals are uncomfortable talking about their racial feelings and behaviors, because they believe they are the only ones who feel that way or respond that way toward racism. The collective therapeutic interviews, therefore, show how their racial life history is a shared experience and an integral part of the social fabric of the society. The way racism operates, then, is to individualize their experiences, and thus give real meaning to the concept of institutional racism. Perhaps this is the reason William J. Wilson had a different tale to tell when he wrote *The Declining Significance of Race.* He and others missed the subjective component of institutional racism, because they lacked an experiential database.

The black elite experience race on an individual level, but it is a shared experience that has particular characteristics for people who are linked to society in a certain economic way. What emerged out of these life histories of successful blacks was that they had achieved objective success—all the trappings of prestige, status, and positional power—yet it was a tenuous success. Ever-present was the subjective component of racism, reminding them of the precariousness of objective success. Despite their statuses, privileges, and successes, they were still black in a racist society. This emphasis on the individual aspect of racism was shifted to the objective institutional aspect of racism in the sixties, thus minimizing the individualization of racial experience and the impact of its psychological damage. It is important, therefore, to see the linkage between individual and institutional racism. Hence, I shall redefine the concept of racism to incorporate both dimensions.

TOWARD A REDEFINITION OF RACISM

Before the late sixties, scholars focused primarily on a prejudice-discrimination model to explain race relations in the United States. The emphasis on prejudice was particularly central to earlier works of prominent psychologists and sociologists.[9] The prejudice perspective emphasized the unfavorable attitudes directed at an out-group because of real or alleged physical or cultural characteristics, while discrimination stressed the overt, unequal, and unfair treatment of an out-group member because of his or her alleged physical and cultural characteristics. This model views racism as more individualistic, episodic, random, subjective, and personal, and its effects are intended to harm.[10]

After the late sixties, Stokeley Carmichael and Charles Hamilton, in *Black Power*, expanded the focus from prejudice-discrimination to institutional racism— a pattern of racism that is embodied in the policies and practices of the folkways, mores, legal structures, and bureaucracies of social institutions that have an intentional and unintentional differential and negative impact on people of color. The following example from Carmichael and Hamilton's *Black Power* illustrates the differences between the two perspectives:

> When White terrorists bomb a church and kill five Black children, that is an act of individual racism. . . . But when in the same city—Birmingham, Alabama—five hundred Black babies die each year because of the lack of proper food, shelter, and medical facilities, and thousands more are destroyed and maimed physically, emotionally, and intellectually because of conditions of poverty and discrimination in the Black community, that is a function of institutional racism.[11]

The concept of institutional racism, unlike the prejudice-discrimination model, shifts the focus from the individual to the system. Its effects are more covert, more systematic, more routinized, and more objective and impersonal. Its harmful effects are both intentional and unintentional.

Institutional racism has remained, since the late sixties, the dominant explanatory model of race relations among academics. However, this emphasis should be refocused to give appropriate recognition to individual racism. This redefinition calls into question previous assumptions that individual racism is more individualistic, overt, episodic, random, and intentional. While these features may be more characteristic of its mode of operation, individual racism, like institutional racism, has a shared component.

Individual racism focuses more on the subjective and personal—the shared patterns of behaving, feeling, and thinking on an individual level; institutional racism stresses the objective and impersonal—the shared structural and organizational patterns on the group level that differentially affect the life chances of people of color. Hence, the subjective and objective patterns are both institutionalized; both operate as part of the basic fabric of society.

In some cases, institutional racism may be mediated through an individual, and the victim of racism may experience it as an act of the individual; however, it is really an institutional phenomenon. For instance, a personnel director acts as an agent for a major corporation that might have an explicit or implicit policy not to hire blacks. The victim of this discriminatory policy does not have the knowledge or the empirical reference frame to separate the organizational policy from the individual act. It is, therefore, important to continue to emphasize individual racism, because although the implicit or explicit policy is embedded in the organizational structure and affects blacks collectively, it is experienced on an individual level. Thus, the two concepts are integrally linked.

In the past, scholars have ignored the tradition of such writers of African descent as W. E. B. Du Bois, Frantz Fanon, and Albert Memmi, who stressed the subjective and psychological impact of racism. These scholars focused instead on racism's structural component. The study of objective racism, as Memmi said about psychoanalysis and Marxism in *The Colonizer and the Colonized*, "must not, under the pretext of having discovered the source or one of the main sources of human conduct, pre-empt all experience, all feeling, all suffering, all byways of human behavior, and call them profit motive or Oedipus complex"[12] or, in this instance, I say institutional racism.

A dual heritage is common among people of color. It is the perennial Achilles heel of the oppressed. Du Bois, Fanon, and Memmi were cognizant of the conflicted nature of the dual heritage among the oppressed and the impact of its psychological damage.

Du Bois, an African American scholar, saw this duality as a universal phenomenon that affects "the collective psyche of peoples of African descent."[13] For African Americans, the conflict emanates from their identity as blacks and as Americans. Du Bois, in *The Souls of Black Folk* at the beginning of this century, called it the double-consciousness.

> The Negro is a sort of seventh son, born with a veil, and gifted with second-sight in this American world—a world which yields him no true self-consciousness, but only lets him see himself through the revelation of the other world. It is a peculiar sensation, this double-consciousness, this sense of always looking at one's self through the eyes of others, of measuring one's soul by the tape of a world that looks on in amused contempt and pity. One ever feels his two-ness,—an American, a Negro; two souls, two thoughts, two unreconciled strivings; two warring ideals in one dark body, whose dogged strength alone keeps it from being torn asunder.[14]

For Fanon, a West Indian scholar, the duality arises from cultural differences. "The Black man has been given two frames of reference within which he has had to place himself. . . . His customs and the sources on which they were based were wiped out because they were in conflict with a civilization that he did not know and that imposed itself on him."[15] For Memmi, a Tunisian writer, the source of the conflict is inherent in the language. "Possession of two languages is not merely a matter of having two tools, but actually means participation in the two psychical and cultural realms. Here, the two worlds symbolized and converged by two tongues are in conflict; they are those of the colonizer and the colonized."[16] He views the middle-class colonized as suffering the "most from the bilingualism," feeling that the "intellectual lives more in cultural anguish."[17]

Du Bois, Fanon, and Memmi suggest that the duality can lead to identity confusion and inherent contradictions—the collective psychological damage done by racism. It is time, therefore, to return to the study of race relations in Du Bois, Fanon, and Memmi's tradition. A redefinition of racism, whether it takes place on an individual or on a collective level, must take into account that it is institutionalized and has a subjective and an objective component. The subjective component incorporates the shared psychological effects of racism—affective, behavioral, cognitive—on the individual. The objective component includes the structural effects of racism and its differential life chances on the group. Perhaps the empirical outcry that rose from critics of William J. Wilson's *The Declining Significance of Race* was not so much that he had missed the empirical mark: rather, he had not targeted the pain, and the cry was more a primal scream.

RACISM DEFINED

Racism, as I define it, is a process of justification for the domination, exploitation, and control of one racial group by another. It incorporates a set of attitudes and beliefs to support and to legitimate the dominant group's discriminatory behavior. Racist dominance is institutionalized, multifaceted, and all-encompassing. It aims to control the cultural, economic, educational, political, and legal standing, emotional and physical health, and the sexual and social interaction of the oppressed group. Racism manifests itself intentionally and unintentionally, covertly and overtly, individually and collectively, and subjectively and objectively. At its root, and sustaining its myriad occurrences, is the unwavering belief that the definers (most powerful group members of a socially perceived category within racist social systems) are inherently superior by virtue of their shared biological or cultural characteristics.[18]

In this definition, the key notion is that racism is a power relationship. It is exercised by the oppressor over the oppressed within racist social systems. Members of the oppressor group are the victimizers who derive privileges and benefits from the racial arrangements within racist social systems based solely on their membership in that socially constructed category. Members of the oppressed group, on the other hand, are the victims who are accorded differential and unequal treatment from that arrangement, based solely on their membership in that socially constructed category. The oppressed group has an identity imposed by the oppressor group and a sense of place in the social order. The oppressed members may internalize or resist the status imposed upon them.

What emerges out of this definition is a re-elevation of the psychological impact of racism. This definition helps us not only to look at the obvious victims of racism, such as the underclass in William Julius Wilson's study,[19] but also to examine the psychological impact of racism on the entire population victimized by it. Previous studies have focused on the psychological impact of racism on the underclass but have ignored the black elite. This study is intended to close that knowledge gap.

Chapter 1, "The Color Line as Reality: Race Lessons, Patterns, and Propositions," shows how the black elite's experiences have been shaped by race, not by the means of production. This chapter takes issue with most Western Marxists who treat race as an epiphenomenon of society. It shows that race is an important stratifying feature in this society. Blacks experience racism across class boundaries; though the experience might be different, it is still tied to the function of racism in this society. Hence, race cannot be solely a class phenomenon, because, in the Marxist sense, class is a collective experience reducible to the underlying social relations of economic production.

Although the reality of the color line is experienced on an individual level by the Talented One Hundred, there is a shared social fabric connecting the threads of these personal life histories. The reader will see these threads in the lessons, patterns, and propositions about the nature of the black experience that may also help blacks to cope.

Chapter 1 notes further that there is a dual value orientation in American society. While there is adherence to democracy, freedom, equality, individualism, progress, achievement, and success, there is also an acceptance of racism and group discrimination. Blacks are victims of these conflicted value orientations and the resulting actions emanating from them. On the one hand, blacks have internalized the values of competition, democracy, freedom, equality, hard work, individualism, success, and achievement. On the other hand, they have overwhelmingly rejected, albeit to varying degrees, racism and group discrimination at the affective, behavioral, and cognitive levels. This dual value orientation is a source of conflict for the black elite. They expend much energy trying to balance conflicts and concerns around issues like universalism versus black pride, Afrocentrism versus Eurocentrism, and individualism versus collectivism.

Chapter 2, "Manifestations of the Color Line: The Impact of Violence," focuses on the psychological impact of racism on the black elite. This chapter shows how racism individualizes rather than objectifies their experiences. Using the universal value of individualism to contextualize the racial experience of people of color denies that there is a collective component to it. Hence, the psychological damage done by racism individualizes the experiences and focuses the problem on the individual.

This chapter also looks at how the oppressor group employs violence and three devices of power—control, dominance, and exploitation—to maintain its racial privileges and a sense of place for the oppressed group. The concept of violence is examined from a Fanonian perspective, which includes physical and psychic violence. Within the broader cultural and social arena, different realms of activities where racism operates are examined, such as education, economics, the media, housing, and sexual interactions.

Chapter 3, "The Color Line across the World of Work," looks at the shared racial experiences of the black elite in the profit, public, and nonprofit sectors of the economy. This chapter notes that since the civil rights movement, the black middle class has made great strides into the mainstream sector of the economy. However, these gains have been tempered by continuous battles with racism in the workplace

Chapter 4, "The Color Line across the World of Academe," focuses on the shared racial experiences of black academicians in higher education. While the black elite in academia have made gains since the sixties, they continue to face

an uphill battle with racism, which affects their quality of life and their retention in the halls of ivy.

Chapter 5, "The Color Line in Social, Religious, and Family Life," deals with
the shared racial experiences of the black elite away from the world of work.
This chapter addresses the impact of social isolation on blacks who live in predominantly white environs. It shows how living in a predominantly white setting can disrupt black professionals' traditional mutually supportive familial,
friendship, and organizational ties that could buffer them from their stress. This
chapter also examines how they cope with isolation.

Chapter 6, "Gender Politics: Through the Eyes of Black Women," focuses on
the black professional woman and her experiences with racism and sexism.
Through the eyes of black women, I look at the issue of sexism and racism in
their interactions with white men, the issue of racism in interactions with white
women, and the issue of sexism in interactions with black men. I also examine
the psychological consequences of the double jeopardy of sexism and racism.

Chapter 7, "Styles of Coping," discusses the variety of shared personal and
collective modes of coping on and off the job. Individuals who internalize their
negative racial experiences, for instance, are more likely to see their failures as
personal inadequacies. Individuals who recognize race as a reality are more
likely to incorporate it as a factor in their interactions and to find meaningful
ways of coping—by externalizing racism and organizing others to combat it.

Chapter 8, "Beyond the Color Line: An Alternative Vision," views the black
elite as players not only in the arena of the United States but also in a global context. This chapter focuses on duality as a stimulus in the creative process. Having
a dual consciousness gives the black elite a special way of viewing the world and
a special sensitivity to the plight of oppressed peoples of the world. Thus, this
chapter addresses the black elite's views on such issues as global racism, human
rights, nuclear disarmament, and the increasing class divide. The black elite look
at these issues primarily from an Afrocentric perspective, which emphasizes, for
instance, human needs over military defense. The failure of whites in America to
benefit from the Afrocentric perspective results in a high cost to them.

Chapter 9, "The Color Line in the Twenty-First Century: Generational Differences," looks at new generations of blacks who grew up in the post–civil
rights era and how their values and worldview have changed from previous generations. It also looks at social factors that underlie these changes, such as the
growing class divide in black America, and their implications for continued
racial progress.

NOTES

1. Since the first edition of *The Black Elite: Facing the Color Line in the Twilight of
the Twentieth Century* (1991), a spate of popular and scholarly studies on the subjective

side of success in a racist society have been published, such as Philomena Essed, *Understanding Everyday Racism* (Newberry Park, CA: Sage, 1991); Sara Lawrence-Lightfoot, *I've Known Rivers: Lives of Loss and Liberation* (Reddings, MA: Addison-Wesley, 1994); Joe R. Feagin and Melvin P. Sikes, *Living with Racism: The Black Middle Class Experience* (Boston: Beacon Press, 1994); Mary Patillo-McCoy, *Black Picket Fences* (Chicago: University of Chicago Press, 1999); Richard L. Zweigenhaft and G. William Domhoff, *Blacks in White Establishment?* (New Haven: Yale University Press, 1991); Henry Louis Gates Jr., *America behind the Color Line* (New York: Time Warner, 2004); Ellis Cose, *The Rage of a Privileged Class* (New York: HarperCollins, 1993); Audrey Edwards and Craig K. Polite, *Children of the Dream: The Psychology of Black Success* (New York: Doubleday, 1992); Lawrence Otis Graham, *Our Kind of People* (New York: HarperCollins, 1999).

2. Not all voices of the Talented One Hundred and the Talented Thirty are heard in this volume. But those you do hear are representative of my population.

3. For method of data collection for the Talented Thirty, see chapter 9.

4. Everett V. Stonequist, *The Marginal Man* (New York: Russell and Russell, 1961), 222.

5. It is not possible to compare this distribution directly with national averages. The Talented One Hundred were asked to indicate their annual income at the time of the interview. Given that the interviews spanned a two-year period, there is no common reference point to examine the income distribution at a given point in time, for example, 1986.

6. Martin Kilson, "Black Bourgeoisie Revisited," *Dissent*, Winter 1983, 87.

7. Barney G. Glaser and Anselm L. Strauss, *The Discovery of Grounded Theory* (Chicago: Aldine, 1967).

8. Bart Landry, *The New Black Middle Class* (Berkeley: University of California Press, 1987); Daniel C. Thompson, *A Black Elite* (New York: Greenwood Press, 1986).

9. Gordon W. Allport, *The Nature of Prejudice* (Reading, PA: Addison-Wesley, 1954); T. W. Adorno et al., *The Authoritarian Personality* (New York: Harper, 1950); Gunnar Myrdal, *An American Dilemma* (New York: Harper and Brothers, 1944); Robert K. Merton, "Discrimination and the American Creed," in Peter I. Rose, ed., *The Study of Society*, 2nd ed. (New York: Random House, 1970), 449–457.

10. Joe R. Feagin and Clairece Booher Feagin, *Discrimination American Style*, 2nd ed. (Malabar, FL: Robert E. Krieger Pub. Co., 1986).

11. Stokeley Carmichael and Charles V. Hamilton, *Black Power: The Politics of Liberation* (New York: Vintage Books, 1967), 4.

12. Albert Memmi, *The Colonizer and the Colonized* (Boston: Beacon Press, 1967), xiii.

13. James B. Stewart, "Psychic Duality of Afro Americans in the Novels of W. E .B. Du Bois," *Phylon*, 4 (1983), 93–107.

14. W. E. B. Du Bois, *The Souls of Black Folk* (New York: Fawcett, 1961), 16–17.

15. Ayi Kwei Armah, "Fanon: The Awakener," *Negro Digest*, 18 (Oct. 1969), 4.

16. Memmi, *Colonizer*, 107.

17. Memmi, *Colonizer*, 120.

18. This definition of racism is in the tradition of such scholars' works as Robert Blauner, *Racial Oppression in America* (New York: Harper and Row, 1972); Feagin and Feagin, *Discrimination American Style*; Carmichael and Hamilton, *Black Power*; and James Jones, *Prejudice and Racism* (Reading, PA: Addison-Wesley, 1972). See also Sunera Thobani, Shyrel Smith Hosseini, and Richard H. Ogles, "Towards a Further

Demystification of the Racist, Patriarchal, Imperialist World System," *Human Affairs: International Journal of Social Studies*, 14 (1988), 3.

The concept of race has been used in many ways to refer to linguistic categories (Aryan, Russian-speaking), to religious categories (Hindu, Jewish), and to national categories (Germans, Poles). Because such varieties of categories have been considered races, they reflect the arbitrariness and artificialness of racial designations. The official classifiers isolate certain social categories, based on an arbitrary selection of physically or biologically transmitted characteristics.

Race is, then, a social creation, not a biological fact. It is a sociopolitical category based on certain perceived inherited physical characteristics. These characteristics are isolated, and their importance, as differentiating features, is overemphasized in different societies. For example, Julian Pitt-Rivers, in "Race, Color, and Class in Central America and the Andes," in John Hope Franklin, ed., *Color and Race* (Boston: Beacon Press, 1968), 264–281, noted that in much of Latin America, skin color and the shape of the lips are less important differentiating criteria than hair texture, eye color, and stature. In the United States, skin color and the shape of lips are important. However, whether one's phenotype is closer to white is not an issue in this country. Traditionally, a person has been defined as black if one has known black ancestry—one-fourth, one-eighth, one-sixteenth, or too minute to be discernible. This classification of race is so entrenched in the United States that the Census Bureau figures have been historically based on it. However, in the 2000 census, an individual had the option to check more than one race.

19. William Julius Wilson, *The Truly Disadvantaged: The Inner City, the Underclass, and Public Policy* (Chicago: University of Chicago Press, 1987).

1

THE COLOR LINE AS REALITY: RACE, LESSONS, PATTERNS, AND PROPOSITIONS

The history of human relations is filled with the conflicts of peoples of different colors and races. At the conclusion of the Copenhagen Conference on Race and Color in 1965, John Hope Franklin, the black historian, wrote, "They had learned that the specter of color and race haunts every nook and corner of the world, consuming an inordinate amount of mankind's energies and attention that are so desperately needed to solve the major problems of peace and survival."[1]

THE COLOR LINE

The color line is a major dividing reality in the United States. The civil rights movement represents an era of personal and collective challenge to end the color line. Jack B. Lane, a forty-seven-year-old public official and a civil rights leader during the sixties, valiantly opposed the old black and white guardians of the dividing line. "The resistance was not just against the system of segregation and white leadership, but part of it was a revolt against the old guard within the black community, because people said it would not work," says Lane. Most of the Talented One Hundred, like Lane, were deeply influenced by this movement, believing it signaled the demise of the color line. Joseph Lowery, the sixty-five-year-old president of the Southern Christian Leadership Conference, expressed well the personal and collective aspirations, hopes, and meaning of this era for most participants in this study:

> I felt good about myself. I guess that might have been the greatest victory of all—self-emancipation. We were free at last from inferiority. Those of us who were active

in the movement shared that. We were like a snake who had just crawled out of its skin. We just crawled out of that body that cramped us and that kept us fearful and inferior. We lost fear. We lost self-hatred and gained self-esteem, because we had taken our destiny in our hands. We had entered an era of self-determination.

When people stayed off the buses, it was as if to say, You can't imprison me. I don't have to ride your bus. I am free. That movement in the sixties shifted the responsibility for our destiny from others to us. Before that we depended on Congress and the courts. Now we said that it doesn't matter what the courts say; we are not going to ride in the back of the bus. So that was a very liberating experience for us. We felt that we could knock out segregation if we could open up institutions to blacks—that we could move up into the mainstream and solve the problems of racial discrimination. No question that we were absolutely sure we could do that. Where we were wrong was the problems are deeper than that. While the overt barriers of discrimination removed the embarrassment, humiliation, and dehumanization as factors in our society, discrimination is deeper than separate facilities.

The color line is deeper than separate facilities or unequal education or residential segregation. Arthur Hoppe, an insightful white columnist, whose article appeared in the *San Francisco Chronicle* in 1968 at the height of the black nationalist movement, summed it up best when he told the story of "Little Black Tombo."

Once upon a time there was a little Black boy named Tombo. He was a slave.

"All I want in life," he said, "is to be free, to be equal and to be a man."

Then one day—Hallelujah!—his White masters freed him. "Now that you are free," they said, "you must work hard to be equal to us."

Little Black Tombo nodded. "Yes," he said, "now that I'm free, I must become equal to you so that I, too, can be a man. How do I become equal?"

"The problem," said some Nice White People, "is an educational one. You must get an education. Then you will be equal to us."

So some Nice White People gave him an education. It wasn't easy. It took years and years and years. But at last Little Black Tombo had an education.

"It's funny," said Tom (for, being educated, he had changed his name), "but I still don't feel equal to you."

"The problem," said some Nice White People, "is an economic one. You must have a good job. Then you will be equal to us."

So some Nice White People gave Tom a job. It wasn't easy. It took years and years and years, but at last Tom had a job.

"It's funny," said Tom, "but I still don't feel equal to you."

"The problem," said some Nice White People, "is an environmental one. You must move out of the ghetto into a nice house like ours. Then you will be equal to us."

So some Nice White People gave him a house. It wasn't easy. They had to pass laws saying other White people had to sell him a house whether they liked it or not. But at last Tom got a nice house.

"It's funny," said Tom, "but I still don't feel equal to you."

"The problem," said some Nice White People, "is sociological. You must dress like us, talk like us, and think like us. Then, obviously, you will be equal to us."

So some Nice White People taught him how to dress and talk and think and they even invited him to their cocktail parties.

The hostess would squeeze his hand warmly (though she never kissed him on the cheek). And the men would clap him on the back and ask him his opinion (but only about racial matters).

This time, Tom didn't say much at all. He grew a beard, put on dark glasses, changed his name to Tombo X and shouting, "Black is beautiful," hit the first two Nice White People he saw over the head.

They were, of course, deeply hurt. "After all we've done for you," they said. "Don't you realize you're throwing away everything we struggled together for? Now you'll never feel equal to us."

"It's funny," said Tombo X, smiling, "but at last I feel like a man."

Hoppe concludes that the moral of this story is, "You can think a Black man is free and equal. But first you must think of him not as a Black but as a man." I would add that the moral of the story is that the color line, like sex and class, is a fundamental reality and a stratifying principle in this society.

Many scholars have ignored race; particularly, Western Marxists have treated it as an epiphenomenon of society. The dynamics of society are explicable only in terms of class conflict and the mode of production. Hence, racism is attributed to the forces of capitalism. In their view, racism can disappear only after the class struggle has been won. Some scholars, like Martin and Cohen, have rejected this traditional view of race as "vestigial, transitory, and generally a disappearing phenomenon"[2]; rather, they see race as a pivotal social structural category.

The color line is a reality, since blacks experience racism across class boundaries. Though the experience might be different, it is still tied to the function of racism in U.S. society. Race, as well as class, is embedded in the institutional structure of society. Hence, race cannot be solely a class phenomenon, because in the Marxist sense class is a collective experience reducible to the underlying social relations of economic production. The black elite's experiences have been shaped by race as it interconnects with class.

This chapter examines the lessons, patterns, and propositions about the nature of the reality of the color line in North America: To be black is to be conflicted; to be black means to watch and walk the tightrope; to be black is to experience the double standard; to be black is to be on perennial probation; to be black is to be never good enough; to be black is to bear the race burden; to be black is to be always in a precarious status; to be black is to be forever in a continuous struggle, personally and collectively; to be black is to be limited by the glass ceiling; and to be black is to wear the mask. Although the reality of the color line is experienced on an individual level by the Talented One Hundred, there is a shared social fabric connecting the threads of these personal life histories, as we shall see in the lessons, patterns, and propositions.

TO BE BLACK IN NORTH AMERICAN SOCIETY IS TO BE CONFLICTED

A dual value orientation exists in American society. While there is an adherence to democracy, freedom, equality, individualism, progress, achievement, and success, there is also an acceptance of racism and group discrimination. Robin Williams Jr., a sociologist, sees the latter two as deviant and contrary to the main thrust of American society;[3] however, racism and group discrimination are the norm and are integral features of the stratification system. Blacks are victims of these conflicted value orientations and the resulting actions emanating from them. On the one hand, blacks have internalized the values of competition, democracy, freedom, equality, hard work, individualism, success, and achievement. On the other hand, they have overwhelmingly rejected, albeit to varying degrees, racism and group discrimination at the affective, behavioral, and cognitive levels. This dual value orientation of American society is, nevertheless, strongly rooted in the black elite's psyche, generating a source of conflict and frequently producing strange fruit.

Thus to be black is to be conflicted in this society. There are many manifestations of this conflict, embodied in what Du Bois called the double-consciousness—the identity conflict of being a black and being an American. Other scholars have labeled it "double vision," "dual reference group orientation," "biculturality," "diunital," and "multidimensional."[4]

The Double-Consciousness Revisited

When I interviewed Bernie Roberts, a prominent social researcher in his mid-forties, he reflected on the omnipresence of the double-consciousness: "The thing which is so discouraging is that when I read Du Bois's writing that he published in 1898, I would still think it is 1898 if you didn't tell me the year it was written, and that's when you feel it's sad. I got on this tie [referring to the fact that taxi drivers in Washington DC ignore him, even when he is wearing a tie], looking nice, and standing in front of the Mayflower Hotel. . . . There are little changes that have occurred now, and that tells me racism is not disappearing."

The duality evolved in Du Bois's novels, reflecting his own personal growth over fifty years.[5] Again, the duality is portrayed differently, depending on the historical and cultural epoch, by writers like Frantz Fanon and his "Manichean world," the never-ending conflict between light and dark in *Black Skin, White Masks*, James Weldon Johnson in *The Autobiography of an Ex–Coloured Man*, Richard Wright in "The Ethics of Living Jim Crow: An Autobiographical Sketch," Roger Wilkins in *A Man's Life: An Autobiography*, and John Edgar Wideman in *Brothers and Keepers*.[6]

Du Bois seems to suggest that the double-consciousness leads to identity confusion and inherent contradictions in the collective psyche of peoples of African descent. Ninety-three percent of the Talented One Hundred also believe it is a problem for African Americans. Crystal Miller, a professor of theater in the Black Studies department at a major university, who is in her late forties, feels, "It presents a divided loyalty of wanting to belong, to love one's country and wanting to be proud of it, but always being somewhat a stranger about one's own experience here. It forces blacks to choose between [being] black or American, and being forced to choose is destroying part of one's self."

Pat Robinson, a fifty-three-year-old judge, who grew up on the West Coast, knows this dilemma. "When you think of yourself as an American, America doesn't think of you as an American. That's the problem. Sometimes you are forced to go back to your blackness, because America won't let you be an American, even though that's the way I grew up thinking. I am going to be smart. I am going to go to school and make it in society. You get a lot of knocks on your head by whites in society, reminding you after all you are black. Everything that's for me isn't for you as a black. That's the real problem—a catch-22."

Though "this system has inequities, it creates the greatest opportunities for the majority of the people. I never thought I would be saying anything like this," remarked Diane Earlinger, a forty-two-year-old pathologist and a manager in a federal agency. Johnson Longworth, a professor of art at a major university in the Midwest, agreed that America offers many opportunities, but he is still not comfortable living in this society. One senses his ambivalence and his poignancy about wanting to love his country and wanting to be proud of it, but his long racial memories have interfered.

> I'll never forget that experience when I was in Brazil at an international festival for the arts, where they brought in black folks from seventeen different countries. And we were in the hotel and different people were talking about their countries. As things developed, a Nigerian said, "I love my country." A Cuban said, "I love my country." A Panamanian said, "I love my country." I couldn't say that, and I have been here all my life. I've accomplished and I've suffered, but I would be hesitant to say I love this country.

There were some among the Talented One Hundred, like Albert Sungist, a sociologist, who remarked that the duality "produces a schizophrenic identity and conflict," the conflict of having to fight for your country during wartime yet being denied the privilege of full participation as a citizen. To this issue, Teresa Hale responded:

> Not since my early impressionable elementary school stage have I really felt pride and patriotism. The rude awakening of the need to constantly struggle for constitutionally guaranteed rights leaves a very bitter taste and a permanent sense of alienation and insecurity. Blacks constantly face issues of racism at home. This reality is so draining that I give little thought and concern for many current international issues that do not impact on my day-to-day existence notwithstanding the nuclear arms race, the African drought, and South Africa.

Being a black American, at some level, poses the dilemma of prioritizing being an American and being black. Like many of the Talented One Hundred, Earnest Ross, a fifty-seven-year-old college professor, stated clearly this dilemma: "Are you an American or are you a black American? You must decide which is going to come first." He said this choice influences the direction of how his "vote, money, or energy will be contributed."

> If you decide to choose being an American, then what you do is act American, even at the expense of blacks. Sometimes it does come to a choice. I have decided that I am a black American. I am interested in black things, black women, and helping blacks.

Although most of the Talented One Hundred admitted that they had not consciously reflected on the prioritization of their identity as an American or as a black, they were constantly reminded of their blackness. For the Talented One Hundred to whom I posed this question, 91 percent identified themselves as black first and American second.[7] Although individuals were not asked specifically what it means to be black or American, they implied that being American meant a sense of patriotism, a sense of belonging to this country, and a sense of sharing in the privileges and benefits of this society. For some, being black meant claiming a geographical and symbolic identification with the continent of Africa and the peoples of African descent. However, for most others, it meant a sense of shared collective consciousness with and responsibility for other black Americans because of racial discrimination.

The dilemma of choosing our identity is an ongoing process that forces us, as Ross suggests, to decide consciously or unconsciously the direction in which we will expend our energy. Listen to Aretha Shield, a thirty-seven-year-old artist who grew up in an inner city in the Northeast, wrestle with the conflict.

> I think it is terrible to live your life split in halves. For someone who grew up in the sixties, the questions I raise are, Am I going to be a black artist or just an artist? What will be the content of my art? Will I be a platform for the people, my race? Am I going to go for art for art's sake—enjoying mainstream America? A lot of black artists find themselves in this predicament which comes out of this double-consciousness. I am one of many black artists who have this search for identity in our work. What am I going to say? How am I going to talk about this American experience? Every artist has to talk about some experience that is reflected in his art in some way. For the black American, this double-consciousness comes out vividly. You can see it when you look at black art. One can visualize this deep internal conflict.

Aretha is referring to the idea that in Afrocentric art, there is usually a positive reflection of the black experience, even when the subject and message appear negative. Black art, like jazz, is improvisational, and it embodies feelings. But, even though it is improvisational, there is continuity and unity in its forms and expressions.

In her own work, Aretha said, "I thought at one point I had to solve this dilemma. I had to come up with this answer and everything would be clear, and I could be the artist that the black community wanted. I felt that would be the thing to do; but now I don't think I can solve this dilemma. I go through periods where the dilemma of the black-white conflict and male-female conflict come out distinctly in my work." At other times, she feels, "I need to balance the pain of that reality. I have to deal with the universal themes of the human condition, because if you cut me, my blood is red like everybody else's. I am a human being first. At this point in my life, I am focusing on universal themes—just the energy of how a flower grows; just the movement of the sky; just a feeling— nothing concrete—where you say this is a man or a woman. I have a need to deal with feelings, and often you can't tell what a feeling is. I am first a human being." In focusing on those elements of her basic humanity, she hopes that the feeling will transcend her work, communicating that feeling to all kinds of people. "I am black and female, and I hope all that will be reflected in my statement. I think that's all I can do. I want to represent the whole planet, not just blacks. I am part of the world," reflected Aretha, as she reacted to the dilemma of being an African American.

Jefferson Barnes, a fifty-one-year-old sociologist at a major university, views the issue as an artificial separation. "I tell my Asian students if they think of themselves as first Asians—Japanese or Chinese—then they haven't been to Japan or China. If you spend some time in sub-Saharan Africa, you'll know how American you are." For Jefferson, the dilemma is more contextual. "In America, you may feel like you are more black American, but if you take your butt out of this country, they'll tell you this right away. In the context of this society, most of the time you are going to feel more black than American. If you live in a white world, they are going to remind you all the time."

Hear Laverne Townson, a forty-three-year-old black American living in Nigeria, as she groped with her contextual identity. "You look upon yourself as an American in Nigeria, but the minute you are back in America, you think of yourself as black." Since Laverne, a successful manager of a bank, has lived in Nigeria for many years, I asked, "Do you feel more like a black American, American, or Nigerian?" She laughed, saying, "In Nigerian society, I tell them I'm Nigerian. But I am American."

Like Laverne Townson, Teresa Johnson, a forty-three-year-old American West Indian, who was born in the Virgin Islands, has a three-way mirror to view the world. "I am West Indian and an American. I grew up as an American West Indian in the Caribbean. There is a three-way cross. You are looking at yourself, and you are looking at someone looking at you as a black person and as a West Indian. A lot of West Indians, even though they are in America, do not want to be here and don't see themselves as Americans."

In contrast to most of the Talented One Hundred, Yvonne Walker-Taylor, the first woman president of Wilberforce University in Ohio, does not see the duality of being a black American as presenting a problem. She felt, as 4 percent of the Talented One Hundred did, that she could not separate the two. "We are black Americans. They go together. It is like asking which comes first—being black or being a woman. They are so tied together, to one another; I cannot separate them. I cannot separate myself from being an American any more than I can separate myself from being a woman. I cannot separate myself from my blackness and have never wanted to do so."

Though 5 percent of the Talented One Hundred claimed their salient identity as American, there is an ironic twist and ambivalence in this claim. Like Walker-Taylor, Joseph Lowery cannot make the distinction between being American or black. "Both are being assaulted. I am assaulted because I am black. I am not assaulted because I am an American, but because I am a black American." He said, "The problem with America is that we are not allowed to claim it. We are treated like stepchildren so we are without a country. And nobody wanted to claim Africa because of its presentation to blacks as an 'ignorant, savage, and dark continent.' Now that Africa has been emancipated, we are not Africans, so we can't claim it."

Lowery rejects the Negro national anthem, even though he feels it is "a great black hymn." "There is only one national anthem and that is 'Oh, say, can you see.'" Laughingly, he said, "I can't sing it. The words are despicable and need to be changed, but as long as that is the anthem, it's mine, because America is mine. I am not going to let anybody abrogate my ownership, and I am not going to abdicate it. So it's my country, and the blackness is somebody else's problem."

He continued, "I am black. I am comfortable with being black. If the Lord says go back and come again in another color, I would choose black. The only difference is I'll shave a few years off my seniority [laughs]."

When the daughter of Ruth Shelly, a fifty-three-year-old sociologist, decided not to stand for the national anthem at a baseball game, the people around her were angry. They called her names. The names that she was called had reference to being black, not being unpatriotic.

"There may be racism and all that, but this is the only country we got. When we sing our national anthem and many blacks sit, it bothers me," said Elizabeth Wright, a college administrator in her fifties who grew up in the South. "I feel a kinship when I stand and sing the "Star-Spangled Banner." If we are going to stay here in this country, we are going to have to relate to it. We are American and we are black. We can enjoy our heritage and put emphasis on our black authors, but undergirding all that, we are American. We worked to make this country what it is, and we should be proud to say we are American. I have some strong feelings about that. We need to get up and say 'I pledge allegiance to the flag' and hold up our heads." Elizabeth was initially somewhat hesitant in expressing her patriotism, remembering an incident fifteen years before when friends castigated her for having "little flags for her centerpiece" at a Fourth of July celebration.

Choosing a salient identity as an American or as a black is one of the many dilemmas of being black in this society. The decision is a process that invariably affects individual and group identity. The drama of the duality also unfolds in many other themes—class orientation versus race orientation, individualism versus collectivism, materialism versus spiritualism, Afrocentricity versus Eurocentricity, integration versus separation, and black pride versus universalism.

Class Orientation versus Race Orientation

How does the double-consciousness affect the orientation of black elite who are moving into the mainstream? Are they likely to adopt a class orientation to identify more with the white middle class or a race orientation to identify more with working-class and lower-class blacks? When a class orientation and a race orientation coexist, do black professionals experience them as contradictory?

Martin Kilson, a social scientist, hypothesized that "status deracialization" increases as blacks move into the mainstream. This upward mobility of blacks affects class identity.

> It allows, above all, new milieus to shape class awareness and identity milieus within which middle-class Blacks derive not mere professional, but also social and political orientations. When reinforced, in turn, by the increasing shift to suburban living among upper-strata Black families . . . we have the essential ingredients of a mainstream Black bourgeoisie.[8]

But does success mean that race matters less? I asked the Talented One Hundred the question, "Would you say in terms of your values, behaviors, attitudes, and lifestyles, you identify more with, that is, feel closer to, middle-class whites or working-class and lower-class blacks?" Seventy percent of the participants stated specifically that they identified with the working class. However, many individuals qualified their statements, admitting they had, as Jonathan Mobutu, a forty-year-old director of black studies and an economist at a major university in the Northeast, expressed, "peripheral white middle-class values, but their core values were working class." In general, they did not mention the lower class. Sixteen percent said they identified with middle-class whites, and 14 percent did not identify with either the white middle class or the black working class or lower class. They were likely to identify with middle-class blacks. They indicated that middle-class blacks were very different from middle-class whites in their values. Others did not identify with either class; rather, they emphasized their individuality.

This question generated interesting responses. Many of the Talented One Hundred often took long pauses, and I was asked repeatedly to restate the question as if suddenly they had become hearing impaired. When they recognized that there were inconsistencies in previous statements, there was an attempt to align their feelings because they did not reflect their beliefs of racial solidarity. One person reminded me that this conflict was reflected in an old folk saying, "They are my color, but not my kind."

Colbert Miller, a thirty-nine-year-old cardiologist, who was still sporting his late-sixties Afro hairstyle, delivered a passionate impromptu oration on the disintegration of race pride, the foibles of integration, and the need for race solidarity and empowerment of the masses.

> The worst thing that ever happened to this country is integration. As we progress, we have a tendency to try to assimilate into the other world, and that is why I think it is the worst thing that ever happened to us. It has kept us from progressing as a black race, because as soon as one of us makes a little money or gets an education, we have a tendency not to support our own institutions, our own people, and our own businesses. People think they are nigger rich,[9] have achieved, and gotten over. We try to get into the other world, and it doesn't make a difference if you are an MD, a PhD, a lawyer, or a major political figure, we are black in this society.

When I asked Colbert if he identified with middle-class whites or working-class or lower-class blacks, he stated middle-class whites. He took a lengthy pause and laughed. Continuing, he said, "I would like to theoretically identify with blacks, but you gave me a group, called lower-class and working-class people on the street, with which I can't identify. I don't say to them I am better than you, but my values do not identify with theirs." Colbert is from a working-class background; his father owned a small restaurant, and his mother worked for many years as a domestic.

Zora Neale Hurston, a popular black folklorist and writer during the Harlem Renaissance, captured well the contradiction between race pride and class orientation in *Dust Tracks on a Road*.

> "My people! My people!" From the earliest rocking of my cradle days, I have heard this cry go up from Negro lips. It is forced outward by pity, scorn, and hopeless resignation. It is called forth by the observations of one class of Negro on the doings of another branch of the brother in black. For instance, well-mannered Negroes groan out like that when they board a train or bus and find other Negroes on there with their shoes off, stuffing themselves with fried fish, bananas, and peanuts, and throwing the garbage on the floor. Maybe they are not only eating and drinking. The offenders may be "loud-talking" the place, and holding back nothing of their private lives, in a voice that embraces the entire coach. The well-dressed Negro shrinks back in his seat at that, shakes his head and sighs, "My people! My people!" . . . What that educated Negro knows further is that he can do very little towards imposing his own viewpoint on the lowlier members of his race. Class and culture stand between. The humble Negro has built-up antagonism to the "Big Nigger."[10]

This conflict between race pride and class orientation plays itself out in other scenes, for example, successful blacks who give lip service to supporting black institutions, as Colbert Miller stated, but support white institutions.

Though race pride and class orientation may be in conflict, they still affect individual and group identity. In a society that values individualism, the collectivism so essential in developing a strong black community is in opposition to the basic orientation of individualism. There is the inevitable tension between self-advancement and group advancement.

Self-Advancement versus Group Advancement

Benson Robinson, a fifty-two-year-old successful entrepreneur, embodied the conflicted drama of the duality. He appeared almost nonracial in his orientation. Yet he said that he identified more with working-class blacks. He said everyone should be concerned about him- or herself, and there are too many blacks on welfare, as well as too many begging in the black community for his help. His philosophy is, "It is not what is good for Benson Robinson, but what is good for Benson Robinson's business," and "begging is not good for business." Despite his philosophy, he spent five hundred thousand dollars for black contractors in 1987 and three million dollars in the past eight years. "People put me down because everybody got to have somebody to talk about. If Benson Robinson were not in business, where would people get this money?"

Tony Michaels, a fifty-year-old corporate manager, has a different philosophy. He described himself as a humanitarian and somewhat of a "misfit" because he has paid a price for his community involvement. Tony said, "The corporations tell you 'I really want you to put something back into the community,' but what they really measure you by is what you are doing in that corporation—the dollars that you bring to them. There is a tendency to write you off to some degree when you put a lot of effort into community service. They won't admit it, but it's true."

Prince Albert, a sixty-one-year-old artist of West Indian descent, feels "all professionals should be primarily concerned with their own advancement. It is an extra burden on blacks to be concerned with the masses first and themselves second. It is the nature of people to be concerned with their own advancement. When they have security, they can help others. In the United States, you have the feeling you are replaceable. So, professional excellence and performance have to be paramount. Otherwise you might not have a job. After that, you can afford to be charitable."

Prince Albert's comments point out an additional demand placed upon the black elite. A strong ethos undergirding the black community is that the black elite have a special obligation to assist the masses. This effort requires energy and commitment that conflict with a demanding career and familial obligations. Despite the fact that the black elite must be exemplary "ambassadors for the race," proving their capabilities and opening doors for other blacks, they still are expected to serve the community. There are often conflicting community, organizational, and professional goals. One journalist remarked that she frequently felt conflict between her sense of professional responsibility to report bad news about the black community and her sense of obligation to the black community. If the black elite do not appear sensitive to the needs of the black community, they are often the target of criticism.

Afrocentricity versus Eurocentricity: The Dilemma of the Black Elite

As upwardly mobile blacks enter the mainstream of American society, they are likely to "confront, at minimum, two options," said James E. Blackwell, sociologist and author of *Mainstreaming Outsiders: The Production of Black Professionals*.[11] They accommodate by adopting the Anglo-conformity model or by adopting cultural pluralism. The former is the dominant group's expectations. The latter model follows the dominant group's Eurocentric expectations in language and values in the world of work and the educational process but adheres to the Afrocentric view in other aspects of daily interaction, such as musical tastes, styles of worship, and linguistic patterns. Hence, there is always a conflict at the personal and societal level to appropriately balance this tension between the Afrocentric perspective and the Eurocentric perspective. When I commented to Clifford Warren, a prominent surgeon, about his collection of African art, he said, "I like everything black. Blackness is my orientation. It determines where I live, what I do, and with whom I practice. I like everything black." His sentence trailed off. Remembering that his wife is white, he looked away, explaining, "I agonized about it and how it is going to be accepted." In contrast, Graham Boston, a forty-four-year-old scientist, prefers to associate, to live, to work, and to worship with whites. He grew up with whites in the Northeast and feels more comfortable around whites than blacks. But when I asked about the probability of his children dating or marrying someone white, he retorted definitely, "No."

Ethel King, a thirty-eight-year-old journalist with a major newspaper, is dating a "Jewish fellow" and has experienced tension about her own degree of blackness. "Am I being a traitor because I am dating this person? Am I going to do less because I am dating this person? You wouldn't have to ask yourself these questions if you were white," said Ethel. She had dated interracially before, but was unable to handle it. However, when she met her present friend, she "liked him so much." Ethel admitted, "I started questioning myself all over again about can I do this. I realized it didn't bother me as much as it used to, and that scared me. So I had to question myself about that. When you are black, you end up doing that so many times. I don't know if a white man would question himself about dating a black woman. I think the sense of who we are is so tied to our blackness and the black community and what people think of us."

King added, "If you let it, the black community will dictate everything about your life—how you write and what you write. If I spend time with this guy, there are going to be people who feel my writing is not going to be valid anymore, because I am writing about the black experience. They will point to me and say, 'How would you know if you are with this white man?'"

There are innumerable manifestations of tension between Afrocentricity and Eurocentricity. For example, individuals who espouse an Afrocentric perspective may not desire to live in a black community, fearing their property may be devalued. Their "creed and deed" are generally consistent; yet inconsistencies arise when they do not want to live in a black neighborhood, to work with black people, or to attend a black college, because they still harbor negative stereotypes of other blacks, even when that environment has been nurturing. Sometimes people were embarrassed to admit these inconsistencies, and at other times they were so enthusiastic and felt so comfortable that they did not conceal their thoughts.

In general, the types of residency or workplace setting, physical appearance, style of dress, or political persuasion were not consistent indicators of Afrocentricity or Eurocentricity. Jonathan Mobutu believes, "Blacks must be bicultural to be successful, unless they function in either a totally black or totally white world at all times. Learning to be bicultural is especially difficult for young blacks. It causes me no specific problem, just inconvenience, because I think I understand how to use biculturality creatively as a tool to fight racism and oppression." Mobutu uses his biculturality creatively when he serves on different committees as a token black in his university. He views his assignment on these committees as an opportunity to gain an understanding of the governance of the university and how it functions so he can better assist blacks.

While Mobutu is managing the duality productively as a weapon against racism, over thirty years ago, sociologist E. Franklin Frazier, in *Black Bourgeoisie*, criticized the middle class for its unproductiveness. He castigated the black middle class of his era for creating "a world of make believe," centered around black business and black society, and hiding their insecurities and frustrations through conspicuous consumption.[12] Since Frazier's scathing indictment, there has been a concern over the consumptive material behavior of blacks as a compensatory lifestyle in handling racism. Although material success is an important value orientation in this society, the concern in the black community seems to be over a lifestyle of excessive conspicuous consumptive behavior versus a lifestyle of personal and collective acquisition of wealth to support and build a strong black community. This crucial distinction is not noted when one hears the outcry that "blacks are too materialistic."

The Trappings of Class

I asked the Talented One Hundred if they believed blacks are too materially oriented. Twenty-one percent were neutral, believing that American society was materialistic and the behavior of blacks was not any different. Vernon Jordan, lawyer and former executive director of the Urban League, like others, felt that he was "not prepared to make a judgment about that. This is a judgment for yourself." On the other hand, 53 percent of the individuals agreed that blacks are too materialistic, usually offering "compensatory reaction to racism" as an explanation.

Pat Robinson thought, for instance, "Blacks put more into material things than do whites. They want you to see the couch they are sitting on. It has to do with the black experience and being somebody. Going into my relatives' neighborhood, you can see one or two new Cadillacs, washed and cleaned in front of their awful houses. That is the only way to be somebody. The kids will throw a rock through the window if you try to fix up the house. You can't advance at work. You can't get status there. It's too late to go back to school and get an education. So what else is there to do?"

Ferdinand Hamilton, an administrator at a large predominantly white university in the Midwest, agreed, saying, "I understand the need to compensate for a lot of inequities. I used to think about that when I went down the dusty roads in Alabama and saw television antennas on dusty shacks. I got to thinking about what else do they have."

Though Jonathan Mobutu agreed with Ferdinand Hamilton and Pat Robinson, he felt "a focus on material trappings is becoming an ideology in its own right. Having a large quantity of these trappings is becoming an end rather than a means. It is becoming a measure of self-worth and success."

Marla Robinson, a forty-three-year-old civil rights administrator, believes we are materialistic; however, unlike others who locate their explanation in the ethos of the American culture, Marla thinks it is a remnant of our African ancestral heritage. "We came from a kingly-type environment, and there is a pride that goes way back. We buy the best, because we deserve the best. Before we were slaves, we were kingly, princely, and scholarly, and we had monuments of ivory and gold. Just like the streams, and like their rhythms, there is a pride that flows in our veins."

Although Hosea Kelley, a psychologist, also thinks blacks are too materialistic, he disagreed with Marla's Afrocentric perspective of materialism. "Materialism is not historically one of our values. It has been one of the destructive values that we've adopted."

In contrast to this view, Jeremiah Moses, a widely respected sixty-five-year-old politician, does not think materialism is destructive. In fact, he believes that materialism leads to an honest work ethic to acquire goods: "I think it is a healthy thing to be materialistic. We wouldn't have so many people satisfied to be not working, because you have to work at it or do something to get it. It's a lot better than going into empty houses, stealing wash tubs and sinks, and carrying them on their backs to get fifteen dollars."

Twenty-six percent of the Talented One Hundred to whom I posed the question disagreed with the statement that blacks are too materialistic. Often they expressed feelings similar to those of Jeremiah Moses.

Leo Aramis, a thirty-four-year-old journalist with a major daily paper in the Northeast, concurred that blacks are not materialistic enough, making the distinction between the acquisition of wealth and the consumption of material things.

> I don't know what is meant by materially oriented. I don't think we are materially oriented enough. I think that when we talk about getting gold chains and driving big cars, we call that materially oriented. And that is not; it's trappings and a hangover from when we could do nothing else. We couldn't buy a house because they wouldn't sell us one. We couldn't invest in stocks. So the only things they would let us have were big cars. So we had big long cars and little bitty houses. And that's where they get this whole material aspect. We are not materialistic enough. We don't buy land, make investments, and perpetuate wealth for our youngsters. We need to get more materialistic and less boggler minded.

One concern is the excessive consumption of physical assets and the lack of acquisitive behavior toward financial assets. Another concern is ambivalence about the acquisition of wealth, which is deeply rooted in an ascetic Christian ethic that views the accumulation of wealth as morally suspect and is reflected in such biblical admonitions as "The love of money is the root of all evil," "For it is easier for a camel to go through the eye of a needle than for a rich man to enter the kingdom of God," and "The meek shall inherit the earth." In the sixties, the rise of the black nationalist movement and other radical groups raised the level of consciousness about the inequities in the distribution of wealth in a capitalistic society. Hence, blacks who were upwardly mobile, acquiring physical and financial assets, were viewed as selling their souls to capitalism or betraying their black identity.

Jonathan Walden, a thirty-nine-year-old minister and social activist, believes, "There is nothing wrong with having material goods in life. My only caution from a religious viewpoint is those things not be put before God. If God is first, we should be blessed to enjoy all that life has to offer."

John Lamont, a fifty-four-year-old physicist at a major university on the West Coast, sees an even more subtle side to the ambivalence toward wealth that emerges out of a racial ethos that somehow "wealth is not for black people," noting, "Martin L. King Jr. once said that the material side has its place. We need wealth in our society. Somehow there is a psychology of equating black to impoverishment. As we develop in this society, one manifestation will be the wealth of that group. And we will somehow have to come to grips with that wealth as well as maintaining a spiritual identity as Afro Americans."

The ambivalent values and attitudes toward materialism that evolved out of a Christian ascetic worldview also have a racial side. On one hand, there is a feeling that wealth is unobtainable for the masses of blacks; hence, there may be a rejection of the idea, but not the class trappings. Second, in a society that values competitiveness and individualism, there is a belief that blacks who amass a fortune will forsake their identity and the black struggle. Joshua Smith, chairman and CEO of Maxima Corporation, the ninth-largest black business in the United States, has captured these contradictions about wealth among blacks. He said, "I have witnessed a number of people who have emerged. I have noticed there is an acceptance of a white lifestyle—having a house in the suburbs and sending their children to private schools. The behavioral pattern of blacks who reach financial success is that they want to be accepted by other groups. We tend to be less active in the group from which we came."

Even though Joshua is referred to as "that black millionaire," he sees his wealth as "new wealth—on paper—but not yet established." Yet, he said, people always comment to him, "The thing I like about you, Joshua, is that you haven't changed." "I say, 'What am I supposed to change to?' I always ask them what they mean, and they comment, 'All other people I know, when they get important, they change.'"

For Joshua, "wealth is a product of achievement. Wealth is a feeling of reward. Wealth is the satisfaction that I am moving in the right direction, that I am helping and will help others, and that I am making a difference. Wealth is something in time, stage, and manner that I want to achieve."

Joshua has some "basic problems about the subject of wealth and black people."

There is a definite dogma that wealth is not for black people. It is very clear. Our politicians talk about the large corporations without any signs or without any beliefs that we could be those large corporations. We talk about the rich as if blacks will not be rich. Rich people are those people over there. Wealth is something for others. I think it characterizes the problem of black people in a capitalistic society. I've said in many of my speeches, we live in a capitalistic society in the United States. I didn't invent it and you didn't invent it. It is driven by motivation to achieve wealth, and it is important that we understand that it is a measure of success. Wealth is a factor that permeates all other factors that we are lacking. We have no political clout. Jews have fewer people, but much more political clout. . . .

Wealth is something we have by the way of income. Blacks earn $250 billion a year collectively. This wealth is equivalent to the ninth-largest country in the free world. There is wealth in blacks, but the wealth is not collective. The wealth is individual, and the earnings are masked by debts. We are in debt. We do not own houses. We do not have our money in the market working for us. We do not have real assets. As a result of not having real assets, even though we have the earning power, we have no influence in this country.

In general, the Talented One Hundred perceived their assets as below those of their white peers, but above those of their black peers. A study by the U.S. Bureau of the Census in 1991 showed that the median white household net worth was ten times that of the median black household—$43,280 and $4,170, respectively.[13]

Andrew Brimmer, a black economist, noted that blacks place more of their money in physical assets than financial assets. This assumption is supported by the fact that 76 percent of the total black wealth is in homes, motor vehicles, and checking accounts, while the percentage for whites is 58 percent. Only 11.6 percent of black wealth is in interest-earning assets, stocks, and mutual fund shares, while 26 percent of white wealth is invested in these ways. Moreover, 56 percent of black households own no interest-bearing assets.[14]

Joshua feels our ambivalent attitudes toward wealth may interfere with our acquiring it. "It constantly baffles me about why we refer to rich people as 'they,' corporations as 'them,' and wealth as not for us. We seem to bathe in being like our peers and we'll go into great debt just to impress our peers, none of whom have wealth. That seems to be our modus operandi. It seems the higher we go, the more debt we go into."

Reflecting, Joshua concluded, "There has to be a basic change when people say 'I am rich. That's good. What have I done wrong?' In other ethnic groups that is why they network for the achievement of wealth."

As we have seen, duality plays itself out in many themes. While it presents a problem, unless the actions of individuals are perceived as a group threat, there is a collective tolerance level for the ambivalence and conflict. Many scholars, however, see the duality as adaptive. Elaine Pinderhuges noted, "While it requires great expenditures of energy and can lead to identity confusion, some Afro Americans are able to become exceptionally clear about their identity and values."[15] Jefferson Barnes agreed:

It presents both opportunities and problems. The opportunities of marginality give an inside view about one's social existence that transcends the ordinary consciousness. If you have a double-consciousness, you understand those things that other people can't possibly consider. It is what happens to women who are able to see the world of men, but men can't see the world of women. Blacks can see the world of whites, but whites can't see the world of blacks. [Like] any group that is disadvantaged, at any level—because we are human and have mental capacity—we sometimes get more insights into a phenomenon than if we had naked power. Naked power strips our consciousness in many ways. Du Bois was correct about that, but I don't think it should be taken to mean a negative consciousness.

Since "blacks can see the world of whites," the duality creates positive and negative charges when black people walk on racial high wires.

WATCHING AND WALKING THE RACIAL TIGHTROPE

"When a Jew enters a room of Gentiles, a Chicano, a room of Anglos, a Black, a room of Whites, there is a common reaction, namely, the minority member will attempt to sense out where there is severe hostility and bigotry," says Johnnetta Cole, an anthropologist.[16] Perhaps this phenomenon explains why American blacks and whites continue to differ in their perceptions of the treatment of blacks. For example, in a Gallup survey of blacks residing in predominantly white communities, 64 percent of whites said blacks in their community were treated "the same as whites," but only 44 percent of blacks believed they were treated equally.[17] Cole calls this trait the "minority sense," noting that "minority subculture teaches that one must detect or at least attempt to detect hostile attitudes and behavior in the interest of self-protection—from protection of one's pride and self-esteem to protection of one's life."[18]

Whether this trait is referred to as the "minority sense," the "sixth sense," or the "race watch," as I call it, it is the protective gauge used in navigating the racial tightrope. Many of the Talented One Hundred see race watching as a twenty-four-hour duty.

"You are on guard all the time. You run the risk of being schizophrenic. You always know you are black, and you are always anticipating white people and how blacks will react to you," remarked Ferdinand Hamilton.

"The society is racist, and you have to figure out how to compete. In order to compete, you have to be by and large better. You have to be more conscious of details than your white peers. You know that people are looking over your shoulder. The same transgressions your white peers might make, you can't afford, because people are envious of where you sit in the first place," said Hamilton.

Agreeing, Jack B. Lane said, "We live in a racist society and we all do maintain a certain guard. Sometimes I may not be conscious of it, but I probably maintain it. I find myself in settings and meetings, and it comes to me every now and then that I am the only person of color there. I say to myself, if I were not here, they probably would be saying something else about black folks. In my presence, they don't say this about black folks. They only feel it, but they do not express it." Jack senses this even though he has not heard anything and has been treated cordially.

Walter Calvin, a forty-four-year-old corporate executive with an international conglomerate, grew up in the rural South, and he believes strongly that it has inured him, and other Southern blacks, giving them an edge on the race watch. "I think Southern blacks tend to have a kind of resilience to racism. You are able to almost expect it, see it, and understand it in ways that people who have not grown up in this kind of environment may not be able to catch the signals quite as fast. Once you know it, feel it, and understand it, you do not get preoccupied with it. You move on," says Walter. "You put a shield over one eye saying I know this is my racism eye, and the other eye I am going to keep on the ball in terms of where I am going."

Keeping one eye on racism and "keeping one eye on the ball" seemed to be the modus operandi for the Talented One Hundred. Jefferson Barnes learned very early the lessons of navigating between two worlds from growing up in a tough "working-class neighborhood of gangs and violence in Chicago." He was the valedictorian of his class, acting the "perfect gentleman" while in school. But when he left school, he acted tough like some of the gang. "I had the task in my early teens of navigating a real tightrope," he said.

Jefferson told me a story to capture the navigation. He was "captain of the boys," and his teacher, leaving him in charge, instructed him to direct the boys to the library for an assignment when he heard the bell ring. "As soon as she went down the hall, we started acting up and talking about each other's mama. I get up and I am doing my little rap. The class is quiet. I look and there is Ms. Jackson. She says, 'Barnes, I am ashamed of you. You go to the back of the classroom; you are no longer in this row.' From that moment on, my standing with the classroom skyrockets. I learned don't go too far in that direction to make this tightrope work," he recalled. It shaped Barnes's view of how you navigate in the world. Learning the rules of the game, he balanced a "cat-like navigational development—a difficult reign," said Barnes. Consequently, when he left his high school, which was 99 percent black, and went to a 99 percent white college, he had "gotten so good at tightrope walking and so good at understanding that you had to know how people were coming at you and how they felt that going into the white man's world was one more tightrope walking."

For successful blacks, walking the racial tightrope is another reality of the color line manifesting itself in many arenas. Marla Robinson talked about the problem of the black administrator/manager in the world of work. Many black administrators who head mixed or predominantly white organizations are concerned about the issue of racial balancing, because they are sensitive to discrimination and often fear charges of reverse discrimination by whites. In her previous position, Robinson recalled, the black executive director of a social welfare agency "hired only whites around her. And when she lost her job, the same people she hired generated a lot of negative publicity about her and were not supportive."

Robinson said that the executive director was "arrogant" and not sensitive to black issues, indicating she did not need the black community because she was supported by the Junior League. After her firing, she became very black and very involved in black organizations. "She is at all the banquets—the NAACP, the National Council of Negro Women, and the Urban League. When she became the executive director, these organizations were the kind I wanted her to join; they could have saved her. If she had been involved with her people, she could have cried on their shoulders and regrouped. Before her firing, I could not get her to go to a black church, and she looked down upon black organizations."

Ned McMillian, a fifty-four-year-old physician, agreed with Marla, saying, "Black corporations are so concerned about discrimination and racial balancing that they'll hire a white over a black. They go beyond the call of duty to show whites that they are okay." He thinks other ethnic groups help one another more than blacks help each other.

John Hubbard, a forty-year-old professor of sociology at a predominantly white university in the Midwest, thinks about "balancing race all the time." Since he is in a tenure-track position, he de-emphasizes race, because he doesn't "want to be perceived as a boat rocker or radical." He said, "That makes me not threatening because I don't harp on race all the time." Even one colleague commented to

him, "I don't think of you as a black faculty—just a faculty." He learned to manage race relations by toning down the discussion on the subject, particularly after
his white students' evaluations reflected that he "talked too much about sexism
and racism."

Davis and Watson's *Black Life in Corporate America: Swimming in the Mainstream* noted the stress caused by the perplexity of deciphering race-related behavior.[19] To succeed in the corporate world, one has to skillfully navigate corporate politics and race politics. Listen to Warner Babbitt, a thirty-nine-year-old
journalist with one of the most reputable newspapers in the country, discuss balancing "how to play corporate Uncle Tom without making white folks uncomfortable. . . . A lot of blacks go into corporations blissfully unaware of political
and cultural differences. We grow up being taught to carry ourselves with dignity and don't be an Uncle Tom. This is great character building, but it is bad
politics in a predominantly white corporation." He thinks whites are Uncle Toms
more than blacks are. "I never thought of carrying my superior's coat; to me, that
was being an Uncle Tom. To them, it is using common sense. I view it as an attack on my dignity. They view it as getting ahead."

Babbitt believes that corporate Uncle Tomism is a prerequisite in his industry. He had to "figure out how to do the corporate Uncle Tom bit without becoming the Uncle Tom in the traditional sense blacks view it. . . . You have to
study it very carefully, because there is a downside to it. If you try to play the
same corporate Uncle Tom as whites, because a number of white superiors do
not see you as on their par, they start seeing you in the traditional role."

There are other issues to balance in the world of work. Thomas B. Thomas,
a thirty-eight-year-old marketing manager from Maryland, knows he might lose
his "fair share of business" when he "dresses for success" or displays other symbols of material success. It suggests to many whites that he is "one step closer
to where they are." When he drove up in his Cadillac, a client asked, "Is that
your Cadillac?" "Yes, it is my car," he replied. "You are overpaid," said the customer, "and you don't need my business."

Blacks walk the tightrope not only with whites, but also with other blacks. In
her administrative position with a federal agency, Diane Earlinger feels isolated
from her black colleagues as well as whites. Since she is in a high-ranking position, blacks mistrust her. They see her as a part of the system, making networking to improve working conditions among blacks more difficult. "Sometimes you are made to feel guilty because you are up there. Why can't you make
the system different? Why don't you take a stronger stand on these issues? You
are getting extra pressure," said Diane.

Walking the tightrope is not confined to Diane's world of work. She also finds
herself balancing it for her children. "It's so difficult for parents. You are always
balancing what is the right thing to do," she said. Before having children, Earlinger and her husband lived in a predominantly white community; however,
they thought it was important for their children to grow up in a black neighbor-

hood "knowing who they are." Although advocates of public education, they were not happy with the school system, and were, therefore, unwilling to sacrifice their children's education. The compromise was to live in a black community and to send their children to a private school "to learn to read, write, and do arithmetic and to balance that with the interaction of their cultural heritage."

Like Earlinger, most of the Talented One Hundred want their children to be citizens of the world, interacting with diverse racial and ethnic groups. Walking the tightrope requires balancing black pride with universal concerns. "There is a need to balance special nurturing from cultural roots, but one must, at the same time, live in harmony with other people," remarked Teresa Hale, a fifty-four-year-old psychologist from California.

The tightrope walking can increase one's feelings of marginality. While growing up in the 1930s, John Daniels, a sixty-two-year-old corporate executive, had to walk between two worlds—his predominantly white school and his black community. Balancing those concerns produced a split personality, "creating a painful marginality" that scarred his adulthood. He remembered his father saying about his success in the predominantly white school, "You are getting too big for your britches."

"The whole racism thing is incredible. There are so many things that blacks who are in a minority situation have to deal with that other people don't," said Cassie Cooper, a vice president of academic affairs at a predominantly black university and in her mid-thirties. "If you walk into a cafeteria and find three or four blacks at a table together and you are with your white colleague, where do you decide to eat? You don't want to give the impression that all blacks want to be together and isolate themselves at a time when you are saying you really want to be a part of the organization."

Bernice Sumlin, educator and former national president of Alpha Kappa Alpha sorority, resolved this conflict by "sitting with her black friends if she sees them at predominantly white gatherings. . . . When there are white friends in mixed gatherings, I'll go over and sit with them."

Being black, one is constantly balancing on the racial high wire in some area of one's life, whether it's professional concerns versus community obligations, individual concerns versus collective obligations, black pride versus universal concerns, Afrocentric orientation versus Eurocentric orientation, or integration versus separation. To be black is to be keenly aware that if one missteps, there is a dual standard by which one is judged.

TO BE BLACK IN AMERICA IS TO EXPERIENCE A DOUBLE STANDARD

Blacks in this society are judged by a different standard than whites in customs, education, employment, health, and housing. These dual expectations are inherent in the nature of a racist society. In reacting to racism, blacks also judge other blacks by a double standard.

Since the double standard is so ubiquitous, I shall illustrate its complexities through a subject that many of the Talented One Hundred candidly discussed—black politics, corruption, and racism.

Said Robert Woodson, "Two out of five black elected officials are facing some legal action. Someone would look at that and say that is an expression of racism, and, therefore, focus attention on what white people are doing." With the increasing number of black public officials under scrutiny for corruption, many blacks adhere to a conspiracy theory. They believe that whites are out to destroy black leaders, diffusing their power base in the black community. But others question the theory. "If the government targets all blacks to be investigated, that is unfair. However, if during the investigation, they found all blacks doing things that were wrong or in violation of the law, they should be exposed," remarked forty-five-year-old Roscoe Champion, a judge. But, he adds, "We should hold white officials to the same standards." Yet we cannot, Robert Woodson argued, "allow racism to be used as a cover for the indiscretion of people. Blacks can exploit the whole racial issue."

Mayor Johnny Longtree, a sixty-five-year-old, knows that "black officials steal and white officials steal. And we can't steal as much, because we are not in as many situations to steal." He feels both blacks and whites are subjected to scrutiny, "but it's more volatile when it's blacks."

Elizabeth Wright feels that some black politicians have invited criticisms and investigations by their actions. Judge Champion agreed that "it invites suspicion when a part-time councilperson with a sixteen-thousand-dollar salary drives a Mercedes-Benz. The larger society suspects black officials. They think we want to line our pockets. They know that prior to getting elected, we didn't have anything. They don't understand how we make so little as part-time elected officials and live on the level that suggests we make two hundred thousand dollars."

As a politician, it is important to be economically independent, advocates Mayor Longtree, also a successful lawyer. He was invited to President Carter's inauguration and to the White House several times for dinner, and he knows one can come to enjoy "that glamorous lifestyle." However, he noted, "most of us who go into politics are dependent on a job. So you get a lot of pressure if you don't make money, because a lot of time must be devoted to the elected office and you can't work on that job. So with that glamorous lifestyle, many succumb to the temptation that is available with money."

Mayor Longtree "never took a quarter," because he understands "there is a double standard. . . . You have to be morally upright if you are black." Joseph Lowery feels it is not "fair to ask blacks to be more perfect than their white predecessors." Yet he thinks "black officials have a responsibility to live aboveboard and to recognize that they are being scrutinized more intensely than their white predecessors. Whether it's fair or not, they have to reckon with it."

Though Robert Woodson believes "there should be a single moral compass and a single means of judging misbehavior," racism has contributed to his understanding that "we have a responsibility not to be like white folks. There is too much corruption going on around black officials. . . . I did not struggle in the civil rights movement to take white pigs away from the trough to be replaced by black pigs. I fought against pigs being at the trough," said Woodson, in a rising voice.

Jack B. Lane concurred that some black elected officials want to copy the worst habits of the majority population, like "stealing, cheating, and lying." But he did not think "we can do it," saying, "I think the young black men and women that came out of the civil rights movement and got involved in politics have a special obligation—a mandate and a mission to inject something very meaningful into American politics. We have to inject some of that ethic, some of that humanity, some of that sense of commitment, some of that sense of caring, and some of that sense of sharing, because of that legacy we have to uphold."

When black officials fail to uphold the legacy, Lowery noted, "people always ask what is it going to do to black leadership?" He quipped, "What did Richard Nixon's downfall do to white leadership? We have had three white presidents since Nixon—one exposed, one condemned, and one banished. I never heard anybody raise the question, does it hurt white leadership? It is a racist notion to suggest that what happens to one black leader, if something bad happens and the allegations are true, discredits black leadership. It is a racist double standard."

Black leaders and black people's trials are ongoing, because inherent in the verdict of the double standard is a life sentence to perennial probation.

TO BE BLACK IS TO BE ON PERENNIAL PROBATION

When Judge Roscoe Champion sat in judgment of others, he, too, was being judged by his white peers and the public to see if he was fair. Champion said that he finally convinced them that "I was not discriminating against whites nor was I giving blacks preferential treatment, but I was applying the law." Having proved that he was competent and fair, his colleagues accepted him. He initiated many changes in the court system. Judge Champion's experience is symbolic of another day's probation in the lives of blacks.

To break down racial barriers, the Jackie Robinsons and the Doug Williamses had to prove themselves in sports; the Jesse Jacksons and the Adam Clayton Powells had to prove themselves in politics. In every arena, there is an admission test and an ongoing evaluation. Said Laura Price, a successful gynecologist, "You can have all the credentials, have finished your internships, have been certified and recertified, and have a successful practice, but when you go to meetings, you will not be recognized." These experiences at white medical meetings have been "crushing for me," she remarked. "Sitting at the back of the bus in the 1950s didn't bother me as much as this."

Being black and female, Laura was sentenced to double probation. When she opened her practice in her Southern hometown as a gynecologist, she noted, "the community was more skeptical because I was female." Even though she described herself as "straightforward, Christian, honest, and educated," blacks were initially hesitant to be treated by her, despite her competence. She said, "I had to work harder. I had to stay in my office and attend to my patients very carefully. I had to go over and beyond the call of duty." With her reputation established, the probation was lifted. The word spread through the black community that "when you call, she will answer. When you go into labor, she will be at your side. She will call in other doctors or do whatever she can to make sure your health is maintained. She is a good doctor."

Laura's office is so overfilled with patients today that she has to turn them away. She has proven herself to the black community, but she is still on probation with both her black male and white colleagues in the medical field. She is the only black female officer in her local Black Medical Association, and black females are still considered to be the lowest caste of members of the American Medical Association.

Diane Earlinger also has a medical degree. Like Laura Price, she has proven herself repeatedly. However, she said, "At this point I have no interest in proving to anyone what I can do. I have no energy [for] trying to prove or educate people considered uneducable, and that is the average smartass white boy [laughs]. There is no incentive for him to change his beliefs and attitudes. His beliefs and attitudes are getting him where he wants to be, so why change them?" Since she believes whites have no vested interest in changing, she is less interested in proving herself and more interested in "making sure the system guarantees opportunities for every black." She knows that no matter how hard one tries to prove oneself, to be black is to be never good enough in the eyes of a racist society.

TO BE BLACK IS TO BE NEVER GOOD ENOUGH

To achieve as much as they did, the Talented One Hundred had to be better than the best. Graham Boston, a scientist and engineer, who has been in a predominantly white environment during his entire life, remarked, "There is no one in my office who can come up to me and say that I'm not good enough. I don't take risks. So when I want something, I work hard at being better than anyone else and at reducing the risk. And it gives me a better opportunity to get what I want. My technique is to be better than anyone else."

Aretha Shield had to learn this painful lesson by trial and error. She had grown up believing, "If you worked hard and had enough talent, people would see the capability. But I live in a society that has a very strict code of passage."

As illustrated earlier in the story of "Little Black Tombo," Diane Earlinger, too, has learned that "there is no way a black person can be successful enough, smart enough, or rich enough to be equal." Even when blacks' intellectual capacity is individually recognized, there are other reminders, said a chief of police. "None of the men will say I am not smart enough for the position. They will come up with all kinds of other things, such as I haven't come through the ranks and I have no experience."

In areas like sports and music, where blacks have traditionally been allowed to excel, they still have to prove themselves. Several months prior to his death, I interviewed Booty Wood, a sixty-seven-year-old former leading soloist who had a long-playing tenure with the bands of Duke Ellington, Count Basie, and Lionel Hampton. He reported that after his illness and retirement from the Count Basie band in the mid-1980s, he had to audition to play at an obscure club. Though he had an established reputation as an excellent trombone player, the nightclub manager would still "go and get some high school trombone player." He said, "Many blacks are left out. You got to be super good to be even considered for a local band." In Dayton, he exclaimed, "they claim I can't play a show. I played shows in Paris and all over the world. . . . Years ago, they would get the least qualified blacks and let them fall on their faces and say they can't play a show," he lamented.

In his fifty years as a member of the American Federation of Musicians union, he has received only one call from the organization. Booty threatened to sue one owner of a night club and was hired. The owner eventually told him he was the best trombone player, although he had been told by others that he could not play.

"White folks just presume black folks are incompetent. It is an authentic presumption, wherever we go and whatever we do," claimed Leo Aramis. "Instead of getting blatant discrimination, you get that presumed level of incompetence and paternalistic kind of thing." He cited an example from his own experience. When Leo sat down to talk with a group of students about the field of journalism and asked them "questions that they needed to be able to answer," his white intern started answering the questions. "I told him to shut up. Why are you answering these questions I am asking them?" Repeated Aramis, "There is a presumed level of incompetence."

A "presumed level of incompetence" is the primary reason Jeraldyne Blunden, the artistic director and founder of the nationally acclaimed Dayton Contemporary Dance Company, has transmitted to her children the race lesson that she learned from her parents: "You have to be twice as good to be almost equal." This lesson was first conveyed during a prize fight in the 1940s involving Joe Louis. She remembered, "Blacks stood still to listen. There were no cars on the street. When he won, you could hear the horns blasting. The black man had to be better than anybody else to get a chance to box."

Like Jeraldyne, Teresa Stanfield, a college administrator, also learned from her parents the lesson that "a black person has to be twice as good to have the same job as a white person." It was the prevailing sentiment of her all-black community in the Midwest. "You had to excel in order to be acceptable."

It is an adaptive strategy of successful blacks to create unrealistic strivings, even when they know they are never good enough in the eyes of a racist society. But they continue to strive, because they are always "ambassadors for the race." It is a race burden each must bear.

TO BE BLACK IS TO BEAR THE RACE BURDEN

"Never being good enough" spurs successful blacks to always be super blacks. They continue to strive, because their personal success is symbolic of the achievement of all blacks. Hence, "individual blacks feel a significant responsibility to represent the race," said Cassie Cooper.

Agreeing, Jonathan Mobutu knows, as black poet Langston Hughes noted, "You are always an ambassador for your race." It is his strategy for dealing with racism. He said, "Whenever I am involved in something, the presupposition is going to be that I am there as a token because I am black. I make it my business to immediately take the offensive and demonstrate that I know as much, if not more, than whites do about their subject or whatever, and that I know about the black experience and am able to pull it into the discussion, so it can demonstrate some additional complexity." With his increasing confidence and his increasing awareness, he has become more aggressive in employing this strategy to "pull more information together" than his white colleagues and thus "control the situation."

In representing the race, one becomes the spokesperson and symbol for the group's failures, its successes, and its causes. Jefferson Barnes is frequently called upon to be the spokesperson on his predominantly white campus. "Whenever there is a problem involving blacks on campus, I get a phone call. It is a case so far removed from white professors that they reach out and grab you." Laughing, he remarked, "I got a phone call at eleven o'clock at night from a high-level administrator, saying 'Barnes, we have a problem.' I said, 'What's our problem, boss?'" There was a rape on campus involving blacks, and the administrator wanted to know, should it be kept quietly out of the newspaper that they are black? "The fact that my race is so invariably relevant that they would call me, even though I was so far from the scene, is ludicrous. Why were they telling me that they had a problem?"

Over forty years before, during World War II, John Daniels was also "far from the scene" when students at his white high school attended a dance on the army base. The white school principal asked him and all the other black students to come to his office the next day. The principal reminded them that whites and blacks should not dance together. Although the few black students who attended the dance on the army base were not involved, black soldiers, who were stationed in the area, had danced with white girls, and the military police were called in to break up the dance. John was deeply hurt by the actions of the principal. He was the perfect ambassador for his race. John was the president of the newspaper staff and very popular, but this dance incident reminded him of the reality of racism. He always played by the rules, saying, "I was particularly bitter at the notion that the principal didn't think I knew the name of this game." He, like his grandfather, wanted to be "well thought of by whites."

Over forty years later, Dira Ridley's thirteen-year-old daughter wants to "play by the rules" of white society to achieve success. Dira mentioned that her daughter is embarrassed by the social behavior of blacks in her school, because they are "loud and boisterous in the cafeteria." She, herself, is also embarrassed "to go through the inner city where people are loud." "Granted, I am using a yardstick and saying that behavior is not acceptable by white standards. In the real world, based on successful individuals, you don't act that way," she said.

As a spokesperson and symbol for the race, a successful black person is also expected to be the expert on any subject dealing with blacks. When Robert Snow, now a city attorney, sat on the moot court as the only black student in his law school in the seventies, he was called upon to respond to all the race questions when the moot board was accused of racism. He said, "I took the first question and the next. It was one of the few times I lost my coolness in public. I arrogantly said I was not going to answer one more race question. I was not there to answer race questions. No one had accused me of racism. If they wanted the question answered, they should ask the board members who were accused of being racist." He later found out from a white partner that there was a prearranged plan to ask him the race questions.

One of the heaviest race burdens the black elite must bear is the notion of responsibility in empowering the masses. Du Bois espoused this idea in his concept of the Talented Tenth. His notion that the black elite should provide leadership is deeply embedded in the black community. This notion embodies a strongly held ethos among various strata of the black community that blacks who are "making it" in society have a "special obligation to uplift the masses." When I asked the Talented One Hundred how they felt about the statement, "Some people feel that blacks who are 'making it' in society have a special obligation to help the masses of blacks," most agreed.

But they do not always feel as strongly as Jack B. Lane, who believes, "Those of us who have been blessed or given an opportunity have a moral obligation, almost a calling. It's in a biblical sense like responding to the Macedonian call. You got to do it. We've been given something special, so a little more is required of us." Having greater resources, they agree with Lane's dictum that more is required of them.

While the idea of the black elite's responsibility for the masses is a popular one, Thomas B. Thomas, a district sales manager for a major corporation, reminds us that often their "creed is not equal to their deed." Many of the Talented One Hundred admitted they and their peers could do more. Few individuals among the Talented One Hundred subscribed to the notion that the responsibility for "uplifting the masses" lies solely with the black elite. Rather, their views reflect a continuum in a synthesis of competing positions. One position sees black poverty, for example, as a complex issue that requires a national solution. Thus, both the government and the private sector should be involved; but the government has the greater responsibility in the solution of the problem. Another position sees a national role for the black elite as having a responsibility in the solution of black poverty.

If the black elite are expected to play a role, what should it be? There are individuals among the Talented One Hundred who think the black elite should play a general role. One general role is political, a role of pressure and politics to make the government more responsive to the poor. Since the black elite have greater resources, another general role is to support the economic development of black institutions and organizations; to provide social services, like organizational skills and knowledge; and to assist in the transformation of values. And they should serve as role models.

But many of the Talented One Hundred rejected these general roles, espousing instead a more specific role. These individuals advocated that "one should contribute according to his or her talent." For example, a physician might organize the community around health issues, while an entrepreneur can provide economic development, training, and jobs. Still others see both general and specific roles for the black elite.

Among the Talented One Hundred were critics of the notion of the black elite's special obligation and responsibility to uplift and provide leadership to the black masses. Prince Albert feels that "all professionals should be primarily concerned with their own advancement. It is an extra burden on blacks to be concerned about the masses first and themselves second. It is the nature of people to be concerned about their own advancement. When they have enough, they can help others."

Ethel King thinks it is "a racist double standard" and an "unfair burden for black professionals to have an obligation to the masses. . . . Why should they feel that any more than a white person who has made it? It should come from the individual. No one should have to point the finger and say every black who makes it should feel an obligation. It does not have to do with being black, but with being human," said King. She believes there is an "inherent danger" that people may come to view the solution to the problem as lying solely with blacks, absolving the government of any responsibility. This view is supported by Bart Landry.[20]

Ruth Shelly views this idea of the black elite's obligation as elitist. "You have a special obligation to yourself, and this notion is elitist. It sounds like the master who felt a responsibility for his slaves. This is setting one group against another," noted Ruth.

Critics further point out that feeling a special obligation implies a lack of free will. If black middle-class individuals want to contribute to the uplifting of the masses, it should be encouraged, but they should not feel it is their special obligation. This ethos may encourage the black elite to contribute to strengthening the black community out of a sense of guilt, rather than out of a sense of concern and commitment.

Similarly, critics say that when the black elite feel it is their responsibility to uplift the masses, it implies paternalism. This view fails to acknowledge self-responsibility in determining one's destiny. Moreover, it suggests that leadership cannot emerge from the masses. It is argued that, while the black elite have greater resources, strengthening the black community requires the collective efforts of everyone, especially since the black middle class, working class, and the poor are bound by the color line.

Ruth Shelly aptly noted that "strengthening of the black community cannot emerge unless there is a collective consciousness." This collective consciousness can come only with a transformation of values, which involves a redefinition of priorities in the black community. Thus, when a transformation of values occurs, a sense of concern and commitment, implied in the notion of the black elite's responsibility and special obligation to the masses, will emerge. But this sense of commitment will be not only the group's concern and responsibility but also the individual's.

Despite the critics, the Talented One Hundred, in general, feel a strong sense of commitment and responsibility for empowering the masses. Like others among the Talented One Hundred, Jefferson Barnes feels it is an "unfair burden," which is "true for any form of injustice. But blacks have a special burden to deal with black issues, and how they deal with them is complicated. It is an extra burden, but we should bear it."

Pat Robinson agreed, "It is an imposing demand, but it is absolutely insidious to take the opposite view."

TO BE BLACK IS TO BE ALWAYS IN A PRECARIOUS STATUS

Jefferson Barnes, Pat Robinson, and most of the Talented One Hundred understand that, in accepting the special race burden of empowering the masses, their destinies are inextricably linked, because blacks' success is so precarious in this society. If Benson Robinson, an entrepreneur and millionaire, can be told by his white customers whom to hire, it reflects the status of blacks in this society. Benson told me that one white manager wanted to impress him, so he hired more blacks. "I had six blacks working in the same area, and a very prominent white doctor told me about two and a half years ago, 'Benson, I would like to talk with you.' He had been a good customer of mine," Benson said. "You have a hell of a good business here. We are all proud of you. You are doing an excellent job, but I feel you are making a mistake. It's good you are upgrading blacks, but I think you got too many at the door." Benson's reply to the doctor was, "'Thank you very much. I'll take a look at it.' I get busy and I don't see a lot of things. . . . One day I decided to go out and look, and I said I do have quite a bit out here. Then I got a couple of more complaints." The customers implied that too many blacks might scare away white customers. Finally, Benson dispersed black employees to his businesses located in mixed or black neighborhoods.

The following stories of John Daniels, Kelly Smith, and Diane Earlinger further illustrate the precariousness of black success. Before his retirement, John Daniels was a senior vice president and assistant to the chairman and CEO of a major corporation. Daniels was more than an affirmative action case, stating, "I had the authority and the blank check from the chairman. I had every capacity to influence. I was on his board. I worked directly for him, and he owned 80 percent of the company. So he gave me a blank check to do anything. I came in at the top and stayed at the top."

Daniels was able to "totally integrate the company and eliminate discriminatory patterns." Before he joined the company, the chairman indicated to Daniels that he was amenable to changes, telling him, "If you say so, John, it will happen." The chairman had supported the first black mayor of his city, and he also encouraged corporate responsibility. "I made sure all the vice presidents were lifetime members of the NAACP. [He laughed.] They would have to make speeches at black schools," said Daniels.

The CEO died, and the company underwent reorganization. The direction of the company changed, and this affected John's influence in the company, so he retired. He had an interested and concerned mentor who was committed to effecting changes, but his untimely death indicated the precariousness of Daniels's influence.

Kelly Smith, a high-ranking manager at an international company, was greatly assisted by her mentor, the CEO, a white male, in getting a promotion, after another white supervisor discouraged her from seeking the position. Within a month of her promotion, the CEO died.

Diane Earlinger became the first top female administrator at her international agency. Although she was the "best-qualified person," her white division directors were upset because they expected to get the job. "After all, they had been there for thirty years and thought they earned it," noted Earlinger. In her first meeting with the division directors, she told them, "I never had the pleasure of working with anyone like you or anyone I necessarily liked or respected, but that has never kept me from getting a job done. I trust that is not going to be a problem for you." She ended the discussion. They left. She said, "What made it tolerable at the time was the top director who supported and sustained me."

Even with his support, she "operated at a significant disadvantage, ending up working two or three times as hard to accomplish half as much." Earlinger remarked that "the sheer level of effort and energy that is required to survive reached the level at some point of diminishing return. Why am I doing it? Is it making a difference for anyone? Why am I doing that and putting up with all this crap?"

When the director resigned, a Mormon political appointee became the director. "This person could not communicate with me." Admittedly, she said, "We both have to assume some responsibility for that relationship." Five minutes before she was to receive an EEOC award from her organization, the new director informed her of his intentions to reorganize her program. "Standing with a donut in one hand and orange juice in the other," Earlinger stated, "he wanted to proceed with the search process as quickly as possible. I would no longer manage that program, and it would no longer exist at the agency. That's how I was told."

When blacks are isolated from one another, the precariousness of their success is likely to increase. While many of the Talented One Hundred understand that isolation may affect their success, there are others who relish the status of token. "They relish being the only black. They want white people to see them in a certain way. They are not concerned about others in the group. They do not see their success as connected to group success. You cannot have individual success in this country as people think you can. It's very much related to group success," said Teresa Johnson. She believes, like Toni Morrison in *The Bluest Eye*, "Some other token can always top you. Some better token can be found."

Stephanie Tahara, a forty-three-year-old public administrator from California, agrees that there is an "inherent danger" for those who relish their isolation. "They will suffer because they are going to get kicked sooner or later." She related a story about a black male colleague who was "the least black of anybody I've seen lately. . . . He was a computer expert, and he was their darling for two or three years. But when the computer system did not run like clockwork, he was psychologically demoted and discarded out of favor. He was a token for a while, but now he is in pain. A colleague was promoted as boss over him. I have never known a black to be sustained as 'darling' for very long."

Joseph Lowery castigated the token who lacks social consciousness:

Those "bougie buppies" [young black upwardly mobile persons] have not yet come to realize that they need networks and that they need to be community conscious. If they haven't gotten there, they are getting there. It is just around the corner for them. Most have begun to realize that it wasn't like they thought. They are not as secure as they thought they were. And what they begin to realize is that for most middle-class black Americans, they are one or two paychecks from poverty, considering debts and obligations. They are right back where their cousins, their mamas, and their uncles are.

It is therefore important, according to Mayor Johnny Longtree, to "always be reminded that when you grow up poor, you remember from whence you came. And if you forget that, you are never going to make it. Lots of blacks don't reach back and pull up others. But as long as I look in the mirror, I know from whence I came. I am not too far from there right now, won't take too much to put me back from where I came."

Mayor Longtree knows there is a continuous struggle personally and collectively, because one is constantly reminded of one's blackness. Aretha Shield was reminded when she took her artwork to her alma mater, a school that frequently purchased the work of prominent graduates. She was told by the school administrator to take her work to the Urban League, commenting, "They might like it." Aretha believed she was in this "never-never land of being colorless with the art." She realized, however, that there was "no way you could escape being black in this country." Others are reminded of this when they or their children are stopped by the police in predominantly white upper-middle-class neighborhoods. Robert Woodson's teenage son was in Wilmington, Delaware, visiting a friend. It was night and he was running down the street. A police officer stopped Woodson's son, placed him against a wall, and frisked him. The police thought he was a suspect in a holdup, and they handcuffed him, taking him to the 7-Eleven store that was robbed to be identified. The store manager could not identify him, so the police released him.

Said Woodson, "When my son called me to report the incident, I asked him how was he treated. 'Was the policeman rough with you? Did he curse you or treat you discourteously?' I was able to make some phone calls, and the policeman was called into the chief of police's office. My son was not mistreated, so I didn't take any action. I had the influence to take action if I had wanted to. I could have dealt with that cop and the system." Though Woodson had the personal influence to "deal with the system," it is clear from this incident that despite class or status, individual influence is precarious when it comes to blackness. Being black is, therefore, a constant reminder of the continuous struggle of the color line both on the collective and personal levels.

TO BE BLACK IS TO BE IN A CONTINUOUS STRUGGLE, PERSONALLY AND COLLECTIVELY

"When I wake up, I am angry. I know what is ahead of me for today. You have to get the people in the office to work on their behalf to fight the people outside the office on behalf of the people within. It is an endless struggle," said Sheridan Williams, a professor, poet, and playwright at a large university. Michael Lomax, the chairman of the Fulton County Commission, and also a professor, agreed. "I am in a world which is not going to encourage the advancement of Michael Lomax, because there are too many other individuals in that world encouraging their own advancement. I have to keep the pressure on. I can't let up. We, as a race, will have to keep the pressure on. We can't desert the NAACP and the Urban League. We went through a period where we felt we could desert the NAACP, the Urban League, the National Council of Negro Women, and walk away from black churches, colleges, and communities." There was a feeling, after the civil rights movement, that "we now have the admission ticket and can go anywhere." But "we have learned," said Lomax, "that it doesn't work, and we are seeing a trend of coming home or reinvesting in our institutions, recognizing that their strength is a reflection of our individual strength, and they are integrally connected, and we must keep them."

In the collective struggle, Jews are an important group role model for blacks. Roger Johnson, a state representative from the Midwest, thinks blacks have to be like Jews. "A group who wants to rise has to help others if they want to maintain some position of power." "We can learn from the Jews," acknowledged Michael Lomax. "They say you will never forget the Holocaust. If you use Jews the wrong way or talk about them the wrong way, they'll be right on you. We have to be vigilant like that. It is persistence. You have to never let up."

Headlines like "Just When Civil-Rights Activists Thought They Could Take a Rest"[21] and "Activists Fight Desegregation Rollback"[22] indicate that the struggle is continuous. Four rulings in the late 1980s by a more conservative U.S. Supreme Court dismantled affirmative action programs designed to assist female and male racial minorities and white females. In the case of *Richmond v. Croson*, the court struck down by a vote of 6–3 the Richmond, Virginia, City Council's set-aside plan that earmarked public contracts for minority-owned businesses. In the case of *Wards Cove Packing v. Antonio*, the court ruled 5–4 that statistics showing that minorities are underrepresented in the workplace are not sufficient evidence to bring a discrimination suit. In addition, the court shifted the burden of responsibility to prove discrimination from the employer to the employee. In the case of *Martin v. Wilks*, the court ruled that whites may bring reverse discrimination claims against a court-approved affirmative action settlement. Finally, in the case of *Patterson v. McLean Credit Union*, the court unanimously upheld the 1866 law used to challenge discrimination in the making of private contracts, but by a 5–4 vote refused to extend the law to racial harassment in the workplace.

Many civil rights proponents view these Supreme Court rulings as signaling an end to gains won during the "Second Reconstruction," which began in the sixties. The racial battle for equality and justice is continuous for oppressed people. President George Bush's veto of the 1990 Civil Rights Bill underlines that reality.

Individuals who are likely to be in the vanguard of the racial struggle are the black elite. Many of the Talented One Hundred, such as Vernon Jordan, have accepted this race burden, because they understand that group mobility requires their collective efforts. "The Talented Tenth have responsibility to those not in the Talented Tenth," says Jordan. "I feel a special obligation to help those who cannot help themselves. I've spent twenty-five years trying to do that."

Joseph Lowery preaches that there are biblical grounds for collective action by the black elite. "The Bible says that the strong must bear the infirmities of the weak." He thinks "all those people who pulled themselves up by their own bootstraps have also learned to lie. We can't separate ourselves, even if we wanted to. They will put us all in the same bucket whether we want to or not."

The belief that successful blacks must assist other blacks in the collective struggle has kept Jeraldyne Blunden going. It is also a guiding principle by which Earnest Ross has lived. "I believe in the principle that it's by helping others that we will make it." The collective racial struggle for him is like a "rubber band. . . . You have to keep the pressure on or else it goes back to its original position. In black-white relations, the pressure must be there constantly." For Tony Michaels, a fifty-six-year-old corporate executive, the collective pressure and obligation to the black community come not only from the Talented Tenth but also from the black masses: "It must exist with everyone." Hosea Kelly believes this collective obligation exists at some level. "Every black person, whether consciously or not, has a concern about blacks, though they may find it difficult to manifest in their behavior."

Jeremiah Moses, along with many of the Talented One Hundred, however, has doubts about young blacks, particularly those under thirty, who he feels "have no realization about the struggle." There is a strong sense that they lack sensitivity and commitment to the ongoing struggle for social justice, because they did not come of age during the civil rights era. They are the product of the "Me" generation. Hence, lacking a collective identification with the black community, their commitment to strengthening it is not seen as a collective concern but an individual effort to pull oneself up by one's own bootstraps. "The buppies have bought into the philosophy that the only way to have upward mobility in corporate America is to shed one's blackness. Act white, talk white, and don't be too closely identified with civil rights organizations. You can give money, but not a check so whites will discover you made a contribution," noted Roscoe Champion. Historian Kufra Akpan thinks that because of this absence of collective racial consciousness among young blacks, "we are in a dangerous position in this society. . . . We are not developing the strong replacement parts for a strong black society with a serious collective consciousness to meet the future challenge. The young people, or most of them under thirty, think this is 'America, the Beautiful.'"

Others are not as critical of the young, viewing them more from the perspective of a life passage and feeling they will become more concerned after their own needs have been met. One person, having criticized young blacks, acknowledged that she "may be looking through old eyes."

Whether or not we feel there should be a collective obligation, Bernie Roberts still maintained, "We must have an obligation, because the blacks who have made it would not have been where they are unless somebody left a legacy for them. People who were unlettered opened up the doors for us. We have an obligation to open up the doors for others."

John Hubbard knows the struggle must be ongoing because "in the eyes of the white power structure, all blacks still are niggers because of the continuous systemic exploitation and degradation. It is the essence of nigger status. It means no matter how successful we are in terms of getting degrees and earning incomes, it is given to us by the power structure and can be taken away." Until we acquire an "independent political and economic base, what we get is at the pleasure of the master." Hence, the struggle is an ongoing personal and collective process to eliminate the glass ceiling.

Like Bernie Roberts, we can be reminded, too, of Johnny Longtree's comments: "People who think they've made it by themselves have to remember if it wasn't for your brothers and sisters down here in this mire, you might not be able to climb over their shoulders to get where you are. You see very few companies where a black man has a chance to be president."

The black masses who were involved in the civil rights struggle and the black nationalist movement, as suggested by Johnny Longtree and Bernie Roberts, helped raise the ceiling of opportunities for the black elite. They understand, like Frederick Douglass, the ex-slave, orator, and liberator, who said at a conference in Canandaigua, New York, in 1857, "If there is no struggle, there is no progress. Those who profess to favor freedom, and yet deprecate agitation, are men who want crops without plowing up the ground. They want rain without thunder and lightning. They want the ocean without the awful roar of its many waters."

TO BE BLACK IS TO BE LIMITED BY THE GLASS CEILING

The Southern Christian Leadership Conference has so many discriminatory complaints that "that they can't cope with them," said Joseph Lowery. The Equal Employment Opportunity Commission is overburdened with racial discrimination charges. There is a glass ceiling on the aspirations of blacks. Sometimes the glass ceiling is clear, and other times it is cloudy. It was very cloudy for a young black woman in Atlanta, who became so enraged with the limits of the glass ceiling that she killed herself and wounded two white colleagues in 1987 when she failed to get a promotion. "The corporate community is a very tension-filled place. There is a glass ceiling, and the glass is getting stained with the blood of those who have fallen by the wayside," says Lowery. "Blacks who are upwardly mobile in the workplace are finding themselves trapped under the glass ceiling and they cannot escape. If they can afford to get out, they ought to get out and do other jobs. Some are sacrificing status and salary. Others are seeking spiritual resources to cope."

In a *Black Enterprise* poll of its readers, 48 percent of all respondents said they thought "the chances for Black managers to advance up the corporate ladder were poor."[23] And more than 61 percent of the respondents said they had encountered racial discrimination in their employment.[24]

Hosea Kelly calls it the "bubble theory." He says as long as blacks behave in a certain way, "they are allowed to live under the bubble, but they can never become a part of it. They have to be a good nigger. The good nigger doesn't challenge too much, doesn't focus on black life too much, and doesn't tie himself to his African heritage."

There was a cloudy glass ceiling for blacks when Claude Kent, now an engineer in his fifties, applied for engineering school in the early 1950s. He had graduated in the upper 10 percent of his class, and it was the policy of his state university to accept anyone in the upper 10 percent of the class. When he went to enroll in the university, the dean of engineering, whose name was White, did not take time to look at his transcript. "He told me," Kent said, "I could not be an engineer and the reason was because I was black, saying, 'You people cannot be engineers.' He said I was welcomed to come there and enroll in an industrial arts course, so I can go back to teach my people carpentry and masonry."

With his mother, he drove to another university in the Midwest. Fortuitously, the dean's name was Mr. Justice. "You are welcomed to come if you want to," he told Kent. "He said I would be the first black in engineering school, and I was going to catch hell from the faculty and students." It was not easy for Kent. He understood that his major "reason for going to the university was not to be distracted by them," but to obtain his "major goal by diversionary tactics. . . . Not having enough money or food, I risked my health to prove myself. I decided that when the going gets tough, the tough gets going. Whatever it takes to make it, I will. Since I was told I couldn't do what I wanted to do, I felt I had to overcome them."

When Graham Boston applied for engineering in the sixties, the ceiling had been raised higher and its glass was clearer. He has achieved top honors in his field, but he also stands as a testament to blacks' progress in eliminating one more barrier. He said, "I am standing on the mountain top and I have done it all. I enjoy sitting on top of this mountain. I know there are people who are trying to pull me off of it and trying to replace me." Even though he is successful, he knows the precariousness of it. His struggle must be ongoing.

While growing up, the Talented One Hundred learned a dual lesson about the glass ceiling. They were told there were limits, but they also heard, as Warner Babbitt did, that "there is a world of unlimited possibilities, if you strive hard enough. . . . No one ever taught me what I couldn't do at home and school. I was always told what I could do, although the rest of the world was saying, 'You can't do these things because you are black.' So when I met the rest of the world I said, 'Uh huh' and went on to do what I had to do."

When Jackie Robinson, Hank Aaron, Doug Williams, Martin Luther King Jr., Mary McLeod Bethune, and Jesse Jackson "hit the ceiling," like countless others, they "went on to do what they had to do" to raise it. Since the first slave ship landed, blacks—from entertainers and servants to actors in the global arena of business, education, politics, science, and technology—have been raising the glass ceiling. They understand that raising the ceiling is a continuous personal and collective struggle. Yet, through it all, because of the conflictive nature of the duality—through the race watching and tightrope walking, through the double standard, through never being good enough, through perennial probation, through bearing the race burden, through the precariousness of their individual and collective success, through the continuous personal and collective struggle—they wear the mask.

TO BE BLACK IS TO WEAR THE MASK

Wearing the mask is an adaptive survival strategy to conceal actions, feelings, motives, and thoughts. Uncle Tom symbolizes the accommodation to an oppressive society.

The black folk genre is also replete with tales about the rabbit trickster and about John, a slave who deceived and outwitted Old Marster, his white master. Similarly, in other areas of black-white encounters, blacks often do not reveal themselves to whites. When whites conduct research involving blacks, for example, it is often difficult for them to obtain information. One does not reveal one's true self. Zora Neale Hurston speculates on the reason in *Mules and Men*:

> The white man is always trying to know somebody else's business. All right, I'll set something outside the door of my mind for him to play with and handle. He can read my writing but he sho' can't read my mind. I'll put this play toy in his hand, and he will seize it and go away. Then I'll say my say and sing my song.[25]

Hurston's astute observation caused me to question the meaning behind the actions of someone I observed while attending a sociological meeting in Florida, in the early 1980s. During a morning session, a respected black sociologist, extolling the virtues of racial progress in America, used racial humor to appease and cajole his predominantly white audience. When he spoke during an evening session, Dr. Jekyll had turned to a Mr. Hyde. Before his more mixed audience, he was militant in asserting the rights of blacks, in pronouncing black pride, and in denouncing the evils of white oppression. Between the two sessions, during a social gathering, he played openly and affectionately with the toes of his white female colleague.

To Ferdinand Hamilton, "The worst thing in the world is to be in a position where you say one thing to white folks and another thing to black folks. . . . You have to be at oneness with yourself to be comfortable with your own commitment." Indeed, from my observations, Hamilton seemed comfortable with his advocacy role in the presence of blacks and whites, not masking his personal or political posture.

Dick Godfather, a federal administrator in his early fifties, knows that blacks mask their posture, "acting one way around blacks and another way around whites." John Hubbard smiles around his white colleagues, working well with them, but doesn't do much socializing. He is most comfortable socializing with his black colleagues. "It's a matter of being comfortable around one's own kind. It's nothing that you say, it's just how you feel. It's vibes. Nothing I can put my finger on. Maybe it's the black vernacular." He is more comfortable "talking with more expletives and profanity in a black setting," because it would be tolerated more by other blacks.

Marla Robinson also acknowledged that she is more comfortable relating to blacks.

> I can comfortably relate to my black boss, but if he were white, I would have to put on a mask or different face. People who read this in the future probably will ask, "Why don't you be yourself?" You can't be yourself. Ain't no use thinking you can be yourself. Anytime a person thinks of you as subhuman, you are going to have to reinforce that you are human, an intelligent being of a higher order. If you let your hair down, it can give them a message or another indication, because their interpretation of your behavior is so important. You can't allow it. You are constantly aware of everything. You can't relax. You can't say, "You ain't going to do it." But I won't say that with white peers, because they are going to see it as someone who does not have command of the English language.

As a journalist, Warner Babbitt frequently wears the mask as a means "to extract information from informants. . . . I understand white folks better than they understand me. I can always figure out where they are coming from, but I can confuse them when I want to," he said. In his tenure as a political reporter with a major newspaper, he "learned to handle whites very well. I could make them love me. I could make them hate me."

Sometimes he uses his cloaking shield to make himself invisible. "When I don't want white folks to understand me," he said, "I do a Ralph Ellison on them. White people are amazingly simple sometimes. They are the easiest people in the world to manipulate."

He cited the time when, as a political reporter, he was interviewing a state senator about "something he shouldn't be doing." Babbitt went into his "little invisible act with him." The senator only "saw a black person coming. . . . The senator was going on and on. I said, 'Excuse me, Senator, I don't understand such and such.'" In a slightly black voice, he asked the senator what he expected and scratched his eyebrow. "He fell for it and started to tell me in various and sundry ways how the program was operated. I said, 'Oh yes' and 'I don't understand.' He would make little funny ethnic jokes. I didn't react. He became so confident that he was speaking to a fool that he started to tell me everything I wanted to know."

When the story appeared in the paper the next day, the senator called the newspaper, saying, "I didn't say that." "He indicated to the editor that this young black guy was slow and didn't understand what he was saying." When Babbitt played the tape recorder back to him, he asked as he unmasked, "Are you sure I got it wrong?" Babbitt knows, like poet Paul Lawrence Dunbar:

We wear the mask that grins and lies,
It hides our cheeks and shades our eyes,
This debt we pay to human guile;
With torn and bleeding hearts we smile,
And mouth with myriad subtleties.

Why should the world be overwise,
In counting all our tears and sighs?
Nay, let them only see us, while
We wear the mask.

We smile, but, O great Christ, our cries
To thee from tortured souls arise.
We sing, but Oh, the clay is vile
Beneath our feet, and long the mile;
But let the world dream otherwise,
We wear the mask.

In this society, the black elite's economic status and achievements do not erase the color line. The acceptance of the color line and the acceptance of the value orientation of democracy, freedom, equality, individualism, progress, and achievement result in a dual value system. While the black elite accept the value orientation of democracy, equality, and freedom, they reject discrimination across the color line. This dual value orientation is a source of conflict that manifests itself in their personal and collective identity. The way the black elite experience the conflict of the color line is on an individual level, though it has a collective component—it is a shared experience. If blacks understand the realities of racism, they can more effectively cope with oppression. In the next chapter, I examine some manifestations of the color line and the impact of psychic violence on the black elite.

NOTES

1. John Hope Franklin, ed., *Color and Race* (Boston: Beacon Press, 1968), x.

2. Michael T. Martin and Howard Cohen, "Race and Class Consciousness: A Critique of the Marxist Concept of Race Relations," *Western Journal of Black Studies*, 4, no. 2 (1980): 84–91.

3. Robin M. Williams Jr., *American Society: A Sociological Interpretation*, 3rd ed. (New York: Knopf, 1970).

4. William E. Cross, Jr., "Black Family and Black Identity: A Literature Review," *Western Journal of Black Studies*, 2 (1978): 111–124.

5. James B. Stewart, "Psychic Duality of Afro Americans in the Novels of W. E. B. Du Bois," *Phylon*, 44 (1983): 93–107.

6. See Frantz Fanon, *Black Skin, White Masks* (New York: Grove Press, 1967); James Weldon Johnson, *The Autobiography of an Ex–Coloured Man* (New York: Knopf, 1912); John Edgar Wideman, *Brothers and Keepers* (New York: Holt, Rinehart and Winston,

1984); Richard Wright, "The Ethics of Living Jim Crow: An Autobiographical Sketch," in Abraham Chapman, ed., *Black Voices* (New York: New American Library, 1968); and Roger Wilkins, *A Man's Life: An Autobiography* (New York: Simon and Schuster, 1982).

7. Whether we identify ourselves as black first or American first merely reflects a larger collective and identity clarity issue about what we should call ourselves in America. There appears to be a continuous evolving identity. About every two decades, we change the name of our ethnic identity. In the 1940s, we changed from colored to Negro; in the 1960s from Negro to black; and in the 1980s from black to African American. The term Afro American seems to survive through each collective identity issue, rather than adding to the debate.

I should point out, also, that embodied in this collective identity issue are such concerns as whether Afro American Studies or Black Studies should be called Africology or Africana studies.

8. Martin Kilson, "Black Bourgeoisie Revisited," *Dissent*, Winter 1983, 87.

9. The term "nigger rich" connotes a standard by which wealth is measured in the black community that is different (usually lower) than in the white community.

10. Zora Neale Hurston, *Dust Tracks on a Road* (New York: Arno Press and *The New York Times*, 1969), 223–224.

11. James Blackwell, *Mainstreaming Outsiders: The Production of Black Professionals* (Dix Hills, NY: General Hall, 1981).

12. E. Franklin Frazier, *Black Bourgeoisie* (New York: Free Press, 1957).

13. "Race: More to be Done," *Hampton Roads Daily Press*, Newport News, VA, Jan. 13, 1991, H2.

14. Derek T. Dingle, "Finding a Prescription for Black Wealth," *Black Enterprise*, Jan. 1987, 39.

15. Elaine Pinderhuges, "Afro American Families and the Victim System," in M. McGoldrick, J. K. Pearce, and J. Giordano, eds., *Ethnicity and Family Therapy* (New York: Guilford Press, 1982), 114.

16. Johnnetta B. Cole, "Culture: Negro, Black and Nigger," *The Black Scholar*, 1, no. 8 (June 1970): 41.

17. Kenneth E. John, "How Are Blacks Treated in Your Community?" *Washington Post, National Weekly Edition*, March 2, 1987, 37.

18. Cole, "Culture," 41. See also Francis Terrell and Sandra Terrell, "An Inventory to Measure Cultural Mistrust among Blacks," *Western Journal of Black Studies*, 5, no. 3 (1981): 180–185.

19. George Davis and Glegg Watson, *Black Life in Corporate America: Swimming in the Mainstream* (Garden City, NY: Anchor Doubleday, 1982).

20. Bart Landry, *Black Leadership: Possibilities and Limitations*, paper presented at the Association of Black Sociologists, Atlanta, Georgia, Aug. 1988.

21. Al Karmen, "Just When Civil-Rights Activists Thought They Could Take a Rest," *Washington Post, National Weekly Edition*, May 1988, 31.

22. Paul Ruffins, "Activists Fight Desegregation Rollback," *Black Enterprise*, Sept. 1988, 25.

23. Richard D. Hylton, "Working in America," *Black Enterprise*, Aug. 1988, 63.

24. Hylton, "Working," 66.

25. Zora Neale Hurston, *Mules and Men* (Philadelphia: Lippincott, 1935), 18–19.

②

MANIFESTATIONS OF THE COLOR LINE: THE IMPACT OF VIOLENCE

"I grew up in a very large family and a very loving home. I had an extended family of grandparents and great-grandparents. We were poor. But we had this great sense of pride and this sense that you got to make things different," said Jack B. Lane, the forty-seven-year-old son of Johnny Lane, a sharecropper and bus driver, and Louise Lane, a domestic.

His parents and grandparents valued education and hard work, frequently reminding the children, "You are not going to get anything unless you work and struggle for it. Go to school and get an education so you won't have to work so hard the way we did." His mother did not want them "to go to the field and work in the hot sun." His family also instilled in the children "a respect for people and a reverence for life. . . . My parents laid a strong foundation," said Jack.

Jack grew up with the signs and symbols of the old rural South during the fifties, a time of racial apartheid. He remembers:

> As a child growing up in rural Alabama, I've seen the signs as we would go down-town, "White" and "Colored." I've seen the symbols and signs of racism. I don't know if I quite understood racism, until I went downtown to the theater and was denied admission, or went to the library and couldn't check out a book.

In his fifteenth year, Jack saw the signs of coming change in the old South. A young minister, Martin Luther King Jr., began reordering signposts. He "heard King and watched the drama of Montgomery" unfolding only fifty miles from where he grew up, and he felt there was a way out and that something could be done. "This man provided for me, like he did for many young people and people not so young, a way out. He provided the instruments, tools, and techniques for dealing with the system of prejudice and racial discrimination."

King and the movement changed forever the course of Jack's life:

> Martin Luther King Jr. and the civil rights movement forced me as an individual, as a black child, as a human being, to literally grow up overnight. If it hadn't been for the movement, I don't know where I would be. It changed my life, and I know I am a different person.

Jack became a leader in the civil rights movement, and it gave him a sense of unlimited possibilities. He was also the first college-educated member of his family.

> The movement gave me a sense that you can do it; you can make it. If you have the sense of stick-to-itiveness and persistence, you can do it. You felt almost invincible. It created a greater faith in the possibility of change and in the possibility of see-ing human beings change, grow, and develop. I would not be where I am if I had not had the experience of the civil rights movement.

At the time of my interview, he was a dedicated public servant who had been elected to a public office.

The civil rights movement, the public policy priority of equal opportunity, and the expanding economy cracked open the closed door to opportunities in the sixties and the early seventies, and thousands of young, gifted, and black Jack B. Lanes slipped through the crack. They arrived at the door of opportu-nity from the cotton belt of Alabama, Georgia, and Mississippi, from the coal fields of West Virginia, Kentucky, and Pennsylvania, and from the burned-out ghettos of Watts, Harlem, Detroit, and Newark. They were the offspring of parents and grandparents who tilled the soil as sharecroppers, who scrubbed the floors as domestics and janitors, and who performed the dirty work and were the source of cheap labor in the factories, mines, and steel mills of the North and South. They were also children of doctors, lawyers, ministers, and teachers. Their traditional career choices—teaching, ministry, and the se-lected few occupations of medicine, dentistry, and law in racially segregated communities—were expanded to more diverse career options for the first time in racially integrated communities.

With this burgeoning middle class, William Julius Wilson, in *The Declining Significance of Race*, asserted that "many talented and educated Blacks are now entering positions of prestige and influence at a rate comparable to, or, in some situations, exceeding that of Whites with equal qualifications."[1] For many aca-demics, including Wilson, this expansion of blacks into the middle class her-alded the decline of racism. But some eschewed this positive prognosis of the state of race relations in America. Sociologist Charles V. Willie, one of Wilson's strongest critics, using data on family income, provided empirical support for the increasing, not declining, significance of race. He argued in the late seventies that not only was racism increasing, but it was especially so for upwardly mobile blacks. He asserted that "middle-class Blacks in racially integrated situations at this period in American history are almost obsessed with race."[2] And "the people who most severely experience the pain of dislocation due to changing times are the racial minorities who are talented and integrated, not those who are impoverished and isolated."[3]

The debate over the significance of class and race as factors in the upward mobility of blacks continues and is likely to persist in the twenty-first century. In this debate, generally, the Talented One Hundred take the position that race is a more salient factor in their life chances than class. When I asked them if racism was declining in the 1980s, 92 percent said it was not. They did believe overt racism had declined since the 1960s, however. While 8 percent of individuals felt racism would eventually disappear, the majority believed it was a permanent stratifying feature in this society. Thus, whether overt or subtle, racism aims to rule the cultural, economic, educational, political, and legal standing, emotional and physical health, and the sexual and social interactions of the oppressed group. The dominant group wants to maintain a sense of place for the oppressed group. Hence, the oppressor group employs violence and three important devices of power—control, dominance, and exploitation—to maintain racial privileges.

The concept of violence is examined here from a Fanonian perspective, which looks at human violence in situations of oppression. It incorporates violence that is defined as legitimate or illegitimate, intentional or unintentional, instrumental or expressive, individual or collective, overt or covert, and physical or psychic. According to Hussein Abdilahi Bulhan, in *Frantz Fanon and the Psychology of Oppression*, "violence is any relation, process, or condition by which an individual or a group violates the physical, social, and/or psychological integrity of another person or group." He states:

> The proposed definition rests on several assumptions. First, violence is not simply an isolated physical act or a discrete random event. It is relation, process, and condition undermining, exploiting, and curtailing the well-being of the victim. Second, these violations are not simply moral or ethical, but also physical, social, and/or psychological. They involve demonstrable assault on or injury of and damage to the victim. Third, violence in any of the three domains—physical, social, or psychological—has significant repercussions in the other two domains. Fourth, violence occurs not only between individuals, but also between groups and societies. Fifth, intention is less critical than consequence in most forms of violence. Any relation, process, or condition imposed by someone that injures the health and well-being of others is by definition violent.[4]

Bulhan's definition allows us to look at violence from a broader perspective and to extend the taxonomy of violence to include personal, institutional, and

structural violence. Bulhan notes that "institutional violence and structural violence involve more complex relations, processes, and conditions than personal
violence. Personality and temperament are more likely to gain primacy in personal violence than institutional and structural violence. Ordinarily, institutional
and structural violence span individuals and generations. . . . Structural violence
in particular imposes a pattern of relations and practices that are deeply ingrained in and dominate everyday living."[5]

Since structural violence is such an integral feature of the attitudes, values,
and mores of individuals who are socialized into the system, it is sometimes difficult to detect. Both the oppressor and the oppressed often construct their social reality around daily interactions or somewhat "ascribed" roles that are taken
for granted. Social oppression involves all three forms of violence. "Oppression
and one of its expressions, racism, legitimize structural violence, rationalize institutional violence, and impersonalize personal violence," writes Bulhan.[6]

In this chapter, I examine how the violence of racism is used as an important
mechanism to maintain control and a sense of place. The oppressor group aims
to control, dominate, and exploit in every major institution and in every facet of
social interaction. In attempting to impose a sense of place and identity, the actions of the oppressor have important psychological consequences for the oppressed group. The violence of racism manifests itself physically, culturally, and
socially. Within the broader cultural and social areas, I look at how racism manifests itself in the realms of economics, education, housing, the media, and sexual and social interactions. I also examine how racist manifestations in these areas have changed since the 1960s.

THE IMPACT OF PHYSICAL VIOLENCE

The most common and fundamental control device is reliance on physical violence. The oppressed are kept in their place by threats of physical injury or ac-
tual acts of violence. The history of black-white relations in this country is replete with physical violence—floggings, lynchings, whippings, murders, and
police brutality.

Prior to the civil rights movement and the opening up of equal opportunity,
the members of the traditional black elite were confined to segregated environments. They lived and attended schools in primarily segregated communities. They were generally employed or self-employed in institutions serving the
black community. The racism that the traditional black elite experienced was
overt, and it was supported and sanctioned by the folkways, mores, and laws of
the larger society. This overt form of racism empowered white individuals to
have personal power over any black person. Thus, individual acts of physical violence by whites were more rampant among the traditional black elite, as we
can see in the stories of Lee Watson, Yvonne Walker-Taylor, Joseph Lowery,

and Ned McMillian. Though individual acts of physical violence are not as pronounced among the modern black elite, violence still remains an important feature, as illustrated later by Renee Stone's story.

Lee Watson, a fifty-nine-year-old college administrator and realtor from Virginia, heard stories of physical atrocities suffered during and after slavery from her great-grandmother, an ex-slave, who lived to be over one hundred years old, and from her grandmother, who lived to be ninety-four:

> In slavery white men feared the slaves' ability to communicate with God. If they were caught praying, they were whipped. They were hanged from their hands with their feet hanging down. They were whipped with a horse whip until the blood ran down their backs. They would scream, "Oh pray master." And the slave master would scream, "Oh pray yourself, damn nigger" and rubbed salt in their wounds. After freedom, the black woman would not be allowed to be seen with a calico dress and the black man with khaki pants. They would be flogged by the patrol.

Her great-grandmother was "taught by white children to read the Bible in the loft. If their parents had caught them, they would have been whipped," said Lee. She was greatly inspired by the stories of her great-grandmother and her grandmother, who reared her, and by their philosophy "to walk like you have something to do; act like someone has a string on you, pulling you forward. Never drop your head. Keep walking." Her mother died when she was four. "Without having a mother, I could have been a prostitute, drunkard, or dope fiend, but I chose to follow in my great-grandmother's tracks as a person who could stand up and be counted," said Lee, as tears overwhelmed her.

When she wiped away her tears, she said, "I knew I was placed on earth by God, and I intend to take my place." Her place in society turned out to be different from her great-grandmother's. At seventeen, she started working. "Calling myself a woman, I took my place in this world and in this society. I had thirteen dollars in change in a tobacco bag. Today, at the age of fifty-nine and divorced, I feel comfortable to say I am more than a millionaire," said Lee, who keeps walking like someone has a string pulling her forward.

While Lee Watson's story illustrates how acts of physical violence are transformed through time and continue to impose psychic trauma in the next generation, the story of Yvonne Walker-Taylor, the seventy-one-year-old first woman president of Wilberforce University in Ohio, one of the oldest historically black colleges and universities in the country, gives us a glimpse of the pre–civil rights violence in the 1920s.

In that era, the Ku Klux Klan was very active. Walker-Taylor, who was from a socially and economically privileged background, said that "when the cooks didn't come and the horsemen didn't show up, it meant the KKK would parade" in front of their home in Raleigh, North Carolina. Although she was born in New Bedford, Massachusetts, her family lived briefly in Raleigh. Her father was an A.M.E. minister and an outspoken social activist who urged his congregation from the pulpit to vote. "While lying in the attic" at age eight, Yvonne was told by her parents that "they were playing a game, and they were going to watch those people."

> I looked out and saw all those white robes and pointed hats. I thought it was the cutest thing. I thought they were clowns. They looked so funny. They planted their cross down in the yard and stood looking at the house and burned that cross. All the neighbors pulled their shades and nobody walked up and down the street. I remember hearing nothing but the crackling of the fire. They all marched away and daddy breathed a sigh of relief and brought us downstairs. He made a couple of calls to the press and the police, but no one did anything about it.

She and her mother were sent back to Massachusetts after whites attempted to kidnap her. "They were trying to force my daddy out of Raleigh, because he was 'too big-mouthed,'" said Walker-Taylor. Her father wanted to be a part of the American dream and vote. Even in the face of violence, he aspired to a higher place for blacks, and he inspired her to fight for the civil rights of blacks.

It was during the Depression of the 1930s that Joseph E. Lowery had his first encounter with racial violence in rural Alabama. It was a bad time economically for whites and blacks. The bad times accentuated the competition between blacks and whites, and blacks' sense of place.

> When I was quite a young lad I came out of my father's business—a little ice cream parlor. I was three-fourths the way out and this big white policeman was one-fourth in the door, and he jabbed me in the stomach with his nightstick and said, "Get back nigger. Don't you see a white man is coming?" I ran home to get my father's pistol and as God would have it, my father came home when I was on the way out of the house. He had never been home that time of day in my lifetime, except on Sunday. But he was there and saw the tears running down my cheeks, and he made me tell him what the problem was. I told him. I finally admitted I had come to get the gun, and he took the gun and said he would handle it. He made a complaint to the chief of police and the mayor. Both told him they understood his problem, but the best thing was to forget it for two reasons: (1) nothing they could do about it, and nothing they would do about it; and (2) that was the only person they could hire in a small southern Alabama town. I grew up bitter for a while about that. But as I experienced the Christian religion, my bitterness faded into determination to do something to change that system and to work with hearts and minds. It was an important event for me because it brought home for me, in a very traumatic way, race relations.

During the midforties, when black men were fighting in Europe during World War II "to make the world safe for democracy," Ned McMillian, then a twelve-year-old boy, did not feel safe in his small Georgia hometown. He learned early his sense of place from the lessons of his parents, who told him, "This is a white man's world, and if you are going to live in it, you are going to live by the rules and regulations that he has set up." His father owned a small restaurant, and Ned saw those rules and regulations when he was working in his father's kitchen. Ned was often "perturbed because every weekend, the police would come down to the restaurant, but no one would call them." He added, "One Saturday night, one hit my father, and I'll never forget that. The policeman drew his gun and my father couldn't hit back." He repeated, "I'll never forget that."

"How did it make you feel?" I asked.

"If I had a gun I could have gotten to, I would have blasted them. I felt there was nothing I could do. I felt bad, because my father didn't have an even chance. I didn't feel he was a coward. He was overpowered. They had the gun. He did not. They had the badge. He did not," said Ned, now a prominent doctor and a social activist for the black struggle.

Not having an even chance has been the norm for blacks from north to south, and from east to west, and from the dawn of slavery to the dusk of the twentieth century. Renee Stone, a perky twenty-six-year-old professor and the youngest among the Talented One Hundred, knows firsthand what it means not to have an equal chance for the American dream. Her perkiness seemed to belie the nightmare of her racial experiences. Perhaps she learned from her parents, both professionals, that "to be successful, you have to wear the mask." The mask was off when she talked about the pain of her elementary school days in the midsixties in an upstate New York all-white neighborhood and her post–civil rights experiences with physical violence.

> It was Ku Klux Klan territory, and my life was being threatened every day, and our house was bombed. I remember sitting on the playground for over an hour on a rainy day, while my parents were trying to get me into this public school. When I was admitted, the school bus would not pick me up. On my way home from school, a high school kid grabbed my shoulder and said, "Nigger, if you go through these woods again, I am going to break you and throw you in the swimming pool." I ran home crying.

Stone's family was highly mobile, moving across many states. In each move, her father challenged the limits of "place." And each challenge brought reprisals. When they moved into a white neighborhood in the 1980s in the Midwest, they were harassed. The neighbors and their dogs would harm their farm animals. On one occasion, her father, a minister, "blew a dog's brains out." She said, "The white folks did not like it, and they threatened to bomb us. They started a fire on the grass." She ended our discussion of her racial experiences by saying, "We had to fight battles with the white folks, the fire department, the health department, and the police department. The fire department excused the fire, as 'they were not trying to burn down the property.' There are so many racist things, I could go on and on."

I could "go on and on" relating the stories of physical violence among the Talented One Hundred, but I shall pause here to reiterate the major points of the story lines.

Reliance on physical violence is the most fundamental control device used by whites to maintain a sense of place for blacks, so that whites may continue their domination and exploitation and maintain racial privilege. Control, domination, and exploitation take place in every major arena of this society, and personal physical violence is an integral feature; but it is less prevalent today than before the civil rights movement.

Race privilege is, as in the story of Lee Watson, whites preventing blacks from praying or reading during slavery years. These practices were used to keep slaves from organizing and revolting. To maintain a cheap source of labor, it was essential to have uneducated and passive slaves. Whether racial privilege is to keep blacks from voting and organizing to obtain power, as in Walker-Taylor's story, or to keep blacks from being economically independent, as in Lowery's and McMillian's stories, "race privilege is not simply economic. It is a matter of status also," says Robert Blauner in *Racial Oppression in America*.[7] To indicate different social status, it is important for whites to keep blacks out of certain neighborhoods or schools, as seen in Renee's account, or to keep black women and men from wearing their calico dresses and their khaki pants, as described by Lee.

Some of the Talented One Hundred who participated in the civil rights movement encountered personal and institutional violence. However, they have rarely encountered it as professionals during the post–civil rights era. But the rise of physical violence in the nation during the past few years, perceived by many as "gone with the wind," may once again subject the modern black elite to physical violence. While the recent incidents of physical violence have been directed primarily at the black working class and underclass, as the black elite move into predominantly white suburbia, they, too, may become victims. The probability of encountering physical violence is increasing, given the rise in campus violence in the late 1980s and the early 1990s. College-educated individuals who participate in campus violence represent the most "enlightened" members of society and thus the hope of a more democratic society. Their overt racist behavior has surprised and shocked those in academe and others throughout the nation.

However, given the fact that most college-age students were not born yet when the civil rights struggle was going on, and given the shrinking economic opportunities, campus violence should not shock or surprise us. Physical violence seems to be related to the downturn in the economic cycle and to the segment of society in which the economic threat is most visible. With the tightening job market among college graduates, racism is a reaction by some white students to protect their interests and to maintain their statuses. Before the late sixties, there were very few blacks on white campuses. At the time they were entering in larger numbers, the economy was expanding. The individual physical violence on campus or in other segments of society is not overtly sanctioned and supported by the larger society, and it is a rarity among the modern black elite. Though a few black elite continue to be physically threatened, like Renee Stone and her family, who live in a white neighborhood, others have not experienced such threats in the past twenty years. But they are still affected by earlier experiences that have left psychic scars.

Most of the Talented One Hundred avoided the closed doors of segregation while growing up in the South. But in the face of physical violence, some were made stronger in their convictions to change the system and their place in it. At the beginning of this chapter, we met Jack B. Lane, who said that the violence he encountered during the civil rights movement made him stronger in his religious convictions and faith.

> It convinced me that I don't know what the end is going to be. I don't know the outcome. I don't know whether I am going to live or not. But I am going on anyway. I am going to take the leap of faith and go. You may get arrested and jailed; you may be teargassed and bullwhipped. But I am going on anyway. You felt like you were involved in a holy crusade, and you came to the point where you were prepared to stare death in the face to arrive at the prize. And that's why we would sing "Keep your eyes on the prize—hold on, hold on."

THE IMPACT OF CULTURAL DOMINATION

The most effective way to win allies among the oppressed is to control their belief system—the way one perceives the world and thinks about objects and events. Cultural domination is more subtle than physical violence, and it is employed as a means of social control. It defines the backdrop for the important socialization process. Language becomes that backdrop and the important symbol and defining tool for the transmission of culture. Language is used to define, validate, and invalidate the oppressed and their customs, rituals, values, and institutions by negating and denigrating them. This integral and universal feature of culture influences people's thoughts and experiences more than is recognized.

The old proverb "Sticks and stones may break my bones, but names will never hurt me" is not an accurate reflection of reality. We recall that Renee Stone had vivid memories of physical violence while growing up in the 1960s. Yet, she could also clearly recall the psychic impact of her elementary school days of being ignored, ostracized, and called names. She said,

> Children would take apples to school to give to their teacher. I would take pretty little maple leaves that I had found on the way to school. The teacher would look at them and throw them in the trash. The teachers never let me assume leadership roles in their little chicken skit. The children teased and called me "nigger."

Such language as "nigger" is used to divide people into categories. Thus, language is pivotal to understanding Frantz Fanon's theory that a Manichean worldview undergirds human violence and oppression. Hussein Bulhan notes in *Frantz Fanon and the Psychology of Oppression* that a Manichean view is one that divides the world into compartments and people into different "species." This division is based not on reciprocal affirmations, but rather on irreconcilable opposites cast into good versus evil, beautiful versus ugly, intelligent versus stupid, White versus Black, human versus sub-human modes. This duality of opposites is not dialectical and hence not an attempt toward a higher synthesis. Its logic is a categorical either/or, in which one of the terms is considered superfluous and unacceptable. Yet in reality, this duality of opposites in the Manichean outlook are [sic] interdependent. Each is defined in terms of its opposite and each derives its identity in opposition to the other.[8]

Out of a Manichean worldview a duality has emerged between the values of Western and non-Western people. In the Manichean worldview, the Western world defined its values as good and superior, and consequently these views were to be extolled. Non-Western values were defined as bad and inferior, and these views had to be denigrated. The cultural transmission of a Manichean worldview has a major role in perpetuating racism through the socialization process, whether consciously or unconsciously. The process of cultural domination for white American children begins when they first hear the nursery rhyme, "Mirror, mirror on the wall, who is the fairest of them all?" They begin "feeding and cutting their teeth on the milk of Mother Racism," said Ruth Shelly, a fifty-three-year-old sociologist. Black, brown, and yellow children have already been weaned from the benefits of its nourishment, because the mirror does not reflect them.

Thus, the oppressor aims to define the reality of the oppressed group, which incorporates, at some level in its ways of thinking, acting, and feeling, both consciously and unconsciously, the definition of the oppressor group. It is necessary for their survival and success in an oppressive system. It is the mark of oppression, as Kardiner and Ovesey recognized nearly forty years ago.[9]

Michael Lomax, the first black chairman of the board of the Fulton County Commission in Atlanta and a professor of literature, in his early forties, expressed well the psychic impact of the mark of oppression. While growing up in Los Angeles, California, in the 1950s, the son of a journalist and a lawyer, Lomax watched the drama of the civil rights movement unfolding from his integrated environment. He knows how racism rules emotional health. Although there was the positive side of seeing blacks "standing up for their rights," there was also a "downside of the movement" for Lomax.

One downside of the civil rights movement was particularly traumatic for him. Between the ages of fourteen and sixteen, he visited Alabama with his family. His mother covered the civil rights movement for their family-owned newspaper. He recalled, "It was a very painful experience. I grew up in an integrated environment where I had protection from such overt hostility and violence. When I went south in the early sixties, it was very violent; black people were vulnerable. It was traumatic, and it took a long time [for me] to recover. My brothers and sisters still refuse to visit the South."

Another downside of the civil rights movement for Lomax was seeing the "negative images repeated over and over again on television" of black children trying to enter integrated schools and being met with white hostility. He said, "These negative images were confusing and harmful and gave a low self-image. It was damaging to the ego. It took me a long time to understand that the negative things that were said by white people about us as a people had unconscious implications. We internalize a lot of it, and we do not realize how strongly we internalize it, until we think about it." He pointed out,

> From day one, my mother may tell me black is beautiful and my church may say that. But every time I turn on the television, everything that is beautiful is white. Everything that is ugly is black. Everything that is good is white, and everything that is sinful is black. These are the values that our society promotes. When I see a beautiful woman on television, she is more likely to have blond hair. When I see a strong, assertive man in a position of power, he is more likely to have blond hair and blue eyes. So all of these images wind up, consciously and unconsciously, causing conflict in a black person's mind.

The preoccupation with skin color created a conflict for him, even within his family. Though Lomax is "fairer" in complexion than most blacks, in his family, he was the least "fairest of them all." "My grandmothers looked like two little old white ladies. I was considered dark-skinned in my family," he quipped. When I asked how his family treated him, he responded, "To be honest with you, there was a conflict. Because of my grandmother coming out of a social hierarchy, which was in part based on skin color, I was not high on the totem pole. I was not as high as my baby brother, who's got blue-green eyes, sandy brown hair, and a white skin tone." He laughed again, saying his brother has a problem trying to figure out who he is.

Lomax said the psychic effect of the mark of oppression was "harmful." "I wanted to change and be like my brother." Lomax never thought of himself as light-skinned. "I always thought I was dark; my complexion is a relative matter."

Lomax knows, like Ethel King, that if blacks internalize those negative images, it can have devastating consequences for their self-esteem. Ethel, thirty-seven years old, is a successful journalist with a major newspaper. But her road to success has been paved with pain, her path deviating more than others among the Talented One Hundred. Although most of Ethel's formative years were spent in a small town in the South, the family traveled a lot with her father, a career military person. She grew up in a supportive and loving family who told her she could become the president. When she was in the eleventh grade, she was among the fifty black students bused to an all-white school with a student body of two thousand. She said,

> I didn't want to be at that white school, because I felt I wasn't wanted. I was always a person pretty much into emotions, and I wanted to feel I was needed and loved.

It was very important to me. The way I acted out was that the white teachers didn't think I was so bright, so I acted out in total confusion and ended up skipping classes. No one understood what was happening to me. There were a lot of other things going on, so the teachers only saw me as this problem child. At the time, I didn't understand myself.

Her image of herself was poor, even though, she defiantly said, "I didn't believe I was less than a white person. I think I had bought into it without realizing it until I went to school with whites. I was believing in some of the things I said I didn't about myself. I was shocked at myself—afraid to raise my hand in class for fear I wouldn't know the answer and embarrass not only myself, but every black person in America."

Ethel King left school and ended up pregnant. Her plans to go to college were put aside. She got married and moved to North Carolina, but she soon separated from her husband. She said, "Things got progressively worse. I became a very confused teenager and got into lots of trouble. I got involved with drugs and the wrong crowd. I got arrested for shoplifting and arrested for possession of drugs." The major turning point for Ethel came when she was arrested in North Carolina for the possession of drugs. She vividly recalled the incident that led to her turning point:

I was about twenty-two years old and my daughter was about three. While waiting for my trial, I spent the summer in jail. I remember looking out the window and seeing my relatives carrying my daughter. They pointed up to the window and waved, as if to say, "That's your mother up there." I said to myself, this is crazy. I don't want anyone else to raise my child. That was always clear, when everything else was muddled. I wanted this child to do well, and I thought I could raise her. I said I am not going to go to jail. I didn't change overnight. It took awhile. I had to look at myself and look at life to try to change myself. I asked, What is this thing called life? How did I get to this point? What is wrong with me? I had to go through a long internal process to change.

After reflecting on this period in her life, she remarked, "I used to associate being black with being down and out and being cool. I used to be ashamed that my family had a lot more than other blacks. When I lived among blacks while growing up, I was uncomfortable with my privileged status, but I didn't feel that way when I lived among whites. I only associated being black with being down and out. So to prove myself as a regular black person, I had to hang in the streets.

"I can look back and say I came a long way," said the sensitive young journalist. Indeed, she has. But there are thousands of young, gifted blacks who never make the return trip from the psychological damage of racism.

Like Lomax and Ethel, Teresa Hale, a fifty-four-year-old psychologist now living in California, grew up in Louisiana and also knows the emotional legacy of racism. While growing up, she learned to protect her self-esteem by ignoring racism.

> I grew up under highly discriminatory circumstances and later worked in institutions that did not serve blacks, both during my early childhood and later on as an adult in California. It was the order of the day, whether overt or covert. There had not been specific incidents aimed directly at me, but overall pervasive, restrictive discrimination. I was accustomed to it. I had developed an armor—blindness. Discrimination was expected and accepted by me as a reality. It still surrounds me. I now know that there are legal approaches which may, with enough time, money, and effort, be effective.

The racism contributed to her feeling "demoralized and ineffectual," but, she said, "I had learned to live with it and, at the same time, to seek dignity, meaning, and self-validation. I am sure this repressive approach has been detrimental to both my mental and physical well-being."

Though the mark of oppression left its psychic scars on Teresa, Ethel, and Lomax, Ethel appeared to sustain more emotional injury. While growing up, she seemed, more than Lomax and Teresa, to internalize the negative emotional pain emanating from racism. Lomax's mother tried to balance the negative images he saw of blacks by instilling positive images to insulate him against emotional injury. Teresa, on the other hand, chose to ignore racism as a way of insulating herself from psychic injury.

The examples of Ethel, Lomax, and Teresa illustrate the psychic damage sustained by the black elite while growing up in America. Most of the Talented One Hundred expressed similar experiences and feelings, depending on their level of tolerance, racial sensitivity, and awareness. Although a few of the Talented One Hundred claimed that they had *never* experienced racism, they described virulent incidents that sounded like those experienced by other participants. While the racial experiences of their youth continued to "touch" the black elite, they faced more psychic pain from racism as they moved into the mainstream as professionals.

Leo Aramis, a thirty-four-year-old journalist, argued that "racism touches everyone. You can't grow up in this society without it touching you." Leo believes that the black elite who lack a clear sense of identity are more likely to deny racism. To succeed by the majority standards in this society, some token blacks feel it is necessary to negate their racial identity. What are the psychological consequences?

The Token Black Elite: Dilemmas and Contradictions

Some black elite, in the quest for success, negate their racial identity. Robert Snow, a city attorney for a large metropolitan city in California, feels this could lead to the denial of racism, which manifests itself in negative attitudes and behaviors toward other blacks.

People who make it all the way to the top ignore a lot of racism. They refuse to deal with racist acts, or they don't see them as racist acts. They don't put any color attachment to it. Even if they do, they don't deal with it. They skirt around it. They have come to the conclusion that they are not black or it is not good for them to identify with being black. It is not uncommon to go to functions and you are the only black. If another black shows up, it is likely to produce hostility. They will avoid you. I sense that many times, even though they are similar in terms of background, education, and income. They see blacks and deny them. There is a recognition, but a sense of avoidance and denial. They believe it is necessary to get where they are going. And some people genuinely believe there is no racism. They believe we bring all the problems on ourselves; therefore, racism is hardly worth talking about. If you are in the process of denying the importance of it, it is hard to admit racism.

Sharla Frances, a forty-two-year-old chief administrator for a large metropolitan area in the South, also questioned the integrity of tokens who deny racism or who say they feel comfortable being "different" in white environs.

I think they feel isolated, but behave in a different way. They know they aren't any different from other blacks. Their success suggests they are. But in their hearts, they know they're not. They pretend they like being a token, but in their hearts, they can't stand it. The people I know in this situation live lives of alienation and frustration. They are angry, hostile, quick to blow up, and standoffish. They are professionally competent, but mopish. In fact, that is the way they may behave in a close context, but from afar they act as though they love it and brag about it. They tell you "I am comfortable being different," but the way they behave is "I hate it."

Graham Boston, an internationally known scientist and engineer, admitted that he did not like being different, but he was accepting it. "I come into an environment and somebody says, 'Hey, you are different.' It makes me look at myself and recognize that I am different now."

John Hubbard, a forty-year-old professor of sociology at a predominantly white university, was also doubtful about the token black who enjoys the status of tokenship.

I think most token blacks are miserable, whether they admit it to themselves or not. Any token black by definition is separated from the collectivity of his or her kind. When you are separated from the collectivity, you are alienated. Separation from others of one's kind, as Karl Marx calls it, "species being," is to be alienated. When blacks are taken apart from other blacks in the work setting, they are estranged from other black people. In this estrangement, alienation, and separation from one's own kind, the individual ultimately, in a spiritual sense, winds up committing suicide, unless they maintain contact with other blacks. I say those who enjoy the status of being a token are fucked up in the head. I see people who enjoy the status of being a token reject themselves and their blackness.

Whether or not one relishes being a token, there are a number of dilemmas and contradictions of being one, says Rosabeth Kanter in *Men and Women of the Corporation*. Her assumptions about token women are applicable to the male and female black elite in predominantly white settings. The social isolation of the black elite, if they lack proper coping skills, contributes to psychological damage and the individualization of experiences. Psychic violence is also imposed when the black elite are denied a reference group with whom to identify. Let us look at some ways the black elite may be affected.

First, the experience of being a token and the lack of self-validation, if one lacks a support system, contribute to isolation and loneliness. Yet, as Kanter notes, the "dynamics of interaction around them create a pressure for them to seek advantage by disassociating themselves from others of their category."[10] The Talented One Hundred reported that in their interactions with white peers and colleagues in formal and informal settings, they are constantly doing a balancing act. Should they speak to or sit with another black at lunch or at a professional gathering? If they sit with blacks, how will this be interpreted by their white colleagues? It is okay if whites sit together. If two or more blacks sit together, it was reported that whites get suspicious. Blacks are also concerned with how other blacks will interpret their behaviors. My participants often reported noticing the lack of eye contact or other body language signaling discomfort displayed by another black while in the presence of whites, suggesting a level of discomfort when other blacks are present. Even in predominantly black settings, there are similar dynamics, but not nearly as frequently as in predominantly white settings. Blacks are more likely to include or defend whites than whites are to include or defend blacks in white settings. It seems blacks emphasize fairness more, perhaps because of their greater sensitivity to oppression.

Second, although the black elite are aware of their racial differences, because of their underrepresentation in organizations, they deny racism or do not talk about it, particularly in the corporate setting. If they do talk about it, they are seen as "too sensitive." They have to play the role of "entertainer" to some extent, that is, they have to "fit in." Blacks often have to be nice, friendly, and cheerful. If blacks express too much confidence, it is defined as arrogance. In general, never mind how unpleasant whites may be to blacks, blacks should be nice to whites. If blacks complain, they are viewed as disruptive and not a "good fit."

Often the victim is made to feel like the victimizer. For instance, when Diane Earlinger filed suit against a former employer, she felt like the victim. Before her employment as the first woman in her present position in a federal agency, Earlinger filed a suit with EEOC against a major corporation for discrimination. She said,

> I became aware of how difficult a decision that is. I only understood at that time why people have a difficult time acknowledging discrimination in an overt way. It's almost as if you are guilty about how you've been treated. It is a strange set

of dynamics. I tended to feel guilty, which sounded stupid, as if to say, "Gosh, I really should be grateful for what they've done for me."

She concluded, "The other thing that happened is that you almost have to acknowledge that you haven't escaped. You are just like every other nigger. You may think for a period of time it is different for you because you've done certain things. But it isn't."

Earlinger was victimized twice. She suffered guilt because she filed a suit against the company that hired her. And even though the EEOC found reasonable cause for discrimination in Earlinger's case, the agency was underfunded and thus unable to act on her case.

When Earlinger filed her discrimination suit against a former employer, she had no idea that in her present position she would one day be charged with reverse discrimination. When Earlinger hired a black person, a white female felt that she should have been hired for the position, so she filed suit against her. (Interestingly, Earlinger was defended by EEOC lawyers in her agency.)

Third, although blacks are highly visible as tokens and may be used to support an organization's image as an equal opportunity employer, they often do not get to participate in major decisions that are made informally. Walter Calvin, one of the highest ranking black CEOs in the United States, said, "The greatest source of current discrimination that I experience is that, even though I am active at a level in the organization that demands exposure to the best country clubs, because I am black, I am not invited to play golf. I have to join a club that is of a lesser quality. I will invite them to play on my course, but I don't get an invitation."

Fourth, when blacks participate in informal gatherings of colleagues, they cannot let their guard down and relax too much. There is a sense that they are being tested. Warner Babbitt said he is convinced that whites have a "drink test, and if you let your tongue get loose" some judgment will be made about that behavior and eventually held against you.

The informal flow of information is another way to neutralize the authority of blacks. Frank Russo said that when he issues an organizational policy, his white assistants frequently withhold information from their subordinates.

Fifth, in the realm of interpersonal interaction, blacks reported, as did Rudy in the prologue, that their positions, status, or ideas were constantly being invalidated. When Diane Earlinger attended meetings, it was often assumed that she was a secretary. In one meeting, the minutes were never taken. A white female who had been sent to take the minutes assumed Diane was the secretary. In another instance, Jefferson Barnes, chairman of a department at a major university and in his early fifties, said that when he wanted to use the library stacks, he was asked to present his ID, even though he identified himself. Pat Robinson, a federal judge, told me that three or four times a year when he called attorneys for a conference and asked their names, they responded to his court clerk by asking, "Where is the judge?" The first time it happened, he said, "I lost my coolness and stared at the attorney." The counselor responded, "You don't have on a robe." His friend suggested that the next time he should handle it by saying, "The judge only handles important cases, and I am the janitor, so I'll handle these crappy little cases," he said, laughing.

Crystal Miller is a professor in the department of Afro American Studies in a university in the West. Even though she has published extensively, Crystal knows what it means to be invalidated. "As a professional black woman, there are numerous instances in dealing with whites where they are making the assumption that blacks are not quite as equal as they are. There are many subtleties." I probed for an example, and she said,

> The white person you are interacting with is not allowing you the validity of your own experience. I was teaching a workshop in liberal arts, as a faculty member, and there were only two other blacks, the only minorities out of 150 participants. We were having dinner—my husband, the two black participants, and myself. The table was comprised of four blacks and one white, which was unusual. We were talking about several things, and we noticed the person who was serving the table was slow in doing that. We were talking about racial issues, and one of the black men said that when slow service happens to him, because he is a black person, he suspects it has to do with race. The white person at the table kept saying, "It may not be that; it may be something else." The black man kept trying to get him to understand that it may not be prejudice on the part of the waitress, but because of the nature of his experience in this society, it was natural for him to consider that. The white person simply could not understand that. He kept saying, "Sometimes I get slow service, so it could be that."
>
> Not allowing that person to have the experience, interpret it, and understand why that person is making that interpretation, and the white person not extending himself to understand that, is an example of a subtle racist manifestation of invalidating experience. The black person was not saying he was being discriminated against—he was saying that this is what goes through his mind.

Crystal further stated, "Professionally, people make assumptions about what you know and don't know. Whenever I introduce myself as being in Afro American studies, the lids go down. The assumption is made that you are pigeonholed in a box. Obviously, you don't know anything, and you are inferior. You are an idealogue. You are an affirmative action case."

Many whites say to blacks that they are in their position because of affirmative action; this is a double-edged sword. The affirmative action policy did allow blacks to enter the mainstream. However, the credentials and integrity of talented blacks who are qualified and who have achieved meritoriously are called into question. Although black achievers have benefited from the policy of affirmative action, some individuals remain ambivalent, because it does not acknowledge individual merit. Furthermore, the charge of reverse discrimination, arising from the affirmative action program, has become the new ideology of white males to maintain their privileges.[11]

So Crystal Miller said about being ignored as filling an affirmative action quota in black studies, "It takes some discussions with the person [to establish] that you are a human being and you follow a discipline as well as anybody else. I don't make assumptions about people who are in the English department. If you say you are a historian, I want to know more about it. It is the kind of sub- tlety that people don't always recognize. They are making assumptions based on what you look like. Blacks make the assumption that people in black studies don't know anything either."

Ideas and suggestions are also picked up only when whites present them. Of- ten, if blacks want to get a suggestion enacted, they may get a white colleague to present the idea. The rejection induces anger, frustration, and a sense of helplessness. If blacks do not understand this racist pattern, they will internal- ize it and decide something is wrong with them.

Sixth, the black elite are symbols of their race and also the exceptions. "You are different from other blacks" is a comment often heard by the Talented One Hundred. It serves to individualize their experiences; however, anyone who fails becomes a negative embodiment of characteristics attributed to the race. The black elite are under much pressure to be "ambassadors for the race."

Graham Boston, who was raised in a predominantly white setting and who prefers to live and work in one, knows what it means to be "different" and to be a "symbol for the race."

> I may be attending a party, and I am the only black person there. Some white peo-
> ple come up to me and say, "Some of my best friends are black." When they say
> that, they say I am different. So if I am in a situation where someone comes up to
> me and says I am different because I am black—that isolates me. I will walk into
> that situation and say I am like everybody else, until somebody comes up and re-
> minds me that I am different. I don't look at myself as black and everybody else as
> white. There is a bunch of people out there. I am one of them and that's because
> of the way I was raised.

Boston said that when he became well known,

> People reminded me I was black. Everybody did. The public did because I was
> unique. The neighbors said I was a unique person. I recognized I was different.
> Surprisingly enough, I thought it was bad. It made me feel different. And I wasn't
> used to feeling different. I felt the same as everybody else. [Did you feel like a sym-
> bol representing the race?] Yes. But I wasn't used to that. I was accustomed to just
> being Graham, just the average person. I don't look at myself as black and as dif-
> ferent from other people.

Even though Graham Boston doesn't look at himself "as black and as differ- ent from other people," a racist society does. No matter how brilliant, talented, or world renowned, the color line is a reality. As Leo Aramis reminds us,

Racism touches everyone. You can't grow up in this society without it touching you. It's like being in a room with people who are throwing mud. Even if you don't choose to throw mud, you are backed up against the wall, even if you choose not to be involved. The nature of mud is that it will splatter on you. There will be mud on your shoes, pants, and skirt, because that is the nature of racism. Blacks who deny racism are either fooling themselves or they have been some-where I haven't been.

THE IMPACT OF SOCIAL DOMINATION

Like cultural domination, the violence of social domination is more subtle than physical violence. Social dominance is employed by the dominant group as an-other way to maintain racial privileges in the socioeconomic arena.

Each year, the *Annual Report* of the Urban League on the state of black America begins with an objective statistical portrait of discrimination in unem-ployment and education, and the impact of racial discrimination on the life chances of blacks—the racial landscape of America. It does not tell us much, however, about the racial layout of the raceway. Is the path smooth or rough? Is it straight or curved?

For many of the Talented One Hundred, the raceway is rough. Roscoe Champion, the soft-spoken honor graduate in high school and college and a backstage organizer in the civil rights movement, described his journey. Cham-pion, a forty-five-year-old judge, grew up in a large Southern city. He knew about discrimination and what it meant to be defined as inferior. His parents explained to him very early that "whites felt superior to blacks and there was a considerable effort to keep blacks down," and he was going to "have a difficult time as a black person." Hence, his mother encouraged him to be successful and to go to college. He had been among the first four black law students ad-mitted to a predominantly white university in the South in the late 1960s. He did well in law school, though he encountered the usual discrimination—being graded unfairly and being ignored or dismissed by professors and students. Af-ter finishing law school, he passed the bar and went to work as one of the first blacks in a district attorney's office.

Shortly after this appointment in the late sixties, he was drafted for the Viet-nam War. He thought he would "automatically be assigned to the Judge Advo-cate General's office, the legal unit of the military," because of his background. He knew it happened to others who were drafted—the doctors went into med-ical service, and his white lawyer classmates had been assigned to the JAG of-fice. But he was given the classification of MOS rifleman. The army's plan for him was "to go to Vietnam and shoot."

This racial arrow left Champion wounded—his blackness invalidated any sense of privilege gained from his status as a lawyer. "It was my first visceral encounter with racism. I got incensed. I was so hurt. I felt an injustice had been done to me. This was the first time I had experienced what other blacks had." When he saw the classification, he assumed it was an error, but it wasn't. He complained to the first sergeant, but there was no result. He wrote to his senators, but they could not assist him. He wrote to the NAACP, the Urban League, the SCLC, and the Office for Civil Rights.

He said, "When the first sergeant got wind of my trying to get my MOS changed to a classification consistent with my training, he called a special formation and announced, 'We have someone with a law degree who thinks he is better than the rest of us and should not be made to carry a rifle and go to fight in Vietnam like men fight.'"

Everyone was aware that Champion was the object of this ridicule, since he was the only one with a law degree. The sergeant continued tauntingly, "The person I am talking about should know that someone long ago went to war with a rifle and had a law degree and received a congressional medal of honor—he thinks he is too good to do it."

Roscoe felt good when the black GIs supported him 100 percent. "They felt the sergeant was after me and it was wrong. They were upset that he had called a special formation to ridicule me. That is why I believe in my people, because they could have taken a different position that you are no better than I am." He had gotten along well with the GIs, remembering that his mother always told him to "respect others and you'll get respect."

One night, while on duty, the first sergeant said, "Corporal Champion, catch the next bus!" Champion said, "I knew I was leaving. God told me. I believe in God—my prayers had been answered." The sergeant was angry and tried to detain him in the rain.

The next morning, he went to the JAG office, and the major said, "'They've been raising hell in Washington about you—the Urban League and the NAACP. I didn't know that you were here with a law degree. We would have sought to have your classification changed, because we don't have any black lawyers.' He asked if I wanted to become a JAG officer. I turned him down because I wanted to get back to civilian legal practice. I will never forget that experience," said Champion.

Although Champion's racial encounter took place in the late sixties, after the civil rights movement, when blacks had supposedly gained legal and social rights, it was more typical of the overt racism experienced by the Talented One Hundred before the movement. Overt racism is still, however, very much a part of the cultural and social landscape. When the Talented One Hundred grew up in the South with de jure segregation and in the North and West with de facto segregation before the 1960s, the racial waters were more turbulent. Since then, the racial waters have calmed.

Within the broader cultural and social areas, it is important to recognize different realms of activities in which racial violence manifests itself. By way of illustration, I have chosen to explore the realms of education, economics, housing, the media, and sexual racism for examples of racial violence.

The Educational Realm

Racial privilege and dominance are not only economic, as Blauner reminds us; they are also a matter of status. Thus, they are an integral part of the educational landscape. While growing up, the Talented One Hundred were likely to have experienced overt racism. Those black elite who grew up in the South experienced legal segregation in education. Although the facilities were generally inadequate, dedicated black teachers, who were denied entry into other occupations, used their creative energies to nurture the aspirations of black students. The black elite who came of age in the North and West were usually gerrymandered into black schools, and their white teachers, with the exception of a few, were often not supportive of their aspirations. In general, the Talented One Hundred who attended predominantly white schools reported exclusion from extracurricular activities. They also often had separate athletic programs, segregated student councils, and separate proms.

Take Albert Sungist, a minority officer at a major university on the West Coast, for example. He has strong memories of his experience in a predominantly white school in a large city. "The most vivid experience I had was with white teachers." He had been speaking softly, but his voice rose several notes when he said, "Sometimes I felt teachers singled me out for special treatment, but I can't put my finger on it. It was most uncomfortable. It created a lot of doubt about my intellectual abilities." His aunt kept up his spirits, reminding him to be "patient, understanding, and strive for what you want." His self-confidence was not restored until he entered college as an adult and was influenced by his white sociology professor. He eventually went on to achieve a PhD in sociology at a major university.

Timothy Brownlee, a forty-eight-year-old public official, and Ronald Fellows, an educator and entrepreneur in his early fifties, had similar experiences with their respective high school counselors. Black males in their schools were discouraged from going to college because of their supposed lack of intelligence. Instead, they were encouraged to become firemen or policemen, to go into the army, or to go to work in a local factory. "I was skinny, nearsighted, and half-deaf; I knew no cop was going to put me on the force. The counselor would show us the test scores. I knew he was wrong," said Fellows. The negative encouragement was also mitigated by his parents who "wanted me to do better than they." Brownlee, who enjoyed reading Rene Descartes, Charles de Montesquieu, and Adam Smith, found himself tracked with the "really slow students." The slow classes were all black except for one or two whites. After a few weeks, his teachers could see that he did not belong in this class. His parents and grandparents were the "striving force" that kept him motivated in school.

Brownlee and Fellows did not know it at the time, but they discovered many years later during their class reunions that their white counselors had told all black males in their classes the same thing. They had attended different schools in different cities in the Midwest.

As we have seen from these examples, in segregated or integrated environments before the 1960s, racism in education was more overt than today in affecting the life chances of blacks. Now, it is more subtle. When blacks enter, in any significant numbers, previously closed arenas, the qualifications become higher. (There were, however, temporary measures in the late 1960s and the 1970s to reduce qualifications as a result of political pressure by blacks.) The screening and tracking process is used to disqualify blacks and poor people from the system. The process begins as early as kindergarten with IQ tests and continues through graduate and professional training with admissions tests. Since the tests are based on white middle-class norms, they are designed to eliminate minorities and the poor from having access to privileges. Blacks are overly represented in basic educational classes as a direct result of the intelligence tests. National intellectual torchbearers, like Arthur Jensen, an educational psychologist at the University of California, Berkeley, provide the ideological support to sustain racism.[12]

In addition to the tracking system, which results in blacks being overly represented in vocational rather than college preparatory classes, the curriculum is also Eurocentric. Hence, the culture of other groups is negated or denigrated. Black children see few positive role models in their textbooks. The black history that is presented is often distorted. Blacks are viewed in stereotyped ways or studied as a problem. These educational policies have a negative impact on the self-concept and success of individual blacks.

Sharla Frances, a forty-two-year-old public administrator for a large city in the South, remembers walking out of her graduate class at a major university in the Northeast in the late 1960s when she read what in her perception was a racist question, "What was the effect of the rising underclass on the state?" The racist atmosphere affected her decision not to obtain a PhD in sociology. Even though her father was a lawyer and her mother, an educator and administrator in the public school system, her white professors assumed, she said, that "I was a deprived black female, disadvantaged, and an unlikely candidate for graduate school, even though I had been admitted solely on my test scores." On one occasion, she complained about an unfair grade; she knew she deserved an A. The professor said, "'Given your background, you should be pleased with your success at the university.' This was a Jewish professor and I was very quick to tell him my parents were educated when his parents were still coming over on the boat," said Frances.

In addition to the curriculum, there is also the problem of counseling, academically, financially, and socially. There is a dearth of sensitive and responsive student support services and personnel in predominantly white educational settings, whether at the elementary level or at the university level, for black students. As the only black on her university counseling staff, Teresa Hale has to be "both an advocate and teacher of black interests and concerns. There is a lack of knowledge and sensitivity to black issues." Teresa said,

> Being a black spokesperson is an awesome responsibility when trying to represent the highly varying values and concerns of Californian blacks. When I speak of diversity within the black community, white opponents who are against special assistance for minorities often seek to use this diversity argument as proof that there are no black values or special needs.
>
> The shortage of relevant personnel has made my work extremely draining and usually misunderstood and unappreciated by white colleagues. The never-ending education, advocacy, and jack-of-all-trades aspect of my work has been devastating to my psychological and physical health. I had to take a disability leave. Fortunately, now there are more minority professional organizations and conferences than when I started in the field. They are a big help, but they are inadequate for the day-to-day, on-the-job lonely struggles.

These more subtle examples of racism can be documented by showing their differential impact on the life chances of blacks. Blacks experience these discriminatory acts by agents of institutions on an individual level. Sometimes they expend much energy analyzing the sources of oppression that adversely affect their self-images and their successes.

The Talented One Hundred are baffled about whether an act is race related or not. Though they observe differential treatment, they also question whether it is their politics, their personality, their physical appearance, their sex, their race, or some combination of these characteristics. Their "minority sense," as Johnnetta Cole, an anthropologist, called it, tells them race is always a relevant factor.

John Daniels, a sixty-two-year-old corporate executive, remembers that in his predominantly white junior high school in Indiana, "the teacher would seat you alphabetically, but I always wound up in the back of the room, and others would be sitting right in front of the teacher. It became clear there was some fiddling with it. In one line, you'll have nine people and the other line, you'll have five people. They deliberately put me in the back. I told my mother and she gave them hell when they moved my seat. It affected my performance in the class in a negative way."

Rosenthal and Jacobson show how subtle attitudes of teachers can affect the performance of students. They told teachers in their study that certain children (randomly picked) were "potential academic spurters." On the basis of tests administered at the beginning of the year and other occasions over two years, "the children from whom teachers expected greater intellectual gains showed such gains." Not only did students perform better on the IQ tests, but also the teachers felt they had a better chance at success in later life. They were seen as "happier, more curious, and more interesting than other children."[13]

The children involved in this study were mostly white. One can only imagine the detrimental and traumatic effects on black children. The insidious patterns of nonverbal behaviors of teachers, like dismissing or ignoring, were constantly reported by the Talented One Hundred who had attended predominantly white elementary and high schools. Their white teachers' silent language was a constant invalidation of their very being and their sense of selfhood. (I could easily predict, by the twenty-fifth interview, that individuals who had attended predominantly white or integrated schools were less likely than those who attended segregated schools to say their teachers had been the most important influence outside the family.)

Sometimes the insidious effects of the silent language are so damaging that blacks react in a manner that is unpredictable to them. Frank Russo, a health administrator, was the first of two blacks to be admitted to his medical college in the late sixties in the South. He recalled some of his negative racial experiences in medical school. While he ignored some experiences, he confronted others. He was accustomed to being ignored by professors and by fellow students who did not want to study with him or to be his lab partner. But, when a professor "flashed up a picture of an obese nude black female and everybody laughed," he walked out of his class and complained to the dean, his white mentor. Russo said, "One of my professors in the lab was so prejudiced that he would not even answer questions I addressed to him. And I was a student. When I had to give lectures and teach the class in lab, he would not look under my microscope to see if I had the right slide. So naturally, I spent a lot of time and did a lot of extra work to make sure it was perfect." His experience is similar to those of others among the Talented One Hundred. They complained of studying and working in isolation. Often they did not have a supportive faculty mentor to successfully guide them through graduate or professional school.

Russo recalled one incident that had a major impact on him and almost caused him to leave medical school. A certain professor had stretched his patience.

> One day I was lecturing, and every five minutes, he would interrupt me and ask a question. He was trying to be disruptive. I understood temporary insanity. I felt myself getting hot, and he kept on interrupting and interrupting. The next thing I knew, I had him around his neck, pinned against the wall. I never remember walking from the front of the class to the back to get him. I had knocked over pots and pans with hearts and lungs all over the floor. I didn't remember any of that. After it was over, it kind of frightened me because I didn't remember. I went to the dean and told him I was going to leave before I killed somebody.

Russo laughed as he recounted the story. He said that he can laugh now because he has learned to better navigate the "racial course."

The Economic Realm

The Talented One Hundred made it through the educational hurdles. But they still had to face the job market.

Though overt racism still rules the economic landscape, it is not as blatant now as it was in the 1930s. John Lamont, a physicist, discussed his father's experience with racism during the Depression. Although John's father had only an eighth-grade education, he was a brilliant, self-taught aeronautical and aviation engineer, who supported the family for a time as a cook on an estate of a wealthy white woman. During his leisure time, he developed inventions in the field of aeronautical engineering and received a patent related to aircraft engines. When the Depression was over, he was unable to pursue his avocation because of his nine-to-five work schedule as a janitor at a gas company in Washington DC. He had aspirations to move up from janitor to craftsman at his workplace. But his ambitions were not the order of that day. He "went to the foreman one day and told him he would like to try for a job as a machinist. The foreman laughed at him and said, 'How do you know how to operate those devices?'" His father said, "I'll show you." It turned out that he knew how to operate them, because he was a skilled craftsman. The foreman became so enraged that he fired him on the spot.

Since the late 1960s, the racial climate has changed. There is legal recourse if one is fired solely on the basis of race. Yet Ferdinand Hamilton, the highest-ranking black administrator at a major university in the Midwest, knows there is still a ceiling in the 1990s. "I've been here sixteen years and I've done my job well," he said. He has lots of respect from his white colleagues, black faculty, staff, and students. His white colleagues comment on how proficient he is as a writer. "Niggers are not supposed to write," said Hamilton. "Even at this stage, you have to prove yourself." Though he has worked hard and earned respect from his white peers, "no one has come and said, 'I've got an opening as vice president of communications.' No one has asked me to apply for it. As long as I am dealing with the black man's issue, I do an excellent job there and that's fine." His white colleagues cannot, however, trust him outside the black perimeter and put him in a "more global setting." Hamilton, the assistant to one of the top white administrators at his university, added, "There is an assistant-to-the-provost phenomenon in higher education."

Though the economic cast of racism has changed since John Lamont's father played the supporting character of the janitor in the 1930s, the leading players remain white. Blacks, as (mostly) employees, are often the supporting cast in every major occupational arena.

As a result of the civil rights movement and the opening up of equal opportunities, most of the black elite became employees in predominantly white settings rather than employers. This shift reflects the trend of the larger society as it moves from a manufacturing to a service-oriented economy. There is often a barrier encountered in the recruitment and screening process—an implicit policy not to hire blacks. The informal interview becomes a way of screening blacks out. Individuals who do not have access to this information may interpret the discrimination on a personal level.

The Recruitment and Screening Processes

The subtle racism found in the recruitment and screening processes elimi-
nates many talented blacks. Studies have found that white-collar workers, like
blue-collar workers, obtain their jobs through informal personal networks more
than by any other method. More importantly, one study found the best indica-
tor of the rate at which blacks applied and were hired for white-collar positions
correlated with the black racial composition within the organization.[14] In fact,
the study suggests this may be more important than the attitudes of personnel
officers. Since job advertisement is usually by "word of mouth" or by other informal organizational processes, blacks are often excluded if their numbers in
an organization are low or nonexistent. A job may be advertised in agencies
where minorities are not well represented. And often, when a job is advertised,
an employment decision has already been made. Black applicants can have the
same or better education or training as white applicants, but their qualifications
remain suspect. The usual assumption is that if you are white, particularly male,
you are qualified. Finally, since the classification of "minority" was legally defined to include white women, Asians, and Hispanics as well as blacks, the
chances of blacks, who struggled in the sixties more than other oppressed
groups to gain opportunities, are greatly diminished.

When a job is available to black professionals, sometimes the qualifications
and standards are increased for blacks. There is an interest in hiring the "super
black," while the hiring criteria remain lenient for whites.[15] Thomas B. Thomas,
a district sales manager, observed that "blacks must have a law degree from
Harvard to work in the legal unit of my corporation, while the majority of these
white guys have degrees from mediocre law schools. These white lawyers would
have a hard time trying to make it in private practice, so they work in corporate
America or as public defenders."

Leo Aramis said whites manifest an attitude of "presumed incompetence" toward blacks. In the eyes of whites, blacks never measure up. Hence, their credentials must be beyond the requirement of whites. Although Jesse Jackson was
the most articulate presidential candidate on issues facing this country, receiving over seven million votes in the 1988 presidential primary, he still had to constantly remind the American public, "I am qualified to be president."

Even when the black elite have met the objective criteria for a position—
educational training and experience—there is an informal interview. Many subjective factors come into play in an interview, such as physical appearance,
height, style of dress, mannerisms, speech pattern, and skin color. In major corporations, black professionals must represent as closely as possible the organizational norms of middle-class whites. Hence, black males and females may be
discouraged from wearing their hair in an ethnic style, for example, braids. If
their physical appearance, dress, or speech pattern is "too ethnic," it is viewed
negatively. When Thomas B. Thomas, for instance, hired a promising salesman,
a muscular, dark-skinned man with a "jheri curl," his supervisor did not look fa-

vorably upon the hiring. Although the young man performed extremely well on the job, Thomas's supervisor constantly harassed him. The supervisor did hint that he was uncomfortable with the hair style and the physical appearance of the salesman.

Abundant studies have been done on the correlation between physical attraction and life chances. People who are perceived as attractive have more opportunities. Since there is a differential racial standard of beauty in this society, racist attitudes and practices may be manifested through "attractiveness prejudice."[16]

If blacks and whites are not sensitive to the subjective factors in the informal interview process, the black elite's chances of being hired are reduced, despite qualifications. Whites, consciously or unconsciously, identify with persons with whom they feel more comfortable. Since whites are likely to feel more comfortable with other whites, blacks may be eliminated from the pool of applicants because of this comfort factor. When blacks are in a position to hire, they can see more clearly the way in which the interview process operates to exclude them.

Frank Russo, the highest-ranking black in a public health agency, said,

There was a vacant position in the agency and the applicants were a very qualified black woman and a very qualified white woman. We were supposed to get together and talk about the two most qualified candidates—the administrative staff—and then vote. There is only one black and that's me. Naturally they voted for the white woman. When I asked the basis for their decision, they started out by saying both were qualified for the job. They thought, however, the white woman would fit in better and a few other nebulous things. I told them, "Let me tell you how it is going to be. We are going to hire the black one if things are that equal between them. While I am here, a black will get the job."

He added, "I knew they had gotten behind my back and decided to get the white one. They sat there and voted in front of me, and it was done strictly on race." Russo knows there is an implicit policy not to hire blacks in management, and the informal interview is a way of screening blacks out. Individuals who do not have access to this information may interpret the discrimination on a personal level. Russo's decision to hire the "qualified black woman" over the "qualified white woman" was also a race-based choice. But he felt it was the only way to increase the number of blacks in the agency.

Kelly Smith, a corporate executive with a major firm and in her late thirties, asked, "Do you think another white will give us a job if a white boy is sitting near?" She noted,

In graduate school, I learned about something called "nonpecuniary gains" that white people derive from working around, being around, and living with other white people. If you have two employees, one black and one white, the black employee has to give something more in order to get the same kinds of benefits that the white employee gets, because the employer gets another benefit from his white employee. This is the nonpecuniary gain, and this is why we are fighting all the time.

Since Kelly is a manager, she has seen firsthand the discriminatory process of the informal interview. She was required to take the course "The Targeting and Selecting Process." According to Kelly,

> There are all kinds of legal mechanisms found in the interview process that people say are objective, while it turns out to be all subjective. It is very discriminatory. There are objectives for interviewing applicants now that are supposed to be legally defensible. They measure people based on a point system with several interviewers asking specific objective questions. But the problem with the "objective" process is that the rating on the answer that the applicant gives is a subjective process. People put in their own biases about how a response should be rated. It boils down to people's biases incorporated into an objective process.

When Kelly was clear on its intent, she stated to colleagues, "It appears that this is nothing more than a legal mechanism to continue discrimination." (Kelly asked me not to print her quote about the targeting and selecting process because she feared that because there are so few blacks in her position, she would be recognized and punished. I decided to print the quote, not to violate her confidentiality, but to show that the informal process is a standard practice in many organizations and, thus, it would be difficult to identify her.) When I asked how long this process had been used, she reported, "In the last two years." This informal selection process has in actuality been used for many years. Perhaps it is being more finely tuned to avoid lawsuits. What is clear from Kelly Smith's comment is how racism operates to individualize a shared process.

Blacks may also be eliminated from the hiring process because their presence might affect business. Thomas B. Thomas was almost eliminated from a company until he convinced the employer to give him a chance. He stated, "When they hire someone white, they don't ask why you hired that white guy or if you think your client base will accept him. That is not even a question." When the company hired him, he broke all previous records. However, his achievements did not provide an inroad for other blacks to enter the company, because they did not measure up to his success. Thomas said, "There is a double standard of measuring blacks. On a group level, blacks are measured against whites, usually negatively. On an individual level, blacks are compared with other blacks." Hence, if an average or above average black does not measure up to the "super black," it becomes another way of controlling opportunities. When another black employee was hired but did not perform as well as Thomas did in the company, he was terminated. The failings of one black symbolize a collective failure of the race.

The "super black" also serves an additional function. That person is a cheap source of labor. Warner Babbitt, a thirty-nine-year-old journalist, said he travels all over the country and has more assignments than a white colleague in his department who writes only one column a week. Yet they receive the same salary.

Sometimes the authority of super blacks is diffused because their energy is diverted to many projects. Frank Russo said,

> When I do something, I try to do it well. Sometimes you have to be careful that they don't keep adding things on to you deliberately, and you can't do them well. I have begun to wonder if it is a deliberate act—all in the name of "you are doing a great job." So you have to be on your toes to know that. What it does is to dilute you too much, because you have to delegate. You can delegate yourself totally out of it. You need to have time to monitor all of your monitors.

In a *Black Enterprise* survey of readers, 60 percent of those who responded said they were "underpaid considering the level of education, skills, and time logged on the job."[17] There may be explanations for the survey's findings. First, when black achievers are hired for a position, they have to confront an internal tracking system. There is an entry-level "place" for minority men and women and white women, although occasionally they are placed on a fast track. In the downsizing of a corporation or a downturn in the economy, those positions are the most vulnerable. Blacks become "the last hired and the first fired."

The black middle class is also more heavily represented in sales and in staff positions in human resources than in the mainline positions in corporations.[18] They are also heavily represented as academics in black studies programs on white campuses or are concentrated in black colleges. And they are overly represented in jobs that depend on federal support.

Many black elite are trapped on the lower rung and become frustrated. The internal training programs are not targeted for the entry level. So when it comes to promotion, the emphasis is on the "best qualified." This usually means the white male who is at the upper level of management and who has acquired the experience. The individuals in my population escaped entry-level positions through the sheer force of their personality, their work efforts, their determination, their acceptance of greater work responsibility, and self-responsibility. And perhaps having the support of a mentor also contributed to their accomplishments.

For instance, when Kelly found out about an opening for a better position in her organization through a friend, she went to her supervisor to indicate her interest. He responded, "I don't think they'll give it to you, because you do not have the international experience." Kelly knew her supervisor had recently brought in a colleague with the same experience she had and he was in a position two steps higher than Kelly. Fortunately, she had worked with a CEO who recognized her abilities. The CEO wrote a letter to her supervisor, stating she had "done a wonderful job and had international experience at a city bank in New York." She eventually got the promotion for which she was next in line.

Another explanation for the results of the *Black Enterprise* survey is the lack of mentors. The Talented One Hundred frequently indicated that they did not have a mentor. They pulled "double duty" trying to perform their duties effectively and trying to learn the politics of the organization. In particular, black women expressed more difficulty finding a mentor. For a black woman in a predominantly white male–oriented setting, social interaction is constrained by the negative, historical, sexual racism between black women and white men. Dira Ridley, a physical chemist for an international corporation, attends group luncheons with her white male colleagues but limits evening functions or personal interactions to avoid rumors that might affect her career.

For Clarence Pinkney, a forty-three-year-old manager with a major corporation, who arrived from the segregated South in the midsixties, not having a mentor meant "a sink or swim approach. . . . More personal initiative was required for the job," said Pinkney, who now ranks among the top blacks in this international corporation. He told me that there was no one to validate whether he was doing a good job. At the time, he was the only black. Others reported similar experiences.

Despite the barriers that talented blacks encounter in the economic arena, their incomes give them more options in the marketplace. However, the option to live where they want to may be denied because of skin color.

The Housing Realm

Racist dominance and privilege are a part of the housing pattern. An analysis of government records of one trillion dollars in loan applications by the *Atlanta Journal-Constitution* found that blacks were rejected more than twice as often as whites when they applied for home loans at America's savings and loans. This study showed that the black-white discrepancy in loan rejections was definitely more prevalent in the Midwest and the plains states than in the South. Throughout the country, high-income blacks' loan rejections were greater than those of low-income whites in "85 percent of the one hundred largest metro areas in at least one of the past five years. . . . In thirty-five of the one hundred areas, high-income blacks were rejected more often than low-income whites in at least three of the five years."[19] Michael Lomax, a highly esteemed public official in Atlanta, was rejected for a housing loan.

Prior to the sixties, most black elite lived in segregated communities. Now, most of the Talented One Hundred who live outside the South are in integrated or predominantly white neighborhoods. Finding adequate housing has presented problems for many at varying points in their lives. In fact, housing was the one area where the Talented One Hundred had encountered the most discrimination. Sometimes the signs were blatant, and other times, they were more subtle. Jefferson Barnes received his degree and "headed for Route 66" in the 1960s, but, he said, "I couldn't spend the night until I got to Amarillo, Texas, in a black part of town." When he reached California and searched for an apartment, the for-rent signs were taken down. When he parked his car, the sign said, "No niggers here."

The signs are not always so blatant. Blacks are often steered toward neighborhoods that are designated as mixed or changing. Black brokers, who could assist them with available housing, may be denied membership in the National Association of Real Estate Brokers or full participation in real estate firms to discourage them from selling homes to blacks.

Sometimes when blacks want to move into a white neighborhood, their housing loans are not approved, even though they are fully qualified. When Leslie Glouster, a health administrator in her early fifties, and her husband applied for a housing loan in a predominantly white community, they were told they did not qualify. But a black real estate broker informed them that another black client, a service station attendant whose wife was unemployed, had received a loan for a house in a black neighborhood. When Glouster challenged the president of the bank, he said ("after fumbling with the paper"), "I'll go over it again." "We were granted the loan," said Glouster. The analysis of the *Atlanta Journal-Constitution* concluded that race is a better predictor of a loan application's success than sex or marital status.[20]

The Media

The message of the media is both overt and subliminal. The effects on an individual depend on factors such as the level of racial awareness and the amount of time spent watching television or using other media forms. Some studies show black children spend more time watching television than white children. Television is the most popular medium and the bellwether for interpreting and defining the popular culture. Television contributes to the individualization of the black experience, because there is the absence of an incentive to obtain information about the experience of blacks. Since blacks are underrepresented on television in programming or in positions of power, this medium contributes to cultural denigration of blacks and other people of color. Other media forms also have the same purpose as television.

The Jeffersons, a black television comedy appearing in the 1970s, and *The Cosby Show*, a black comedy in the 1980s, show how the black elite have been portrayed by the media. In the pre-1980s on *The Jeffersons*, the black elite were portrayed in the tradition of E. Franklin Frazier's *Black Bourgeoisie* as materialistic and as status seekers in a tenuous socioeconomic position. George Jefferson, the leading character, is depicted like the "Kingfish" on *Amos and Andy*, but in middle-class trappings. George is short and nonthreatening. He plays the role of a greedy, insensitive buffoon who wants to forget his humble origins. He is dominated by two strong, aggressive black women—his wife and the maid.

On the other hand, *The Cosby Show* projects a positive image of the black elite as having made it. The Huxtables—Claire, the lawyer-wife, and Cliff, the doctor-husband—are egalitarian in their social interactions. The show, however, lacks a race consciousness, and there is a benign view of the black experience.

While these shows project different images of blacks, the genre form is comedy. Blacks are still viewed in the role of entertainers. Putting these comedies aside, the truth about how blacks are treated by the media lies somewhere between these comedies. How the media handled Jesse Jackson's campaign by defining and invalidating his candidacy illustrates this point.

In 1984, the media asked, Should Jesse run? Note that the media frequently referred to Jackson by his first name and white candidates by their last names. In 1988, the question became, What does Jesse want? The media ignored him, because they assumed he was "unelectable." They were not presenting his political agenda and issues; instead, they were comparing him, as a black leader, with Martin Luther King Jr. Black leaders and other individuals are compared with one another, not with whites. When the media mentioned Jackson, it was usually because of his view on Palestine and his remark about "hymie-town."

In the meantime, other candidates began to incorporate Jesse Jackson's populist themes and issues—South Africa and drugs—into their campaigns to dilute his strength. Even when he came in second or third, ahead of other candidates in primarily white areas, he was ignored as a part of the political analysis. The question became, Can he win white votes?

Finally, when Jackson won the Michigan primary, a stunning victory over Dukakis, the media asked, Can Jesse win? The media claimed that they were soft on Jackson, blaming him for their failings and implying Jackson had gotten away with minimal criticism. He was then bombarded with much critical coverage to make up for the previous failure to recognize him as a viable candidate.

Along the way, the media were defining, interpreting, and setting limits on the aspirations of blacks. Jackson did represent the aspirations of blacks and a large segment of other Americans, even though the media individualized that by asking, What does Jesse want? When Jesse Jackson received seven million votes, came in first or second in forty-six contests, and elected over twelve hundred delegates to the Democratic National Convention in Atlanta in 1988, he had made an impact. His issues on South Africa and drugs became part of mainstream debates of all candidates—Dukakis labeled South Africa as "a terrorist nation," and Bush labeled it as "a racist nation."

At the Democratic convention, the media commentators asked if Jesse would disrupt it or disrupt Dukakis's campaign. They followed with questions like, How can Jesse be controlled or kept in line? Peter Jennings, anchorman for ABC, asked during an evening coverage of the convention, "Can he be contained on the reservation?" Jackson was aspiring for the highest office in the country, and agents of the media were so intimidated that they did not even conceal their feelings.

Jackson's electrifying and candid speech during the 1988 Democratic National Convention caused a temporary paralysis in analysis by the articulate Dan Rather, Tom Brokaw, Walter Cronkite, and Eric Sevareid; even Ted Koppel lost his train of thought when Jackson appeared later on *Nightline*. On the major networks, ABC, NBC, and CBS, no one could provide insight into this historical occasion.

Jackson's ideas were powerful, and perhaps, as he often said, his time had come. White commentators could not overlook their own personal responses or those of the audience—black, brown, red, yellow, or white. Some, like Sevareid, wanted to confine the impact of Jackson's speech to the "articulation of his people's needs." On the other hand, Walter Cronkite recognized that Jackson had gone beyond this. However, he viewed Jackson as the conscience of the nation, providing moral leadership, and Dukakis as the managerial leader. Seemingly, blacks could now play in this new arena, but only in the role of a moral leader, not as a manager of the country. Finally, Cronkite validated that Jesse Jackson was the best orator in the country. While this is a noble recognition, it has its downside. Other blacks, not whites, will be compared to him, like the athletes and entertainers who are now recognized as among the best, because they proved themselves beyond a reasonable doubt.

The next question the media posed was, Can Jesse reconcile with the Democratic party to win the election? The media will continue to raise questions about Jesse Jackson and other blacks who move beyond the color line. However, the media have not yet raised questions about their role in perpetuating the color line by denigrating or negating an accurate collective portrayal of the black experience.

SEXUAL RACISM

Lisa Allen, an attractive forty-one-year-old professor of history at a major university in a border state, is well liked by her colleagues. Yet, she has to carefully tread the tightrope with her white male colleagues on the issues of being collegial and being aware of the unspoken dynamics of sexual racism. While speaking, her white male colleagues may touch her hands, arms, or back. Though "the touch" may be a mere friendly gesture from colleagues, she is still somewhat wary. Admittedly, only one colleague has referred to her "dark beauty as mysterious and exciting," but being touched still makes her wonder. She is also reluctant to go out to lunch or dinner alone with her white male colleagues.

Lisa is addressing the dynamics of sexual racism in this society. The relationship between black females and white males has a long history of negative familiarity— a history of sexual exploitation by the white male. The black woman in this society has been portrayed as sexually exciting and unrestrained. So Lisa is unsure whether "the touch" from her colleagues is a part of that negative history or whether it is a friendly gesture from a warm colleague.

Sexual racism is also a part of the landscape of the color line. Calvin Hernton, in *Sexual Racism in America*, and Charles Herbert Stember, in *Sexual Racism*, have dealt candidly with sexual racism between blacks and whites and its impact on blacks.[21] Along with sexual myths about black women, Hernton and Stember also discuss the preoccupation of whites, particularly the white male, with supposedly black male supersexuality and the sexual purity of the white woman. These are myths that govern interactions between the races and among blacks. The construction and manipulation of the myths by those in power have functioned primarily to maintain their social and economical privileges.

Although attitudes toward interracial sex vary by race, religion, occupation, education, age, region of country, and sex, sexual racism is embedded in the fabric of this society. When Thomas B. Thomas, director of marketing and the only black in his position at a major company, is away on business with his white colleagues, they feel comfortable telling racial jokes; Thomas seems "different" from other blacks they've heard about, because he is smart and hardworking. The common racial joke in his workplace is, "When you get out of the shower in the morning, there are three wet spots on the floor," said Thomas, who appeared very embarrassed as I probed. (The three wet spots supposedly left by a black man are two footprints and the print made by his very large penis.) He also mentioned that sometimes when he is on business and is assigned a room with his white male colleagues, "they try to sneak around and catch a glimpse of me, so they can go and tell if it is true"—the myth of the black male's extraordinary anatomical sexual endowment.

The myth applies not only to adult black males, but also to children. One story told to me during this research took place in Huntington, West Virginia, in 1987. There was a conversation among white nurses in the local hospital about black males' penises. One nurse took out a ruler and responded to a newborn black male's cry, "If you cry or need attention, you are so beautiful and gorgeous, and with what you got between your legs, you got it made."

Although interracial marriages have increased since the 1967 Supreme Court ruling that struck down state laws prohibiting such marriages, the mores are still strongly against them. Thomas said, "You can commit corporate suicide if you bring your white mate to visit the company or marry a white woman." He said that some black males think it helps them to advance, but he has seen the careers of black men, who had been placed on the fast track in the corporation, halted. The white woman becomes a source of rivalry between black men and white men. "Once a white woman goes black, she can never come back," said Thomas, indicating that she is stigmatized for having any sexual interaction with black males.

"I can't have white women talking to me too long about anything, because rumors will spread, and they will hunt around and try to catch you," said Thomas. Two well-known politicians echoed similar feelings. One sixty-five-year-old mayor said, "I don't fool with white women. I stay away from them if they get too close. I limit their time." The other sixty-five-year-old politician said, "I am scared of them. They'll trick you." He thinks that white men use them to entrap assertive black men who have openly challenged the system.

The comments of Thomas and the two public officials reflect some of the collective dynamics of sexual interaction. On an individual level, however, many of the Talented One Hundred had dated interracially and reported mostly positive experiences. Ten percent—mostly males—were married to or had been married to a white person. One professor described his marriage as "stormier than most." Others had long, stable marriages, like the jazz musician and his white wife of twenty years, whom I interviewed separately and together.

But there were many contradictions and ambivalences surrounding interracial sex, dating, and marriage. They were especially pronounced when I asked, "What is the likelihood that your child/children will marry or date someone from a different racial background?" While a minority strongly disapproved, in general, the majority gave a restrained and tacit acceptance, saying, "I'll respect their choice. It's their decision, but I prefer that they marry black." They cited difficulties their children might encounter with society, the problems their interracial offspring might encounter, and how these issues might affect their racial identity and consciousness.

Veronica Pepper, a psychologist in her late fifties who is interracially married, did not like it when her son by a previous marriage to a black man married a Hawaiian. "My husband is white, so I am not a good one to talk about this. I was very upset when he married. I felt rejected. There are not enough black men, so I am saving one for another black woman. I think men choose more, initiate more, and so it reflects your choice. I felt personal rejection as well. My grandson is multiracial. He's got some black in him, but you would not necessarily see it. I have two white grandchildren, but I want a black child," said Pepper. She stated that she had expressed those thoughts only to her husband, but "my son knows how I feel about interracial marriages."

Pat Robinson's ex-wife is white. He told me he was very concerned when his son would date only white girls. But recently his son has been dating a black girl. "I am very pleased," said the judge, smiling. "I don't know how I would feel if my son got married to a white woman." I asked, "How do you think you would feel?" He answered, "I would be open because I married a white woman. If I had a preference, I would rather for her to be black. I think he would be happier." He thinks his son has a "racial identification problem that kids of interracial families have."

Sexual racism, like the racial landscape of education, economics, housing, and the media, was more overt prior to the 1960s, when conventional mores and legal restrictions limited interracial marriage and sexual and social interactions between blacks and whites.

THE RESPONSE OF THE BLACK ELITE TO OPPRESSION

How does one respond to oppression? Does one deny it? Does one ignore it? Does one accept it? Does one withdraw from oppression or reject it? Is there a dominant mode of adaptation or a mixed mode?

When I approached Ruby Dee, actress, poet, and writer, for an interview and explained my project, she said, "I am more concerned with justice than racism.

I keep my head above the clouds and choose not to deal with racism, and I look beyond it." Although she agreed to the interview, I never had the opportunity to find out how she kept her head "above the clouds."

Individuals among the Talented One Hundred are diligently ignoring, denying, avoiding, and withdrawing from racism and "keeping their heads above the clouds." But as the sensitive young journalist said, "The nature of mud is that it will splatter on you," even when one does not *choose* to throw it or be involved with it.

While the Talented One Hundred may ignore some acts of racism, they may be particularly sensitive to others. Bernie Roberts, a social researcher, is rather adept at handling racism. But he admitted that he is very sensitive to taxi drivers in Washington DC who ignore him.

> The thing that bothers me, as an adult, is that here in Washington, I can't deal with not being picked up by a taxi cab. It has blown my mind. I still have to deal with that. But I haven't recovered from it. It is the one act of discrimination that I can't figure out. It baffles me. But I have to explain why blacks don't want to pick me up either. My friend tells me, "They think black males will accost them." But I observe black taxi drivers passing black women to pick up white women.

When Pat Robinson was growing up in the 1940s, he coped with racism by avoiding it. Yet it did not avoid him when he became the first black member of a varsity baseball team in the early 1950s. The coach wanted his players to be fit. In his apparently customary pep speech, he somehow forgot that Pat was a member of the team when he said, "I want all of you to run around the field five times and the last one back is a niggerbaby." Robinson says, "I was stunned and there was clear silence. It was one incident I'll never forget." The university named the baseball field after the coach and wanted the players to attend a dedication ceremony in his honor. "I would not show up to honor that son-of-a-bitch," Robinson said. "To them, he is a good old boy. For me, [that incident] left its scars and seriously interfered with my affection for the school." This had a real emotional cost for Robinson. He had been very involved in extracurricular activities, feeling fully included then, but now dubbed himself as the "official Negro." "It seemed as though they said we ought to have a Negro and I was that Negro," he said of his predominantly white alma mater.

Over thirty years elapsed before Robinson reassessed his way of looking at his college experience. "I got angry at myself for having such little insight back then. It took me thirty years to realize this was not what I thought it was." He had played football during his freshman year, and the death of a player brought the college teammates together in 1985. He looked forward to sharing fond memories. When they gathered, "there was a lot of drinking and war stories and what you've been doing all these years." Robinson's voice lowered to a whisper. "I had the weirdest experience, because I realized I never belonged there. I didn't realize it back in 1951 when I played with them. When the other players were recalling incidents, I said, 'I never did that with you guys. I didn't know about that.' I played football and kind of goofed around a little with the guys, and then went to this rooming house where other black athletes stayed, and it was nothing like that." The highly esteemed public official's voice trailed to silence. When his thirtieth-year graduation anniversary came up in 1986, he recalled, "I remember I didn't go and I had planned to. I said it is going to be just like the other one—why should I go?"

Denial is a way of masking the pain. It is time consuming and unproductive for many to remember the painful incidents. Ethel King "did not remember" two important discrimination lawsuits she had filed. It was only through extensive probing that I found out about them. One suit was filed against a restaurant that did not serve "colored people," and the other was against a realtor. "It was one of the most heartbreaking cases for me. I would cry and couldn't get over the fact that the realtor had been so blatant." When the court found the realtor not guilty, she remembered that the realtor "jumped up and said, 'Justice has been served.' My girlfriend was in tears, but I couldn't cry. I was so angry, I said this is why people throw Molotov cocktails." Tears flowed freely from her eyes as she recalled this incident thirteen years later.

"For what reason do you think you had difficulty in recalling these experiences?" I asked. She replied, "I was so angry and hurt. I could see the power of that anger. If I could get that angry, I couldn't live with it, and what happens is you put it so far back, it doesn't immediately come to mind. But you never, never forget, and once I start thinking about it—it's amazing." There was laughter when I told her others had done the same. "I thought I was the only one," Ethel responded.

Claude Kent, an engineer, is good at ignoring the impact of race. When I asked the racial composition of his neighborhood, he said repeatedly, "I don't know." I became impatient with his unusual response. Finally, I asked, "Do most of the people in your neighborhood look like you or do they look like her?" I pointed to a white female who was within view of his office. Finally, he acknowledged his neighborhood was predominantly white.

Denial and avoidance are coping mechanisms used in handling racism. They may be functional or dysfunctional to individuals, depending on the situation. There was a feeling among the Talented One Hundred that "they could not dwell on racism; they must move forward." They use a mixed mode of coping, depending on situational factors.

Nevertheless, we can see, through the experiences of Pat Robinson and Ethel King, how the psychological effects of racism are deep and lasting.

Occasionally, individuals accept the blatancy of racism without questioning. Benson Robinson, a successful fifty-two-year-old entrepreneur, grew up in a predominantly white community. He is among the wealthiest of the Talented One Hundred and among the wealthiest in the country. For Benson, race is not a salient issue in his life. His mother taught him that "people are people regardless of their race," and he responds to people on that basis. He was among

the few individuals who stated that they had never encountered racism. However, during our interview, Benson recalled that a competitor who heard he was
opening a new business said, "Doesn't that damn nigger have enough money?"
Benson hires mostly whites in his business. (You may recall that when Benson's
white manager hired six blacks, some white customers complained he had too
many blacks working for him.)

When I asked Benson if he had ever hired a black manager in his business,
he said that he had hired two. But they did not work out, because they stole
from him. "I have a problem, and it's my biggest problem that I'll share with
you. Black people, for some reason when they get in a position, they get slick.
They don't want to work anymore. They try to find an easy way to make it," said
Benson, who works a fifteen-hour-a-day schedule. He likes to deal with people
in an honest manner. Turning the question, he asked, "Where do we get that
mentality? You are a sociologist; tell me."

Benson's son, a college student with whom I had a chance to interact, does not
share his father's philosophy. He said, "I would assess my target market, but it
would not deter me from hiring qualified people, and if it turns out they are black,
I would hire them. If they were not qualified, I would not. If they were white and
not qualified, I would not hire them. I would certainly not hire them just because
they were white!" We were out of the earshot of others, but the son whispered,
"My father is a compassionate person, so I know that prejudice has to bother him."
He cited examples of his father's white employees who left racist notes, like "Nigger, clean up," in the bathroom for the black janitor. (I did not have a chance to
ask the father about such notes because I spoke with the son after our interview. I
also did not want to violate the confidentiality of the son's conversation.)

Benson's candid response to racism reflects a lower level of racial awareness
and sensitivity, unlike most of the Talented One Hundred, whose levels of
awareness were higher. In general, they rejected many detrimental aspects of
the Eurocentric perspective and incorporated an Afrocentric one to buffer
them against racism. They emphasized the importance of maintaining black institutions, preserving black culture, and teaching black history. Their responses
were not, however, unidimensional; at some level, they were multidimensional.

The Talented One Hundred expressed contradictions and conflicts in the
three components of their personality—cognitive, behavioral, and affective. Individuals who had a higher level of self-awareness sought to justify their inconsistencies and bring them in line. Multilevel conflicts and contradictions are en-
demic to a racist society.

The individual awareness level—shaped by such factors as age, regional differences, racial composition of environment in formative years, racial experiences, and academic discipline—is along a continuum. Racial responses are
multidimensional, depending upon the situation and the historical time period.

Let's look at Dira Ridley's response to racism. As a physical chemist in her
late thirties, she is strongly influenced by her academic training. When I asked

if she had ever been discriminated against, she responded, "Yes, I have felt discrimination, but I can't scientifically prove it to you." Although she intuitively senses racism, she needs hard empirical data to prove it. She feels also that "scientific data will lead to greater enlightenment," particularly among natural scientists. Dira strongly believes in science solving problems. Interestingly, in the light of Dira's analysis, the data show that in the natural sciences, blacks are the most underrepresented racial group.

The concept of the "race man," as Alfred Moss noted in *The American Negro Academy*, was more prominent before the rise of specialization in the academic disciplines. Black professionals had a greater allegiance to ameliorating race conditions than advancing in their particular discipline.[22] Jonathan Mobutu feels that this emphasis on greater specialization by black professionals will lead to individualization of the black experience and, hence, a more nonracial orientation.

The individualization of their experiences may not allow the black elite to see their individual fates as being integrally linked to one another and to the masses of blacks. Moreover, the individualization of racial experiences may contribute to psychic damage. For instance, the black elite may become gatekeepers preventing other blacks from achieving. Michael Lomax, who was extremely candid in our interview, wanted me to use his real name. Perhaps he felt his candor would assist others to examine their actions. He said, "At an earlier point in life, I tried being a gatekeeper. I've gone through periods where my self-esteem was not high enough that I felt comfortable having other blacks around."

Lomax, the chief architect for the inaugural National Black Arts Festival in Atlanta, is now working to change the image of blacks. He is addressing not only the external issues of blackness, but also his internal conflict, although it has taken him a while. He said,

> I am angry about the conflict inside of me or angry that I am black. I have a legitimate reason to be angry, but I am not going to change my racial identity. So I have to learn to accept myself and determine whether it is appropriate to fight against those negative images and to recognize them and not allow them to seep in and affect those positive images of myself.

If blacks do not understand this hidden agenda of racism, the result is inaction. If they do understand the hidden agenda of racism, they can externalize it and create messages from their subjective and objective experiences, as Lomax did, that will lead to action.

SUMMARY

This chapter focuses on the psychic impact of the color line on the black elite, in cultural and social areas and within the different realms of activities where racism is manifested, such as education, economics, housing, the media, and sexual relations. The oppressor group aims to impose a sense of place for the oppressed group by employing violence and three important devices of power—control, dominance, and exploitation—to maintain racial privilege in every social institution and facet of social interaction.

The concept of violence is examined from a Fanonian perspective, which looks at human violence in situations of oppression. This definition extends the limited concept of physical violence to include psychic violence.

An emphasis on individualism, a major value orientation in the United States, contributes to individualizing the racial experience. Using this universal value of individualism to contextualize the racial experience of people of color denies that there is a collective component also. Individuals sometimes do not link "the personal troubles of milieu" and "the public issues of social structure," as sociologist C. Wright Mills noted in *The Sociological Imagination*.[23] If blacks do not understand the hidden agenda of racism, reactivity may result. If they do understand the hidden agenda, the black elite can externalize their response and create messages from their subjective experiences that will lead to proactivity.

NOTES

1. William Julius Wilson, *The Declining Significance of Race* (Chicago: University of Chicago Press, 1978), 151.

2. Charles Vert Willie, *Caste and Class Controversy* (Dix Hills, NY: General Hall, 1979), 157.

For other critics of Wilson, see Harry Edwards, "Camouflaging the Color Line: A Critique," in *Caste and Class Controversy*, Charles Vert Willie, ed. (Dix Hills, NY: General Hall, 1979), 98–103; Robert Hill, *Economic Policies and Black Progress: Myths and Realities* (Washington, DC: National Urban League, 1981); Alphonso Pinkney, *The Myth of Black Progress* (Cambridge: University of Cambridge Press, 1984).

3. Willie, *Caste*, 158.

4. Hussein Abdilahi Bulhan, *Frantz Fanon and the Psychology of Oppression* (New York: Plenum Press, 1985), 135.

5. Bulhan, *Frantz Fanon*, 136.

6. Bulhan, *Frantz Fanon*, 137.

7. Robert Blauner, *Racial Oppression in America* (New York: Harper and Row, 1972), 27.

8. Bulhan, *Frantz Fanon*, 140.

9. Abram Kardiner and Lionel Ovesey, *The Mark of Oppression* (Cleveland, OH: World, 1962).

10. Rosabeth Moss Kanter, *Men and Women of the Corporation* (New York: Basic Books, 1977), 239.

11. Michael D. Woodward, "Ideological Response to Alterations in the Structure of Oppression: Reverse Discrimination, the Current Racial Ideology in the U.S.," *Western Journal of Black Studies*, 6, no. 3 (1982): 166–173.

12. Chukwuemeka Onwubu, "The Intellectual Foundations of Racism," *Western Journal of Black Studies*, 3, no. 3 (Fall 1979): 157–167.

13. Robert Rosenthal and Lenore F. Jacobson, "Teacher Expectations for the Disadvantaged," *Scientific American*, April 1968, 22.

14. Joe R. Feagin and Clairece Booher Feagin, *Discrimination American Style* (Melbourne, FL: Robert E. Krieger, 1978; rpt. 1986), 47.

15. Feagin and Feagin, *Discrimination*, 52.

16. Daudi Ajani Ya Azibo (Donald Allen), "Perceived Attractiveness and the Black Personality," *Western Journal of Black Studies*, 7, no. 4 (Winter 1983): 229–238.

17. Richard D. Hylton, "Working in America," *Black Enterprise,* Aug. 1988, 63.

18. Sharon Collins, "The Making of the Black Middle Class," *Social Problems*, 30, no. 4 (April 1983): 369–382.

19. Bill Dedman, "Blacks Less Likely to Get Home Loans," *Dayton Daily News*, Jan. 22, 1989.

20. Dedman, "Blacks Less Likely."

21. See Calvin C. Hernton, *Sex and Racism in America* (New York: Grove Press, 1965); Charles Herbert Stember, *Sexual Racism: The Emotional Barrier to an Integrated Society* (New York: Elsevier, 1976).

22. Alfred Moss, *The American Negro Academy: Voice of the Talented Tenth* (Baton Rouge: Louisiana State University Press, 1981).

23. C. Wright Mills, *The Sociological Imagination* (New York: Oxford University Press, 1957).

③

THE COLOR LINE ACROSS
THE WORLD OF WORK

The door of opportunity swung wide for Jack B. Lane and other talented blacks in the late 1960s and early 1970s. The winds of change, spurred by the civil rights movement, an expanding economy, and the shift from a manufacturing to a service-oriented economy, produced the largest black middle class in America, by any definition, in nearly four hundred years. It also created unprecedented career choices. Blacks could now sit on corporate boards and school boards and choose from a range of careers, from architect to astronaut, corporate manager to mayor, and scientist to school superintendent. Bart Landry, for example, found "no less than sixty-five different titles held by Black males" in a 1976 national survey of middle-class blacks and whites.[1]

The old black middle class, unlike the new black elite, was confined to traditional occupations of teaching, ministry, social work, medicine, dentistry, and law in segregated communities. The new black middle class is increasingly in the white suburbs, where the majority of new, white-collar, middle-class jobs are being created. A *Washington Post* article, "The Integration of the American Dream," noted that this new black middle class, unlike the old black elite, is "emerging and succeeding by the standards of the majority White culture in mainstream American careers. One result is that class is becoming a more important predictor of behavior than race."[2]

Though class is an important predictor of some behaviors, race continues as a salient variable in the lives of the black elite. Articles such as the one in the *Washington Post*, describing the success of the black elite who are moving into mainstream careers and into corporate boardrooms, reflect an accurate surface portrait. "But scratch the surface and another reality appears," says Bart Landry, a sociologist, in *The New Black Middle Class*. He knows the workplace "is still not color-blind."[3] Acknowledging that the "racial climate has greatly improved," Landry senses too that there is still a chilly racial wind, swinging back the door.

THE "GILDED GHETTO": BLACKS IN CORPORATE AMERICA

When Clarence Pinkney, a forty-three-year-old, started at X Consumer Products Company in the midsixties, he was one of the first black professionals ever hired. Now blacks compose 7 percent of the management, and *Black Enterprise* lists the company as one of the fifty best places to work.

The popular literature about the triumphs of successful blacks furthers the perception that profound changes in the boardrooms of corporate America have taken place. For instance, in 1988, *Black Enterprise* ran the cover story "America's Hottest Black Managers," stating,

> They represent some of the most powerful men in corporate America. Their decisions determine whether the world's largest corporations will reap millions—even billions—of dollars in profits. They influence what the nation eats, buys, and drives, as well as how it communicates. They are America's twenty-five hottest Black managers and they are putting their bold signature on big business.[4]

Evidence from the Equal Employment Opportunity Commission (EEOC) supports the significant growth of black officials, managers, and professionals in corporate America within the last two decades.[5] Clarence Pinkney exemplifies this trend. In more than twenty years with the X Consumer Products Company, he has moved from an assistant advertising specialist to a top position in personnel management. He expects to continue his progress in the company.

For a brief period, it seemed corporate America held promises of unlimited opportunities for young blacks. But during the Reagan era, these triumphal opportunities began slipping away. From 1980 to 1985, the number of black male managers increased only slightly from 2.7 percent of white-collar managers to 2.9 percent, a decrease in the rate of growth from the previous five years.[6] The retrenchment in the commitment to affirmative action by the Reagan administration and corporate downsizing were clear signals that blacks were losing ground and experiencing added trials. A conference board survey of business leaders ranked affirmative action for minorities and women as twenty-third out of twenty-five human resources management issues.[7]

Not only has the rate of growth for black employment in corporations slowed down, but even fewer blacks are moving up the corporate ladder, particularly into the senior executive level. There is a sense of ghettoization of black professionals working in corporate America. Many blacks who enter the corporate world remain at entry-level positions. They are also likely to be employed in staff positions rather than line positions. They are channeled into such human resource areas as community relations, public relations, and personnel relations. These jobs are the most vulnerable to shifting economic winds. Moreover, they are less likely to prepare blacks for upward mobility or the fast-track positions.

The Talented One Hundred who are employed at the senior executive level in corporations confirmed the earlier assessment of John P. Fernandez's work, *Black Managers in White Corporations*, published in 1975, and Edward W. Jones Jr.'s research on the status of black managers, which appeared in an issue of *Harvard Business Review*.[8] According to Fernandez, Jones, and the Talented One Hundred, there are several shared concerns in such areas as (1) recruitment, retention, and retrenchment; (2) quality of life; and (3) the balancing of the role strain and role conflict sometimes inherent in their political and professional positions.

Recruitment, Retention, and Retrenchment

Many barriers exist for blacks entering corporations. As noted, the literature supports the importance of informal networks in obtaining a position for both blue-collar and white-collar workers. In addition, corporations are most likely to hire individuals with whom they feel more comfortable. The lack of commitment to affirmative action by the federal government and the private sector helps ease the pressure to hire blacks. Also, there is still reluctance on the part of some corporate managers to recruit blacks. They feel their clients are unwilling to accept blacks, and they are uncomfortable about taking risks with their own careers. Thomas B. Thomas, a thirty-eight-year-old regional sales manager for a large corporation, said senior executives in his company continue to use this rationale, despite his success.

When Thomas went to work as a sales manager with a major corporation in 1971, the district manager did not want to hire him because he felt employing blacks would affect the company's white clientele base. Thomas convinced the manager to hire him. "You are either the biggest 'bullshitter' I've ever met or the best sales manager," the district manager said to Thomas. "The only way you can find out is to hire me," retorted Thomas. He broke all previous sales records in the company in an all-white area, and each time he broke a record the white district manager "moved up a notch." Thomas thinks whites "measure the successes or failures of all blacks by one another," so he always works hard and performs better than others to cope with racism. "If I were of Caucasian descent, there would be no stopping me in the market, but I lose my fair share of business because they know I'll move one step closer to where they are," concludes Thomas. He believes it is important to have more blacks in the corporation. Hence, Thomas has actively recruited other blacks, but has not met with much success.

In contrast to Thomas, Duane Dennis, a thirty-two-year-old stockbroker for an international investment firm in the South, did not have any difficulties in the eighties being hired in an industry that has until recently excluded blacks. Less than a dozen investment banking firms in the nation are black owned. In 1987, only one black firm had a seat on the New York Stock Exchange.[9] "It is an industry," Dennis said, "that survives by the confidence of people investing a large sum of money with brokers to manage." Since there are negative stereotypes about blacks being poor managers of money and incompetent business persons, I asked if he thought it mattered being black in this industry. Dennis does think "it matters a lot." He believes, like Thomas, that he has to be better than other brokers to succeed. While he has been successful with both whites and blacks, who make up 60 percent and 40 percent, respectively, of his clients, he has encountered racial incidents. Said Dennis,

> When I talk with white clients on the phone, they are receptive. [He said his speech pattern does not sound typically black.] But when I go to the office to pick up the check, they are taken aback. I remember only one incident in which a client wanted her money returned, an older white female, who was going to invest a large sum of money. In the course of two months, we had spoken four or five times on the phone, building up rapport. Once I got to her place and she saw I was black, she literally developed heart trouble at the door. She said that she had chest pains and would mail the check, but would need time to recuperate. Needless to say, the check never came. A phone call beat me back to the office. She indicated that she never had any professional relationships with blacks, and that she prefers having an older white male to manage her money.

To minimize such overt racism, Dennis learned to appear in person to meet his clients, commenting, "I want them to make sure they know with whom they are dealing. I don't want any more surprises."

In contrast to the response of his white female client, Dennis had a favorable reaction from clients who live in an all-white community known for its overt exclusion of blacks. When his white clients offered to mail a check to him after a phone consultation, he wanted to make certain they knew he was black. He said, "They were initially shocked, but they ended up telling me that they felt more comfortable with an honest black broker than a dishonest white one." When other white clients meet Dennis in person, they make comments like, "I thought you were Jewish over the phone," or "I thought you were short and Italian." Dennis does not think these comments are inappropriate or racist. "I smile when they say that. I think it's a way of establishing rapport. If they say something that is offensive or inappropriate, I'll let them know. I react to the comment, not the person behind it. I would react the same way if the person making the comment was black." Black clients have also been surprised to see a black stockbroker, but upon further probing, he admitted, "No blacks have ever made such comments."

Many competitive and highly skilled young blacks, like Duane Dennis, are entering new career paths in finance. Previously, not only did they lack information about career opportunities in finance, but racism was the major factor blocking their paths. Prior to the election of black mayors and the appointment of black public officials, white investment firms were selected to manage municipal accounts, even though blacks contributed a large portion of those funds. However, in the 1970s, these investment firms discovered the need to hire blacks as entrées to black mayors. Thus, greater opportunities in public finance have become an avenue of upward mobility for many blacks, but the more lucrative business in corporate finance continues to elude them.

Although some corporations, such as accounting and investing firms, have aggressively recruited blacks, there is still a problem in retention. In a *Black Enterprise* report on corporate racism, Joyce Johnson, chair of the National Association of Securities Professionals, notes, "It's almost like a blood bath [is taking place] in some of these major firms. . . . They are hiring minorities left and right, but they're firing them within six months."[10] These issues of evaluation, promotion, and retention concern many blacks in corporate America.

Evaluation, Promotion, and Retention

Having acquired the proper credentials to enter corporate America—maybe even MBAs and PhDs from Ivy League schools—blacks still find the workplace is not color-blind in its evaluation, promotion, and retention. A survey conducted of black MBA alumni of the top five graduate business schools found that 84 percent believe that considerations of race have a negative impact on ratings, pay, assignments, recognition, appraisals, and promotion. Ninety percent of the participants also agreed with a statement that subtle racism pervades their own companies, and more than half said the racism is overt.[11] Thus, the evaluation, promotion, and retention process may be affected by these conscious and unconscious racist attitudes and behaviors, as indicated by a 1982 survey of the class of 1957 Ivy League graduates. When asked if blacks are as intelligent as whites, only 36 percent of the Princeton class, 47 percent of Yale, and 55 percent of the Harvard class agreed with the statement.[12] These graduates are now in the age cohort to be promoted into senior corporate positions. One can speculate about the impact of their belief not only on hiring but also on evaluating and promoting.

The Talented One Hundred who work in corporations frequently reported experiencing or observing overt discrimination in the appraisal and promotion process. Thomas B. Thomas mentioned that his wife, a regional manager for a major company, earned excellent ratings, but just prior to evaluation and promotion, her personnel file was partially destroyed. Usually, appraisal and evaluation take more subtle forms. For instance, when a white manager behaves assertively within the corporation, it is often interpreted as positive. But if a black manager acts similarly, this may be negatively interpreted as arrogance. This racist perception and interpretation adversely affect evaluation. The person may be labeled "not a good fit," thus impacting the chances of moving up the corporate ladder. More importantly, however, the Talented One Hundred reported that supervisors often stated that the reason for nonpromotion was a lack of qualifications.

Take Kelly Smith, a high-ranking officer in an international corporation, for example. She knows that she was qualified for the next rung on the corporate ladder, the highest position in her field. Even her boss maintained that she is better than others, although he claimed she didn't have the qualifications for a position in international affairs. "I have more qualifications than others. The only advantage they have over me is that they've lived abroad. My qualifications are in excess," said Smith, who has an MBA from a prestigious university. She thinks it is very difficult to distinguish corporate politics from racism. She admits that "many bosses keep their subordinates behind because they feel the promotion will have a negative impact on them. This, I feel, is corporate politics." But she thinks it was racism when her supervisor said she did not have the qualifications to do the job. "It is very difficult to assess corporate politics; often people get muddled and don't know how to behave. It gets mixed up in terms of the subtleties of corporate politics and racism."

Since Kelly was promoted to her present position, she has seen many persons, several steps below her level, promoted to her level. She even hired a man and a woman who are now at her level. "I have not been promoted, and the reason is that the next position is a big step," said Smith. She does not think the company is ready for a black, particularly a woman, to be promoted to the high-ranking line position. While there are two blacks in the corporation who rank higher than she does, they are employed in staff positions. Kelly said,

> They've been given the position of external affairs, basically where you give money away. They do not have line functions where corporate decisions are made. So you can see it is a very powerful position, and many people would not want me to have this high-ranking line position. What I think the company is likely to do if they promote me is to ship me out to some country to be in charge of some division of a country. It would be a position of authority, but it would take me out of a line position, and I may be out there for life.

A disproportionate number of black managers are in staff positions in the field of human resources. Many blacks who entered corporations in the late 1960s and early 1970s had liberal arts degrees. Thus, they were more likely to be hired in staff positions as affirmative action officers, community relations experts, or personnel managers. Since blacks are disproportionately in human resources areas, they are vulnerable to downsizing in the corporation. EEOC officials who are in human resources are also being phased out or have little power. They, too, have to walk the tightrope in protecting their own positions by not pushing too fast and too far in helping other blacks. Although blacks entering corporations today have a greater chance than ever before of being promoted, they may be ghettoized in entry-level positions. In such industries as banking and finance, they are often stuck in public finance rather than corporate finance, where the opportunities are more lucrative. Being clustered in certain positions limits their chances of upward mobility.

Quality of the Workplace

The literature on black managers suggests they experience alienation, isolation, loss of identity, and culture shock in varying degrees. In his research on black MBAs, Edward W. Jones found that 98 percent of the participants believed that corporations have not achieved equal opportunity for black managers; 90 percent perceived the climate of support was worse than for their white peers.[13] Rosabeth M. Kanter, in *Men and Women of the Corporation*, found that the culture of corporate administration is influenced by the numerical dominance of men, while the quality of life for women was influenced by their proportion in the organization.[14] It was not surprising when the Talented One Hundred in the corporate world said they lacked supportive mentors and informal networks to assist them in reaching the next step of the corporate ladder. Since the middle-management level has very few blacks, their numerical minority affects their chances of finding a mentor. Kelly Smith sees it as "unfortunate that blacks in the corporate world have very few mentors they can count on." She feels fortunate in having had them: "I've had people who have served as mentors to me—one was an Egyptian CEO—but the others were white. I have been very fortunate to have had them, but I don't have any at this point."

Even though Kelly has climbed the corporate ladder by her own merit and with the support of a few mentors, she found that the competition becomes keener and fiercer at the top rung. A *Black Enterprise* survey of readers supports Kelly's experience, indicating blacks who have the highest level of education and income were the most likely objects of discrimination.[15] Kelly feels she has reached an invisible ceiling and the possibility for her promotion is slim. She described the organizational climate in the United States as not supportive. However, when she travels abroad, her clients and staff treat her courteously and respectfully. Kelly reiterated that her colleagues and supervisors think she has too much power. "They want to dilute my power, undermine me, or ship me off to another country." One means of diluting her authority was to ask her to share her Cuban secretary, whom Kelly had hired and promoted to executive secretary. This presented some serious problems. Said Kelly, "She was extremely loyal to me. Now that she reports to two other men, her allegiance is to them. I have asked her to do certain things for me and she has gone behind my back to my boss to tell him she does not want to do these things, prior to discussing them with me. That is totally unheard of." Kelly maintained that a white secretary, whom Kelly described as "an envious little white girl," helped "pollute the mind of the Cuban, who has a Latin mentality that says if she works for a man, she owes him more allegiance."

In describing further the quality of her life in the workplace, Kelly pointed out that she is hassled by her boss and others about the way she dresses and about the type of car she drives.

> I am a very bright, confident individual and qualified for the position I have. But the white folks on the job can't stand the fact that I have the money and the material goods. My dear boss mentioned this to me. Some of my colleagues are on my level, some beneath, and a few above. It is not that they can't afford them. It is just that they don't think I should have them. About three years ago, I bought a Mercedes-Benz. I am an officer of this company and paid to make financial decisions. How on earth do they think I can make a better financial decision than I make for myself? I invested my money in a Mercedes-Benz, which I thought was a reasonably good investment.

Since her white colleagues were envious of her, the new boss appeased them by restructuring her department. When Kelly asked,

> "Why are you restructuring the department?" He replied, "People are envious of you. It is not that you can afford to buy a Cadillac and others can't afford to buy a Cadillac; it is just that others think you should be driving a Ford." He didn't say my Mercedes-Benz, because that would have been too clear. The people are envious of the way I dress, the way I look, the car I drive, my behavior, and the power I have. I am an officer and make a lot of decisions. They would like to find something wrong with what I do. But they can't, because I know it better than they know it. They are constantly looking for something to nitpick.

When Kelly leaves the workplace, home is not a total refuge from racism; not even the nightly comfort of her bed brings her peaceful sleep. "I can't sleep—my mind is racing—because I can't figure out how they are going to come at me next. So I have to work twice as hard to think about this person and what is going on and to try to figure out what they are going to do next."

Even though Kelly is unable to sleep some nights because of the race watch, she warned, "Blacks could destroy themselves if they internalize the stress from racism." To cope with racism, she said, it is necessary to always "be the best at what you do and to be persistent, because you never know who is watching you." She reminded me of the CEO who noted her performance and promoted her just one month prior to his death. Though Kelly, a political moderate, understands the importance of working hard, being competent and independent, she is also keenly aware of the political landscape. It is important for blacks not to "confine all their energies to working within the corporation," said Kelly. "Blacks should have outside contacts with political organizations of strength and power. If you can't get what you need on the inside, you need to develop an external base in order for someone to think twice about doing something adverse to you." Kelly lives in a politically active black neighborhood in the South where many public officials also reside.

"Although the corporation where I work is powerful, my colleagues do not know who I know and what power I can engender."

Like Kelly, Walter Calvin, also a top-ranking black senior vice president in an international conglomerate, has had "to figure out what they are going to do next." In fact he became so "fed up" with trying to figure things out, he told his superior, "Include me in this act or move me." He was transferred from the domestic to the international side of the parent company. Walter has not encountered much discrimination as an executive within the international side of the corporation. However, he still faces it when he represents the company. He said,

Even in Europe, where whites are not accustomed to blacks getting off a corporate jet, they stare at me as though I am a ghost. I can be in a crowd of my white counterparts in London or in Frankfurt and it is as though I am—[He did not complete the sentence]. I've had instances like this happen to me. It goes something like this: [A waiter asks] "What would you like, gentlemen, to drink?" And everyone answers and he says, "And you, sir?" [Laughter] It is as though I am the guy who is carrying everyone's bags. In many instances, I've been the senior officer in that setting and that has happened here and abroad. As a senior vice president of a world-class corporation, I should be able to go, because of the stature and the status of this job, anywhere on earth I might choose. But because of the color of my skin, I am being denied access to the privilege that this job affords me.

Prior to his transfer, he had no mentor and was not a part of the social and informational network of the organization. This was a serious problem for Walter, who described his life as "a constant daily trauma of literally chipping away at a block, just trying to get your foot in the door, and getting around the table where decisions are made. I went through this experience for three years, and it affected me psychologically. This experience nagged at me for over a year. It took me a long time to get over it." Walter recalled one experience.

I shall never forget one incident where I felt extremely isolated. There was a marketing meeting in Chicago, and the marketing segment leaders had to make presentations before our colleagues. I kept asking the team leaders who were talking about how the presentation should be made, "What are you looking for?" I never received an answer. I came to the meeting with all my storyboards for advertising and storyboards for marketing strategy. I found out when I got to the meeting that it had started thirty minutes before I was told it would. I was scheduled to be the second person to make a presentation. Yet, I was put on hold until the next day. You can imagine what this does to you when you're ready for a presentation. I never got the rules for the presentation. Everybody else had the rules except me, even my white marketing groups who were at a lower level. I was never invited to sit in on the marketing strategy meetings.

In spite of the frustrations, Walter succeeded. His success in the corporation in the early 1980s epitomizes the aspirations of blacks seeking to move up the corporate ladder. But he felt that he could not share his "daily traumas" with other aspiring blacks, so he coped with his racial traumas alone. Now he feels it is important for blacks to maintain outside networks to relieve stress encountered on the job. Walter, a liberal Democrat, has "gotten his foot in the door" and, finally, he can take his place "around the table to influence decisions." He is working internally and externally with groups and individuals to divest his company's vast holdings in South Africa. Walter's and Kelly's experiences are typical of the Talented One Hundred in the corporate world.

Looking inside the newsroom, we get another glimpse of the quality of life behind the scenes from Warner Babbitt and other journalists. Life in the newsroom can be difficult if one does not understand the interfacing of corporate politics and racism. Said Babbitt, "I had a white woman editor who had an absolute attitude about black men who had balls. She could only deal with a eunuch, but not a black who is a man and enjoys being a man. She took great pride in berating me in front of the entire desk, chiding, 'That is your problem, you always think small and here you are focusing on that small union. You must think big and have bigger stories.'" He didn't listen to her, but continued to pursue the story. When the story became an international daily headline, he said, "I beat everybody with the story." Yet, he didn't get any credit for his work. Instead, Babbitt said, "I got constantly reprimanded by her. . . . I couldn't figure her out. I was doing my work." Not only did he feel the editor was racially biased, he admitted it did not help her attitude toward him when he "screwed up politically with her." Unknown to Babbitt, his editor and another editor were competing for the same story. One asked him to do the story, but when he completed it, he gave it to the other. "*They* thought I was playing both ends of the stick," said Babbitt.

Politics interface with race in the newsroom, affecting the quality of life for black journalists. "You are seen as a black first and not a reporter," claimed Babbitt. Hence, this perception strongly influences the life chances of blacks in the print or broadcast media. "[Black] reporters do not get the good assignments, the meaty or plum stories, the front-page stories, the foreign desk and national assignments, the positions as editors, managers, and publishers, or enough feedback on their work," said Leo Aramis, an associate editor with a major newspaper. These limited assignments and opportunities obviously affect their evaluations and their chances for moving up the ladder.

The quality of life in the newsroom is further affected by the nature of the work. Journalism, one of the most stressful occupations, is extremely competitive, and being black increases the stress. "People will cut you in the back; they do play politics," said Babbitt. "I went around thinking that if I were smart, they would let me do what I had to do. They didn't have very many black reporters on the national desk. Only one at the time. Even now, the desk is called the White Citizens Council. This paper has never been able to maintain more than two black reporters out of a staff of forty or fifty on its national desk. Only once briefly did they have four, and I was one of them."

Caustically, he asserted, "We were all doing nothing, covering what I call RUMP and RUIN. RUMP is refugees, urban affairs, minorities, and politics. RUIN is refugees, urban affairs, immigrants, and Negroes. The only difference is when we weren't covering RUMP, we covered RUIN. The white folks wanted to know how the Negroes were going to vote." A colleague, who left the national desk, forewarned Babbitt, "You can stay here on this national desk, but the white folks aren't going to let you go very far, because they consider politics and the state department their property." "It turns out that he was exactly right—all the things that have to do with the running of 'Great White America,'" remarked Babbitt. "I always ended up working on Sundays, and it was considered penalty work. Their stars do not work on Sunday, and the paper does not have a fair way to allocate Sundays. One black and three white women ended up running the national desk. I would call it 'Affirmative Action Sunday.'"

Ethel King, also a journalist for a major paper, agreed with Babbitt, but pointed out, "I used to think the media were leaders because we pointed the finger at everybody else. Many people think that, and I try to clear up that misconception. Racism is everywhere." For this reason, Ethel does not pour her whole heart into the corporation as she feels most black males do. It is important for her to maintain outside interests in writing and in a supportive network of family and friends to sustain her in the newsroom.

Supportive mentors or a network on the job would have greatly assisted Walter Calvin and Warner Babbitt; however, their experiences are typical of others in corporate America. According to a *Black Enterprise* poll of its readers, participating in a survey on working in America, 66 percent said they didn't have a mentor to assist in advising them in their careers.[16] A similar finding among the Talented One Hundred showed that 62 percent of them did not have a mentor. Bebe Moore Campbell, in "Black Executives and Corporate Stress" in the *New York Times Magazine*, noted, "Blacks are trying to learn an ingrown system without coaching and mentoring. They can do it, but it takes longer. And some are paying a heavy price in stress."[17]

Unlike most of the Talented One Hundred, Tony Michaels, who entered the corporate world in the late 1950s in the Midwest, has been fortunate in having many mentors to guide his career. "I had people willing to go to bat for me," said Michaels. Earlier in his career during the late fifties, when Michaels faced racial discrimination, he was confrontational in coping with it. His mentor, having risked his own position in hiring him, advised him, saying, "I know your make-up, drive, and competitiveness. Anytime you do anything different, be sure you are right. People all over the country are trying to prove you are wrong. You know you are right. I am right, and we are going to show them we are." So he persuaded Michaels not to be confrontational, imploring, "Let me do your fighting for you."

Jews and white women, having their own history of marginality, were identified as the most likely mentors for the Talented One Hundred. Jeraldyne Blunden, a dancer, was the first black student of her Jewish mentor. "She was a big influence on what I did," said Blunden. Certain white ethnic and religious groups, like the Mormons, were the least supportive. Three of the Talented One Hundred reported negative experiences with Mormons, who make up a small percentage of the white population in the United States.

Leo Aramis views the role of a mentor differently from others. He said, "We got to stop this nonsense about a mentor being a surrogate parent or buddy. A mentor is someone who can help you do what you need to do, so you can do your job better. If that person can be a surrogate relative, that's fine. But if not, that's all right, too." Warner Babbitt sees merit in this position, though he has had mentors. "Several editors helped me out and moved me along," remarked Babbitt. One woman assisted him "to write and conceptualize a story and not be satisfied with 'he said, she said,' and how to grasp the context." Yet it was a white colleague who gave him the best strategy for survival in the corporate jungle of journalism. "You see yourself as working for this newspaper. You have to see yourself as working for Warner Babbitt, who is selling something to the newspaper. And if you see it that way, your job would be a lot more fun," advised his colleague. He started to work on stories on Fridays to "hold them away from the great white male editors. [When] my good lady friend editors would come on Sundays, I would spring the story on them. Since Sunday is dead, it was a great idea. The story always went up on page 1 on Monday."

There may be a greater expectation among young blacks of having a supportive mentor and network. Blacks who were directly influenced by the civil rights and black nationalist movements may view themselves as more willing actors and initiators in the face of adversity, thereby feeling less daunted by obstacles of racism. A discussion among journalists during an annual meeting of the Association of Black Journalists illustrates the differences between professionals who came of age during the civil rights era and those of the post–civil rights era. During the conference, young journalists who had worked five years or less in the profession were invited to share their concerns and to obtain feedback needed to upgrade their technical skills. Leo Aramis discovered "some young people came close to having psychological problems, despite the fact that they had grown up in integrated neighborhoods, gone to integrated schools, gone to the best journalism schools in this country, and had been accepted by whites in those settings. They went into the newsroom and got hit by racism. We had one girl sitting there crying, 'They never invited me out to lunch.'" Leo retorted, "I told her she was not there to go to lunch and somebody should have told her." Other young journalists complained they did not get the best stories, assignments, or promotions. Responding to the young journalists, Leo reminded them that "I had to fight for it. . . . They came in thinking if they busted their butts, they would be accepted by white folks. I came knowing I would never be part of the group. I had to demand it."

Leo also found that some of the younger journalists who had been in the profession as long as four years "still could not write a story lead and did not grasp or didn't even know how to organize a story." They felt they were in a position to move up. "But they weren't, because no one in their shop was helping them," said Leo. "They weren't telling them you are doing this wrong and you need to work on this. Either their copy was changed on the desk or the people would print it the way it was written." He strongly believes "they need to find someone to look at their work" and "there is someone they can find."

In spite of the lack of mentors and supportive networks, the Talented One Hundred are succeeding and functioning in corporate America. As Leo suggested, most came to corporate America "knowing they would never be a part of the group." But they continue to view themselves as actors of their destiny, in spite of racial roadblocks. They understand that as ambassadors for their race, they must bear its heavy burden of continuing to move forward.

A myth runs through corporate America that companies are "color-blind." A silent conspiracy of both blacks and whites pretends race is not a factor in the workplace. "Discrimination is ever present but a taboo topic. . . . If you want to move up, you don't talk about it."[18] Hence, some blacks feel that to associate with other blacks or to hire a black secretary or a black manager is viewed as suspect by whites or is seen as "too black." Dira Ridley, a physical chemist in a major consumer products company, thinks "if you are seen with another token black, it may be okay. However, if you are outspoken about race and you are associating with other blacks, it weakens your security. The crumbs thrown out are like a bird in the hand, whereas the collective power of blacks might be far away." So, many black elite do not wish to upset the status quo, even though their inaction may conflict with their political orientation to assist other blacks with moving up the corporate ladder.

Dira Ridley, who described her political orientation as vacillating between moderate and liberal, did not fear risking "the bird in the hand" when she helped to organize professional black women in the corporation where she works. Dira understands the importance of the collectivity, asserting,

> I am a firm believer that while one individual may progress, it is important for the group to progress. I didn't think black women in the organization had anything to do with what I was doing. I was doing extremely well. In fact, one of the reasons I signed the letter to investigate the attrition rate of black women in the company was because my manager said I was doing extremely well. I didn't sign it out of spite; I think I could have progressed in spite of getting a consultant to come in to evaluate the status of black women. I think I am that good. If I put into perspective what it takes—not only knowing something, personal interaction, and that comfort factor—I could have made it. The question is, Have we made this true for the broader group? I was interested in black women and not Dira Ridley, knowing that if the environment of black women changes, it would help me as well.

When greater numbers of blacks enter the workplace, race issues become more salient, and the quality of life seems to improve. The larger the number of blacks, the greater the likelihood of having supportive networks and mentors who can assist in learning corporate politics. When *Black Enterprise* selected the twenty-five most successful black managers in corporate America, it was found that black and white mentors who were well placed had a major impact in shaping their careers.[19] Many of these managers were employed by companies that *Black Enterprise* listed as the fifty best companies for blacks to work in. As blacks move into positions as managers, they can hire and mentor other blacks. Leo Aramis believes it is easier to fight his battle against racism because 18 percent of the professional staff in his company is black. If you challenge the system alone, you are likely to be isolated. Leo challenged an editorial endorsement by his newspaper of a white mayoral candidate over a black one. He challenged it because a black mayor was being compared with a black candidate. (The comparison involved the late Harold Washington of Chicago.) "I saw it in the computer and thought it was racist. I put a note on the end of it and told them I thought it was patently offensive and shouldn't be in the paper. We don't compare Jewish mayors, Polish mayors, and Italian mayors. The editorial endorsement was stereotypical, and I wouldn't work for anyone where that would appear in the newspaper. It was rewritten." Of course, he admitted, "I had to be prepared to quit if they didn't change it. . . . But it helps being at a paper that has as many black folks as my paper does," said Leo. "One of the black editors came to me [after the editorial incident] and said, 'You know, man, I really enjoy being at a paper where once in my life I don't have to be the only one to fight every fight.' I fought this one, and the next one he might fight. Next time somebody else might fight one. It's not just always one person who is picked out as the rabble-rouser who jumps up and down every time so he can be ignored, pushed out, or sabotaged. So that makes a difference."

Despite racial obstacles, the Talented One Hundred continue to work diligently to move up the corporate ladder, believing they should be promoted on merit instead of patronage. They also expressed the fervent belief that if you work hard enough and do your job efficiently, "someone will recognize your abilities." The black elite learned to cope with all the contradictions inherent in the workplace by treading the tightrope carefully. Edward W. Jones, in "Black Managers: The Dream Deferred," captures well the role strain and dilemmas of blacks in corporate America.

Running the gauntlet means smarting from the pain of prejudice even as white colleagues deny that your reality of race has any impact. It means maintaining excellent performance, even when recognition is withheld. It means being smart but not too smart. Being strong but not too strong. Being confident but not egotistical to the point of alienation. Being the butt of prejudice and not being unpleasant or abrasive. Being intelligent but not arrogant. Being honest but not paranoid. Being confident yet modest. It means seeking the trust and respect of fellow blacks and

acceptance by whites. Speaking out on issues affecting blacks but not being perceived as a self-appointed missionary or a unifaceted manager expert only on black
subjects. Being courageous but not too courageous in areas threatening to whites.

It means being a person who is black but not losing one's individuality by sub-
mersion into a class of "all blacks," as perceived by whites. Defining one's self while
not contradicting the myriad definitions imposed by white colleagues. Being accepted as a leader for whites and not being seen as an Uncle Tom by blacks. Being
a person who is black, but also a person who is an authentic human being.[20]

For some, "running the gauntlet" is physically and psychologically risky. In
increasing numbers, the black elite are going to work for black corporations.
More importantly, however, some are using their expertise and skills gained in
corporate America to start their own businesses.

ENTREPRENEURSHIP: FORTUNES AND FRUSTRATIONS

Reginald Lewis, the megadeal maker, made a fortune in his buyout of the
billion-dollar Beatrice International Corporation. It catapulted him from number six to number one on *Black Enterprise*'s list of the Top 100 Black Businesses
and to perhaps being the most influential black businessman in America. His
success signaled a shift in the role of black entrepreneurs as national and international players in the marketplace. Since the civil rights movement, some top
black businesses have expanded to the general market in construction, automobile dealership, manufacturing, and computer systems. Others continue to
serve primarily black clientele, particularly those in the cosmetics industry,
publishing, and real estate. The vast majority of black businesses still cater to
black clientele. These businesses are mostly sole proprietorships that are service oriented, such as automotive repair shops, beauty parlors, grocery stores,
and cab companies. According to the Census Bureau, individual proprietorships accounted for 95 percent of all black businesses in 1985.[21] Black businesses increased about 50 percent from 1977 to 1982, but sales receipts declined during this same period.[22]

With the decline in sales receipts, there is an increasing concern that black
businesses might disappear unless more of African Americans' estimated income of $250 billion is recycled back into the black community. Having greater
options in the consumer marketplace, blacks do not patronize black businesses
exclusively. Also, Asian and other minority-owned businesses have begun to replace establishments owned by blacks, eroding further the wealth in the black
community.

Black Enterprise magazine's board of economists sees the low level of self-
employment as a primary obstacle to creating wealth in the black community.
These economists claim that individuals who own equity in businesses are more
likely to have higher incomes than the general population. "People who are in

business have five times the net worth of people who work for salaries. So if you are going to improve the wealth base of a people, you have to have more entrepreneurs and successful businesses,"[23] said one *Black Enterprise* economist.

Many impediments exist for blacks who would like to become successful entrepreneurs. Like others among the Talented One Hundred who are self-employed, Joshua Smith, a nationally known entrepreneur who owns a computer services company, pointed out some common concerns and obstacles of black entrepreneurs. He asserted that "race plays a major role in business development." First, he said, "Race is critical because when we had major businesses during the period of segregation, we also had a black business market that was a captured market. That market was there because black people were unable to choose where they could buy. So in order to meet the supply side of things, blacks had to develop businesses. We did develop businesses to fit an available consumer market that couldn't go anyplace else to do anything. People can be successful entrepreneurs when conditions are right to support them." However, as a result of integration, he thinks "the rug to the consumer market was pulled." Blacks "went everywhere and bought everywhere. They have got to get away from that freedom consumption. It means the markets for blacks have completely gone in terms of any loyalty to black businesses."

Black consumers' estimated total income is $250 billion. However, said Joshua, "less than 5 percent goes to support black businesses. We have reached a chicken and egg situation. If we don't have businesses, we can't create the business, and that must change." For black businesses to thrive, "they must produce or provide a service to the overall society, basically to the white community. [My] business is not unlike other businesses; we don't have black customers yet. We have basically institutional customers and federal government customers." He believes that "there is a heavier burden on black businesses than what exists in other ethnic communities. If the community supports the business, it has a chance to grow up. No one is going to tell me that every Chinese who opens a Chinese restaurant knows how to run one. You can't tell me that every Vietnamese who goes into the market has a family background in that area. That is not true; but they have in place a support system to buy from one another." Joshua thinks that "since blacks have no loyalty, they will patronize a Korean or Vietnamese restaurant that has taken over a black restaurant in the black neighborhood. We are so used to exercising freedom of buying that we haven't gotten out of this pattern. Now we have gotten so accustomed to not seeing black businesses that we don't expect to see them."

Tony Brown, a television personality and columnist, organized the Buy Freedom national campaign to promote black businesses and to challenge the black community to move from freedom consumption to stewardship. Blacks, he asserted, spend almost 95 percent of their income on goods and services controlled by nonblacks and thus "export 1.7 million jobs annually from the black neighborhood and import unemployment, welfare program dependency, and a defeatist attitude."

Not only is there a relative lack of support for black businesses within the black community; blacks find it difficult to acquire the necessary capital for investment from both the government and the private sector. When Thomas B. Thomas was self-employed, for example, one reason for the failure of his business was the lack of capital to bid on federal contracts. "You had to put up 10 percent to bid. If the bid is a million dollars, not many small businesses have the capital to let you hold that amount for ninety days until the final bid." Thomas mentioned that when he tried to get private funding, the funding company wanted to take 60 percent of his company. He claimed that some supposedly joint ventures of minority-owned enterprises are actually owned by major white corporations who have financial control.

While there are various set-aside programs in the federal government for minority businesses, according to Joshua Smith, "When we get outside that set-aside market, we fall flat on our face, and that's unfortunate," because often small businesses lack capital. Approximately 80 percent of all black businesses fail. But, Joshua pointed out, "80 percent of all small businesses fail, and blacks have primarily small businesses. Hence, they are no more likely to fail than white businesses."

Joshua agreed with Thomas that when an entrepreneur wants to generate capital to start a business, the finances are often not available to blacks. "Black people do not have assets. We own only one-tenth of one percent of the assets in this country; even though we have income, our assets are abysmal. So there is a perception that the black person is not a good risk in the banking or financial services. If such a perception exists, you would not want to loan money to that person either." He claimed, "These perceptions are not only in the white community, but in the black community. Black people are the harshest critics about black businesses; therefore, the perception is simply prolonged and enhanced. So blacks have a harder time in gaining access to capital."

Joshua noted that although the negative perception about black business is strong, it is inaccurate.

> There is a definite perception in this country about black businesses. It is unfortunate that no one goes back to the days when businesses were thriving. Who the hell did black people buy from when they couldn't buy from white people? They bought from black businesses. There were role models in black businesses. People expected to see successful newspapermen, insurance people, restauranteurs, grocers, and furniture dealers who supplied all the needs to the black community. We are losing those role models today. So there is a perception out there that black businesses are inferior businesses and black business people aren't very businesslike people—none of which is true.

The truth is that black businessmen, like James Paschal, a successful restauranteur in Atlanta, have been serving the black community for years. When the Paschal brothers wanted to expand their restaurant business and build a hotel and lounge in the early 1960s, they were able to obtain the capital from a black bank. The Paschal Brothers' Restaurant has been in business for over forty years. Several presidents and international dignitaries have visited the restaurant. It has been called the place where "politics get under way in the morning." James Paschal said Martin Luther King Jr. held several of his strategy meetings for the civil rights marches at his restaurant, including the Selma march. The Paschal Brothers' Restaurant was deeply involved in the civil rights movement, providing food and getting students released from jail. There is a saying around Atlanta, recalled James, that "when election time comes, the local politicians who do not meet at Paschal Brothers' Restaurant in the morning can rest assured that they won't be elected." Though blacks are still supportive of his business, he admitted, we "have lost support to white establishments."

Joshua Smith sees another important factor contributing to the difficulties of entrepreneurs, and that is the loss of incumbent rights.

> As a result of desegregation and the breakup of black businesses, we lost something that is so critical to competitiveness. We lost incumbent rights—that is, the company that has the contract or the job. It is the organization on the inside, the company that is working every day with problems and the future needs of the client. The incumbent is breaking bread every day with the client and is developing a sense of comfort with the client. When it comes to bids on new opportunities where there is an incumbent already present, it poses a basic obstacle to black businesses. We are not incumbents. By virtue of not being incumbents, we don't have the comfort or confidence. We haven't had that opportunity to build up relationships. We are new, unknown, small, and black. All these factors are negative in terms of who will be the winning contractor. So when black businesses submit their bids, it is very unusual for a company who has not dealt with a black business to throw out an incumbent that they've been dealing with for years to get this unknown with all the perceived negatives. So, by lack of incumbency, we suffer a lot. Incumbency is very important to understanding how a market reacts and what a market does to any kind of opportunities.

Thomas B. Thomas can relate to Joshua's comment about incumbent rights and the difficulty in obtaining contracts from white businesses because of the negative perceptions about black businesses. When Thomas was in business, he had to "hire a white bird dog to sniff out business. Whites go out and develop an interest in your product and service, and we would come in and close the deal. The reason we have to do that is because if we go after clients who are Caucasians, they have a real problem with giving you a piece of the pie." Thomas admitted that "some blacks have been very successful at playing the government game. How they do it, I can't speak for them. But I do know they have made a lot of money. For me, I had a horrible time."

In contrast to Thomas, Joshua has "made a lot of money" from federal contracts. But he has not hired a "white bird dog." Despite some difficulties, Joshua has been able to sniff out his own business prior to and since his graduation from the Small Business Administration's 8(a) program in 1986.

Joshua attributes his success in part to his ability to take risks when he sees an opportunity. He said that "the only things that will show up on your doorstep are trouble, mangy dogs, and other people's opportunities." He feels that blacks do not want to take risks in entrepreneurship.

> Black people, to a great extent, are unwilling to make the transformation from secure corporate positions into the entrepreneurial role. That is driven a lot by our standard of living. If we have things tied up in homes, we obviously have to make the mortgage payments. We are strapped by other financial limitations in terms of our standards of living. So it makes it very difficult to make that move from the secure to the unknown, because we've committed ourselves to our yearly outlay. So we don't have the flexibility to make a move, nor do we have the assets. Our families are not wealthy. We do not inherit money. So we lack the financial support to provide the security to take risks. We are cautious about what we have and want to maintain that. The end result is that black businesses are small, and these businesses have an abysmal mortality rate.
>
> Having said that, the only way blacks are going to secure any kind of position of autonomy is through economic avenues. The power base of economics is entrepreneurship, which has a spirit that is driven by the attitudes on the part of the people that it is something that we must do. So there is a need within the black community to produce more successful entrepreneurs and larger black-owned and controlled firms. It is a matter of resources, role models, perceptions, and access to capital. All of these factors make it difficult for black businesses to make it. It seems inevitable that if black businesses don't become a priority, we are guaranteed to continue to slide into dark channels.

Joshua said he is successful also because he carefully plans his career paths. He cautions aspiring entrepreneurs to avoid "starting a business and learning while you are on the job, because it is too costly. You have to learn on somebody else's operation. You have to bring people into your business that have knowledge that you don't have. So many businesses fail because of the ego of the person who started it. You bring people in who will challenge you and not acquiesce to you. In order to attract good people, you have to have integrity and a good track record yourself."

Still, no matter how talented one is and how hard one works, opportunities for black entrepreneurs like Joshua Smith seem inextricably linked to the public sector, particularly those opportunities provided by the federal government. But the recent Supreme Court ruling in January 1989 on set-aside programs may have a continuing negative impact on black businesses. Two months after the Supreme Court ruling, the Georgia State Supreme Court struck down Atlanta's affirmative action program, one of the most effective programs in the nation. Only days after the Georgia ruling, Michigan's set-aside program was declared unconstitutional.

PUBLIC SERVICE: PUBLIC SERVANT OR PUPPET?

With the equal opportunity policies of the federal government in the 1960s and the increasing political control of large cities by blacks, the ranks of middle-class blacks in public service began to swell more than any sector of the economy. Yet even before 1960, the government was an important source of black employ-ment and upward mobility. In 1960, for instance, 13 percent of white managers and 21 percent of black managers and administrators were employed in govern-ment. The proportion of black managers and officials was 62 percent greater than that of whites. By 1970, 27 percent of black managers and 11 percent of white managers and administrators were in government. The proportion of black managers and officials increased to 133 percent greater than whites, noted Sharon Collins in "The Making of the Black Middle Class."[24]

A significant number of blacks have benefited from the federal government legislative policies to gain economic parity. But, according to Collins, the "struc-ture of opportunity within which the middle class has grown is still character-ized by inequality. The Black middle class emerged from special political and legal protection, and it occupies a useful but powerless market position in U.S. society."[25] She argues that the opportunities available to blacks are more de-pendent on political pressure than economic trends. Moreover, blacks are overly represented in positions dependent on federal funds, positions that are most vulnerable to shifts in the political winds. Middle-class blacks are in posi-tions in those sectors of the economy that serve the needs of blacks. Since these positions are heavily dependent on federal funds, they are also vulnerable to political winds and pressures.

The number of blacks holding senior policy-making and managerial positions in the federal government rose during President Jimmy Carter's tenure, but dropped when President Reagan took office. The number of blacks holding presidential appointments dropped from forty-four in 1950 to twenty-one in 1981; dropped from nineteen in 1982 to fifteen in 1983; and climbed from nineteen in 1984 to twenty in 1985, remaining at that level until 1987.[26] In 1988, Reagan appointed the fifty-one-year-old Lt. Gen. Colin Luther Powell as the national security adviser, the first black ever to serve in that position. Sub-sequently, George H. Bush appointed Powell as the first black to head the Joint Chiefs of Staff, and the president has continued to appoint blacks as senior pol-icymakers.

Seemingly, whatever gains blacks have made since the 1960s are the result of race-oriented policies. Collins maintains that researchers often ignore the types of organizations in which blacks earn their income. "Black workers' functional relationship" is to "Black consumer networks and the dependency of class mo-bility on government rather than free market forces."[27] The government-supported jobs created new opportunities for blacks, but Collins maintains they were the result of "a policy-mediated situation—not a market-oriented situa-tion."[28] She indicates four federal policies that created opportunities for the growth of the black middle class: the Equal Employment Opportunity Com-mission, the Office of Federal Contract Compliance Programs, the federally funded social welfare services, and the federal contract set-aside programs. Many of the Talented One Hundred, who had high-level positions as officials

and managers and who benefited from the federal policies that created opportunities for the black middle class, found themselves at the mercy of political
tides. When the federal funds ceased or decreased, so did their economic security.

Blacks who are in mainline positions in government are not immune to
racism. While the government has sometimes vigilantly served as a watchdog
for the enforcement of equal opportunity policies in other sectors of the economy, it has not guarded its own door. Like the black elite in the private sector,
those who were public servants repeatedly reported feeling powerless even
when they were in mainline positions as opposed to administrative and staff positions. Often those individuals in mainline positions were reclassified, removed, or ignored. The Talented One Hundred reported that another common
discriminatory pattern is to restructure departments or divisions to neutralize
the authority and power of black managers. Stephanie Tahara, for example,
works as an administrator. She managed ten divisions for a county government
before a reclassification and reorganization of her division. Her experience was
typical of the isolation and the quality of life for blacks in public service. She remarked,

> If I succeed in managing well ten divisions without turmoil, I am not recognized.
> If a white person does it, he/she will get a promotion. The criteria are always
> changing. I was given a huge division to manage with a reclassification, but it never
> materialized. The person to whom I reported was an assistant director, and he was
> evil. The director was neutral, but he allowed certain things to happen, and that
> made him evil. The director had wanted me to take this job, but he allowed this
> man to persecute me. The assistant director never gave any positive reinforcement,
> and he was forever finding the most nitpicking issues to be concerned about. He
> would arbitrarily assign an impossible deadline for a project. One way to deal with
> it was to be superficial, but that was a catch-22 and another setup.

Since there was a pattern of systematic discrimination of black professionals
and managers in her county government, Stephanie, who described herself as
sometimes a political radical, was instrumental in helping to organize a Black
Managers' Association to combat racism.

When Dick Godfather, the highest-ranking black civil servant in a federal
agency, was removed from a position, his response was more accommodating.
He received outstanding evaluation and performance ratings by his superior.
Yet he was removed from his position, "so a white boy could have my job. . . .
No one said anything was wrong with my job performance. They just trans-
ferred me to a less satisfying job, saying it was for the sake of the organization."
At first Dick got very angry "and began calling people that precious name that
black men have a way of calling people. . . . Then I just felt hurt," he said. Hav-
ing a strong racial consciousness, Dick realized he "could not give up." He felt,
"Black men get caught in that situation." Masking his feelings, he decided to

"accommodate to make sure a black remained in a position of authority." Eventually, Dick said, "the other guy screwed up the job, and three years later I got the job back—it became a more powerful position."

At the time of the interview, Dick administered about thirty different national educational programs. In his position, he has assisted numerous black educational institutions.

Sharon Georgia, a forty-two-year-old city attorney for a large municipality, believes "if you mask your feelings, you can move through the system." But the situation is so intolerable that she cannot wear the mask or become a puppet. Sharon, an outspoken activist, made a guest appearance on a radio program to discuss how she was treated by whites. She said, "The city manager raked me over the coals for 'playing politics.' You know they [her white supervisors] don't listen to black radio stations on a Sunday afternoon. But the next morning, they were calling in to request the tape." She was angry. Unlike Dick, Sharon is unable to mask her feelings.

> I won't go anywhere in this job because of my personality. White folks consider me as arrogant and caustic. My bosses, black and white, don't like it. If they are bull-shitting, I might tell them. When you are in a corporate environment, there is a certain way you act. I don't fit into my job because of my personality as well as race, but I can separate personality from race and sex. For example, I have a white colleague who was given a higher position, more money, and better equipment than I. That is partly racism, or maybe partly sexism. When that happened, I got upset and angry, but I didn't internalize my anger. I know I am going to face racism, so I move on and don't get locked into the system. I will tell the motherfuckers to take this job and do what they want to do with it—but there is a price you pay and you got to be willing to pay that price. It can be termination or ostracism from the community. When I first started to practice law, I was recognized as an outstanding young black woman. Now I am seen as that wild woman—that witch—because I will tell white folks to kiss my ass. Some black folks say be careful. White folks can hurt you if you move on to another job.

Sharon's response to this warning was, "When I came to city hall, I had a reputation, and when I leave, I'll have one." Historically, blacks who were unable to wear the mask were killed off, isolated, or labeled "crazy nigger" or "bad nigger." Yet, they were often instrumental in initiating positive social changes that moved blacks forward.

THE NONPROFIT SECTOR: VICTORIES AND VICISSITUDES

Some problems cited in the corporate sector are applicable to the public sector as well as the nonprofit sector. There are, however, distinct concerns associated with the nonprofit sector of the economy.

In 1968, Jeraldyne Blunden founded the Dayton Contemporary Dance Company in Ohio, a nonprofit, tax-exempt corporation with the commitment "to enrich the cultural environment of the Dayton community through the art of dance." Having performed at the American Dance Festival, her company is now nationally acclaimed, and her goal is to "establish and maintain a world-wide reputation with strong capabilities in the fields of jazz, ballet, and modern dance." She is victorious, in spite of the vicissitudes she has encountered over the past twenty years.

Like blacks in the for-profit and public sectors of the economy, blacks in the nonprofit sector, too, are ghettoized and stereotyped in roles and positions, whether as visual or performing artists, as administrators and managers, or as social activists. Blunden speaks to the issue of stereotyping blacks in certain roles, saying,

> The professional dance world was not ready for blacks to do anything other than tap dance, jitterbug, swing their hips, tap their feet, and pray. [Laughs] When I joined the regional National Association for Ballet, we were the first black company that did straight modern dance. It was different. They weren't used to seeing us do that. And little by little, we were accepted, because we could do other things than tap dance. That was something we had to prove. If we had a dance or piece based on spirituals, whites loved it and we would get a standing ovation. If we had a piece from Western Europe or something from the Renaissance or classical music, there was little said. The fact that we danced it well was accepted, but more audience members would say, Why didn't you do something that was finger-popping? They are now getting over that because companies like the Dance Theatre of Harlem and Alvin Ailey do everything. They can do finger-popping-type pieces and the German composer's *Streams*. It is important that we keep those two black companies and their international focus so people will know that we can do other things.

Securing and distributing adequate funds are issues for those employed in non-profit agencies, whether service-oriented or concerned with the arts. When Blunden started going after corporate money, "funding corporations decided they could not support two dance companies and indicated they didn't need two." The intention was to eliminate funding for her dance company, considered in the top five black dance companies in America, and continue to fund a white company. "The percentage of funds the white dance company receives is higher. There is an inequity in funds. The artistic performance and reputation should have some merit," said Blunden. "Our needs are just as great as other arts organizations' in the city, but we are treated differently. They make you jump through more hoops." To become a part of a mainstream funding source, the dance company was required to move to larger headquarters. The company is still not a full member of the arts organization in the city. "When we first applied for membership, they turned us down, in 1982," said Blunden. "We kept applying, but instead of making us a full member, they created a [new] category, calling us an associate member. Never before or since has anyone been an associate member of the arts organization in the city. I don't think they will ever use it again. There are always new criteria. No matter how good our artistic product, and I do think we have a good one, it will never be equal in the eyes of the people who have the money. I personally feel whites see us first as a black organization, not as an arts organization. If they could wash away the color, we'd rate very high."

Since those in the arts community will not "wash away the color" of her predominantly black dance company, Blunden selects influential black community leaders as board members to fight funding battles. This allows her to devote her energies to the creative process and to actualize her dream "to have an internationally known company that works fifty-two weeks a year." She knows "being successful is part and parcel of surviving in doing what you really want to do. So you must rely on yourself. That is where the motivation, ideas, and creativity have to come from, and in my business you start with a dream."

SUMMARY

Since the civil rights movement, blacks have made great strides in the mainstream sector of the economy. However, these gains have been tempered by continuous overt and subtle battles with racism in the workplace. In spite of black professionals' credentials and career experiences, they are more likely than whites to be ghettoized into staff positions in human resources. They also have several areas of concern in workplaces: (1) recruitment, retention, and retrenchment; (2) quality of life; and (3) the issue of balancing personal stress and role conflict inherent in their professional positions and their personal politics.

Entrepreneurs find that the negative perception about blacks in business makes it more difficult for them to obtain capital for expansion and startup. In addition, since the civil rights era, the support of the black community has eroded, because black consumers have more options in the marketplace.

Because of the triumphs and trials of life in corporate America, the fortunes and frustrations of black entrepreneurs, the public servant or puppet role of blacks in the public sector, and the victories and vicissitudes of blacks in the nonprofit sector, the Talented One Hundred are politically sophisticated and cosmopolitan. They understand both the political and the racial landscapes, which help them to more effectively cope in the workplace.

NOTES

1. Bart Landry, *The New Black Middle Class* (Berkeley: University of California Press, 1987), 88.

2. Joel Garreau, "The Integration of the American Dream," *Washington Post, National Weekly Edition*, Feb. 8–14, 1988, 6.

3. Landry, *New Black Middle Class*, 112.

4. Derek T. Dingle et al., "America's Hottest Black Managers," *Black Enterprise,* Feb. 1988, 81.

5. Derek T. Dingle, "Will Black Managers Survive Corporate Downsizing?" *Black Enterprise*, March 1987, 51.

6. Dingle, "Will Black Managers Survive."

7. Dingle, "Will Black Managers Survive."

8. Edward W. Jones Jr., "Black Managers: The Dream Deferred," *Harvard Business Review*, May–June 1986, 84–93.

9. Nathan McCall, "Making Fast Money in High Finance," *Black Enterprise*, Feb. 1987, 54.

10. Derek T. Dingle and Constance M. Green, "When the Tough Get Going," *Black Enterprise*, Aug. 1987, 50.

11. Jones, "Black Managers," 86.

12. Jones, "Black Managers," 88.

13. Jones, "Black Managers," 86.

14. Rosabeth Moss Kanter, *Men and Women of the Corporation* (New York: Basic Books, 1977).

15. Richard D. Hylton, "Working in America," *Black Enterprise*, Aug. 1988, 64.

16. Hylton, "Working in America."

17. Bebe Moore Campbell, "Black Executives and Corporate Stress," *New York Times Magazine*, Dec. 12, 1982.

18. Jones, "Black Managers," 85.

19. Dingle et al., "America's Hottest Black Managers."

20. Jones, "Black Managers," 91–92.

21. "Facts and Figures," *Black Enterprise*, Aug. 1987, 39.

22. "Facts and Figures," *Black Enterprise*, June 1987, 96.

23. Derek T. Dingle, "Finding a Prescription for Black Wealth," *Black Enterprise*, Jan. 1987, 48.

24. Sharon M. Collins, "The Making of the Black Middle Class," *Social Problems*, 30, no. 4 (April 1983): 373.

25. Collins, "Making of Black Middle Class," 369.

26. "Fewer Blacks in High Positions," *Dayton Daily News and Journal Herald*, May 22, 1987.

27. Collins, "Making of Black Middle Class," 370.

28. Collins, "Making of Black Middle Class," 371.

4

THE COLOR LINE ACROSS
THE WORLD OF ACADEME

Jefferson Barnes, a fifty-one-year-old tenured professor, is head of an academic department and a research institute at a major university. Having published widely, Barnes is respected by colleagues within the department and in the larger academic community. Barnes serves on several key committees within the university. He is very political, describing his present political orientation as liberal to radical on most issues. With a direct line to the chancellor, he has been successful at obtaining more funds and equipment for his department, recruiting more blacks on campus, and improving their quality of life. Barnes exemplifies those blacks in academe who have successfully negotiated the professional, political, and racial landscape in higher education since the sixties.

Prior to World War II, black faculty and administrators were deliberately excluded by law or tradition from predominantly white universities. William H. Exum, in the article "Climbing the Crystal Stair: Values, Affirmative Action, and Minority Faculty," noted,

> The first few Blacks to be accepted as faculty were obvious anomalies. For example, in the 1850s Charles L. Reason became professor of arts and letters at New York Central College, a school founded by abolitionists. Later exceptions were clearly "superstars." A Black Jesuit priest, Father Patrick Healey, who rose from instructor to become president of Georgetown University in 1873, is one example. On the other hand, W. E. B. Du Bois, the internationally acclaimed Black scholar, held a position as assistant instructor of sociology at the University of Pennsylvania from 1896 to 1897, but was never offered a permanent post there or in any White college or university. When Blacks did begin to receive faculty status in the twentieth century,

recognition was belated, or dependent upon special funding. William A. Hinton began as an instructor at Harvard in 1918. He spent twenty-six years at the rank of instructor and three as lecturer before finally being appointed professor in 1949—the year before he retired.[1]

Black administrators and faculty are a relatively new phenomenon on predominantly white campuses. Prior to the civil rights movement, they were confined largely to black campuses. As a result of the civil rights movement, the enrollment of black students increased. With the rise of the black nationalist movement and the assassination of Martin Luther King Jr., colleges and universities began recruiting black students aggressively.

When black students arrived on white campuses, they found a dearth of role models; they protested and called for more black faculty. The black colleges were a major source of talent from which black faculty and administrators were drawn, creating a brain drain in those schools. Many black academicians were lured away by the promise of greater research opportunities, higher salaries, more leave time, and reduced teaching loads. In addition, some believed they were playing a viable role in furthering the process of integration and equal opportunity. However, in contrast to Barnes's success in academe, a disproportionate number of black administrators and faculty hired since the late 1960s and early 1970s have found their paths of opportunities littered with perils.

Blacks in academe, like those in the private and public sectors of the economy, continue to face obstacles in their effort to attain a higher quality of life, cope with the strains of role conflict in the workplace, increase their numbers in academe, and obtain tenure. While only a few blacks successfully find their way to traditional departments in white academia, the career paths of many black academics are blocked at the lower ranks in nontenurable positions that are affiliated with special programs for minorities.

In higher education, blacks represent less than 5 percent of the total faculty. It is estimated that from two-thirds to three-fourths of black faculty remain concentrated in historically black colleges and universities, and since the late 1960s, in black studies departments on white campuses. They are also less likely to be employed in the most prestigious colleges and universities.[2]

The problem of recruitment of blacks in higher education in predominantly white colleges and universities relates in part to supply, demand, and distribution. Though the concentration of PhD holders in historically black institutions decreases the available pool of black faculty, a survey of minority PhD recipients found several other explanations of why this pattern of supply and demand exists. First, there has been a sharp decline in the number of blacks receiving doctorates. The sharpest decline occurred from 1977 to 1986, when the number fell from 1,116 to 820.[3]

Second, blacks, as well as Asians and Hispanics, are entering academic employment at a smaller percentage than ten years ago. Third, black PhDs have

the lowest faculty promotion and tenure rate of any group. A nine-year longitudinal study of minority PhD recipients revealed that black faculty were less
likely to be promoted or to receive tenure at the same rate or in the same time
span as Asian American or Hispanic faculty. In fact, Asians' promotion and
tenure rates were higher than the national average. Promotion and tenure are
affected by the quantity of research in higher education. The data indicate
blacks are predominantly in administrative and teaching positions, Hispanics
are in teaching and research, and Asians are in research.[4] Thus, the differential
rates in job assignment may explain in part differences between ethnic groups.

Blacks are also distributed disproportionately in education and the social sciences, while their participation in the natural sciences and engineering is minimal
and appears to be decreasing. Black students earned only 222, or 1.8 percent, of
12,480 doctorates awarded to U.S. citizens in graduate science and engineering
programs in 1987. In contrast, in 1978, there were 278 blacks who received doctorates in science and engineering, 2.1 percent of the total doctorates awarded.[5]

Although there is a problem of supply, demand, and distribution, Jewel
Prestage, in "Quelling the Mythical Revolution," notes, "The institutions in
quest of Black faculty are the sole source of such faculty. The dearth of available Black academic talent is a direct consequence of their failure to produce
such talent."[6] Often, commitment to and leadership in equal opportunity is also
lacking from administrative officials. One reason is that, in higher education,
"the ideologies of merit and autonomy provide a legitimate 'nonracist' basis for
resisting demands for racial change as embodied, for example, in affirmative action programs."[7] In the search and recruitment process, there is the issue of
how to estimate the pool of available racial minority candidates; an underesti-
mation of applicants will result in lower hiring goals. Potential candidates are
often overlooked because of the way in which the position is advertised. In evaluating and processing candidates, universities desire "minority superstars, but
may be less willing to gamble on minorities than on Whites."[8]

Even when blacks are invited for interviews, they are frequently treated in-
sensitively, which discourages them from accepting a position. According to
Lisa Allen, a forty-one-year-old PhD from a major university, who interviewed
at a large, predominantly white public university in the Northeast in the late
seventies, the climate was hostile. She declined her faculty appointment.

> I learned from a more humane colleague that others in the department felt I had
> an advantage over white candidates, because I was black and female. It was their
> reason for giving me a hard time. The department scheduled a grinding agenda
> from 8 a.m. to 11:30 p.m., without a break. I had to meet with each faculty (about
> fifteen), to teach a class, and to make a two-and-one-half-hour presentation. Dur-
> ing the presentation, I was constantly interrupted with snide remarks about my
> findings and methodology. I was angry and frustrated. I felt [that] if this interview
> was any indication of how I would be treated in the department, I didn't want to
> be here. So I accepted a more congenial college.

While Lisa Allen was able to glean a sense of the quality of her academic life during the interview process, others do not feel the impact until their arrival on campus as faculty and administrators. The quality of life is related to the number of blacks. When there are fewer blacks in a predominantly white institution, there is greater social isolation.

ROLE STRAIN AND ROLE CONFLICT IN THE ACADEMIC MARKETPLACE

Black academicians like Jefferson Barnes have integrated into predominantly white university settings; yet they maintain their black identity. Understanding the political and racial landscape, they are able to work with whites. They expect racism. Barnes said, "I am never surprised by racism. I never assume there is a minimum of racism among white colleagues and friends, so I don't get angry when it comes up. My question is, How is it going to be manifested? Is it going to be with a billy club or with knights in hoods, or will it be subtle discrimination of talk at the faculty club?" Understanding that racism exists, Barnes acts with political expediency when "it doesn't override black concerns." While he has learned to negotiate the political and racial tightrope in academe, there are others who are apolitical and nonracial. They enjoy their status as a token black in the university and ignore racism.

For most academicians, however, the social isolation in predominantly white universities is an issue. "It is tough for the individual who is a pioneer," said Cassie Cooper. Having worked at both black and white institutions in higher education, Cassie, vice president for academic affairs at a black college and in her late thirties, feels that there are more identity conflicts in white settings.

> It puts the person in a position of cognitive dissonance. There is a lot of pressure to perform well that I don't think you find for a white person in the same situation. A black must represent the whole race. You want to do a good job and not let the race down. There is tremendous pressure for an individual to stand out. Not only do you want to do well for yourself—whatever the position dictates—but you are doing it as the first or only black person. There is only the problem of trying to fit in. What do you do? On the one hand, if there are other blacks in the situation, you want to be a part of the black group. However, if you are going to be successful, you have to be a part of the white group. You have all these identity issues to deal with. You want to move upward, doing the things that any person, black or white, in that situation would do to be successful. Yet, you don't want your black colleagues to think you are out for your own selfish motives, because you identify with them.

When black colleagues are perceived as concerned solely with their own professional self-aggrandizement at the expense of their black identity, social pressure is frequently brought to bear upon them. They are reminded that, although they may have achieved meritoriously, they owe a great deal to "the blood, sweat, tears, and the backs of the student movement"[9] in the 1960s and 1970s. Hence, they have an obligation to share their knowledge and to participate collectively in the empowerment of black faculty, staff, students, and the larger community.

The literature on the quality of life for black academicians indicates that there is limited social interaction between black and white colleagues. Black administrators, however, do appear to have more contact with whites. If academics limit their interaction with white colleagues, their access to important networks of mentors and sponsors is affected, thus impeding their upward mobility in the university. Having powerful allies and advocates can assist them in getting their research published by established journals and publishing outlets. Mentors can also assist new academicians in learning how the system operates. While some of the Talented One Hundred in academe had white mentors at some point in their careers, they were the exception rather than the rule. And there are few blacks in top positions to act as mentors at white colleges and universities; when they do exist, they are often isolated from one another because of their heavy involvement in academic activities. Even when blacks are teaching in black studies, Crystal Miller, a professor of theater in Afro American studies, noted, "it doesn't mean everything is peachy creamy. There are problems we have with one another, like not supporting each other, jealousy, envy, and sexism. It may be exacerbated because we are in a powerful white setting."

Not having mentors and supportive networks can affect the evaluation process, preventing individuals from successfully climbing the academic ladder. Jonathan Mobutu, an economist and director of black studies at a predominantly white university in the Northeast, attributes the difficulties of a black professor, who was denied tenure at the university in which he teaches, in part to not knowing the system. He maintained, "There are other factors going on in higher education. Once you get tenure, you can goof off; so you have people coming in reading the *New York Times* and *Wall Street Journal* and going to lunch. The brother is doing that too; but as an assistant professor, you don't do that. Your behind is supposed to be over in the laboratory demonstrating how hard you are trying to get publications. It illustrates the need for a black network to facilitate new faculty entry into higher education, to let them know about the culture and the informal agenda as opposed to the formal agenda." Professor Mobutu, who has a progressive political orientation, is working to create an office of minority faculty development to assist the newly arrived and those who are not fully established in buttressing their credentials for promotion. This office will also provide them with mentoring and support for research, travel funds, and grants.

Mobutu also feels that blacks do not get support from white colleagues because whites have a "lack of respect for the academic and service activities of black faculty." This colors the perceptions of white faculty and students toward black faculty. Having a negative image and lower expectations of black faculty, Mobutu asserted, "any white student feels he/she has the authority to challenge one's credentials, while they will never do that for a white faculty member." Students feel "more comfortable challenging a black woman" than her male counterpart. There is still "the macho image of the black male that if you get in my face, I'll knock you down."

The barriers black faculty encounter are as much with their colleagues as with white students, maybe even more so, claimed Mobutu. Colleagues assume that the expertise of blacks, unless they are in the natural sciences, is limited to the black experience. Mobutu cited a personal encounter in which he sensed disrespect from a white colleague and told how he coped with it.

> There is a course taught at the university on nuclear war, and it involves the invitation of guest lecturers to come and talk on specific topics. I got a call from the coordinator saying that he heard I knew about the economics of war and the defense buildup. Since you are an ambassador for your race, I always arrive early. "There goes those Negroes again; they are always late." So I arrived early and sat in the front row. There are no blacks in the class. This guy walks in the class; he has never seen me before and he looks around and says, "Well Professor Mobutu has not gotten here yet, so we'll do this. . . ." I said, "Wait! I am here." I am sitting with a suit on. [Since the professor could not readily identify Mobutu, he assumed Mobutu had not arrived, which indicated his tendency to stereotype blacks as always late.] The white students' perception was to pick up what was going on. The guy started to hem and haw. So I do my thing and whatever I am talking about I try to make sure I bring a correct and comprehensive perspective to bear, and the students appreciated that. They wanted to continue the discussion.

The lack of respect and sensitivity toward faculty may be expressed in overt ways. In the late 1980s, when Mobutu and his boss had a luncheon engagement with the director of a project to improve science education, this stereotype was evident. During lunch, Mobutu asked the director if black secondary teachers were a part of the science education program. The director answered, "We had one, but she dropped out. I don't know if black folks aspire to know anything about science." "This statement was made to my face," remarked Mobutu. "It is personal racism, but it projects a broader stereotype." The stereotype is that since there is a paucity of blacks in the natural sciences, it is the result of a lack of interest or intelligence. "In that kind of setting, you can't always respond to it the way you like. I wanted to reach across the table, snatch him, and beat his butt. But I had to handle it in a different way, and that exacerbates the frustration. It is part of what black males and females experience daily on white campuses." Mobutu handled the situation by trying to correct the perception of the project director and convince him that blacks were indeed interested in science.

In facing social isolation, a lack of respect, the lack of support services, and taxing professional obligations, black academics are still expected to perform their "buffer" role in the university with black students and with the black community. It produces a dilemma, creating role strain and role conflict. Sense the tension and conflict from walking the academic tightrope as both Teresa Johnson and Crystal Miller articulated the dilemma. Said Teresa,

> Blacks have to do more. We have to develop a department, participate in the community, and involve ourselves with our students. I don't think most people do that. We wear tons of hats in order for us to keep what we think we have for our folks on campus. So you have to do double duty all the time. There are committees on affirmative action, graduate minority, et cetera. There are only forty-five or fifty of us in this university of forty thousand population. Can you imagine how overwhelming? There is a continual amount of energy being exerted. They need more of us. They are getting a lot more [for their] dollar [from] each of us, and they are overworking us.

Teresa, a political progressive, copes by attempting to balance her professional obligations and service activities.

Crystal Miller, a radical Democrat, echoed the sentiments of Teresa Johnson, raising questions about the expectations of black professors on predominantly white campuses.

> Minority people who work in white universities are a rare breed. It is important to our community that we interact and provide service in some way, help out in the school system, work with community groups, and speak to various groups. In a university, that is translated into community service. How much do you do? How do you value that when it comes to evaluating someone's work for promotion? Community service is not as valued, for example, as giving a talk at a church versus presenting a paper at the MLA, though it may be more effective in the long run in helping young people. However, a promotion depends on standards set by the university. What do you do when the church calls up and asks you to give a talk? Do you say, "I am sorry but I have a paper I have to give." Can you take the time to do it, or do you find a way to do the community service as well as academic work? You have double demands placed on you; you have a choice to ignore one and go with the other or try to satisfy both. I try to satisfy both. I don't believe I would be here without the support of the community of people who didn't have the opportunity I had. I feel I have an obligation and debt to pay to my community.

William Ofodile, a Nigerian professor of anthropology in a traditional department at a large, predominantly white university, acknowledged that the demands of the educational systems are in conflict with those of the minority community.

> The minority community expects you to do more applied things, but the academic community is not looking for that. I serve on committees that convey to the black faculty whether he or she is making it. I feel black Americans see things in a different perspective. The black candidates do not publish. They want to solve problems rather than deal with theoretical and methodological problems. Sometimes blacks have difficulties in balancing the two things.

Ofodile does not try to balance professional obligations with community concerns. Instead, he has chosen to concentrate his efforts on research and publishing.

For administrators like Ferdinand Hamilton, who is also a well-known scholar, there is a constant balancing of professional growth and administrative duties. Black administrators are hired as interpreters for the needs of black students, faculty, and the black community, and those of the white administrators, faculty, students, and the larger society. "It presents potential problems, anytime you have to serve two masters or wear two hats," said Ferdinand, a vice provost for minority affairs and special assistant to the president of a predominantly white university in the Midwest. It requires constantly walking a political tightrope to be recognized by various factions within and outside the academic community. "There are certain expectations the university has and certain expectations my black constituents both on campus and within the community have. They can be counterproductive to what you are doing. You have to do a lot of in-fighting." So he finds that the most productive way to balance on this tightrope "is to let people in the community do the fighting for you or whatever is necessary. Otherwise, you cut your nose off to spite your face, and you won't be here to do what you can do," said the politically active liberal Democrat.

Black administrators in higher education are likely to be "a special assistant-to-someone phenomenon."[10] Most black administrators in predominantly white universities are denied access to power and have limited authority, except for black studies and minority affairs. Ferdinand Hamilton has used his position to influence university policies. He has recruited minority administrators, faculty, and students and improved the quality of their lives on campus. These changes have also improved the overall quality of the university's educational process through cultural diversity.

The quality of the environment affects the retention of black academicians. Much talent is lost from higher education when they are unable to successfully function because of the role strain and conflict and the impact of social isolation inherent in their predominantly white settings.

Although retention of black academicians is affected by quality of life, there is also a formal process that factors importantly in retention. Once black academics enter the halls of ivy, the issues of evaluation, promotion, and retention become important. John Lamont, a tenured professor in the physics department at a major university, for example, has been recognized by the university for his brilliant contributions to the scholarly community and to all humankind. In his case, the goals of academe, which subscribe to the "pursuit of knowledge," "fairness and reason," "free inquiry," and "value neutrality," have been realized. But too often this is not the case. Since universities are bureaucracies, these ideals do not mesh with the reality of how bureaucracies function. (We sometimes forget universities are bureaucracies with their own goals, needs, and norms.) Most colleges and universities have a merit system for hiring, promoting, and retaining. However, "it is not an objective, competitive system, but rather a patronage system of merit. Publication, achievement, and performance are important in such a system, but so are ascriptive traits, personal qualities of style and manner, conforming behavior, mentors, and sponsors."[11]

Even though there is an "objective system" in place for the evaluation of scholarship, how is it derived and from what source? At the core of the evaluation process are epistemological concerns about the nature of knowledge itself—such questions as, What is knowledge? How is knowledge generated? Who are the dispensers of knowledge? What knowledge becomes the acceptable truth? And by what mechanism does it become the acceptable truth?

Evaluating the Black Scholar and the Afrocentric Perspective

Though blacks, like Jefferson Barnes and John Lamont, are hired in traditional departments in predominantly white universities, most black faculty are concentrated in black studies programs, or they hold a joint appointment in a traditional department and black studies. One reason for hiring black scholars is that they offer a new source of knowledge. Yet, some of these scholars face the problem of how that knowledge is evaluated and how it affects the promotion and tenure process.

Black scholars often challenge the traditional body of Eurocentric knowledge and scholarship in terms of content, theoretical paradigm, underlying worldview, and methodology. Consequently, they produce knowledge that is new and is derived from an Afrocentric perspective.[12] Hence, in evaluating the scholarship of blacks in academe, the traditional Eurocentric producers of knowledge are in conflict with the emerging Afrocentric perspective.

There are problems created by the divergent worldview. Professor Jonathan Mobutu, a director of black studies, discussed the differences in the Eurocentric and Afrocentric perspectives in scholarship and the problems they present in the evaluation of that scholarship.

"In the Afrocentric perspectives blacks define themselves relative to the continent of Africa and our origins in Africa as a principle point of black studies," said Mobutu.

> It means building upon the knowledge that we have a classical African civilization and blacks have always been actors, shaping their own destiny, as opposed to being victims at the hands of other powers. Black people have been the ancestors who produced the major contributions in the modern world, even though Europeans have been co-opted into making believe that somehow Greece and Rome emerged out of the sky. It also means that in trying to improve humanity, a principal focal point is those activities which focus on trying to re-elevate African people to their former role as teachers of the world, as opposed to being treated like children of the world.

One historian once said that "Africans are certainly my brothers, they are just two hundred years my younger brothers." We are correcting that notion and getting people throughout the African diaspora to understand that the situation people of African descent find themselves in is only temporary and simply not consistent with the historical record of the black experience.

Mobutu also believes,

Black studies has attempted to interject the study of wholeness into the human condition. Beyond that, there is also the task to do the same thing for the natural and the physical sciences, that is, try to reinterpret and see how they impact one another in meaningful ways. This worldview contradicts the Western way of thinking, because we don't have the tools to prove it. Western science requires that you come up with some kind of symbolic representation, using some kind of number system. If you are talking about consciousness or one's connection to a broader reality, you can't measure them. So you have to choose some other way of understanding that you can use or evaluate, other than the Western science way of manipulating the environment.

Out of the Afrocentric perspective, we get important information about the black experience through oral traditions—art, music, et cetera. The data are embedded in there and not reducible to numbers. It is data on what people are thinking and what they want to achieve. These sources of knowledge have been relegated to a subordinate status by Western science, which suggests that this is the best way of knowing something and understanding something. It's Western science that comes up with replication, verification, and falsification.

Mobutu concluded that scholars in black studies are trying "to understand and link African ways of understanding the universe as opposed to Western ways. It is a challenge because it is not acceptable to traditional science. It depends on who is in academe and who decides what constitutes knowledge and what isn't knowledge."[13]

Like Mobutu, Tefe Fusi, an ethnomusicologist at a predominantly black institution, understands and needs to vigorously defend these fundamental differences in worldview and philosophy of the Afrocentric and the Eurocentric perspectives. The Afrocentric sounds and elements of music—time, rhythm, and form—for example, are often misunderstood in the context of the Eurocentric tradition. Listen to Fusi as he discusses some differences in worldview.

Western orientation is intellectual, and the African orientation is intuitive and wholistic. And there is always a conflict. The worldview is different. The African concept of sound is totally different from the Western world's. Traditionally, African sound is considered as a wave length that establishes a link between the visible and the invisible worlds. And that is why we are able to use music, the raw material of sound, to put into structural patterns. Those patterns are meaningful to those societies in which the events are taking place. We are able to use the medium of organized sound as a link between the invisible world and us. Music, to us, is not art form for entertainment. It relates directly to the psyche and is, therefore, psychologically conceived. Thus, music becomes a spiritual element in our lives.

Fusi, an African, selected his doctoral thesis at a predominantly white university in this country. He said, "The white faculty members were against my doing something on my own traditions. At first, I didn't understand their reasons, but later I concluded they wanted to remain the experts, and it would have been a challenge to their authority." There was resentment when he decided to study his own culture. He believes this was the reason for the subsequent denial of the assistant professorship, which had been promised to him upon completion of his doctorate.

Now that Fusi is a widely respected ethnomusicologist, lecturing across the country, he constantly stresses to his white colleagues that a knowledge of African philosophy is crucial to understanding the significant difference between African and Western elements of musical expressions and styles.

> You see, this is my argument with white folks about the philosophy of Africa. How are they going to argue and tell me how I feel about my music and what constitutes what I feel about it? I am in the middle of the stuff. I have experienced rituals in which people use music, and they've gone nuts listening to a particular type of song. Who is going to tell me—a white person for that matter—that because of this element and that element, that is why people are going through that state of mind! There is no way any white man in this room—I say when I go places—[can say that it is] because of this rhythmic element or melodic element in music that we feel that way about it! They don't like it, but there is no way I am going to stop telling it the way it is. All we are trying to do is develop an African philosophy.

In "The Study of Music as a Symbol of Culture: The Afro American and Euro-American Perspective," Robert W. Stephens, a musicologist, concurs with Tefe Fusi that the musical traditions and styles of Afro Americans and Euro Americans are different. For instance, the former traditions arise from an oral culture and are more spontaneous and intuitive, while the latter derive from a literal culture and are more structured. "Many implications flow from this observation; the most crucial is that products of the literal culture may misunderstand products of the oral culture, or vice-versa." Not surprisingly, "such misunderstandings have occurred and played a central role in the relationship between Afro Americans and Euro-Americans."[14] The differences in these cultural traditions affect musical styles and the use of musical elements. "Since the dominant group reflects Western European musical values, it views them as the benchmark by which to judge all others,"[15] thus adopting feelings of cultural and musical superiority.

Similarly, misunderstandings and negative interpretations within the context of traditional academe are made about the professional discipline of Afro American studies that has emerged within the past twenty-five years. While a number of black studies programs proliferated during the upheavals in the late 1960s and early 1970s, few developed into full-fledged university departments with control over budgets and faculty. Critics of black studies continue to challenge their academic validity, refusing to accept the discipline as having a legitimate place in higher education. This results in "the failure to understand fully the emergent field of Afro American Studies and the special circumstances of its professionals that leads to failures of fair and accurate assessment of the nature, scope, and quality of their work both as academicians and as administrators."[16]

Hear Teresa Johnson, a professor of Afro American studies at a major university in the West, discuss the demands, problems, and responsibilities confronting black professionals in the field of Afro American studies.

> I am in Afro American studies and Afro American literature. It has been a field that has been resisted by the educational system here in this country. So you need to do three times as much as other people around you to make whatever you do count. It's not that you have to do more publishing, but you have to do a lot more work to publish.

The many obstacles for black academicians who want to write about the black experience, she believes, are "a major factor why many bright young people are not choosing academe." Teresa pointed out, "When I did my first book on black women novelists, colleagues sent out queries to other white scholars, and the overwhelming response was there was no such field. So you overdo the proving. You have to really make it clear that it is a scholarly field. You have to go out there and educate people who think they are educated."

The university holds a regents professor's position, an appointment that is reserved for exceptional people in the arts. James Baldwin, the novelist and essayist who died in 1987, was a regents professor. But, Teresa asserted, "We had to persuade the educational establishment that James Baldwin in 1978 was really a fine writer. We had to convince them that he wasn't a radical browbeating crazy." When she invited Paule Marshall, the African American writer, to the campus, most of the committee was unfamiliar with her. "I literally gave them lectures on who she is. Not until recently did people here admit that we have great Afro American writers. Not until Alice Walker won the Pulitzer Prize was she recognized by this university. . . . It makes her established." Teresa said,

> It has taken years to make it clear to people that the writing I and others do is to acknowledge the great black writers. It is a continual plugging away. So if I write about those writers and their works are not considered great, now what would my work be considered? I think that is the trial of people in other fields of Afro American literature. People will discuss race relations, but they won't necessarily see that there are great writers and thinkers among black people. They may be interested in whether blacks and whites can get together, or they can think of us as problems. But when we talk about our contributions and the things we do and the way we set our stan-

dards, that's another matter. There is a continual striving that we have to do here to make this point clear. I really do think given my attributes, if I were in a more racially privileged situation, I would be far beyond where I am now.

Teresa senses "there is a ghettoization of ethnic studies." Other departments within the university resist accepting courses from the black studies program. For example, "The English department doesn't want to accept black literature." She also noted that when scholars are in an ethnic field, "it is not considered an important field . . . even though the person may be a first-rate mind." Because they are in the ethnic field, they are not chosen for positions in other departments. She raised the question, "Why aren't there any blacks in history?" There are "top white scholars in Afro American studies at this university. But it doesn't mean you don't hire a black in history." She wonders if it is a threat to hire a black scholar in the same department with a white scholar whose field is in the black experience.

It is clear from the responses of Jonathan Mobutu, Tefe Fusi, and Teresa Johnson that the emergent discipline of black studies challenges the state of Western knowledge, its paradigms, and its philosophies. The new knowledge, paradigms, and philosophies that evolve out of this new discipline are unfamiliar to traditional academe. Problems exist in evaluating this new scholarship, but not because it lacks merit. "Black studies" has a negative image in traditional departments, not only because it is new, but also because it is associated with a less powerful group in the society. A lack of sponsors in established fields to serve as advocates for this new scholarship adds to the problem. Hence, since publication of research is an important criterion for evaluation in promotion and tenure, black faculty members are not retained or promoted at the same rate as white faculty.

Even when blacks are engaged in research, promotion and retention may still be difficult to obtain. Said Mobutu:

> White faculty do everything they can not to tenure a black faculty. They come up with every excuse they can, such as not a good colleague, meaning you didn't go to their parties and get-togethers and your research is not mainstream enough. If you do research on the black experience, it doesn't count or it is not published in the right journal, like the *Western Journal of Black Studies*. It is not the same as if published in the *American Journal of Economics and Sociology*.

He cited an example of a colleague who had been denied tenure because of the nature of his research. "This professor is doing path-breaking research in hypnosis, using a black and white sample. He published in black journals." But his white colleagues are saying "he has not published enough."

Even when one has "published enough," there is still the issue of quality. One case that received national attention supports Mobutu's contention. Dr. Sandra A. O'Neale, a forty-nine-year-old former professor at Emory University in Atlanta,

Georgia, was twice denied tenure in the English department. The Phi Beta Kappa graduate from the University of Kentucky doctoral program filed a civil rights lawsuit against the school, alleging race and sex discrimination.[17]

Dr. O'Neale, whose areas of interest are in nineteenth-century American literature, African American literature, Biblical literature, and black feminist studies, has published twenty-nine articles on black Americans. While some colleagues contended she was denied tenure because her research is too black oriented, other faculty and administrative officials maintained "the decision to deny tenure was [based on] the questionable quality of her published articles." One tenured white professor stated, "There are members of the English department who do not regard the works of the authors she writes about or the periodicals in which she publishes as important."

William Ofodile has published extensively in mainstream academic journals and with major publishers. But when his tenure was initially denied by his department, unlike most African Americans, he did not attribute it to racism. Said Ofodile, "I was turned down for tenure the first time I applied because I had been there only four years. It hurt me. It wasn't how long you've been there, but what your productivity was, and I had met that. I don't think it was racial, but a growing glut in the marketplace." After another reputable university offered him tenure and a professorship, the university reversed its decision, giving him tenure and promoting him to full professorship. "I didn't ask for it. It was due to the quality of my work and the offer from the other university," said Ofodile. He has a different perception of race relations than his African American colleagues. Ofodile said he has not experienced racism. "I will not say it's because of the quality of my work, but I have done well as far as my work is concerned." When I broached the subject of racism with another African professor at a black university, he mentioned that he had to be resocialized like African Americans to be sensitive to racial cues. It was not a part of his socialization process in Africa. Perhaps Ofodile has not learned the subtle racial cues or has chosen to ignore them. Some academics, particularly blacks, are critical of Ofodile's research on minorities and the educational process. They reject his idea of blaming the victim and criticize his lack of an Afrocentric perspective. Said Ofodile about his critics,

I am not angry with anybody. The acceptance of my work is split with both blacks and whites. There are whites who support my work as indicated by invitations to speak and to contribute to journals and books. They think it is new and needs to be listened to. People who are involved in solving social problems—blacks, whites, Hispanics—have problems with my work. I can understand their positions intellectually. Since I am from Nigeria, I can stand back and look at the issue as a marginal person. I can ask questions that both blacks and whites don't ask. Since there is a pressure to solve problems, some people don't go beyond that. And I do feel victims sometimes contribute to their own demise. I want to explain why that is as opposed to letting the differences be explained biologically. My good friends no longer talk to me because they think I am blaming the victim.

Walking the Academic Tightrope

Although publishing is more important than teaching and service as a criterion in the evaluation process for promotion and retention at most colleges and universities, blacks are still expected to fulfill an important service role. Minority academicians are "buffers, mediators, and interpreters between students and institutions, expressing the needs and interests of each to the other."[18] However, "the institution puts pressure on you to provide services without including it as a part of the evaluation process. And now it comes from the top position of president, so you can't say you prefer not to serve, because you are not tenured. He makes the final decision on tenure. So you are caught between a rock and a hard place," asserted Mobutu.

Albert Sungist understands what it means to be "caught between a rock and a hard place." When he was denied tenure, he was a faculty member in an experimental ethnic college in the West that was strongly interested in recruiting minorities and the poor. He said many faculty were recruited "under the rubrics of affirmative action, giving us a negative label. . . . Most of us in that college were not viewed favorably in some corners of the campus because we were minorities. There was a minority person who headed the college; many people hated the college as well as the black provost," said Sungist. "I got caught between the old and new policy with this experimental college. The old administration emphasized service; the new administration emphasized publishing." He attributes his tenure denial to the confluences of racism, elitism, and changing standards.

Sometimes standards change at "a time when new groups of populations are moving into academe—blacks, women, and Hispanics. It is a tool to control a subset of a population," claimed Mobutu, adding, "in the fifties and sixties, you didn't have to be a good researcher or an excellent teacher to get job security. But these same people are now changing the standards to judge new faculty under the guise of quality education. You have to publish or perish. If you look at them, they don't have the publications." It is no coincidence that standards change when a diverse population enters academe or any new marketplace. A *Newsweek* report noted that as Asians enter American universities (particularly prestigious universities) in increasing numbers, administrators are beginning to change the standards. Instead of looking at their high test scores and grades, they are adjusting admission criteria to keep Asian Americans' numbers low. Berkeley, for instance, revised its procedures in 1983 to give more weight to essays and extracurricular activities, areas in which Asians have generally not fared well.[19] Because of protests from Asians, this overt policy was changed.

Black academicians in predominantly white colleges and universities often serve two masters. Many blacks hold joint appointments, for example, in the English department and black studies or ethnic studies. Having to fulfill two separate roles and requirements may affect their tenure and promotion at review

CHAPTER 4

time. Serving two masters can produce a conflict over academic standards. Crystal Miller described such a conflict:

> What is valid scholarly work? Is it valid to do an anthology of a work or one of your authorship? Some disciplines in the university would say an anthology is less valuable. Do you accept these values or do you challenge them? These are the pressures blacks are under. When you don't agree with these values, you can be punished or fired. I don't fight all the battles, but there are some that are too important not to fight.

Retrenchment in affirmative action, along with problems in the evaluation process, results in the loss of many black faculty from the halls of ivy. Though some black academicians are in traditional departments, most are concentrated in black studies or hold a joint appointment in a traditional academic department and black or ethnic studies. Administrators usually are in staff positions related to minorities. The black academicians often experience social isolation because of their low numbers. They also have to balance their professorial duties with service-oriented concerns related to black students and the black community.

Academicians who want to offer a broader vision of knowledge often find that the Afrocentric perspective is rejected. This affects the retention process.

Despite the perils, the Talented One Hundred in academe continue to cope successfully, because they have learned, like those individuals in other sectors of the economy, to successfully negotiate the political and racial landscape. They also know the importance of a political and social network.

Kanter states in *Men and Women of the Corporation*,

> There is a small positive psychological side to tokenism: the self-esteem that comes from mastering a difficult situation and getting into places that traditionally exclude others of one's kind. If the token can segregate conflicting expectations and has strong outside support groups with which to relax, then perhaps a potentially stress-producing situation can be turned into an opportunity for ego enhancement. This benefit may accrue only if there are buffering networks to shield the impact of social isolation and of the tokenism found on the job.[20]

SUMMARY

After black students protested in the late 1960s about the lack of black faculty and an absence of the contributions of people of African descent from the academic curriculum, black teachers and administrators were hired. These academicians, many of whom left traditionally black institutions, were hired to develop, administer, and teach in the newly founded black studies program. In general, blacks, especially women, found an alien environment that was hostile to producing alternative paradigms of thinking and seeing the world that challenged the traditionally patriarchal, Eurocentric perspective. White colleagues and mainstream publishing outlets did not readily accept their new knowledge as valid. Thus academicians encountered much role conflict as they struggled to balance their Afrocentric concerns with the traditional requirements of the academic life and with tenure, promotion, and service to their students, their university, and their community. Yet they endured and served as catalysts for women's studies and other emerging programs in multiculturalism.

NOTES

1. William H. Exum, "Climbing the Crystal Stair: Values, Affirmative Action, and Minority Faculty," *Social Problems*, 30, no. 4 (April 1983): 384.
2. Exum, "Climbing," 385.
3. Shirley Vining Brown, "Increasing Minority Faculty: An Elusive Goal," *MGE Research Profiles*, 1, no. 3 (Princeton, NJ: Educational Testing Service, 1988): 1.
4. Brown, "Increasing," 2.
5. Barbara Vobejde, "Blacks in the Sciences," *Washington Post, National Weekly Edition*, Aug. 15–21, 1988, 38.
6. Jewel L. Prestage, "Quelling the Mythical Revolution in Higher Education," *Journal of Politics*, 14 (Aug. 1979): 769.
7. Exum, "Climbing," 390.
8. Exum, "Climbing," 391.
9. Edward Jackson, "Blacks on White Campuses: Problems and Perspectives," in Julia C. Elam, ed., *Blacks on White Campuses* (Lanham, MD: University Press of America, 1983).
10. Andrew J. Chisham, "An Assessment of the Role of Black Administrators in Predominantly White Colleges and Universities," in Julia C. Elam, ed., *Blacks on White Campuses*, (Lanham, MD: University Press of America, 1983), 55–67.
11. Exum, "Climbing," 393.
12. According to Molefi Kete Asante, Afrocentricity means "literally placing African ideals at the center of any analysis that involves African culture and behavior." Molefi K. Asante, *The Afrocentric Idea* (Philadelphia: Temple University, 1987), 6. Moreover, Asante states, "the Afrocentrist seeks to uncover and use codes, paradigms, symbols, motifs, and circles of discussion that reinforce the centrality of African ideals and values as a valid frame of reference for acquiring and examining data." Molefi Asante, *Kemet, Afrocentricity and Knowledge* (Trenton, NJ: African World Press, 1990), 6.
13. While the discipline of black studies questions the Eurocentric paradigm of thinking and knowing, it also faces challenges from within its borders. The increasing presence of black women scholars in the higher education academy has raised issues about the field's male-centered approach and its exclusion of the contributions of women of African descent in this country and throughout the African diaspora from the development of black studies, its curriculum, and its leadership role in Africana studies professional organizations. For example, Delores P. Aldridge founded the first black studies undergraduate program in 1971 at a major white institution in the South, Emory University in Atlanta, Georgia. Delores P. Aldridge and Carlene Young's work in *Out of the Revolution: The Development of Africana Studies* (Lanham, MD: Lexington Books,

2000) highlights some trailblazers who struggled against multiple odds to make their way in academe. See Lena W. Meyers, *A Broken Silence: Voices of African American Women* (Westport, CT: Berin and Garvey, 2002); Lois Benjamin, *Black Women in the Academy: Promises and Perils* (Gainesville: University Press of Florida, 1997).

14. Robert W. Stephens, "The Study of Music as a Symbol of Culture: The Afro American and Euro-American Perspectives," *Western Journal of Black Studies*, 10, no. 4 (1986): 181.

15. Stephens, "Study of Music," 182.

16. Russell L. Adams, "Evaluating Professions in the Context of Afro American Studies," *Western Journal of Black Studies*, 5, no. 3 (Fall, 1981): 140.

17. Sam Hopkins and Ann Hardie, "Professor Denied Tenure Sues Emory," *Atlanta Journal and Constitution*, Dec. 24, 1988.

18. Exum, "Climbing," 395.

19. Eloise Salholz, "Do Colleges Set Asian Quotas?" *Newsweek*, Feb. 9, 1987, 60.

20. Rosabeth Moss Kanter, *Men and Women of the Corporation* (New York: Basic Books, 1977), 240.

5

THE COLOR LINE IN SOCIAL, RELIGIOUS, AND FAMILY LIFE

Bernice Jackson, fifty years old and a social work administrator, is among the few black managers employed in a racially mixed social services agency in a large Midwestern city. Her relationship with her white colleagues is warm and cordial. They work cooperatively as teammates on joint projects. They participate in the office celebrations of birthdays, promotions, and bon voyage parties. But this work-inspired congeniality does not extend beyond the work day. Bernice Jackson returns to her black neighborhood and her black friends.

Twenty years after the death of Martin Luther King Jr., *Newsweek* ran a cover story, "Black and White," asking, "How integrated is America?" Did the winds of change that brought many blacks into the mainstream of the world of work also take them into the educational, political, and residential arenas and the social and intimate spheres of whites? After twenty years, some sectors of the workplace have become more neutral meeting grounds for blacks and whites, but the winds of change left a chill in their social and political worlds. Churches, neighborhoods, and schools are largely divided by the color line. Few work-inspired friendships go beyond the workplace.

Unlike Bernice, who returns to her black community after work, increasing numbers of black elite find themselves living and working in a predominantly white world. One consequence of this is a growing sense of social isolation. For blacks who live and work in communities where there is only a small black population, this social isolation can be intense and stressful.

The article, "Young, Black and Bored" in *Providence Sunday Journal Magazine* raises the question, "Where do you go after work if you're a Black professional in Rhode Island?" The retort: "Home—to call the moving van?"[1] A similar article in

Ebony asks how blacks fare in Vermont, "The Whitest State," which is less than 1 percent black.[2] Although most middle-class blacks live in states with a higher percentage of blacks, isolation is a concern for those who are moving into the mainstream.

The expanding economic, educational, political, and social opportunities for blacks have resulted in greater opportunities for mobility and interaction in the white world, thereby creating new sources of stress. Sociologist James Blackwell, in *Cities, Suburbs, and Blacks*, notes that as blacks move into the mainstream, isolation is an increasing phenomenon, resulting from the disruption of social ties to the group of origin.[3] This pattern is typical of the persons I interviewed. Seventy-one percent of the Talented One Hundred grew up in black neighborhoods, 15 percent in white neighborhoods, and 14 percent in racially mixed or transitional neighborhoods. At the time of the interviews, only 44 percent of the Talented One Hundred lived in black neighborhoods, 35 percent in white neighborhoods, and 21 percent in racially mixed neighborhoods, usually over 70 percent white.

This mobility pattern is different from that of previous generations of blacks, who migrated to the North during the great migration or to the West Coast during World War II seeking jobs in the defense plants in California. While they were uprooted from their Southern origins, many extended-family members moved together, usually settling in predominantly black communities. The black elite, on the other hand, often settle with their immediate family or alone in a white neighborhood. Overwhelmingly, the Talented One Hundred felt that when you live and work in a white community, isolation is likely to increase. In her dissertation, "Life in Isolation: Black Families Living in Predominantly White Communities," Beverly Tatum, studying upwardly mobile blacks, reported that "some parents lamented that they no longer experience that collective community spirit and cohesiveness."[4]

Many salient factors contribute to the isolation of the black elite in white settings. One is the issue of balancing Afrocentric and Eurocentric concerns. Blacks who work in the corporate world spend an increasing amount of time nurturing their careers. To climb the corporate ladder, it is essential to interact socially outside of the workplace, where important business transactions take place. If blacks expect to be successful in the workplace, they have to increase their interactions with whites outside the office. These social functions are more instrumental than expressive. In their quest for upward mobility, some blacks feel they must assimilate totally, adopting the lifestyles and values of whites. Hence, their business and social contacts become increasingly white.

Joseph Lowery sees an inherent danger in this isolation. Said Lowery, "There are people who choose to be isolated. They live in white neighborhoods, join white churches, send their kids to white schools, and completely divorce themselves from the black community." Whether or not the black elite freely choose an all-white setting, it can be stressful, particularly since there is no reprieve from the continuous onslaught of racism. While the black elite may be accepted on the job, they may not be accepted in their community. If the black elite patronize a neighborhood restaurant, they may be concerned about whether they will be seated near the kitchen or be treated courteously. (When an acquaintance of Jonathan Mobutu, for example, went to her neighborhood restaurant, the waiter brought her a slice of watermelon along with a glass of water.) Some of the Talented One Hundred reported that when they go to their neighborhood stores, more identification may be required of them to cash checks, and the police may stop or follow them to see if they live in the neighborhood.

Even on vacation, the black elite might not find relaxation from racism. While Diane Earlinger's family was vacationing at a beach resort in the South, her teenage son spotted a white female classmate. They started conversing, and Diane observed the scowling faces of whites. She felt uneasy about their expressions, fearing for her son's safety.

These continuous bouts with racism, on and off the job, can put the black elite who live in isolation from other blacks "at high risk for emotional collapse," said Joseph Lowery. "Those folks are taking off all their shields. And they are going totally out there, exposing themselves to the atmospheric pressure, and many collapse. They have become very frustrated, because sooner or later, they are wrong about their acceptance. They hit that ceiling, becoming frustrated and not knowing where to turn." Sometimes, Lowery said, they return to the black community; other times, "they stay there and live in anguish."

Blacks are concerned about the danger that Lowery posed; they want to retain their balance on the tightrope between Afrocentric and Eurocentric concerns. Having come of age during integration, many of the Talented One Hundred are reevaluating, over twenty-five years later, the impact of integration. They understand the need to keep their racial identity by maintaining a strong black support system in their familial, educational, religious, political, personal, and social spheres.

LIVING IN A PREDOMINANTLY WHITE NEIGHBORHOOD

While many black professionals live comfortably in the black middle-income neighborhoods dotting the suburbs of many large cities of this country, there are still not enough homes for the expanding black elite. In other smaller communities, the black population may not be large enough or may be too dispersed to form a black neighborhood. Greater opportunities in the workplace along with the increased options in housing resulting from fair housing laws have had a major impact on residential patterns. Many blacks look to predominantly white neighborhoods for housing. But blacks in predominantly white communities interact less with their neighbors than blacks who live in black communities. If other black families live nearby, they are more likely to interact with each other than with their white neighbors.

Increasingly, middle-class blacks live in isolated white communities, away from their extended families, their black peers, and their black communities. Often this pattern disrupts ties with their traditional support system. The strong extended family has been recognized as an important feature of the African American tradition.[5] It is an important source of emotional, financial, and social support. Shimkin, Louie, and Frate's research on the black extended family found that the family network served as a facilitating agent in migration and urbanization and fostered educational and economic advancement.[6] The extended family continues to be a significant resource for the black middle class. According to sociologist Harriette P. McAdoo, "Whether or not they had moved up recently, and whether they had moved out to the suburbs or stayed in the city, today's Black middle-class families have kept an important part of their roots, the networks of mutually helpful family and kin who helped them rise."[7]

Pat Robinson, like many others among the Talented One Hundred, lives in a predominantly white neighborhood and is geographically distanced from relatives. Sometimes his desire to help the "black masses" and his relatives creates a dilemma for him. "I have a lot of poor relatives back home. The question I face is, 'Where does it go? What do I do?' I can spend my time helping my relatives. I am a federal judge, but I have to remind people of my roots."

Since many black elite are the first generation to succeed in the professional mainstream, they "assume an important position in their family hierarchy," said Bebe Moore Campbell in an article about their plight, "Black Executives and Corporate Stress." They are frequently called upon by family members for "financial assistance, career guidance, and even psychological counseling."[8] This expectation of mutual aid can sometimes be a drain on their resources. They may find themselves assisting siblings and relatives who may be on welfare or drugs or who may need their financial or emotional assistance in other ways. While the black elite might value family ties, these often conflict with personal aspirations. While some blacks remove themselves from their familial network, others remember their own precarious success, a mere stone's throw from poverty.

Blacks who live in predominantly white communities miss being in the presence of relatives, sharing and supporting one another. Many of the Talented One Hundred expressed concern about relatives, particularly elderly parents whom they left behind to fend for themselves. Jonathan Mobutu lives in a comfortable, predominantly white college community, but he is concerned about his widowed mother, who lives over 250 miles away in a large city. Since she lives in a high-crime community, his own comfort is disturbed by her lack of security. She protects herself with a gun, which almost cost him his life. During a weekend visit to his mother's home, Mobutu sat in a chair where a gun was placed in a ready position for any intruders.

It is the "dichotomy and tragedy of being a so-called successful black," remarked Johnson Longworth, because "you always have that string tied to that other reality. You cannot do things comfortably knowing that other reality exists."

Longworth cited an example of a black vice president of his university who was chairing a meeting when he received an emergency phone call. "He came back with a long face. Later we learned that his mother had been mugged in Chicago. A vice president had to jump on a plane to Chicago because his mother got mugged." Thus, while the black elite might be geographically removed from their social origins, they are emotionally wedded to the daily struggles and concerns of their extended families, black friends, and the black community.

FRIENDSHIPS AND SOCIAL NETWORKS

Since the amount of interracial contact outside the workplace is limited, peer networks are important support buffers for the black elite. Here they can have the conflicting expectations inherent in their racial status validated by others, thus reducing the stress of isolation. The Talented One Hundred seek validation from black friends and close associates, even when they live and work in predominantly white settings. When I asked individuals if their friends or social contacts were black, white, or racially mixed, 62 percent said their friends were primarily black. They reported feeling a greater level of trust and comfort with blacks. They also wanted release time from "race watching," as expressed by one individual. "You always have to watch what you say and what you do in the presence of whites, whether it is in a social or business environment. You can't be free. There is a sense of being watched."

Marla Robinson agreed, asserting, "I would share some things with blacks that I would not share with whites. I don't believe in discussing my private life with white people. I don't want them to know me that closely. I don't trust what they'll do with the information. I have never leveled with a white person, despite having had close friendships with white women."

Thirty-four percent of the Talented One Hundred had friends and social contacts of different races. Many reported having very close white friends, but indicated their closest friendships were with other blacks. Remarked Robert Woodson, "I have black and white friends, but I have a deeper relationship with my black friends than my white friends. We share more in common. There is much more to talk about, for example, a common culture and childhood experience. You can share, and the range of things you can explore from someone of your culture is greater. There are nuances and subtleties that you accept that become a part of you and the interchange." Woodson perceives there are distinct differences in the way blacks and whites conduct themselves in social settings in his environment. "We can drink, dance, and be very friendly with somebody else's woman, but there are acceptable limits no matter how much you have been drinking. Your hands do not suddenly wander, nor do you begin to take certain liberties . . . in the name of camaraderie or good times. We are conservatives when it comes to that. Whites are freer. I am always on guard for whites maybe exceeding the boundaries of kidding, comradeship, and saying and doing something that breaks across the imaginary boundaries."

John Daniels, who also has racially mixed friendships and social acquaintances, said his five or six best friends are the blacks with whom he grew up. He and his wife are comfortable with both blacks and whites. But his black and white friends may not be comfortable with one another. Therefore, his racially mixed affairs are usually small dinner parties. When he had a surprise birthday party for his wife, it was all black. "If we had whites, it would not be the same. The mixing capacity of my black and white friends may not be compatible. They are not comfortable with one another. So the party takes on a different tone," said Daniels.

The social contacts of the black elite are primarily black, while the business and professional contacts are 12 percent black, 60 percent racially mixed, and 26 percent white. This pattern suggests that there is exclusion outside the workplace that operates in both directions.

In his study of black managers in white corporations, John Fernandez found that the "percentage of Black and White managers who belong to racially mixed and unmixed organizations are quite similar," but "there is a large difference in their degree of contact at social functions. The Black managers have a great deal more contact with Whites at functions not related to work." Moreover, white friends of black managers are usually not from their workplace.[9]

I found that most of the Talented One Hundred belong both to racially mixed and to all-black organizations. They hold memberships in black sororities and fraternities and civil rights organizations, which Daniel Thompson, in his book *A Black Elite: A Profile of Graduates of UNCF Colleges* categorizes as (1) black caucuses, established by blacks who belong to predominantly white organizations; (2) parallel organizations, established by blacks to enhance professional advancement outside of the main parent organization (e.g., the Association of Black Psychologists); and (3) the traditional civil rights organizations (e.g., the NAACP).[10] Some blacks belong to a number of organizations, but others are not active, often because of the demands of their jobs.

Blacks have historically used their fraternities, sororities, lodges, and civic and social organizations to solve personal and community problems. They serve as "service centers, information exchanges, forums for jobs, and business-related and support mechanisms in personal development," noted sociologist Lawrence Gary.[11]

THE BLACK CLASS DIVIDE: POLITICAL CONSCIOUSNESS AND POLITICAL AFFILIATIONS

The Talented One Hundred have a high degree of participation in social and civic organizations, and they are politically conscious and very active. Among researchers, there is a strong perception that as blacks move upward in the social structure, their social, professional, and political orientations and affiliations become more class linked than race linked. This perception is fueled by the fact that increasing numbers of blacks have moved into the middle class since the 1960s.

With the rise of a significant black middle class, there is growing concern within the black community that it is becoming two separate societies. One society is an affluent middle class that has moved to the suburbs. This group feels isolated from the black masses. The black elite sense a lack of support from the black community and feel "put down" for their achievements.

The other society is an inner-city underclass that feels trapped by poverty, crime, drugs, violence, rampant teenage pregnancy, and high unemployment. They feel deserted by the black elite and resent them for moving up and leaving them behind. The result has been tension between the two societies, a troubling concern for many. Leo Aramis, a thirty-four-year-old journalist, who lives in a predominantly white neighborhood in the Northeast, expressed this troubling tension between the two strata of society. While Leo would prefer to live in a predominantly black neighborhood, he chose a white neighborhood because, in part, he said,

> I can be close to work, and in part, I don't want to come back and all my stuff is gone. It is obvious that black-on-black crime is a severe problem. It is often that black professionals are unwittingly the buffer zone between lower-income and less-educated black folks and whites. So the next time there is a riot, the neighbors are going to come and get middle-class blacks. They aren't going to come and get white folks first. I think we have unwittingly put ourselves in that position. It is that distant feeling that [explains why] brothers in the neighborhood are saying the niggers can't relate to this person, and he is no more than a honky to me. And he got more than I got. The divide and conquer mentality never existed like this before.
>
> I think it is one of the reasons our cities and neighborhoods have dissipated. As professionals, we have moved out to the suburbs to get away. We have taken that Talented Tenth that led our neighborhoods away from black neighborhoods. It used to be doctors, lawyers, teachers, and preachers could not get away. They had segregated housing patterns, and they had to live there. So you take all these leaders away and what you have left is not the most positive leadership. And so we have rampant drug use in our community, drug sales, and gangs running things. You got little girls and boys with no positive role models.

While pointing out the tension between the black elite and the underclass, Leo affirmed, "I am not going to move into the black community because it doesn't work. But it does not stop me from being deeply involved in the community."

Middle-class blacks do become the buffer group between the dominant white group and the black masses. Hence, we can see that individual success contributes to individualizing of racial experiences; it prevents blacks from seeing the hidden agenda of the dominant group. This hidden agenda is manifested, for example, in the social policies created by the government, which have primarily benefited middle-class blacks. Such public policies, like the equal opportunity policy of the late 1960s, created an available job pool for middle-class blacks during a period of social unrest and during an expanding economy. Affirmative action was one program that resulted from the public policy priority of equal opportunity. Robert Woodson feels that:

> the affirmative action program is only useful to some blacks, not all blacks. It is only useful to blacks in the first two tiers of the work force, but it doesn't have a damn thing to do with the unemployed dishwasher who needs training and economic development. So we have to be clear and not use all blacks when it is convenient; but when we talk about crime, only some blacks commit crime. But when we talk about affirmative action, we are talking about all blacks. I think the middle class needs to be truthful in advertising. We need to be accurate and not make these pervasive statements. We tend to disaggregate when it is convenient to us, for example, crime. But we aggregate when we say affirmative action helps all blacks. I think the civil rights leaders are engaged in a bait and switch game. We use the conditions of poor blacks to say we need affirmative action. But when we look at who it helps, it is middle-class blacks. The black middle class may not be conscious of its attitudes and behaviors, but it is a consequence.

On the other hand, the benign policy of the welfare program, which is designed to benefit the poor, expands in times of social and economic upheavals and contracts in times of stability.[12] It also serves the function of reinforcing the values of hard work inherent in the Protestant ethic. Welfare recipients are viewed as deviants because they do not conform to the norm; thus, they are treated like pariahs. This group also creates a source of cheap labor and is exploited economically in other ways by the dominant group, and, as Robert Woodson noted, may be consciously or unconsciously used by the middle class to maintain its status. Since more black women than black men are on welfare, there is not only the question of class but also of gender. Woodson, like others, castigated the black middle class for its lack of involvement in "changing economic policies so the flow of investments can come to low-income communities" and its lack of involvement in identifying policies that are beyond class and race. Instead, middle-class blacks are likely to focus on setbacks in affirmative action policies or race-oriented policies that are likely to benefit them. This is the reason why Robert Woodson feels "there is a growing schism between the middle class and the growing underclass." The consequences of these social policies reflect the underlying tension between the rising black middle class as a buffer group and the underclass and how this tension has been diverted from interactions with the dominant white group.

The members of the buffer group, despite their privileges, are likely to occupy positions that are vulnerable to a downturn in the economy. It becomes clear how the individualization of the black elite's experience prevents them from seeing that their own precarious status as members of the buffer group is intertwined with the masses. If they understand the hidden agenda of racism, the black elite can externalize it and create messages from their subjective and objective experiences that will lead to action. But if they do not understand the hidden agenda of racism, reactivity and inaction result. Nowhere is the issue of reactivity and inaction more pronounced than in the tension created by the widening gap between the middle-class black and the poor black, diverting energy from strengthening the black community.

Although there are class distinctions, in general, the Talented One Hundred felt that living away from the black community would not stop them from being deeply involved in it. They strongly identified with the social concerns of the masses of blacks. About 75 percent of the Talented One Hundred have a liberal political orientation; they manifested that concern in their vote for Jesse Jackson in the 1984 primary and stated they would vote for him in the 1988 presidential campaign. They believe that the government should be more responsive to the poor by developing social and economic policies to ameliorate their social conditions.

Research shows that, whatever their economic status, blacks are more liberal on social issues than whites. A 1986 Gallup poll, commissioned by the Joint Center for Political Studies on the attitudes of blacks and whites, found that "eight in ten Blacks, compared with three out of ten Whites believe the federal government should make efforts to improve the living conditions of minorities, and about 86 percent of Blacks, but only 55 percent of Whites, feel the government should spend more on social programs."[13]

In general, the Talented One Hundred wanted more progressive policies in welfare reform, involving meaningful training, more child care, and improved medical benefits for recipients. In voting for Jesse Jackson's progressive social and economic agenda, they symbolized their collective identification with the masses. There does not appear to be a mass defection from a liberal political orientation. (My interviews with the Talented One Hundred suggest that equating political orientation and political party affiliation is too complex a correlation. However, I found, like Daniel Thompson's study on the black elite,[14] that the Talented One Hundred are largely affiliated with the Democratic Party.)

Since the New Deal, the Democratic Party has espoused more liberal causes, while the Republican Party is viewed as more conservative. Only 5 percent of the Talented One Hundred identified themselves as conservative; 28 percent claimed to be moderate; 38 percent, liberal; 13 percent, radical; and 14 percent said mixed, meaning they were liberal on some issues and conservative on others. The 5 percent of Republicans among the Talented One Hundred reported their political orientation as conservative or moderate. Thus, the perception that as blacks move upwardly in society their political orientation is likely to become more class linked than race linked is unfounded, judging by the Talented One Hundred.

I found race still an important factor in the voting behavior of the black elite. As suggested in a *Washington Post* article on the black middle class, there was much disillusionment with the 1988 presidential election.[15] With the election of President George Bush, the Republican administration has expressed an interest in recruiting blacks into its party. Those middle-class blacks under thirty-five appear more receptive than older blacks. Whether such an emerging pattern materializes, the shifting of political orientation and affiliation among young middle-class blacks from a race-linked to a class-linked orientation remains speculative.

Since there appears to be a changing political orientation among the young black elite as a result of social isolation, the black church becomes the critical institution that continues to bridge the gap between the classes.

RELIGIOUS AFFILIATION

In *The Strengths of Black Families*, Robert Hill notes the importance of a strong religious orientation. Being in a hostile society, "Blacks have used religion as an important coping mechanism."[16] Said Bernie Roberts, a social researcher, "The more I see black people, the more I see we got over because of our religious orientations. We talk about the material aspect of blackness, but black people are religious people. Religious people do not put their emphasis on material things. We are religious people, even if we don't go to church."

The church has historically been an important resource in the black community. The church is a status giver for those with a lowly status in the larger society, thus affirming their dignity and worth as human beings and serving as an anchor for those with little support. "The black church is my anchor, and it is for a lot of black people. When you go to a black church, you will be on the same level with PhDs, maids, farmers, street sweepers, and you are home," noted Jack B. Lane.

William D. Watley, in the *Roots of Resistance: The Nonviolent Ethic of Martin Luther King, Jr.*, agrees, noting that "the all-pervasive character of racism . . . brings together in Black congregational life a unique blend of persons from various walks of life who have not only the same ethnicity, history, and culture, but also a common oppression by racism. It is not unusual in the Black church to find the 'Ph.D.'s and the no D's' sitting on the same boards and exercising the same power."[17] Hence, the black church is the place that provides a safe harbor and spiritual refueling to anchor blacks in the racial storms.

The church provides many additional functions. Said Benjamin Quarles, a black historian, "The church served as a community center where one could find relaxation and recreation. It was a welfare agency, dispensing help to the sicker and poorer members. It was a training school in self-government, in the handling of money, and in the management of business."[18] The church also acts as a training center for intellectual and moral leadership. Noted Bernie Roberts, "I can speak well because I learned to do so in church. I learned poems at a very early age. I feel comfortable speaking, no matter how large the audience. I saw Martin Luther King Jr. and Andrew Young speaking at my church. It is a training ground."

Because the church serves so many vital functions, Marla Robinson, who lives in a predominantly white community and whose son attends a white school, insists on going to a black church. "It is very important for [my son] to have a kinship with the black church and the black community, because of the whole ceremony of the black church, its hymns, and its spirituals. The church has impacted upon us politically, economically, and socially, and it has provided a leadership role. He does not have black friends in the neighborhood. He does in school, but they go their separate ways." It is the reason for Jack B. Lane's strong belief that the church should be there for a young black person to "have something to lean on."

More than 95 percent of the Talented One Hundred had "something to lean on" while growing up. The church served an important function in their lives. Seventy-one percent held membership in the Baptist or African Methodist Episcopal denominations, 49 percent and 22 percent, respectively; the other 25 percent membership was about evenly distributed among Apostolic, Roman Catholic, Congregational, Episcopal, Christian Methodist Episcopal, United Methodist, and Unitarian churches. And there was one Christian Scientist. The few who claimed no church affiliation acknowledged that they attended church. Presently, 69 percent of the Talented One Hundred are members of predominantly black churches.

Many of the Talented One Hundred, such as Laura Price and Yvonne Walker-Taylor, have grown more committed to their faith. Price, in addition to her medical practice, is an ordained minister in her Baptist church. She has no ambivalence about her practice of medicine and her religion. "There is no separation of the physical and spiritual being." Said Laura, "I have always thought of my medical practice as the ministry because of the type of work I am doing. I sincerely believe any good work that you do and you are dedicated to is God's work." Yvonne Walker-Taylor, a life-long member of the A.M.E. church, attributes her success and tenacity to the church and to her father, an A.M.E. bishop. She thinks her strong spiritual A.M.E. background has given her "that impetus and added confidence in self."

John Daniels agreed with Walker-Taylor. That is his reason for maintaining a dual affiliation with a white Unitarian church on the West Coast and the A.M.E. church of his childhood in the Midwest. He became a member of a Unitarian church "because the belief system was close" to his own. Yet, he maintains his alliance with the black church. He said, "It had a major influence on my early development. . . . I don't want to conflict with my mother, my brothers, and sisters who are A.M.E. I feel very much at home in black churches."

So does John Lamont, a theoretical physicist, who, like John Daniels, maintains his black church membership in his Southern hometown. He also attends
a mixed church in his West Coast community. As a young adult, he explored
many faiths, including the Baptist, Catholic, Episcopal, and Methodist. But as
an adult, he realized that his Southern family church was "used surreptitiously
as a school where family members learned to read during slavery years, while
white people thought it was used for church." As a young adult going through
an intellectual odyssey, he said, "I began to think of myself as a member of my
forefathers' church, the little colonial church in the rolling hills." He started to
identify with this concept of family religion. "What I was looking for was just
right in my family."

Twelve percent of the Talented One Hundred, like John Daniels and John
Lamont, attend a predominantly white or mixed church in their present communities. Sometimes, black people attend predominantly white churches because there is no black church in their community or no black church of their
religious preference. Both a decline in overall affiliation with church denominations and changes in denominations were prevalent among the Talented One
Hundred.

Those individuals who grew up as members of the Baptist or A.M.E. denominations had the greatest decline in membership. The former declined
from 49 percent to 37 percent; the latter from 22 percent to 16 percent. The
Presbyterian denomination gained the largest number of converts, from 3 percent who had religious origins in this denomination to 8 percent of individuals
who presently are members. The change in religious orientation may account
for a significant drop in church attendance and membership. Seventeen percent of the Talented One Hundred claimed they had no church affiliation at the
time of the interviews, as opposed to less than 5 percent while growing up. Others said they were members, but attended infrequently or not at all. Teresa
Hale, who lives in a predominantly white community and seldom attends
church, explained how her religious orientation evolved.

I grew up in a hell and brimstone religious atmosphere where there could be no
joyous living. God was fearsome, awesome, and all-judgmental. My baptism was
largely motivated by fear of hell and fear of God—not from the love of God. Once
on my own, I left the church. It had never been a true resource for me. However,
I paid a high cost for this separation. I was plagued by fear of impending doom,
loss of soul, extended burning in hell, and separation from my family and loved
ones. At times there were transitional value changes—agnosticism and attempts to
stand wholly on my own two feet. At this point, my spiritual development is a high
priority. I no longer see God as a white father in Heaven. Growing up in the racially
segregated South with a tradition of white supremacy, getting those little Sunday
school cards picturing Jesus (who was white in terms of my Louisiana reality) and
understanding God as exacting, watchful, and all-judgmental was somehow alien-
ating to me. I never felt that I was a real member of this family. I never felt "saved."

I now realize I want and need a spirituality that speaks to day-to-day living rather than a focus on the hereafter. I am presently much attracted to Eastern doctrines, especially Buddhism, as well as Christian teachings that deal with living and coping with daily life. I am also much sustained by many of the hymns and gospel songs recalled from my early Christian affiliation. Now, I pray a lot, seeking Christian fellowship with others.

I am contemplating joining a black Baptist church, but am somewhat concerned about the inherent petty politics as well as the church covenant that forbids the use of alcohol, even though I drink very sparingly. It is mainly a matter of principle. In any case, I feel that I am deeply religious. God is the major force ultimately.

While some of the Talented One Hundred have left the church because of changes in their religious orientation (e.g., the service was too emotional and anti-intellectual or too concerned with spiritual fulfillment at the expense of social and political empowerment), others, like Teresa Hale, continue to maintain strong spiritual beliefs. Now in their mid-fifties, they are seeking religious affiliations, because they feel the need for a spiritual resource and because they have a better understanding of the role of the black church. Moreover, having rejected their traditional faiths, they are now reevaluating their importance politically and as a foundation for their children's ethical and moral growth. They want to provide their children with an identity and a moral and social support system that is unavailable in their predominantly white world.

Jonathan Mobutu, forty years old, exemplifies the return of the black elite to the church. He said that after twenty-three years, "this is the first time I have actively participated in church. It happened because of a better understanding of the roles played by the black church. I am also concerned about the socialization of my children." He is now a trustee in a new black church started in his predominantly white town. The church is affiliated with both the Baptist and the Methodist denominations.

Jonathan Mobutu grew up in the Baptist church in a large inner city. At eight years old, he was a junior deacon. He attended church on a regular basis until he was about fifteen. Though his estrangement from the church started when he was eleven years old, he was forced to attend. At fifteen, he left the church, "dissatisfied with its beliefs, doctrines, and values." He maintained that even prior to the emergence of his Afrocentric consciousness, he was uncomfortable with a white Jesus. Since he did not understand the role of the black minister and the church in African American society, he felt alienated. "I didn't understand the role of the minister until I undertook Afro American studies. The minister is a spokesperson for his congregation and a buffer for the white community and unemployment. The church had to provide spiritual rejuvenation in order for blacks to get through another week of racism or through other problems." Being an inquisitive young man, he didn't think the "minister was bringing a level of intellectual discussion to the sermon. . . . There were questions I would ask and the minister could not provide appropriate answers. I thought I was smarter than he was; I wasn't getting what I wanted." Mobutu was also un-comfortable with his "uneducated minister," who used phrases like "more bet-ter" and would mispronounce words such as Job, saying *job* as in work instead of *Job* as in the Bible. . . . "I am no longer embarrassed by my childhood min-ister. Having studied black religion, I can appreciate both him and the church," said Mobutu.

During his twenty-three-year break with the church, Mobutu continued to search for a spiritual base. He left home to attend a white college, and there were no nearby black churches. He attended a white church one Sunday, but, he said, "the service was so different that it alienated me. It was a Baptist church, but the emotions, the feelings, and the call and response dimensions of the service were not there. So it projected nothing of the black experience and the church with which I was familiar." After his marriage, he occasionally at-tended the Catholic church to which his wife belonged, but he could not "buy the theological presupposition." He therefore played the albums of Malcolm X, claiming "that was my religion." Mobutu continued to explore different philo-sophical and religious orientations—Islam, the philosophy of Ghandi, Eastern philosophies, and African ideology and traditional religions. "These religious and philosophical inquiries laid the foundation for exploring the spiritual di-mension of my personality," Mobutu said. His spirituality evolved more, he stated, "when I started to appreciate and understand better some Eastern philosophies about how life can be intertwined and how life paths can connect for specific reasons."

In blending diverse philosophical and religious orientations, Mobutu has ac-quired a measure of inner peace. Unlike the "hell, fire, and brimstone" church of his youth, his present church is Afrocentric and its minister a Pan-Africanist. In his sermons, he emphasizes human liberation and black liberation. The min-ister is actively involved in the South African movement, including leading protests. At last, Mobutu has found a comfortable shelter in which to retreat from the oppressive storms, a sanctuary where he can be comforted and chal-lenged.

However, Mobutu is concerned about his children, who live in a predomi-nantly white neighborhood, because they have not found a sanctuary where they can be comforted. Like Mobutu, others among the Talented One Hun-dred who live in white communities are also concerned about their children and the impact of social isolation on their identity in the community, the school, and the social sphere.

BLACK CHILDREN IN WHITE COMMUNITIES

The world of the Talented One Hundred differs significantly from that of their parents and their children. In general, their parents had minimal or no contact with whites in an egalitarian environment. On the other hand, their children have greater contact with diverse groups. The degree of assimilation increases with each generation. Robert Woodson, fifty years old, discussed his parents', his own, and his children's interactions with whites and how the three generations differ. This pattern is typical of many families who live in racially mixed or white communities.

> I guess my mother never had to adapt. [His father died when he was nine.] They just worked for white folks and they went their way and did their work and came back to the black community. White people were never discussed in the family, in the neighborhood, or in the black community. Race was never talked about. They listened to Joe Louis [the boxer] on the radio and celebrated the victories of Roy Campanella [the baseball player].

They accepted the values of the black community. Woodson agrees with the "values and perspectives" of his parents. But he also differs from them, claiming, "I have to interact in a much larger way with the white society. My interaction is going from home out there and coming back. I pretty much have the same social milieu of my parents inside. The definition of my social life is all-black."

On the other hand, Woodson's children have "whites as playmates. You do what you have to do in your environment. If the only kids your age are white, then you play with those kids." Yet he admitted that "even though the kids play, the families are not as close as they would be in an all-black community. We are cordial to one another, but we very seldom visit back and forth, except that the black families do. My children go to a black church and interact with other black families. We have our own black enclave in suburbia." Woodson's neighborhood is one-fourth black. In greater numbers, middle-class black children will be born in predominantly white settings; they will live, work, and die in these settings.

Elam Coke, a dentist in his early forties, thinks it is good that blacks are mixing more with whites. He feels "it helps people think in terms of individuals rather than black-white." Timothy Brownlee, a public official, concurs that integration has its virtues. While his integrated experience has made him cautious, it has prepared him to "deal with people on a one-to-one basis and you get to know them well. . . . Blacks and whites in segregated settings have a distorted view of black folks and white folks," and racially mixed environments seem to lessen this perception.

Jack B. Lane also likes the idea that his son has the "freedom to choose" from a predominantly black, a racially mixed, or a predominantly white setting. Yet he wants to shape that preference by the type of neighborhood he chooses. For himself, Jack would prefer a black neighborhood, but he does not have a preference for a workplace setting. He would have liked a mixed educational setting for himself, feeling it would have prepared him to "cope to live and serve in a mixed environment." Jack feels that if he had gone to a racially mixed school, he would be "in a better position to understand the makeup and mode of the majority population." But, on the other hand, he is not so sure, saying, "I would not be who I am and what I am if I had attended a mixed school. I am what I am because, to a large degree, I came through an all-black school. Because of the situation of segregation, it made me tougher." In his early days in the civil rights movement, he stated, "I wouldn't say no. I wouldn't say yes. I wouldn't give in. The guards said they were going to arrest me; they would arrest me. I would come back the next day. . . . I wouldn't have the appreciation for black history or wouldn't be collecting black books if I had grown up in a mixed setting." Increasingly, with global communication, Jack feels he must prepare his child to adapt to a world that is different from that of his youth. But he is concerned that more cultural and structural assimilation will be at the expense of his son's cultural heritage. "It is important for black children to know something of their past. When children forget their past, they don't seem to be anchored. They live between two worlds and sometimes three worlds." Jack has "seen young people get away from the black world. They become marginal people. It is very important for all of us, particularly a young child, to have something to lean on."

When black children do not have "something to lean on," such as when they are not securely grounded in their cultural heritage, an identity crisis is likely. Mobutu said his oldest daughter "got messed up in terms of trying to deal with her identity. It was a very painful process, but she came through it." His daughter was reared in an all-white environment, and she identified with her "classmates and their families, and not with her own." But when it came time for dating, her white girlfriends "didn't worry about her." Since she, like her father, attached herself strongly to people, she was "devastated by her friends." He had to seek counseling for his daughter. Mobutu said the white counselor wanted to ground the problem in a family crisis, rather than understanding the impact of racism on her. As his daughter became more Afrocentric in her perspective, she developed an organization to help other black children to cope.

The literature supports the view that a racially homogeneous environment appears to have positive effects on the self-esteem and the group and personal identity of black children. Frank Russo, a forty-three-year-old public health administrator, did not need any studies to confirm his conviction that "children in predominantly white settings have a tendency to place more value on not being black." He related the following incident about his three-year-old son.

When I wanted to buy my son a black male doll, he became very adamant about not having one. His home is in a white community. He attends nursery school in a white community, and his teachers are white. The black male people he sees in the environment are not on the same level as whites. I am sure there are some intangible things that went on in my three-year-old, but the bottom line is that he was adamant about not having a black doll. My wife, who is fair-skinned, said to him, "Daddy is black. Don't you love Daddy?" It was almost as though he went into a still pause, as if he were thinking. It means even at that age level, there is some unconscious programming going on in that environment.

Tefe Fusi, an African, is aware of the negative "unconscious programming" of his children in this country. The children in his predominantly white community refer to his children as "black African potatoes" (African American children also call his children names). When they come home crying, Fusi tells them, "You have to understand that you are in this society and you are black." Tefe Fusi sends his children to his African country every two or three years in the summer. "It gives them a positive self-image and reinforces their Africanness."

Many of the Talented One Hundred were ambivalent about the impact of a predominantly white setting on their children, recalling the impact it had on them. Mayor Johnny Longtree, sixty-five, and Judge Jeannette Gear, in her late thirties, feel that being in a predominantly white environment affected their personalities. "It warped my personality, making me introverted. It's not natural for a man or woman to want to be alone. Even today I don't like a lot of people around me. I was alone during most of my years of growing up in a small white community," remarked Longtree.

Whether the Talented One Hundred grew up in black, racially mixed, or white settings, they understand that racism is persistent. Unlike Tefe Fusi, who can send his children back to Africa, they have no place to go to reinforce their African American heritage. Hence, most parents find it necessary to inculcate in their children "race pride" and the "race lesson." On the one hand, they identify imposed limitations because of race, and on the other hand, they encourage unlimited aspirations and being equal as an American. Often, the young offspring of the Talented One Hundred have encountered limited experiences with racism in their predominantly white setting. Yet, the parents feel they should prepare their children for a larger society that may not be as accepting of them.

Cassie Cooper, for instance, likes the idea of her child living in a mixed setting and sees advantages in it. "I was making an observation recently when she attended a birthday party as the only black child. She was quite comfortable and happy, seemingly unaware of her blackness. I think there is something to be said for the positive side that race is not a factor. At her age, had I been the only black child at the party, I would have been most uncomfortable." But Cassie also feels uneasy about her child's assimilation.

She does not want her child to "lose sight entirely that she is black," because her race will be a reality in this society. "No matter how stable the community and educational situation you grow up in, you are going to have to deal with problems of a racial nature, and you can't get around that. I want her to understand the history of black Americans and what they have been through. I want her to understand the situation her dad and I have been through and how the situation has improved, but to understand why that is. Even though it has improved, it is not what I would like it to be," said Cassie.

Dira Ridley, like Cassie Cooper, said her daughter is also further along in race relations. "I am there intellectually," Dira said. However, her daughter "doesn't see black as different from white, and that is good. . . . In junior high and elementary school, people tend to look at factors other than color. But I tell her that in the twelfth grade when people are competing for the National Merit Scholarship, it might be different. If I tell her about race, it will not be an abnormal data point." Dira's daughter has only one black among her circle of friends. Her interaction with other black children is limited, because her black community is small, with an older population. A top-ranking student in her predominantly white school, she does not interact with the blacks who are in lower tracks (toward whom she harbors some negative feelings because of their boisterous behavior). However, Dira thinks her daughter's views will "broaden about blacks when she meets more middle-class blacks with attitudes like middle-class whites."

In fact, where black children have limited contact with other blacks, they have a sense of discomfort in their presence, particularly with lower-income blacks. This problem may be accentuated if the child is an offspring of an interracial union. Pat Robinson noticed that his son had some racial identification problems when he was about thirteen years old. "He started acting really strange after the busing of black kids to his white junior high school. The tough black kids were doing a number on him, taunting, 'Are you with us or against us? Are you white or black? Who are you with?'"

Jeffrey Falcon, Kevin Poston, and Regina Moon are children of interracial unions, and they have asked those questions many times of themselves.[19] They have walked between two worlds, sometimes feeling they belong to neither. While they were growing up, blacks called them "halfbreed," "honky," "spic," and "zebra." Whites just called them "niggers." Whatever racial identity they have personally assumed, they have been frequently reminded that they are seen as black by the larger society.

Jeffrey, a very fair-skinned, twenty-one-year-old junior at a predominantly black college and the offspring of an Italian mother and a black father, grew up in a racially mixed neighborhood (65 percent black, 35 percent white) in a small Midwestern city. He came to grips with his identity very early. Said Jeffrey, "I have always felt closer to blacks than whites." His racial identity has solidified since he attended a black college and learned more about black history. While he was growing up, he was acutely aware of the identity crisis in himself and other children of interracial unions. Many of his mixed friends identified more with whites. They wanted also to excel academically. Jeffrey said, "By excelling, they wanted to further distance themselves from their black heritage, thus decreasing their chances of being stigmatized as dumb and inferior by whites."[20] At school activities, when asked to identify relatives, his racially mixed friends would point to white aunts, uncles, and grandparents, wanting to be associated only with them.

Pat Robinson learned from his mother, a domestic, only a month prior to my interview with him in 1987, that his son, then a twenty-six-year-old, had denied his grandmother when he was thirteen years old. While Pat's mother and her grandson were strolling in the park, he saw some white friends nearby. Pat reported that his son started "acting really strange, like he didn't know my mother. He didn't want them to know his grandmother was black." I asked, "When you heard this story thirteen years later, how did you feel?" "I was furious. I don't know what I would have done then. I probably would have cried rather than being furious," said Pat.

Kevin Poston, a twenty-three-year-old senior at a black college and the offspring of a white mother and black father, grew up in a predominantly black neighborhood in the Midwest. He, too, agonized over his identity. He said that one day in elementary school, "I looked at whites and saw that I wasn't that color, so I put down black on my school form." His racial awareness grew after attending a black college and learning of the "oppression of black people. . . . I became angry and my relations with my mother became rocky. I started treating her like other white people. It was very traumatic. I told her things I can't say on this tape. But I can kill myself now for saying them." Kevin has come to terms with his racial identity and mixed heritage.

Regina Moon, a fair-skinned twenty-year-old, on the other hand, seemed to be struggling even harder with her identity than did Kevin or Jeffrey. Her mother is white and her father, black; they are divorced. She grew up in a liberal, racially mixed community in Ohio and attended a black college. She identified herself as mixed and accepts herself as "an individual, identifying in some circumstances with blacks, other times with whites, and sometimes neither." She feels closer to black men and white women than to white men or black women. While growing up she felt that black girls were jealous of her and white men found little interest in her as a dating partner. But Regina feels closer to her black relatives than her white relatives, irrespective of their sex. When her mother and father married, her mother's parents and relatives did not "talk with their daughter until after she divorced her black husband." Regina said she feels like an outsider with her white grandparents and relatives. She has heard them say "nigger" too often. "Once my grandmother told me, 'You are really pretty.' But she said it like a black person couldn't be pretty," said Regina.

Although Regina, Kevin, and Jeffrey have had their racial identity conflicts, they see advantages in their mixed heritage. But Pat Robinson thinks being racially mixed has left some confusion in his son. "He is not scarred, and there are not any heavy psychological problems, but it shows in his dating. He tends to date more white girls. Recently, he has been dating black women," said Pat.

To many black parents, selecting a person of another race signals an identity crisis in their children, even when their dating opportunities might be limited, especially if they live in a predominantly white community. Hence, the issue of interracial dating and marriage is a sensitive one with black parents. This topic surfaced frequently during the interviews. The Talented One Hundred know the likelihood of their children dating interracially is greater than their own, since there is more extensive contact with other ethnic groups. For parents who live in a predominantly white community and who would like their children to date blacks exclusively, it becomes a quagmire. Take Ellen Strawberry, an administrator in a nonprofit agency in the Midwest, as an example. She wants her children to date other blacks, but there are few black teenagers in their predominantly white neighborhood and school. She commented, "If some white person approaches them for a date, they are quick to tell me, 'Mom, you should have thought about that when you placed us in this setting.'" Her son, who recently started to date, boasted to a friend, "I am going to the good life now," by which he meant he had a chance to date white females.

Historian Kufra Akpan has a daughter. When she went to the prom with a white boy, Akpan was upset. "I said to her, 'You couldn't find a black person? You have humiliated everybody and black people everywhere. You are stepping on them and your dad. How would you feel if I dated a white woman?'" He attributed her action to an integrated environment. "I thought she was weird. She's coming around now. She married a black man. The children evolved over a period of time. While living in a black community, they were race conscious. But they became integrationists after we moved into this mixed neighborhood. I think their integrationist mode had to do with their living in an integrated community. They got socialized in spite of me in that white community. My children's friends were uncomfortable with me. I didn't encourage their friendship. They were trying to be human, trying to be racially unconscious, and trying to act like they were growing up in the racial melting pot of America." Yet, he believes that subconsciously they always understood their blackness. "They had a reminder because I was always negative," said Akpan.

Encouraging Afrocentric behavior and identity can prove expensive, especially if there is a limited pool of blacks from which children can select a dating partner. Jonathan Mobutu's daughter and her friend could not find black dates in their high school to take them to the prom; Mobutu had to import their dates from another state, providing for their transportation and other expenses. His daughter is particularly interested in attending a black college after this and other experiences in the white community.

Diane Earlinger's children attend a predominantly white school, but she makes it clear to her children "that the only thing they are to bring from this environment is reading, writing, and arithmetic. I don't expect them to bring home a white girl, and I certainly don't expect them to bring home a white value system."

The Talented One Hundred who reside in predominantly white communities are particularly sensitive to the importance of imparting the race lesson to their children, who often identify themselves as being "only American" and who sometimes resist this lesson.

Said John Hubbard, echoing the feeling of other parents among the Talented One Hundred, "Strangely enough, I think my children are happy with black-white relations. They think I talk too much about blackness and point out too much discrimination. When I look at television, I point out the subtle racist messages that come across. I point out racism in advertisements and comic books. I point out all the incidences of institutional racism. They acknowledge it exists." But his children say, "It is not important, Dad, not to us." "They want to be accepted by their white friends," said John.

John and his wife are very race conscious, but his children, admitted John, "see us as going too far. They feel we overplay the issue of discrimination in this society, mainly because they haven't seen it on the personal level as we did. My wife's father's barn was burned down by some jealous whites. She has seen what hostility can do when directed toward blacks. Our children haven't experienced discrimination firsthand. They think everybody is equal, and we're all the same." John and his wife raised their children in the teachings of the Baha'i faith, which advocates that everyone is like "waves of the sea, leaves of one tree, and flowers of one garden. . . . Race doesn't make a difference in one's worthiness in the sight of God and in the sight of each other. We've taught them that and they've taken it to heart." While they stress the universality of humankind, they also impart another message. Though universal human acceptance is a part of the Baha'i faith, "the larger society still sees [blacks] as second-class citizens, and their options are going to be limited based on their race. I have told my children and shown them about racism, but they don't quite believe it or accept it yet." John's children have mostly white friends, and John is concerned about their lack of contact with other blacks and is considering moving to a black community. He feels his all-white community has contributed to an identity crisis and psychological problems in his youngest daughter; she has been involved in shoplifting.

The conflicted dual message in the socialization process is viewed, nevertheless, as an important adaptive strategy. But it is sometimes cumbersome to impart this dual message of survival. Marla Robinson, whose teenage son lives and attends school in a white neighborhood, said,

> I am seeing my child as not willing to be accepting of what you have to do to survive. My child is unwilling to bite his tongue, and it is unfortunate that he has to do it. I tell him in the real world, it is a game, and you have to learn how to play it. It goes against my grain, and it annoys me that I have to talk like this, but in reality it is true. I would not be a good parent if I didn't tell my son those people he will be dealing with see him as black first, and I don't want my son to go out there and think he will be equal to them from their perspective. I want him to feel he is better than the element he is dealing with, but he is not a free spirit in America. He should work toward being that, but in the interim, he has to survive and learn how to deal with them, but not give up everything.

Diane Earlinger thinks today's young people feel entitled to education and jobs. "If that is not turned around about the time these children are twenty to twenty-five, they aren't going to do as well as they did in the 1960s. These kids aren't going to take it. There is a built-in inherent right that they expect with their generation. I am very concerned about my kids."

Some black elite feel that this sense of entitlement stems from parents' failure to discuss racism with their children. Many parents, having escaped poverty, feel embarrassed by their negative, overt racial experiences prior to the civil rights movement. They never confront the issue of racism with their children or discuss their social hardships, thus contributing to their children's lack of social consciousness. Still others believe that the black elite have become "so preoccupied with materialism and being white, they fail to pass on our noble heritage." Lacking a sense of black struggle and not feeling as eager for success as their parents, they are therefore not as motivated to achieve or work as hard. The black elite are concerned that the young blacks—the children of the elite—who have greater resources and privileges, will not pass on the wealth, knowledge, and skills to their children or to the black community, this society, and the world.

The black elite's children must be aware that to be black and to work toward being a "free spirit in America" means a continuous struggle to fight oppression and to establish one's identity. It is essential for parents to transmit the "race lessons" and "our noble heritage" as coping mechanisms. In an integrated environment, particularly an educational setting, some parents fear that these race lessons are not being transmitted, resulting in "confusion among young people under twenty and contributing to their lack of sensitivity to the race struggle." Though Frank Russo sees advantages and disadvantages of a diverse setting for educating black children, he thinks students should be in a "setting where they can emphasize their total blackness as opposed to dealing with everybody's value system, since we have a tendency to get lost." His children live and attend school in a white neighborhood.

Benson Robinson Jr., the twenty-four-year-old son of a successful entrepreneur (introduced earlier), agreed with Frank Russo, responding quickly when I asked about his educational experience in an exclusive white private school. "I wish somebody would write a book about the danger of steeping black children in predominantly white settings." He thinks there are "some real dangers in terms of identity and being different." He recalled his first day of school as a first grader in that setting. "I remember the experience like it was yesterday. I was the only black in a class of thirty-five whites. The teacher asked the students to introduce themselves. Since I was so preoccupied with playing, I was the last to stand up. When I stood up and introduced myself, the students and teacher sighed." During the break, "I remember the kids running over to me and rubbing their hands through my hair. . . . Am I that different from the rest of them to cause this reaction?" he thought. His parents made him feel "good enough" about himself "to ward off the feeling of being different."

Benson remembered feeling uncomfortable about being different in the third or fourth grade. "It was during the time when you begin to notice little girls and valentines with I love you," he said. "I noticed I didn't get as many valentines as other kids, and I was not included in their activities. That was a rather difficult experience for me." But, he noted, the isolation was "offset by my participation in the Jack and Jill," a social club for the children of middle-class blacks. The organization was very important to him because it "reaffirmed that your values are correct and those differences that are so apparent do not really mean anything. The group also reaffirmed the fact that blacks are capable of professionalism and can perform the same as whites. In the white environment, I was just there. The environment addressed their needs, not mine." Yet, he admitted, "the white environment helped me to relax and not pay attention to color barriers all the time." On the other hand, "you were always reminded that they were there." Benson cited the advantage of having equal opportunity in instructional development but noted the disadvantage of not having positive role models and "not having access to one's black cultural heritage."

Suddenly, he shifted again to the emotional impact of his educational experience. "In any society or time period, the worst crime is to be different. I was different. Even though I was different, I spoke the same as whites. I could afford the same toys and better. I enjoyed skiing. The more I think about it, the more I feel someone should address the dangers of being in that environment, where there is no reinforcement." It is a contradictory situation. "Every day was spent in a see-saw way. It gets to be confusing after a while, and that's where the danger lies."

In a 2004 update of black children who are reared in isolated white communities, Brooke Obie, my undergraduate research assistant, supports the conclusion of Benson Robinson Jr. She found in her study, based on in-depth interviews and a survey of one hundred undergraduates at an HBCU (historically black colleges and universities), that black students tended to have a positive self-identity and a negative group identity, which seems to indicate they have internalized racist notions and images of African Americans.

BLACK CHILDREN IN PREDOMINANTLY WHITE SCHOOLS

When Teresa Johnson's daughter performed extremely well on a national mathematics test, Teresa felt particularly proud. She also felt "much pain" when her daughter cried "because she would be in a class with no blacks." She is not in mathematics anymore, since she did not want to be set off from her black peers.

The Talented One Hundred were concerned about the quality of their children's educational environment. Like Teresa Johnson, they were aware of the inherent danger of denigration or negation of the black cultural heritage in white schools. Marla Robinson's sixteen-year-old son, for example, was "kicked out" of his private white high school for challenging his teacher about her lack of knowledge. Chiding her, he said, "I don't believe you are a biology teacher who is teaching a unit on blood and you don't know Charles Drew, the black scientist, who discovered blood plasma!"

At least 79 percent of the Talented One Hundred reinforced the importance of black history and culture in their interactions with their children. In addition, 78 percent said they keep in contact with relatives who live in primarily black communities to reinforce a positive group and personal identity in their children. The school, one of the important agencies of socialization, can have a powerful impact on children. It mirrors the societal values. Education is seen as an avenue of upward mobility and "the great leveler," as Michael Lomax believes, but it also preserves the status quo, directly and indirectly reinforcing discrimination toward and stereotypes about blacks in the classrooms and in the curriculum.

Warner Babbitt, a journalist, has three children in an upper-class, predominantly white public school. "White folks who are accustomed to black people not achieving believe, whether they admit it or not (as nice as they are, when they smile in your face and say all the things they are supposed to say), that black folks are inherently inferior. It doesn't matter about your background. They know black middle-class children are different from black lower-class children, but still, deep down inside, they really believe they are inferior." His thirteen-year-old daughter is the only black in a program for gifted students. But, he said, "she constantly runs into the problem, more than the white kids, that she couldn't have written a particular essay, because blacks don't write that well. She is treated as special, like she is some kind of affirmative action quota, although she scored in the 99 percentile on the SAT. They can't take that away from her. We have to explain to the teachers that she is where she is because she works hard and is intelligent. Whites are accustomed to teaching bright white kids, but not bright black kids who want to excel. However, if black kids have parents who will kick the school's ass, they also get taught."

In the twenty-first century, black children are still being called names like "nigger," "pickaninny," and "chocolate mousse" by whites. They have been discouraged from taking mathematics, though their parents are doctors and scientists. Some white teachers feel black children aren't capable of handling it. Marla Robinson, who pays five thousand dollars a year to send her articulate, bright son to his white private school, said his white teachers asked him "if his parents spoke ghetto English or regular English." Black children have also been discriminated against by classmates with the tacit approval of teachers. Michael Lomax's daughter's experience clearly illustrates this point. He said, "My daughter attends a very exclusive private school, where there is a waiting list. It has an open-class system, not structured. Even without that structured element that is associated with private schools, there is a race and class structure in the school." One day, his daughter came home very upset, saying, "'[So-and-so] is having a party at school and I am not invited.' I said, 'Who is [so-and-so]?' And she said, 'A little white girl.' I said, 'Who is invited?' And she said, 'Everybody except me and [she named a little girl who is an East Indian].' The only two not invited were girls of color. I was mad. I had a long talk with her and indicated, 'There is a lesson you are going to have to contend with because wherever you go, there are going to be people who treat you badly or hurt you because of the color of your skin.'"

Lomax wanted to make certain that invitations excluding children of color would never be sent out through the school's mail. "I am going to be really mad if you do that again. I am going to scream and yell," said Lomax to school officials. He observed that "all little black girls, when they reached puberty level, leave this school."

For Lomax and his daughter, the experience wound up being a creative learning experience. "I helped to negotiate and nurture my child through a difficult racial experience, but one which did not traumatize her," said Lomax. When parents don't deal with it, "it is one of those layers of unhealed wounds for that child, because she will then say, 'I didn't get invited to the party because I am not worthy. I am unworthy because I am black.' You can't allow her to run the risk of feeling something is wrong with her because she is black. As long as it is an integrated environment, people are going to assault you because you are black. What you have to understand is it is their problem, not yours. I told her, 'No one is ever to try and restrict you or hurt you. You must stand up and fight back.'" His daughter encouraged her schoolmates to talk about the experience and "she and all the girls cried. She got mad. Her classmates responded, but they had to deal with their mommies who told them not to invite [the two girls] in the first place."

Lomax noticed that "even though the kids who are in the second generation after integration are taking it for granted, it is not satisfying emotionally to them. . . . My daughter has said to me, 'I want to go to a public school, not private. I want to go to a public school where there are more black people than this one.' It means she won't ever be enchained by the myth that it was something that she missed and she was excluded from it. She saw it, looked at it, found it unsatisfying, and sought something else." In assisting his daughter to negotiate race relations, Lomax views his role "not as an authoritarian parent, but an authority, like a reference book. You can go to that authority and get some information that can be helpful."

More parents have also begun to look at integration, and finding it unsatisfactory, they have begun to check their "reference book" about whether to send their children to white schools. Like Lomax, their "reference book" has added new data, causing them to rethink the integrationist hypothesis. Laura Price, a gynecologist, said, "My children were exposed to a predominantly white educational system very early. Many times I thought maybe I pushed them into it too early. Oftentimes, they were unhappy and wanted to change schools. Some emotional disturbances did occur. I was so set on offering the best academically successful environment." Although her children are grounded in the black church and the community, their white educational experience left a legacy of unhappiness. Laura went to a predominantly white medical school, but she believes that because she had the "highest positive exposure to blackness" during her formative years, she was able to cope more successfully. "It was so entrenched in my brain, heart, and soul that black is great that I was able to cope with integration better than my children," said Laura.

More parents, like Laura Price, have begun to evaluate the quality of education in a predominantly black versus a white setting. During the sixties, there was a strong belief that integration offered the best academically successful environment. The Talented One Hundred, who came of age or who were young adults during the civil rights movement, are now questioning the negative impact of integration on their children (though 36 percent said the ideal educational setting for their children is a racially mixed one). Sixteen percent would like their children to be educated in a black school at certain periods in their lives and to attend a predominantly white or mixed school at other points in their educational cycles, usually graduate school. Many parents expressed interest in their children attending a black college. Jacqueline Fleming's *Blacks in College* supports the notion that the black college is more nurturing; blacks do better academically in black colleges than in white colleges and universities, and their graduation rate is higher.[21] (I might add that 34 percent of the Talented One Hundred preferred a black educational setting from kindergarten through college for their children.)

The Talented One Hundred who preferred a black or a racially mixed educational setting at different stages of their own and their children's lives seem to look nostalgically on the era of segregation. While pointing out its negative aspects, they were quick to note the positive ones. Priscilla King and Jack B. Lane echoed the sentiments of many individuals when they described the advantages of the segregated system in the South. Said Priscilla, who is in her early fifties, "I am very glad I was raised in the South and had black teachers. The teachers encouraged your success and encouraged you to feel good about yourself. There was a sense of black pride. We sang the Negro National Anthem and did things relevant to black people. The teachers were involved with you, not only at school, but also outside the classroom. So I never felt inferior to anybody."

Jack B. Lane also felt his black teachers had a positive influence on him at a very early age.

> Most of my teachers would come from out of town. They would spend the week in the community, and then would go back to town. I guess for the first time you saw people with an education. They paid attention to us. They encouraged us. During Negro History Week, we had to cut out pictures from black publications—*Jet*,

Ebony, *Pittsburgh Courier*, and the *Afro American*—of famous black individuals, like Booker T. Washington, Ralph Bunche, George Washington Carver, Marian Anderson, or Willie Mays. The act of participating in Negro History Week, putting together a scrapbook, and having the teacher say, "You can be like these individuals," inspired me. If these people could do it, then you can make a contribution.

When I asked the Talented One Hundred who were their greatest influences outside the family, the largest number of them indicated their teachers. It is interesting to note that white teachers had little or no positive impact except in the case of a few persons who attended predominantly white schools or had mostly white teachers. One of these exceptions was Tony Michaels, the only black student in his class, whose white teacher told him she expected him to be "better than the rest" of the students. Jonathan Mobutu's white second-grade teacher told him he could grow up to be president. And Sheridan Williams remembers her white teachers were supportive. But for the most part this pattern did not prevail.

Since the number of black teachers is declining significantly and the population of all minorities is rising, it is important to ponder the implications for black students. According to a 1987 survey by the National Education Association, only 6.9 percent of the country's public school teachers are black. By the turn of the century, minorities may make up more than 40 percent of the public school enrollment, while composing less than 5 percent of the teachers.[22]

David Benton, a forty-seven-year-old artist, never had a black teacher in school. "Knowing what I know now and having gone through such an experience, I would opt for a black institution because of the added positive role models." He is thoroughly amazed that he has come through such an experience and "has a wholesome attitude about blackness."

Looking at the impact of integration and the declining number of black teachers, Teresa Stanfield, a college administrator, lamented, "When we had a community in which black adults could band together and protect our youngsters from the psychological effects of racism, there were many good things about it. Now we are in a situation where that can't be. I don't know what is going on in public schools. I think [black students] have a sense of inferiority. They do not feel good about themselves, even though they may show bravado."

The Talented One Hundred are rethinking the educational process and are beginning to encourage their children to attend black colleges. Walden Wilmington, a geneticist, thinks it is important for his thirteen-year-old daughter to attend a black college to reinforce her cultural heritage. Students can also develop leadership qualities in black colleges. "There is no affirmative action program. A black college is affirmative. You can do anything you want," asserted Tony Michaels. Leo Aramis equated the black university with the church. "The black university is a place like a black church. Black folk have an opportunity to be somebody. You might have been a janitor all week long, but on Sundays you were a deacon in the church. You might have cleaned floors all day long, but you might be a missionary in the church. It is good for your self-esteem and community. This sense of community needs to be gained before you get out there in the marketplace." Perhaps the sense of community gained while attending a black college is the reason why Thomas B. Thomas, in his late thirties, will make a deal with his children when they are ready for college. "I have a deal. If they go to my black alma mater, they will have a free ride. If they go to another black school, they will be provided with 50 percent of their tuition. And if they go to Harvard, they will not receive anything."

Most individuals I interviewed were not as adamant as Thomas, who had only black teachers in a predominantly black school in Cleveland. He is strongly in favor of black colleges.

> When I arrived on campus, it was the first time I had seen any black people in such prominent positions. The only blacks I had seen who wore suits during the day were one black lawyer and one black doctor in town. When I went to a black college, I saw this group of people who were dressed up when they went to work. And they were teaching people. . . . I had never been in that atmosphere. It was a unique experience, because for the first time, I saw how people were walking around and talking about how great it was to be black. I had never been around a group of people that felt so good about themselves and what they were able to do. And most importantly, they were interested in explaining what atrocities had been committed on blacks. We met some very powerful people on the campus, people who knew so much about being black in this country and what we have to do to improve our plight.

Prior to entering a black college, Thomas B. Thomas felt that "if you put black folks and white folks together, whites will outscore blacks." He also believed "black always meant bad. Black cat meant seven years of bad luck, and bad guys wore black hats. I knew everything good was white and everything bad was black." His parents did not challenge this assumption. Having grown up in the oppressed rural South in the thirties, they, too, were "children of bondage."

Despite the fact that many of the Talented One Hundred are encouraging their children to attend black colleges, others continue to hold negative perceptions of black schools, even when they graduated from black colleges and universities and found the experience nurturing. When Judge Roscoe Champion, speaking before the Jack and Jill, an organization for children of professional blacks, asked how many children were going to college, all raised their hands. When he asked how many had any black schools under consideration, no one raised a hand. He asked parents of the children to stand if they had attended an all-black school. "All the parents had gone to black schools, and their children did not have any black schools under consideration. The kids sensed something was wrong with that. The kids said, 'Black people who went to black schools were not successful,' even though two mayors had just spoken before them and now a judge. The kids felt bad. Their parents came up to apologize, not knowing they had done that to their children." He thinks "most blacks who went to all-black schools do not attribute their success to them. They say they made it in spite of the black school. They say, 'I overcame an inferior education and made it.' We don't feel a sense of obligation to convey to our children that they can get a quality education. Instead, we want to convey to them we overcame a poor education, so the children begin to look at white schools. Black education is regarded as inferior. We are not grateful. When you finish a black college, it is like you are saying, 'I went because I didn't have the opportunity, but if I had a chance, I would have gone to another school.'"

Opponents of black colleges, Jacqueline Fleming noted, argue that "the poorer resources of black colleges intellectually undermine the students attending them. Segregated institutions are anachronisms in contemporary American society and have outlived their usefulness." The proponents of black colleges, however, point out that these colleges are "places where Black students can learn without the constraints of minority status or the tension engendered by the hostile undercurrent in Black/White interactions."[23] Jacqueline Fleming's research supports the strengths of the black college in educating black youths and the historical role it has played in producing black leaders.

Another concern surfaced in my talks with the Talented One Hundred: Which environment better prepares students for coping in a white society? Thirty-six percent and 4 percent, respectively, preferred a mixed environment or predominantly white environment for their children. Overwhelmingly, the major reason was to give them a "competitive edge" in negotiating in a white world. But defenders of black colleges, like Thomas B. Thomas and Kelly Smith, argued that white universities do not provide blacks with the necessary coping skills. Said Thomas,

The people I've met who have gone to white schools (there are exceptions) who have all the credentials and names behind them seem to approach life with their hands out, like "someone owes me something, because I am a graduate of Yale. And I am entitled to all rights and privileges pertaining thereto." So, therefore, when they walk out and say "I am from Yale," they act as if the corporation will fold over and offer them a job. There is a direct correlation between performance and pay. I don't care where you went to school. If you get on the job and you don't perform, you don't stay very long. It's the real world out here and they want something for what they put out. So I've got friends and associates from major universities unemployed because their attitudes are such that "I am entitled to," rather than "give me a chance and I'll make sure that I'll do what I am supposed to. Let me in the door and the job will get done. It has been instilled in me that I have to perform and to be better." You get this at a black school. At the white school, it seems to me that they are trying to avoid you. The majority of black students don't go back to their white class reunions. Who are they trying to reunite with? There is nobody with whom to reunite, except a few who banded together because they had to unite against the numbers. There is value to black colleges and universities.

Kelly Smith agreed with Thomas. She also felt that one's coping skills are different if you grow up in a white environment. She cited examples of two friends who grew up in a white community. One attended Yale as an undergraduate and went to Harvard Law School. And the other attended Harvard as an undergraduate and went to Yale Law School. The former worked for a senator and a major corporation, but when he moved to the South to work, she said, "he was disillusioned. He could not do well in that environment because of discrimination. His coping skills were at a minimum. This guy thought he was just as good and equal as whites, and they were going to deal with him that way." The latter friend was "unemployed for two years," said Kelly, "because he was unable to cope in the real world. He internalized his failures."

Sharon Georgia, a civil rights attorney who has counseled upwardly mobile blacks, observed that blacks who lack a strong racial awareness and coping skills are more likely to internalize acts of racism and corporate politics as personal failures.

> I've heard black clients say "I am just as smart" when they do not get the position. They are psychologically unable to handle it, because some blacks truly believe being black does not matter in the organization.
>
> I find that blacks in white organizations who understand who they are and what it means to be in an organization don't suffer those kinds of consequences. They don't have to see a psychiatrist and psychologist or don't have ulcers. They move with the flow of things. They say, "I know what I am in this organization. I know I am good. I'll play the game and I'll fight to go on." It's people who don't understand who they are that internalize racism, have psychological problems, and end up getting into trouble on the job. The higher you go up in the system, the greater the pressure. If you don't bring some guns to fight that, they'll kill you off, and they will render you impotent by making you dysfunctional.

SUMMARY

Black professionals who live as well as work in predominantly white environs are more likely to become socially isolated from the black community. Since there is continuous discrimination on and off the job, this isolation creates stress. Living in a predominantly white community also disrupts the black professionals' traditional supportive familial, friendship, and organizational ties that could buffer them from stress. To cope with the stressful impact of social isolation and color barriers, the black elite maintain contact with family, friends, and social organizations like the church within the black community.

The perception that as blacks move into the mainstream, their political consciousness becomes more class linked than race linked is not supported by the comments of the persons interviewed. The Talented One Hundred have a strong concern for issues that affect the black masses. They understand that group mobility is bound by the color line and not the class line in America.

The black elite who live in predominantly white settings are concerned about the quality of the educational and social environment of their children. When black children are in predominantly white settings, there is a battle for their hearts and minds. The continuous exposure of children to such Euro-centric values as individualism conflicts with the need for a collective racial consciousness.

NOTES

1. Ken Weber, "Young, Black and Bored," *Providence Sunday Journal Magazine*, April 12, 1987, 6.

2. Laura B. Randolph, "The Whitest State," *Ebony*, Dec. 1987.

3. James Blackwell and Philip Hart, *Cities, Suburbs and Blacks* (Dix Hills, NY: General Hall, 1982).

4. Beverly Tatum, "Life in Isolation: Black Families Living in Predominantly White Communities," PhD dissertation, (University of Michigan, 1984), 225.

5. Robert Hill, *The Strengths of Black Families* (New York: Emerson Hall, 1972).

6. Dimitri B. Shimkin, Gloria Jean Louie, and Dennis A. Frate, "The Black Extended Family: A Basic Rural Institution and a Mechanism of Urban Adaptation," in Dimitri B. Shimkin, Edith M. Shimkin, and Dennis A. Frate, eds., *The Extended Family in Black Societies* (Chicago: Aldine, 1978).

7. Harriette P. McAdoo, "Black Kinships," *Psychology Today*, May 1979, 67. See also Harriette P. McAdoo, ed., *Black Families* (Beverly Hills, CA: Sage, 1981), 103–169.

8. Bebe Moore Campbell, "Black Executives and Corporate Stress," *New York Times Magazine*, Dec. 12, 1982.

9. John P. Fernandez, *Black Managers in White Corporations* (New York: Wiley, 1975), 25.

10. Daniel C. Thompson, *A Black Elite: A Profile of Graduates of UNCF Colleges* (Westport, CT: Greenwood Press, 1986).

11. Lawrence E. Gary, "A Social Profile," in Lawrence Gary, ed., *Black Men* (Beverly Hills, CA: Sage, 1981).

12. Francis Fox Piven and Richard A. Cloward, *Regulating the Poor: The Function of Public Welfare* (New York: Pantheon, 1971).

13. "Facts and Figures," *Black Enterprise*, March 1987, 32.

14. Thompson, *A Black Elite*, 112.

15. Gwen Ifill and Dan Balz, "Middle-Class Blacks Are Down Beat about the Campaign," *Washington Post, National Weekly Edition*, Oct. 3–9, 1988, 6–7.

16. Hill, *Strengths of Black Families*.

17. William D. Watley, *Roots of Resistance: The Nonviolent Ethic of Martin Luther King, Jr.* (Valley Forge, PA: Judson Press, 1985), 29.

18. Benjamin Quarles, *The Negro in the Making of America* (New York: Macmillan, 1964), 162.

19. I conducted personal interviews of children of interracial unions in May 1987. See Maureen T. Reddy, *Crossing the Color Line: Race, Parenting, and Culture* (New

Brunswick, NJ: Rutgers University Press, 1994).

20. Alvin Poussaint, psychiatrist, notes that children of interracial unions are high achievers, as quoted in Lynn Norment, "A Probing Look at Children of Interracial Marriages," *Ebony*, September 1985.

21. Jacqueline Fleming, *Blacks in College* (San Francisco: Jossey-Bass, 1984).

22. Charles Whitaker, "The Disappearing Black Teacher," *Ebony*, Jan. 1989.

23. Fleming, *Blacks in College*, 1–2.

6

GENDER POLITICS: THROUGH THE EYES OF BLACK WOMEN

Yvonne Walker-Taylor reminisced:

In the beginning, I didn't like being a girl. I had discovered at the age of five that people would come into my father's home and would ask, "Is this your only child?" "Yes," he would say, and they would say, "Oh, what a shame! It's not a boy." I heard that so much I began to feel totally inferior.

One day I was sitting under the steps, my favorite spot, waiting for my father to come home. If I got hurt, I began crying when he came down the street to get his sympathy. I was consoling myself when he came up, and he said, "Baby, what are you doing?" I said, "I am trying to kiss my elbow." "Why are you trying to kiss your elbow?" he inquired. "The kids told me if I could kiss my elbow, I could turn into a boy." My father took me on his knee and told me that he loved me just as I was, and I didn't need to change into anything.

When I was old enough to understand, he constantly reinforced and increased the philosophy that "You are a woman; you have brains, so you can do anything you want to do!"

"Never underestimate yourself," said the seventy-one-year-old Walker-Taylor, the first woman president of Wilberforce University, one of the oldest black colleges in the country. At the tender age of five, Walker-Taylor was precocious enough to understand the consequences of sex and gender on her life chances. But, too often, when the impact of racial oppression is examined, black females and males are grouped together, muting these differences despite the fact that each experiences oppression differently.

Since blacks were brought to this country, the black woman has embodied the contradictions of both her gender and her race. In *Women, Race and Class*,

Angela Davis notes that during the nineteenth century, when femininity meant embracing motherhood and being a homemaker, this did not extend to black women. They were "breeders" and "sucklers" for whites. Their offspring could be "sold away like calves from cows." Black women were homemakers, but outside their homes as cooks and servants for whites. They also tilled the soil alongside black men. Black women were not too "'feminine' to work in coal mines, in iron foundries, or to be lumberjacks or ditch-diggers."[1] Thus, while white women were viewed as the "weaker sex," black women needed to be strong to survive the hardships of slavery. As the "weaker sex," white women were desexed, idealized, and placed on a pedestal of purity, while black women were dethroned and sexualized. Black women were, therefore, sexual objects available to white males. In addition to the physical punishment of lashings and mutilations endured by both black men and women, black women were often raped.

Historically, the gender roles and stereotypes of black and white females in the United States have been in opposition. Black women have been portrayed as Aunt Jemima,[2] who is strong, domineering, matriarchal, and sexually uninhibited, while, in contrast, white women have been stereotyped, particularly in the South, as sexually restrained, gentle, and docile. Since there are so many contradictions and myths inherent in the gender role and image of black womanhood, I examine the drama of sexism and racism through the eyes of black women. While I recognize the plight of black manhood in this society, it is not the primary focus of this chapter.

SEXISM AND RACISM

How does one distinguish between racism and sexism? According to Yvonne Walker-Taylor,

It is hard to distinguish between the two. You never know if white men discriminate against you because you are black or because you are a woman. It would be interesting to be a man for a little while to see if it's the same thing. As a category, women are discriminated against. I find there are similarities between the way women are treated, whether black or white. But we have a double jeopardy.

For instance, when I attended my first conference of academic deans, I noticed that the nuns in the room could command attention. They raised their hands and would be recognized. "Sisters, you have something to say?" they [white male deans] would ask. I noticed this particularly if they wore habits. They don't think of the nuns as women; they are desexed, and their opinions are respected.

When I wanted to make a comment, I was overlooked. I was the only black face at the conference. After I had been dealt by for two sessions, I said, "Wait just a minute." I stood up. I have always been outspoken. I said, "Sir! I am completely visible. Of that I am sure, because I am the only black face here. So I know you see me. I want one good reason why you won't recognize me so I can say what I have to say." He said, "I wasn't aware . . ." [She imitated his "hem haw" embarrassed response.] "Well, thank you very much. I may be heard now."

I have fought for everything I got. This is what I meant by double jeopardy. It is a constant fight. You can never relax and say I don't have to fight. A man will not pay you any attention if you don't command and demand attention. I don't mean being a jackass. I mean dealing with it in a respectful and dignified way. One thing that will disarm a man is respect.

Thirty-seven percent of the Talented One Hundred are women. Like Walker-Taylor, "they can never relax," knowing they have to fight on two battlefronts. But they cannot clearly identify the enemy—their race or their sex. Hence, the overwhelming majority of the women of the Talented One Hundred recognize the confluence of both race and sex as salient variables in their professional and social interactions. As Crystal Miller acknowledged, "It is hard to distinguish, because the black woman is in a particular kind of category that carries with it a lot of historical baggage. Her experience in the United States has been unique. I can't separate them. They are intertwined."

Even those, like Teresa Hale, who attempt to distinguish between sexism and racism by looking "at the language, the underlying assumptions and consequences" still conclude "that sometimes the situation is confounded by a combination of both racial and sexual components, making the distinction extremely difficult."

The appointment in the late 1980s of the Reverend Barbara Harris, the first female bishop in the worldwide Anglican communion, illustrates the confluence of sexism and racism. Though her sex appeared more salient in the controversial appointment, much was made of her race. Indeed, they are interactive. Black men and women are still the last to be hired and the first to be fired. They are underrepresented in senior-level positions, particularly black women, who represent, for example, only 1.8 percent of the officials and managers of major corporations, according to the Equal Employment Opportunity Commission. Black men represent 2.7 percent; white women compose 21.1 percent of officials and managers.[3] Even among *Black Enterprise* magazine's "25 Hottest Black Managers" in corporate America in 1988, not one woman was listed. According to the magazine, women made up less than 1 percent of the 125 final candidates. Only one or two of these women headed major divisions and had a direct "impact on the financial status and direction of the company."[4]

Although black women are underrepresented in high-level positions, it would be unfair to ignore or underestimate the changes in their occupational distributions. In 1940, 60 percent of working black women were employed as domestic workers, compared with 11 percent of working white women, who were mostly poor European immigrants. Presently, more than 50 percent of working black females hold white-collar positions, which are primarily clerical.[5] Between 1970 and 1985, the most significant changes took place in the occupational distribution of employed black women. In 1970, for instance, 42 percent of all employed black women worked in service jobs, dropping to 30 percent by 1985. In contrast, technical, sales, and administrative occupations rose from 26 to 38 percent. In 1970, black women represented 12 percent of managers and professionals, compared with 18 percent of white women; in 1985, black women composed 17 percent of managers and professionals, and white women, 24 percent. Between 1980 and 1985, the percentage of black women managers and professionals remained the same, while that of white women managers and professionals increased slightly, by 2 percent.[6]

A *Black Enterprise* survey of its readers indicated that sex and race are important variables in explaining these variations in the percentage of black managers and professionals. While it appears from the survey that blacks are much less affected by sexual discrimination at work now than in the past, most of those who reported such discrimination were black women. Forty-five percent of the women stated they had encountered sexual discrimination, compared with only 15 percent of the men. Also, a larger percentage (57 percent) of women in the poll stated they had encountered racial discrimination. The survey suggests that as both black men and women move up the corporate ladder, they encounter increased resistance and are perceived as posing a greater threat, particularly the black male.[7] The traditional role of the man as the breadwinner has made the black man more of an economic threat to the white man.

John P. Fernandez's study on *Racism and Sexism in Corporate Life* further supports the *Black Enterprise* survey results that black male managers at the highest levels are likely to feel greater obstacles in the workplace.[8] Fernandez's research is illuminating, particularly since he looks at the following groups by race and sex: Asians, blacks, Hispanics, Native Americans, and whites. While each minority group in this country has encountered discrimination, it has differed in kind and degree. The history, skin color, and size of the minority group are salient variables in predicting the treatment of each group by whites. Fernandez believes that the "greater burden of racism appears to have fallen upon the Black race for a number of reasons: the bitter legacy of slavery, its darker color, its larger numbers, and its location throughout the country."[9] Fernandez's study found that blacks are the most critical of discrimination in the workplace, followed by Hispanics, Asians, Native Americans, and whites. With regard to women, black women were the most critical of discrimination in the workplace, followed by white, Hispanic, Native American, and Asian women.[10] Since blacks are at the bottom of the social structure, it is not surprising that they are the most sensitive to inequality in corporate America. In particular, black women are sensitized to racial and sexual discrimination.

Let us look, for example, at the corporate life of Dira Ridley, a PhD research physical chemist in a Fortune 500 consumer products company. Her story of working in corporate America in the late 1980s reveals racism and sexism in the workplace. Dira feels that she is quite competent.

I think I am good, and people say I ought to be section head. But I've heard my manager say in performance appraisals that I work too hard, and I shouldn't work as hard. I should waste more time. It means to go around and talk. They are trying to delay a promotion for a black woman. But I never want it said that I didn't work hard enough.

I am opinionated and would not hesitate to tell anyone exactly what I think. If a white male said it, then, it would be great. It shows leadership. I get back I shouldn't have said that. I am aggressive. Aggressiveness in a man is exactly what they want. Yet they assign me certain projects because I am aggressive and outspoken. On the one hand, it is good for the assignment, but on the other hand, it is bad because I am a woman. A white woman was also told not to work as hard and burn herself out on a project she had initiated, because they would have to promote two women. They want to delay my promotion.

Though Dira Ridley's primary task is to unravel the scientific mystery of how certain compounds and elements react in the laboratory, she is also forced to unravel the mystery of the social elements of racism and sexism operating in the world of work. Said Dira,

I have individuals who report to me and who also report to white males, and their response in getting things to me is slower than getting things to the white males. I grant that our styles are different. It is tough when I look at things with a single variable faction to try to assess whether something is due [to my being] black, especially as a female. My guts tell me it is because I am black. White women have moved quite well in this company to the same degree as white males or even black males—all more than black women. White women have more project responsibilities and people responsibilities than black women. To me, it implies that in order for black women to be hired, they have to be better than white women and men. That is a fact. The reason we have not advanced is due to color.

We wanted to know why black women were not moving up the corporate structure and why their attrition rate was higher than other groups. We now have in place an accountability program that addresses the kind of training given to black women and how they are progressing. It has become a model, not just for developing black women, but people. And it has been implemented throughout the company. We've helped a number of black women to be promoted.

Despite some progress made by black women in her company, Dira thinks the lack of upward mobility is also influenced by a comfort factor.

They don't ask black women what kind of career they would like, and what kinds of support they need to develop their careers. This comfort factor was not in place with white males to think that a black woman would want anything but a job at an entry level. With the new program we initiated, they are becoming sensitized, and hopefully, they can see the black woman not as a liability, but as a help to them, and their careers will also progress.

Meanwhile, they are less likely to take you under their arm to be mentored, and that's what you need. They have great people who work in this company. Anybody who works with this company can be a CEO. Whites were in the top 10 percent of their classes; blacks were also in the top 10 percent of their classes. The people who succeed in this corporation are the ones who take an interest in certain people. White males tend to mentor white males, and they tend to act like them. In the 1970s, black males also organized in this company, and since it is consumer product oriented, the company cannot afford adverse publicity. Hence, it was a politically astute decision to advance black males and reward whites for mentoring them as well as white women, who are moving along with the women's movement. So all of these things have permitted everyone to advance, except black women. Black men are more likely to have rapport with white men. They are more predominant in management positions than black women. This company is conservative. Hence, if a black man plays tennis with a white man, there is no question about that. If a black woman does the same, the connotations are enormous for the black woman. We need to create a corporate environment where black women can be mentored without the other connotations attached.

One of the "other connotations attached" to the entry of black women into this new egalitarian setting is the notion of white males' sexual attraction to the black female because of the image of her unrestrained sexuality. This was the reason why Teresa Johnson, whose interest is black women's studies, became so concerned about the plight of black women. She remarked,

One of the things that was so amazing to me as a black woman is the sense that somehow we are close to being whores. For this reason, I got interested in black women. The ocean is important to me, so in college, I used to walk near the lake, and inevitably, I got these sexual calls from white men. I was sixteen years old, with pigtails. I can't remember the exact names I was called, but they were names that had to do with whores and sluts by white males. I was out there as a sexual creature in a way I knew young white girls were not. That was something I also felt consistently even when I was in graduate school in New York at Columbia. I would walk into a hotel to rest with my suit and the whole thing and would get that look. "Hey girl, what you're doing?" It was perfectly clear I wasn't a prostitute. That happened then and it is still happening now. I went to a conference last year, and for the entire three days, there were white men who assumed I was a street walker or a call girl.

Whether the black woman is in the professional or social arena, this image prevails. Dira Ridley, along with other professional black women in her organization, is working to shatter this perception as well as others through organizing. In working with senior executives in organizations, she said, "we are hoping to make it profitable to mentor black women." Dira Ridley would like to be a vice president in the company. She asserted, "For a black woman to even think she can become a vice president of the company is clearly shooting for the moon. Not only has a black woman just risen to the head of research in the company, but she is also the highest-ranking black woman. She is only one level above me. The vice president is at least four to five levels from me. My task in getting there is to convince a predominantly white male organization that a black woman can do it."

In coping with racism, Ridley believes it is essential to have "internal personal goals and to work toward them." She said, "While you may not achieve them, continue to make strides, feeling happy as you move toward those goals. You check the small challenges off: The goal is the moon. You may never get to that goal, but you are satisfied that you are moving in that direction."

Contrary to experiences like Dira Ridley's is a perception that black women have an advantage in the marketplace over white men, white women, and black men. Cynthia Fuchs Epstein, in "The Positive Effects of the Multiple Negative: Explaining the Success of Black Professional Women," suggests that sex and racism can sometimes operate as an advantage if employers wish to hire a black woman to fill the affirmative action goals of race and sex.[11] For most of the women I interviewed, this perception is merely an illusion. Aretha Shield articulated well the majority view, saying, "For every door that opens, ten doors close in my face."

"This double-minority status has worked against Black women like a double-edged sword," said Vanessa J. Gallman, an editor at the Tallahassee (Florida) Democrat, who wrote about this work myth in Essence magazine. "On the one hand, we face both racism and sexism in the job market, since most employers haven't given a second thought to affirmative action. On the other hand, our double status distorts what few gains we have made, leaving only stereotypes and misconceptions about what we can't change and what so many claim is an unfair advantage."[12]

The literature does not support the notion that it is an advantage to be a black woman. Black women are still at the bottom rung on the economic ladder. They earn less than black men, despite a pervasive sentiment that black women are more readily hired and promoted than black males.[13] There is a sense, as expressed by Veronica Pepper, a psychologist, that "black women are less of a threat than black men to white men, since women, in general, are given more latitude because they are not taken as seriously." This, too, can be a double-edged sword. A study of biracial groups concluded that black women are perceived differently in the sexual role than white women and differently also in the racial role than black men.[14] White society has "historically allowed more assertive behavior from black women, because black women are considered to be less dangerous."[15] Even though collectively they may be less of a threat to white men than black men, the women interviewed believed that white men were personally threatened by them. "White men are most threatened by me," said Stephanie Tahara. "Therefore, I am reluctant to express myself fully. When I do that, I get chopped up. I have to mask my intellect and other being."

The entry of new recruits who are different from others in professional and social situations may pose a threat to those around them. Said Diane Earlinger, who is the only female, the only black, and the youngest manager in an international agency, "I am different from others in my setting. It's not only unusual to be a black, but also a woman pathologist. There is a level of discomfort when you are not an old white male. Old white males are accustomed to interacting with old white males. They are uncomfortable when you come from a different perspective. They don't know what your motivations are. There is no level of trust, irrespective of competence."

Whether the black woman is less threatening to the white male than the black male is merely one of many polemics in black-white interactions. Perhaps Teresa Hale best summed up the feelings of many of the female Talented One Hundred when she noted that whether the contact between black females and white males is on a professional or personal level, "racism and sexism can be so intertwined, one could be overwhelmed by critical analysis and fine distinctions. The task is so exhausting that I limit these relationships to the greatest possible extent."

This avoidance by Teresa Hale may be understandable given the historical reality of black female–white male encounters in this country. I discovered, however, in the process of interviewing, that there is still another avoidance in black-white dynamics. The Talented One Hundred females tended not to acknowledge the silent tension of racism underlying black-white sisterhood. Perhaps it is because theirs is a fragile bond collectively, although individual black women reported deep friendships with white women.

BLACK-WHITE SISTERHOOD: THE FRAGILE BOND

It was Sojourner Truth who challenged the myth of the weaker sex in 1851 at a women's rights gathering in Ohio. With her voice roaring like the mighty water of the ocean, she electrified the audience with the frequently quoted refrain, "Ain't I a woman?" noting,

> I have ploughed, and planted, and gathered into barns and no man could head me! And ain't I a woman? I could work as much and eat as much as a man—when I could get it—and bear the lash as well! And ain't I a woman? I have borne thirteen children and seen them most all sold off to slavery, and when I cried out with my mother's grief, none but Jesus heard me! And ain't I a woman?[16]

The echoes of her mid-nineteenth century refrain can still be heard by women of color in the twilight of the twentieth century. Sojourner Truth's words confronted not only sexism, but the racism and classism inherent in the earlier and the contemporary women's movements that have characterized the fragile bond of black-white sisterhood.

Unlike contemporary black women, Sojourner Truth and her nineteenth-century black sisters were pioneers in the struggle for racial and sexual equality. These women understood the confluence of race and sex. The voices of contemporary black women, however, have been largely silent. This impelled Bell Hooks, in *Ain't I a Woman?* to remind black women that Sojourner Truth's refrain at the women's convention in Akron, Ohio, more than one hundred years ago is applicable today.

> At a time in American history when Black women in every area of the country might have joined together to demand social equality for women and a recognition of the impact of sexism on our status, we were by and large silent. Our silence was not merely a reaction against White women liberationists or a gesture of solidarity with Black male patriarchs. It was the silence of the oppressed—that profound silence engendered by resignation and acceptance of one's lot. Contemporary Black women could not join together to fight for women's rights because we did not see "womanhood" as an important aspect of our identity. Racist, sexist socialization had conditioned us to devalue our femaleness and to regard race as the only relevant label of identification. . . . We were asked to deny part of ourselves—and we did. Consequently, when the women's movement raised the issue of sexist oppression, we argued that sexism was insignificant in light of the harsher, more brutal reality of racism. We were afraid to acknowledge that sexism could be just as oppressive as racism.[17]

The few women of the Talented One Hundred who participated in the women's movement noted, like Bell Hooks, that they were met with "hostility and resentment from White women."[18] Listen to Stephanie Tahara, a county administrator in California, describe her experiences with a local chapter of the National Organization for Women.

> I was attending a NOW meeting with a friend, and I noticed there was a coolness toward us. If it were a group of black women, there would have been a sense of joy in joining in the fellowship. That warmth wasn't there with us. But they were more relaxed with one another. I sensed a wariness with us because we were two blacks out of thirty. You got the sense they were asking, "Why are you here? We said this was a woman's group, but don't get crazy. We are not sure about you. Are you here to mess up something?" I do know there was a distance, and we weren't included in the sisterhood.

Hooks believes, "White women liberationists saw feminism as their movement and resisted any efforts by non-white women to critique, challenge, or change its direction."[19] Teresa Johnson's involvement with the women's movement lends credence to Hook's perception. Teresa, who is presently involved in black women's groups, was at one time active in NOW. When I asked what happened, she sighed and said, "What a question!"

> I worked hard to have good relationships with white women, and I think some I have managed to work well with. But often, it is difficult. I don't think they realize their sense of privilege as whites. White women do not want to deal with our issues. Of course, they will deal with women like me who are academically successful, because there is a liberal feeling you ought to be included.

But I have to continually push the issue of black women's concerns. I say to them, "If you are going to talk about the feminization of poverty, the people who are the poorest in this country are black mothers." I take out the statistics and say, "If you want to do something, you have to start with this." There is a resistance among white women. Some don't understand the issues. Even when some try to understand, the terms they put it in indicate they are living in another world. Since I deal with black women in my academic field, many white feminists would say I am not dealing with the issue of sexism. They view it as being diluted with race. We exist in categories. They are arguing who is pure. I've gone to many meetings where white women will say my race is not a central issue to the women's movement. The movement also assumes you exclude black men. How can you not talk about black men or men of color and not be concerned about them?[20]

While the largely white middle-class women's movement in this country has conveniently used race to help define and clarify the problem of the movement, Jerrie Scott, a linguist whom I once interviewed about black women and feminism, noted that the women's movement has not recognized "race in the solution of the problem, or recognized the contributions of black women to women's liberation." Stephanie Tahara concurred with Scott's analysis.

In the early 1970s, I experimented in sisterhood, and I could clearly see white women were as racist and threatened as anybody else. For example, the county commission on the status of women hired a director from South Africa, and now what does that tell you! She is still there. She has been protected and cared for by the power structure. The woman is exceedingly condescending. We were always at war with her. A friend of mine is on the commission, and she could see how they made decisions about women of color. She gleaned they despised them. If you bring up an issue from a racial perspective, they freak out. We were holding hearings on sexism and the media, and I decided I was going to testify. I talked about ethnic stereotypes in the media. It went beyond the sexism issues, and the white women were saying that I, along with other blacks and Japanese, was being disruptive and negative. I pointed out that just the previous week on TV, I had seen only Asian whores, black whores, or maids. I said, "Can you deal with that or not? If you can't deal with that, get out of my face." I should not get out of the arena; these white women should, because they are phonies. The white man does not pretend to be your friend; I know he is the oppressor. But here comes some person talking about sisterhood, and they don't have the slightest idea what it is about. They want to embrace me, saying we are in this together. No, stay away from me! The white man will say I know I am going to rip you off and you know it.

Black women achievers feel keenly this double sting of racism and sexism. Some of the females of the Talented One Hundred find it difficult to reconcile their common interests with white sisterhood because of racism. Said Marla Robinson, director of a state civil rights commission, "I have thought about joining NOW. I am concerned about environmental issues, nuclear issues, day care issues, and the comparable worth issue. I think it is important for black women to be part of an organization doing that kind of thing. But right now, I can't hold their hands and sing the Sistersong."

Stephanie Tahara's experience with NOW suggests that white women may not be interested in their black sisters "holding their hands and singing the Sistersong."

> White women indiscriminately support each other. Their agenda says we don't care whether [you are] Republican or Democrat. I heard it from a NOW political caucus. Although they indiscriminately support one another, they will not support black women. And that's not vicious, just smart. They are saying the power needs to be contained within a certain group of women. Yet I don't understand how they can support all women. I don't suspend my intellect. I want to know what is a woman's position on important social issues.

I interviewed Lena Faulkner, a candidate for a major political office. She did not receive support from NOW, the League of Women Voters, or any of the major organizations headed by white women, although her agenda strongly supported women's issues.

Perhaps Bell Hooks's statement merits further investigation. She concludes in *Ain't I a Woman?* that black feminists who participated in the movement found that sisterhood for most white women did not mean "surrendering allegiance to race, class, and sexual preference, to bond on the basis of shared political belief that a feminist revolution was necessary so that all people, especially women, could reclaim their rightful citizenship in the world." She asserts that the feminist ideology gave "lip service to revolutionary goals"; it was "primarily concerned with gaining entrance into the capitalist patriarchal power structure."[21] Statistics confirm that white women are ahead of both black females and males and other women of color in their climb to the top of the workplace. For example, of the women corporate officers in Fortune One Thousand firms in 1986, 96.7 percent were white, 1.9 percent were Asians, 0.9 percent were black, 0.5 percent American Indian/Eskimo, and none were Hispanic.[22] It is in this arena that the reality of the white feminist ideology clashes with that of men and women of color. Since there are more white women than black men and women in the United States, it is expected that they should have greater numbers in positions of power. However, many blacks believe this rapid mobility has been at their expense, since the affirmative action programs, used to advance racial minorities, have also included white women.

Numerous blacks strongly disagree that white women should be considered as a minority. "The white man is going to hire the white woman as a minority. I dislike white women piggy-backing and moving up, and we don't have sense enough to do something. Nobody seems to be complaining about it. Since the Reagan era, there is an arrogance that you dare not question it. There is an attitude that I can do anything I please and you better stay in your place. I didn't see this attitude very much in the 1960s. It's what my mother and aunt experienced in the

1950s, but I certainly see it in the 1980s," said Marla Robinson, a forty-three-year-old administrator from the Midwest.

For many, race is seen as a greater barrier to overcome than sex. Edward W. Jones Jr., who writes about black managers in corporate America, said, "If the comfort level is a big factor in an invitation to enter the executive suite, it is understandable that White women will get there before Blacks. After all, the mothers, wives, and daughters of top officers are White women, and they deal with White women all their lives—but only rarely with Black men and women. And they are likely to view White women as being more their own social class than Black men and women."[23]

Marla Robinson feels keenly the double sting of sexism and racism:

> I feel if I were a white female, I would be further ahead careerwise and moneywise. There are no questions about that. I know it. I have looked at people who have started with me. Considering what I've done and what we each had to offer, they have advanced more rapidly than I. [How does it make you feel? I asked.] It makes me feel like shit. I have become so hostile. It's a new feeling for me. At each stage of life, you take on new battles. Your exposure is so different; you have more insights and your focus becomes less general and more specific. So at this point, I really have a lot of hostility toward white women.

Although Robinson was initially hesitant to discuss the tension between black and white women, she was among the first of the Talented One Hundred women to openly and candidly talk to me about it. Therefore, when I interviewed Crystal Miller, a former director of the Women's Studies Resource Program at a major university, I was particularly interested in her experience. Miller left her position over four years ago, but her memories of her tenure are still vivid.

> Black women were very much a majority. We were one of three centers who had a truly integrated staff. I won't say we dominated, but we were truly more than half. We also had one or two Chicanos and Asians from time to time. The staff would change frequently. I felt white women on my staff and those in the university who were not on my staff had the greatest trouble in accepting supervision from a black woman. It was very difficult for them. They were not accustomed to it. They resisted any suggestions and corrections I made. One person just didn't do her best work. She tried to find another job, circumventing me and going to the administrator to whom I reported, hoping to discredit me. She bad-mouthed the center, was not supportive, and made what we were doing look bad. I think we were doing exciting, wonderful things, and it became a major center in this region of the country.
>
> There were always good and supportive faculty to work with, but there were others who had the "Miss Ann Syndrome," where some white women consciously or unconsciously expect a black woman to serve [them]. In a professional sense, the person who serves becomes the staff person. If you are in a meeting you are expected to take minutes or follow through on all the nitty-gritty details. Since I was

an administrator as well as faculty, they expected me to do that. It was indicated who was supposed to carry out details. They would say you are so able as an administrator. I may be wrong, but I equate that with the black mammy servant that can always take care of everything. She can do it all. So let her do it. She is strong and able. She can take care of the kitchen and the children. This mammy role is transferred to the professional world. It is that kind of thing, and for that reason, that some people were really quite surprised and distressed when I left the position. Colleagues assumed, for some strange reason, that this was supposed to be my career, but I never saw it that way myself. My leaving to some was like losing a good servant. I am sure they didn't say that consciously. But I see them unconsciously feeling Mary Jane is leaving, as if no one else will do the job well. I think that kind of attitude is exacerbated by the color line in this setting.

When Crystal Miller said the "mammy role is transferred to the professional world," it represents an amalgam of the past and present in the workplace, a painful reminder to black women of the intertwining of classism, racism, and sexism in the United States as symbolized by the relationship between "Mary Jane" and "Miss Ann." Until the last few decades, the majority of black women in the United States worked as "Mary Jane," the domestic, serving "Miss Ann" and her family. These memories are still fresh for the Talented One Hundred—no less than 36 percent had mothers who were employed as domestics or service workers, 24 percent and 12 percent, respectively.

Dorothy Bolden, founder and president of the National Domestic Workers' Union, senses, like Crystal Miller, that the symbols of "Miss Ann" and "Mary Jane" are deeply woven into the black-white female socioemotional interactions, which are inextricably linked to the power struggle of class and race. Bolden, who started organizing black domestics in Atlanta in the late sixties, said, "When I was invited to speak before several white women's groups, I heard more of 'I thought my maid was happy and pleased.' How could she be happy when she didn't have a good pair of shoes, when she had to wear men's pants, and when she had to take care of her children, too, on $25 or less a week!"

When the regional director of the women's bureau in Atlanta wanted to set a salary of $12.50 a day for domestic workers in 1969, Bolden organized the workers. Speaking before the director and an audience of domestics and their white employers, she led the protest, saying,

Nobody can set a salary for me if I have to get on my knees to clean a bathroom and to wipe around the commode, inhaling the piss of her husband who missed the commode and having the piss to dry on the floor. When I put water on it, I refreshen it up and I have to clean it up with a rag. I don't think anyone can set my salary.

Whether professional or domestic, as Crystal Miller and Dorothy Bolden note, black women may still be viewed as a strong, reliable source of cheap labor for the families of white women of privilege. Even when black women and white women meet as equals in the professional arena, there is still a clash of race, class, and often culture, as Teresa Johnson pointed out:

> I have never thought of myself as someone who needs to be taken care of. Although sometimes I might think of myself as wanting to be cared for, I grew up with a sense of handling my own life. It doesn't have to be through a man. I think this is true for black women here as well as the Caribbean. I think for many white women, this is not true. So I think there is a difference in the way they are coming at the gender question. They are trying to build up a life for themselves rather than through the accomplishment of men. I am not idealizing black women as strong, but we deal with other kinds of problems. White women spend a lot of time dealing with a sense of self-identity.
>
> The irony of the situation is that in mixed women's groups so many of the white women are married to men who are professionals. And between the two, they are making a whole lot of money. Many black women are not. We are single mothers, working for ourselves.

In 1987, Reynolds Farley, University of Michigan sociology professor, using data from the census bureau, found that only 30 percent of black women between the ages of fifteen and forty-four were living with a husband, compared with 55 percent of white women in that age bracket. According to the study, black women also delay marriage longer and are more likely to divorce than white women.[24]

Teresa Johnson sees black women and white women as having different priorities. "When white women would say, 'Let's have a meeting,' I would say, 'I have to go home.' They can often set meetings at various times, because they have a maid to do their work. And we can't do that." When a black woman can afford domestic help, like Diane Earlinger, she may be unable to obtain it. She reported that several black domestics refused to work for another black woman, even though she would pay more and would treat them better. This reflects an ingrained sense of inferiority toward themselves and other black women. For some domestics, it is more prestigious to work for a white female.

Though race, class, and culture may collide in the workplace and the social arena, black women, such as Crystal Miller, often feel a kinship with individual white females. However, collectively, this kinship is like that of a distant cousin. Remarked Miller, "I feel a kinship or sisterhood with some individuals, but not in general. Because of my experience at the women's center, I assume that kind of sisterhood has to be proven. Prior to holding that position and when I was younger, I was more willing to give people the benefit of the doubt. Now I don't always make those assumptions. I can't help but be more cautious than before."

There is still another reason why many black females express wariness toward their white sisters. Their fragile bond of sisterhood has been further weakened by the complex and sensitive issue of sexual racism and interracial relations between black males and white females and between black females and white males. Here, the ambivalence, contradictions, myths, and stereotypes unfold on the racial stage, playing themselves out in complex scenes.

BLACK-WHITE SEXUAL RELATIONS

Since the 1967 U.S. Supreme Court ruling that struck down laws prohibiting interracial marriage, there has been an increase in these unions. Although interracial unions are still a very small percentage of all marriages, one can gauge this increase not only by statistics but also by the amount of attention given this topic in the popular literature, particularly black periodicals like *Essence* and *Ebony*. Black men are more likely to participate in interracial unions than black women. Seven out of ten of these unions involve black men and women of other races, primarily white.[25] Many people believe that because black men and white women have historically been denied access to one another, the attraction between them increased. This attraction is supposedly heightened by racist sexual myths—the myth of black male super sexuality and the myth of the sexual purity of white females. This increase in relations between black men and white women has exacerbated the tension between black women and white women, between black men and white men, and between black men and black women (particularly college-educated black women).

According to the American Council on Education, the enrollment of black men in U.S. colleges and universities declined by thirty-four thousand between 1976 and 1986, the largest decline for any racial or ethnic group. The percentage of black men, ages eighteen to twenty-four, in college, declined from 35.4 percent in 1976 to 27.8 percent in 1987.[26] This pattern has repercussions for the marriage potential of college-educated black women; the number of available black males is further reduced.

Many black women feel rejected by black men who date or marry white women. For instance, when Leslie Glouster, a health administrator, attended the annual meeting of the National Medical Association, the black medical organization, she and other members were invited to tour the homes of several prominent black doctors in the city. She observed, "In homes we toured, we were greeted by a white woman [wife] at the door."

The sting of rejection black women feel is heightened by the black male's rationale for choosing a white mate. The white female is seen as more physically attractive, less domineering, and more intelligent and supportive. Many black males have internalized negative images of black women and have accepted these positive stereotypes of the white female.

Black women, on the other hand, have generally not dated or married outside their race until recently. Since black females have been viewed as sexual objects and in the slavery era were sexually abused and raped by white males, theirs is a history of negative familiarity. Hence, black women have been reluctant to establish interracial relations. This pattern, however, is changing, according to the U.S. Census Bureau. In 1987, there were fifty-six thousand black women married to white men, eleven thousand more than in 1980.[27] As more black women enter the workplace as equals, they consider white males as partners. This pattern is motivated particularly by the shortage of black males, though some women may also be attracted by the power of white males and the belief that white men treat them better. Despite the recent trend, Teresa Johnson thinks the black female–white male relationship is more difficult than the black male–white female one, because "the black woman carries the culture, and there is all that history of slavery that comes to mind."

Many black males react strongly to this new trend, even when they approve of black male–white female relations. They feel they are losing control over their women. Since the trend of black female–white male egalitarian interaction is so recent, it is not clear how white females may react, or whether it will increase or decrease the tension between black women and white women.

There are many motivations for interracial unions. While some are based on mutual attraction and respect for one another, others may be motivated by racist sexual myths. In an *Essence* magazine discussion of interracial relations between black men and white women, one fifty-year-old college professor was quoted as saying,

> I grew up in Alabama where to look at a White woman could mean trouble. I always wanted to know what they were about. Then with the television telling you every day that they were the most desirable women in the world, I always wanted to own one. Now when I go home and my wife meets me at the door, or brings me something to eat, I feel that I am just as well off as any White man. I know it sounds a bit out of left field, but I am satisfied in America. I have what the White man says is the best there is.[28]

Still others might see, as Crystal Miller suggested, an advantage in interracial relations. Since a white mate does not experience discrimination, you don't have two people who have wounds to deal with. The impact of racism on a black couple imposes a tremendous stress on their relationship. While there is now a greater tolerance for interracial relationships in the society, there is still a strong resistance by whites. And to many blacks, like Jonathan Mobutu, it also poses a psychic dilemma; there is a higher comfort level dealing with one's own race. Others do not object to racial relations as long as the couple is aware of its motives. "And that's where it is difficult," asserted Teresa Johnson. "Are they really seeing each other as individuals, or are they seeing each other through stereotypes? I think that is the problem."

SEXISM IN BLACK MALE-FEMALE RELATIONS

In addition to sexism and racism encountered by black women outside the home, they must also battle sexism on the home front. Although historically the black male-female relationship has been more egalitarian than that of whites, black males have been socialized to accept the patriarchal value of male dominance, even when they could not exercise it. Hence, black females first experience sexism in the home or within the black community.

Diane Earlinger's first encounter with sexism was in her home. In the mid-sixties, Diane, a gifted student, wanted to attend a medical school away from home. Her mother, a housewife and a former home economics teacher before marriage, and her father, a civil engineer, decided that there were not sufficient funds to send both son and daughter away to school. It was more important for Diane's brother "to have that advantage." Diane felt sacrificed. "I was not angry at my parents, though I might react differently now. It was disappointing to me that I didn't go away to school. Clearly, my level of achievement in high school was such that I had an opportunity to go to the best white Ivy League schools," lamented Diane. Even though she was a talented student, she could not apply to the National Medical Association, a black organization, because fellowships were awarded only to black men. Despite the fact that Diane successfully completed a high school that prepared students for professional careers, when she asked for literature on medicine, she said, "the counselor gave me a carton full of literature on nursing. When I graduated from medical school, I sent him an invitation, along with a picture, and he came. He said he was glad I had not listened to him." (The counselor was white.)

Like Diane Earlinger, Laura Price, also a gifted student, first felt the sting of sexism in the home. When Laura expressed interest in attending medical school in the early 1960s, her mother, a director of Christian education at a Baptist church, supported her aspirations. But her father, a minister, did not. Remarked Laura,

> The sons were the ones you pushed, and the daughters were to be sweet and pretty and to finish high school and that's all they had to do. If they went to college, they were to teach school and work in the church. He was very enthusiastic about getting my brother into medical school, but didn't do the same kinds of things to get me in. When I got in, he was very surprised. Yet, he didn't deny me my tuition, books, or anything I needed. However, he would have been very happy if I had done a little less. It was my mother who emphasized if you have the ability, you can do anything. If you want to specialize after medical school, you can. On the other hand, my father said, "It's okay if you want to go to medical school, and that's a little unusual to start with, but you don't have to specialize."

Unlike Diane Earlinger and Laura Price, who grew up in middle-class families, Laverne Townson, a forty-three-year-old bank manager who lives in Africa, came from a working-class background. Her father, a clay-mine worker, did not encourage her to attend college. But her mother, a domestic, gave greater encouragement to Laverne to attend college than to her sons. She wanted her daughter to be independent in case her husband "turned out to be no account." For black women growing up in the South before the civil rights movement, the only alternative to domestic or service work was to teach. Hence, daughters were encouraged to attend college more often than sons. Being a teacher as opposed to being a domestic would protect them from sexual harassment of white males.

In general, black women attended college in greater numbers than black men prior to the civil rights movement. Since 1976, black male enrollment has dropped by 7 percent, while black female enrollment has increased. This pattern is not only likely to exacerbate the existing tension between the sexes, but, more importantly, it will have an impact on the gender competition in the marketplace.[29]

The examples of Diane Earlinger, Laura Price, and Laverne Townson illustrate the sexist attitudes within the family. As women move outside the home and into the workplace, sexist attitudes and behaviors continue to prevail. They are particularly pronounced with successful women who have moved into the traditional male purview. A good example is Yvonne Walker-Taylor, the first woman president of Wilberforce University, a small African Methodist Episcopal institution in Ohio and one of the oldest black universities in the United States. When she sat under her doorsteps as a five-year-old, trying to kiss her elbow and turn into a boy, Walker-Taylor may have sensed the beginning of a long journey—her "struggle against all odds."

As president, the outspoken and energetic Walker-Taylor has waged many battles with the bishop of her district, who is the chairman of the board and quite influential in the operation of the university. When I interviewed Walker-Taylor in her Wilberforce office prior to her retirement in January 1988, she spoke candidly about her presidency.

The bishop is so against me. He came into this district the first board meeting to get rid of me. That's a known fact. This man has a reputation of not wanting women in high places. He does not want to ordain women. It's a part of his pattern. He came in and told me, sitting right here in this office, that the only reason I was president of Wilberforce University was because my father was the president, and they wanted to give that honor to his daughter. He said, "I was against it, but I went along with it. So I made up my mind that when they assigned me to this district, you were going to have to go." I said, "So it took you three-and-a-half years to do it, didn't it?"

Even though the bishop was talking to me this way, I would say, "Oh, bishop, I am so sorry to hear you say that. It really breaks my heart because of my father, who died in 1955. I wonder what he would think of you. You said you knew him and respected him." [Her voice trailed off.] I said, "Bishop, you have a daughter, or don't you care about any woman at all? Bishop, I am going to fight you as long as I can, because I plan to remain president until 1988." [Laughed and lowered her voice.] He said, "No," and I said, "Yes." But there was never one time he could say I didn't respect him. I said, "I respect your position. My father was a bishop. I respect all bishops. But I do not respect your ideology. I will never embarrass you, but don't press me too hard because I have the ear of the church and you know that, sir."

"Yes," he said, "some of my colleagues have been after me about me being on you." I said, "They see the unfairness of what you are doing. But my father taught me to love my enemies. So I rather translate that into respect, because I could never love you. Love means more, and I could never give you that. When you and I meet publicly, we will put up our little fronts, and to me that is a bit of hypocrisy, but in our church, it is necessary. And it will make me a bigger person, because everyone knows what you are doing. The fact that I can smile and you can hug me in public and kiss me on the cheek with your Judas kiss does a great deal for me in the eyes of the church." I said, "Sir, I may someday be elected to the Judicial Council, and I may see you down the line. One never knows." We parted and he went and announced my retirement. [At the General Conference of the A.M.E. Church held in Fort Worth, Texas, in July 1988, Walker-Taylor became the first woman elected to the Judicial Council, the highest judiciary body of the A.M.E. Church. The nine-member council is an appellate court elected by the General Conference.]

How I hung on those three-and-a-half years is just the way I am telling it. Every board meeting he would try to get a search committee to look for a president. I would "sir" him to death and ask on what grounds. Fortunately, the board of trustees thought I was doing a magnificent job. He was the only one, except there was another person who supported him. And he was a chauvinistic guy who graduated from Wilberforce in 1932 and should have been off the board a long time ago. He stayed on my case like the bishop. But I am smarter than the bishop. I know I am. He does not know anything about the operation of the school, but I never threw it up in his face. I let him stumble into mistakes, and I'd say, "Sir, if you did this, it might straighten it out." He would do it and things would smooth out. And he'd say that worked, so I would get through that board meeting. But I would always provide a little snag, and he would have to come to me to find out what you have to do about it.

As a black woman, you have to be better than everybody. You have to stay way ahead, and you have to have enthusiasm for life. You can't keep me down long. Oh, Lord, yes! That bishop would call me sometimes and my secretary would come in and I was sitting here like I was under the desk. I could be so low. It doesn't last long. I snap right out of it. It is faith in the fact that my destiny is in the hands of the Lord and no man can stop me from that which is to be mine. I should have been president a long time ago, but each step of the way I got slapped down.

"I am tired and worn out with the fight. I am seventy-one years old." Her youthful looks belie her age. "I took on this job when most people had retired." Looking at her watch, she remarked, "The average person would be packing to go to New York, and I am sitting here talking with you." Walker-Taylor had a speaking engagement that same day in New York. She described herself as having boundless energy.

For Laura Price, like Walker-Taylor, sexism did not stop at her father's doorstep; it followed her into the medical profession. Although she owns her medical building and her patients are women, she still must interact with male colleagues. As the only woman officer of her local Black Medical Association, she found that it was necessary to remind her male colleagues that women are qualified to serve as officers in the organization. Said Laura, "Where are the women being nominated for these committees? We've had rapid growth of black female doctors in this city. So it is past time for a woman to hold an office. They have us on committees, but they didn't have us holding office. They are aware now when nominations come through that it would be a good idea to put a woman's name on it. If I am on the committee or out in the audience, I will say, 'Where are the women?'"

Teresa Johnson, the first woman appointed to the Afro American Studies department at her university, could repeat Laura's refrain, Where are the women? "I was the only woman for a very long time. I was practically invisible to the men. When I was coming up for tenure, they didn't even know it, because I was not taken seriously. I was not that important in the realm of things."

Though she was ignored, her presence was not totally invisible. When Johnson was appointed to her faculty position in Afro American studies, she received anonymous hate mail in her campus mail box from black men claiming she was taking away their jobs. Reflecting upon the men's attitude, Teresa pointed out that "black women were involved in the civil rights struggle; however, there is a division when it comes to jobs and positions. There is less emphasis on togetherness. I felt isolated and disappointed in our men."

While Teresa Johnson faced harassment from black men about taking jobs away from them, Diane Earlinger encountered sexual harassment. Diane once served as a faculty member at a black medical school but left because the environment was not nurturing and was overtly sexist. Diane was propositioned to have sex, even though she was married to a physician. "I never encountered that among my white colleagues, so I reacted with a great deal of haughtiness and arrogance. There were consequences. I was not promoted. It was a ghastly experience. I am not generalizing about the experience. But I hear that black women in similar environments tell the same story. I had only one experience, but I prefer not to think that it is typical," said Diane.

Too often, sexual harassment is a reality, especially where successful black women are socially isolated from supportive networks of other women. Jonathan Mobutu observed that in higher education, "black males tend to be called on to support black males and females because of the nature of sexism and the division of social walls, which makes black men more available. Black women have families and more responsibilities of child rearing and cannot be as flexible. . . . So I wound up having to spend a lot of time supporting black women. I prefer to see them use a black woman as a role model. I find that to be a difficult type of role. Some black males might use the needs of black women to exploit them,"[30] noted Mobutu.

The dimensions of sexual politics are endless. When women leave the workplace, sexism again follows them back to their doorsteps. Bebe Moore Campbell, in *Successful Women, Angry Men*,[31] shows that the power struggle continues in the two-career marriage. While many men give lip service to equality of the sexes, their behavior suggests they have not been fully liberated. In addition to their careers, women continue to perform the traditional household tasks and to assume more responsibility for childrearing. For women, there is an ongoing tension between career aspirations and familial duties. And black women are doing a double balancing act, walking both the racial and sexual tightropes.

When Teresa Johnson was married and had a small child, life was difficult. Said Teresa:

> Having a child and being a faculty person, most men can't understand that at certain times, you have to go home. You've got a baby to pick up. There is very little consideration of being a mother. I told my male colleagues [when her child was a baby] that you have a wife. While you have somebody to pick up [your child], I am expected to do that. The men wanted you to give all to the job. It didn't have to be that way. It could have been arranged otherwise. Men have privileges because they have wives.

Diane Earlinger agreed that balancing career and family duties poses overload dilemmas. "As a woman, you really don't have the luxury to say at some appropriate point and time that you can take a hiatus from your career. This usually means no coming back, because it is assumed that you are not serious about your career. So at certain periods of time, it meant not doing certain things well either professionally or personally. The personal obligations of women are very different from men."

Single women do not escape sex role stereotyping. They also have to deal with the attitudes of their partners toward their careers. They have to prioritize, deciding whether their career goals or their relationships are more important. Teresa Johnson, forty-three years old, finds younger men and women are more accepting, personally and professionally, of parity. But she senses from men her own age a message about her career that indicates, said Teresa, "I am not really real. I am just putting on. I am trying to be an ambitious, successful woman— the big black woman. I am not really involved in what I am doing. I am just trying to be secure."

Whether the black woman achiever is single or married, her race, class, and sex interface in perplexing ways, contributing to confusion, contradictions, and dilemmas of status. Since she occupies a marginal position in society, chances for isolation are increased.[32] For the black woman elite, class, culture, race, or sex may stand between her two worlds. Consequently, she finds herself on the edges of both, often operating without an anchor, which contributes to her social isolation. There is, said Diane Earlinger, a lack of nurturing of black women.

> There are fewer support systems. Very often, you find other black women are antagonistic, and in some ways envious and jealous because you've accomplished things they may have wanted to, but haven't. Seemingly there is no desire to be supportive of people who have made it. There are no exchanges of services like car pooling. I've become very isolated in many ways and have generally tried not to depend on other

people to be supportive. And that's when you go into the superhuman role for women who are not given any relief on the domestic side, and who have taken on the professional obligations and responsibilities as well. One becomes very lonely and isolated, and at some point, I miss the social interaction I would like to have with other black women.

Diane also feels isolated from the women of her profession because of the low percentage of women in the field of pathology and the kind of institution in which she is employed. An attempt was once made to establish an organization of black women physicians. She was actively involved, but it fizzled. Said Diane, "The young unmarried women were different from the older married ones. One of the first activities was a lingerie party to which lots of single men were invited. It was difficult to relate to something like that, and I considered it inappropriate under any circumstances. I was on the planning committee to develop a charter and purpose, not to plan a lingerie party." She has made several attempts to participate in women's organizations, but has found them unsatisfactory because of petty jealousy.

Similarly, Yvonne Walker-Taylor has not found support from other women. She thinks "women are jealous and they dislike for the sake of disliking. When women get in high places, they don't pull one another up. . . . My preaching is you reach down and bring somebody up. I wanted another woman to take my place when I leave the presidency," remarked Walker-Taylor.

Marla Robinson's experience has been different from those of Yvonne Walker-Taylor and Diane Earlinger. Although she lost friends as she moved up the career ladder, she remarked, "I am finding more beautiful black women who are appreciative of me as a person and proud of me. I don't know if it's because we have matured or because we believe that if we don't support one another, no one else will."

Perhaps black males and females are both beginning to understand that their destinies are linked. Recently, Teresa Johnson observed signs of change in her Afro American Studies department. "There is much more information and knowledge, and it has gotten better. It hasn't happened easily. But there is more of an awareness to have both points of view in the department. I sense there is a change. What the power structure has set up, we should not necessarily be imitating. Since there are so few black faculty, we need one another," said Teresa.

If black men and women do not recognize they "need one another," they have failed to understand how they are inextricably linked in the struggle against oppression. Moreover, this sexual politics saps energy from the racial struggle, thus creating social isolation and additional stresses. In struggling alone, the black woman is often victimized by her own strengths. Said Jerrie Scott, a linguist, "The woman is burdened down and feels she must save the world, save the children, save the black man, save the white man and woman, save everyone except herself."

SUMMARY

Historically, the black woman has been in a peculiar position in this society. While she has generally accepted the dominant patriarchal values of this society, there are conflicts when she attempts to live up to the expectations of the black male and the larger society. Similarly, black males, having also accepted the dominant patriarchal values, find they, too, are caught in a double bind. In trying to meet the expectations of society and the black female, they also get confusing and mixed messages and may be unable to live up to these demands. For both males and females, this dilemma creates conflicts in life expectations, which result in tension between them. This energy could more effectively be directed toward support for one another and not toward support of traditional values. There is a need to redefine the traditional dominant patriarchal values, so males and females can be a resource for one another. Increasingly, seminars on black male-female relations have begun to address these issues. Black male research institutes are also emerging, like those at Albany State College and Morehouse College, which examine the present and future status of black men. This growing awareness should reduce tension between the sexes, creating a more supportive environment in predominantly black, mixed, or white settings.

In the next chapter, I look at how black men and women cope with oppression and social isolation in this society.

NOTES

1. Angela Davis, *Women, Race and Class* (New York: Vintage Books, 1983), 10.
2. Sue K. Jewell, "Black Male/Female Conflict: Internalizations of Negative Definitions Transmitted through Imagery," *Western Journal of Black Studies*, 7 (Spring 1983): 43–48.
3. Sharon R. King, "At the Crossroads," *Black Enterprise*, Aug. 1988, 47.
4. King, "At the Crossroads," 47.
5. King, "At the Crossroads," 48.
6. "Facts and Figures," *Black Enterprise*, April 1987, 39.
7. Richard D. Hylton, "Working in America," *Black Enterprise*, Aug. 1988, 66.
8. John P. Fernandez, *Racism and Sexism in Corporate Life* (Lexington, MA: D. C. Heath, 1981), 61.
9. Fernandez, *Racism and Sexism*, 19.
10. Fernandez, *Racism and Sexism*, 19.
11. Cynthia Fuchs Epstein, "The Positive Effects of the Multiple Negative: Explaining the Success of Black Professional Women," *American Journal of Sociology*, 78, no. 4 (Jan. 1973): 912–935.
12. Vanessa J. Gallman, "What to Say When Someone Tells You, 'It Pays to Be a Black Woman,'" *Essence*, March 1983, 89.
13. Karen Fulbright, "The Myth of the Double-Advantage: Black Female Managers," in Margaret Simms and Julianne Malveaux, eds., *Slipping through the Cracks: The Status*

of Black Women, 3rd ed. (New Brunswick, NJ: Transaction Pub., 1986). See also Francine D. Blau and Marianne A. Ferber, "Occupations and Earnings of Women Workers," in *Working Women: Past, Present, Future* (Washington, DC: Industrial Relations Research Association, 1987), 55–59.

14. Kathrynn A. Adams, "Aspects of Social Context as Determinants of Black Women's Resistance to Challenge," *Journal of Social Issues*, 39, no. 3 (1983), 69–78.

15. Edward D. Jones, "Black Managers: The Dream Deferred," *Harvard Business Review*, May–June 1986, 91.

16. Davis, *Women*, 61.

17. Bell Hooks, *Ain't I a Woman?* (Boston: South End Press, 1981), 1.

18. Hooks, *Woman*, 190.

19. Hooks, *Woman*, 190.

20. Clyde W. Franklin II notes a similar argument is made about men of color in predominantly white male groups. See Clyde Franklin II, *Men and Society* (Chicago: Nelson Hall, 1988).

21. Hooks, *Woman*, 188.

22. "Facts and Figures," *Black Enterprise*, Aug. 1988, 43. See also Fulbright, "Myth," 36.

23. Jones, "Black Managers," 91.

24. "Blacks Have Less Incentive to Wed, Study Says," *Dayton Daily News*, March 17, 1989, 4a.

25. Orde Coombs, "Black Men and White Women," *Essence*, May 1983, 82.

26. Bill McAllister, "The Plight of Young Black Men in America," *Washington Post, National Weekly Edition*, Feb. 12–18, 1990, 6.

27. Laura B. Randolph, "Black Women/White Men: What's Goin' On?" *Ebony*, March 1989, 156.

28. Coombs, "Black Men," 138.

29. "Facts and Figures," *Black Enterprise*, April 1988, 39; McAllister, "Plight," 6.

30. For a discussion of black male-female relations, see Delores P. Aldridge and Willa Hammons, "The Structural Components of Violence in Black Male-Female Relationships," *The Journal of Human Behavior in the Social Environment*, 4, no. 4 (2001), 204–226.

31. Bebe Moore Campbell, *Successful Women, Angry Men* (New York: Random House, 1986).

32. Lois Benjamin, "Black Women Achievers: An Isolated Elite," *Sociological Inquiry*, 5, no. 2 (Spring 1982): 141–151.

7

STYLES OF COPING

> . . . Out of the huts of history's shame
> I rise
> Up from a past that's rooted in pain
> I rise
> I'm a black ocean, leaping and wide,
> Welling and swelling I bear in the tide.
> Leaving behind nights of terror and fear
> I rise
> Into a daybreak that's wondrously clear
> I rise
> Bringing the gifts that my ancestors gave,
> I am the dream and the hope of the slave.
> I rise
> I rise
> I rise.
>
> —Maya Angelou

Racial discrimination is a major stressor in the lives of the Talented One Hundred. Faced with an ongoing onslaught of oppression, what makes them rise? Do they still hear the voices of their parents reminding them, "You got to be somebody." "You have to get an education." "Remember, a little learning is a dangerous thing; you must continue to learn." "If you acquire knowledge, no whites can take it from you." "The fight today is with the mind and not the body"?

The Talented One Hundred continue to achieve their goals, climbing mountains as academicians, as corporate executives, and as entrepreneurs. They maintain a steady pace by holding on to external and internal support systems in the face of adversities.

Bruce P. Dohrenwend and Barbara S. Dohrenwend, social scientists, have hypothesized that upwardly mobile individuals are more likely to have "achievement-related stress—events that exert pressure on the individual to change his customary activities to a new set of higher status activities," for example, entering a high-status occupation. Lower-status individuals are more likely to have "security-related stress—events that exert pressure on the individual to change his customary activities to a new set of lower status activity," for example, losing a job.[1] The stressor is the source or cause of strain, while stress is its effect.

Dohrenwend and Dohrenwend's idea of stress is relevant to upwardly mobile blacks. Since there are achievement-related stresses that are caused by the social isolation of blacks in pursuit of their goals, what is the price of their success?

Social isolation of upwardly mobile blacks can lead to internal stress, which often manifests itself in physiological disorders, for example, hypertension or behavioral disorders, even suicide. In his research on suicide, sociologist Robert Davis notes that suicide has increased significantly for young black males between the ages of twenty and thirty-four,[2] the category that is characteristic of the talented and highly educated. Robert Staples, sociologist and author of *Black Masculinity*, maintains that "for the Black college student or graduate, the cause of suicide may be related to the high expectations he has for success and the frustrations encountered in overcoming the persistent barriers against reaching his potential that result from racism."[3] Other studies have reported similar stress patterns, as manifested in alcohol abuse and health problems, among black men. Likewise, Dolores P. Aldridge in "Black Female Suicide: Is the Excitement Justified?" suggests similar concerns among black women.[4]

Though stress is a major factor in the lives of the Talented One Hundred, initially they did not report that it had any effect on their health. Males consistently rated their health as excellent or good, despite specific physiological disorders. Only after extensive probing was I able to obtain the following account of Ferdinand Hamilton's health. Said Hamilton, who is in his sixties, "I feel good, but my health is probably marginal. I've had five major operations in the last five years. I had a ruptured esophagus which poisoned my body. I had two major operations within two weeks. I had a pecan shell lodged in my throat. I had three ribs removed. I had problems with my arteries, and I had a six-way bypass on my heart. But I still walk seven miles a day."

Males were more reluctant to disclose health problems than females. However, both men and women tended to deemphasize negative health problems. (Their reaction is in sharp contrast to that of welfare recipients, who are more likely to highlight any health concerns, even minor ones.[5])

Despite economic backgrounds, racism is a major stressor in the lives of blacks and affects their health status. When racism is interwoven with sexism, there is an additional stress factor for black women, as noted in *In and Out of Our Right Minds: The Mental Health of African American Women*, a volume edited by Diane R. Brown and Verna M. Keith.[6] One can only speculate whether the stress resulting from social isolation led to the emotional collapse of Sheba, my brilliant friend, or to the suicide of Leanita McClain, a talented young journalist. An article entitled "To Be Black, Gifted, and Alone," by Bebe Moore Campbell, is based on recollections about Leanita McClain, the first black to become a member of the *Chicago Tribune's* editorial board, thirty-two years old and winner of several top awards in journalism, and interviews with black women corporate executives. Before committing suicide, McClain wrote of her social isolation: "I have fulfilled the entry requirement of American middle class, yet I am left, at times, feeling unwelcomed and stereotyped."[7]

The way Campbell summed up the plight of executive black women validates the sentiments of the Talented One Hundred, particularly the women. "Corporate racism, they expected. What was unexpected was the various degrees of culture shock, isolation, and alienation that black women experience as they attempt to acclimate professionally and to assimilate their culturally distinct selves into organizations that reward uniformity."[8]

Individuals react differently to the negative stressful emotional impact of racism and the resulting social isolation. Some are proactive, others are reactive. Those persons who are proactive incorporate racism as a major impediment in their lives, but they accept some responsibility for overcoming it. On the other hand, persons who are reactive blame themselves for the negative emotional stress emanating from race or else they blame the system. At one extreme of the continuum, individuals who fail to incorporate racism as a factor in their lives are more likely to internalize negative stress and engage in self-blame. For example, if individuals who are competent fail to receive promotions, they are likely to blame themselves instead of the discriminatory system. At the other extreme of the continuum are individuals who not only incorporate racism as the overriding factor in their lives, but view it as the sole cause of any negative stress. Hence, they are more likely to engage in system-blame. To accept total self-blame or to attribute total system-blame for the stressor of race can lead to reactivity.

Roscoe Champion cautions us "to be realistic about the nature of the society we live in," noting,

Race is a factor in America. Sometimes it is obvious, sometimes not. Don't become so sensitive to it that you'll have a chip on your shoulder and you'll allow your anger and bitterness to sway your judgment. You have to confront it—sometimes head on—and sometimes you circumvent it. The situation dictates the strategy. But don't let it turn you into a bitter person where you'll use racism as a crutch for your failures in society.

The main thing for a black man or woman not to do while growing up in this society is become so sensitive they allow the problem to control them. I see people get bitter—outstanding, brilliant black people. When they start to allow race to eat at them to the extent they see race in everything, they start faulting white people for everything, even when they have control over some things. Any black man's failures are justified in terms of race. They get so bitter, claiming that all white people are no good. A black moderate is an Uncle Tom. It eats away at them. They lose their perspectives and their personalities change. They grew up in this society, and they know racism is out there. So why let it take hold of you and destroy you or neutralize you? Then no one respects you. They start talking crazy. For instance, if you make a decision from the bench, they'll say, "White people got to him." Those people are unrealistic.

The overwhelming majority of the Talented One Hundred, like Roscoe Champion, successfully manage their stressful emotions by becoming actors in the situation rather than being acted upon—defining the situation rather than being defined by it. Growing up in the South was enough for Vernon Jordan, a lawyer and former executive director of the National Urban League, to act against racism and the anger and pain caused by it. "My victimization by the process of desegregation was sufficient incentive to act." When Jordan was struck down in Fort Wayne, Indiana, by a racist assassination attempt, it did not embitter him. Recalled Jordan,

I spent ninety-eight days in the hospital. It took me out of commission for ninety-eight days, but it didn't affect my life otherwise. I am not one to carry around anger and resentment, because I think they are negative. Therefore, you put whatever effort behind you and move forward. I don't think you should get angry. You should get even. I don't think you can outwit the opposition by being angry at the opposition. I think you have to outwit the opposition by being smarter than the opposition.

Blacks overwhelmed by anger frequently become cynical, which can lead to a passive worldview. "The problem with cynicism is that it is as debilitating as naïveté," claimed Warner Babbitt.

If you constantly look at the limits of proscriptions, the tendency is to behave within those parameters. If you choose instead to look at the possibilities, however impossible, the possibilities may become realistic. You'll find a way of getting around those limits. I choose for my basic sanity to do the latter and build around limits.

The Talented One Hundred have chosen "to build around limits" of racism. They exhibit a high level of self-efficacy. Albert Bandura, a psychologist, has described this concept as the ability of people to "produce and regulate events in their lives."[9] The Talented One Hundred indicated they have a high degree of control over their lives; the more objectively successful the individual, the higher the sense of self-efficacy. (In contrast, welfare recipients have a more passive worldview, a sense of inefficacy.[10])

Unlike individuals who have a low degree of self-efficacy, which can lead them to place the onus of responsibility for their failures on the system or on themselves, individuals with a high sense of self-efficacy are likely to see self-responsibility and system responsibility as interfacing. While acknowledging that a racist system contributes to constraining opportunities and producing negative stress, they incorporate both self-responsibility and system responsibility for overcoming barriers to opportunities.

Michael Lomax eloquently articulated the need to acknowledge both self-responsibility and system responsibility as dimensions in coping effectively with racism.

> I've begun to understand more strongly that as a people, we have internalized the negative images whites have about us to the extent that we have low self-esteem. And that low self-esteem affects behavior. If you don't think well of yourself because you are black, that can affect your academic performance, job performance, and personal relationships. I think it has affected me. The more I come to understand that it is not just the white man with his foot on my neck but my internalizing some of the negatives about myself as a black that has really liberated me from that chain psychologically. I've been able to deal more forthrightly with myself and the areas in which I want to compete. I've been able to deal forthrightly with black and white people. I think a lot of black people have not recognized there are two sets of change—the external and internal change.
>
> We need to recognize that we have to fight a battle on more than one front of racism. We need to recognize that a lot of our problems are internal to us and to the group, and we should focus on that. Too often we say, "It is 'the Man.'" What we don't see is our adaptations of negative values, and we got to confront ourselves. I have a hard time blaming teenage pregnancy and drug abuse on "the Man." Certainly racism is involved, but there are individual and social issues which must have a dimension to the solution which says the problem is inside ourselves.

In accord with Lomax, Robert Woodson claimed,

> A lot of our leadership is misleading our people into believing that because racism exists, ending racism has to be a precondition of our achievement. And therefore there is little you can do, because white people are responsible, and unless racism ends, we don't have any responsibility for ourselves. That is a destructive message that is being communicated to our young people. I think that needs to be challenged. The victimizer might have knocked you down, but it is the victim's responsibility to get up. It's not white people's responsibility to see that I get up; it's my responsibility. These experiences of racism have made me tough and given me drive.

Woodson, fifty years old, developed this race lesson and drive for self-improvement while serving as a young man in the armed forces.

> After two years of running to bars and running around while in the army, I stopped and said, "I'm not going to be like a lot of black people who say white people got

their foot on my neck. The way not to become a part of that is to prepare yourself."
I turned some of that energy and anger into achievement. I had more training than
all the whites in my squadron in missile science and technology. So they had to rely
on me even though they outranked me, because I was the only one who knew how
to run the dials. I learned from this experience that the way you get control and influence is through achieving.

Woodson adds that racism is inevitable, so we should expect it and incorporate
it into our strategy for coping. "The race thing is less important than some of the
class questions. Racism is a given. I expect white people to act like white people.
When I go to a corporation, I see the whole workplace is white. I just expect it."

PERSONAL COPING STYLES ON THE JOB

Since "racism is a given," the Talented One Hundred have developed a variety
of personal and collective styles of managing the stressors of race as well as class
and sex, both on and off the job. These styles include being a race ambassador,
being professionally competent and working hard, having self-knowledge, assessing the environment, being unpredictable, gaining knowledge for personal
and social action, prioritizing battles, creating options, burning and building
bridges, and using biculturality as a weapon against racism.

Being a Race Ambassador

Rosabeth M. Kanter examined the stressors experienced by "tokens" in *Men
and Women of the Corporation*. She indicated that individuals identified as being categorically different are singled out as representatives of their category, as
symbols rather than individuals.[11] Black professionals are mindful, whether at
the conscious or subconscious level, of the implications of tokenism and have incorporated this race lesson into their coping modes. Jonathan Mobutu said that
his "basic strategy for dealing with racism is knowing, as Langston Hughes [a
black poet] suggests, 'You are always an ambassador for your race.' I know whenever I am involved in something, the presupposition is going to be I am there as
a token because I am black." Therefore, Mobutu has to be better informed and
better prepared than his white colleagues to receive some semblance of respect.

Inherent in being a race ambassador is the underlying assumption that blacks
have to be better than whites to succeed in this society. Hence, the black elite
cope by being professionally competent and working hard.

Being Competent and Working Hard

"There is no substitute for being the best. There is no situation that is ideal,
but you learn how to make the best of it. I was taught to get things done and do

things right," said John Daniels, a corporate executive. His grandfather taught him this lesson early as an effective way to cope with racism. "I picked up from my grandfather that you should be as smart as possible, get as many tools or collect as many weapons [as you can] to help you to deal with racism."

Being better prepared than others helps Graham Boston, an engineer-scientist, to reduce the risk of failure. "I don't like to take risks. Therefore, when I want something, I work hard at being better than anyone else, and that reduces the risk and gives me the opportunity to get what I want." Kelly Smith, a corporate executive, believes that "it is important to do the best you can at all times, because you never know who is watching you. This is an adaptive pattern, being the best and being persistent." After being denied a promotion by an immediate supervisor, it was a white CEO who noted Kelly's competence and recommended her to a higher position in the international corporation where she works.

Thomas B. Thomas's field is sales and marketing. To be successful, he acknowledged, "I have to be good at what I do. It requires preparation in this business as any other business. I stay up and study." Thomas's parents got him started early in a winning mode. He recalled,

> My father was very athletic; and being athletic, you had to win if you were going to be recognized as the best. As a result, this attitude carried over to everything. My mother had the same kind of attitude, but she directed it toward education. Nobody was supposed to read better than you or write better than you, because you recognized the problem you would have coming home with less than your best on your report card. So you take the two attitudes of my parents and put them together, and they mesh in the competitive attitude which says whatever you put in front of me, I'll take care of it.
>
> My father also told me that in sports you don't have any friends, because the guy across from you will knock you down if you let him. The same thing applies to business. I don't have any friends. I am only going to get where I am going by being the best. If I were to walk into any of my clients' locations, sit down and talk to them and not have the information already consumed in my brain and ready to give it back out to them, they would not talk to me. Even when I know more about their business than they do, they will turn around and give the business to one of their friends. I am not going to be their friend. We have zero in common. I don't go to church with them. The only reason they'll sit down and talk with me is because they know I am bringing something to the table. If they listen to me, they'll probably gain from that. That gives me the forum to do my song and dance. If I get that opportunity, I'll get the business, because no one else is going to be that prepared, that knowledgeable, and that ready to serve their clients.

While competence, commitment, perseverance, and hard work are effective coping strategies, many black elite revel in the competition with whites or with themselves to prove their capabilities. Said Jeremiah Moses, "When I walk into the room and see white people, I know I am superior. I know how to handle myself and don't have to worry about it. I have built myself up. Instead of having an inferiority complex, I have a superiority complex, because I can do it better. I like to match wits with them in whatever I do."

Earnest Ross "likes to match wits" with whites, too, but unlike Jeremiah Moses, he carefully sizes up his opposition.

> If I am next to you and you are next to me, the race is on. It has colored my whole career. I compete against those I know I can [beat]. You compete for something based on knowledge. If I sense a person's knowledge level is greater than mine, I would not compete. I have been able to get what I want by competing in this way.

For others, the process of professional competence becomes an endurance test to prove one's skills and intelligence against the most difficult odds. Dira Ridley feels, "It becomes a true test of putting my skills—intellectually and personally—to move up in that society. Now, I want to know how I stack up against the toughest odds imposed on an individual. That isn't to say I would move up quicker in a black environment. I want to test my skills with those who have the power." Claude Kent is challenged to prove his professional competence when others define his limitations. "When someone tells me I can't do something, I show them I can. So discrimination makes me only more determined to be successful."

Thirty-four-year-old Walden House, who has a PhD in biology and received all his educational training in a predominantly black setting and who has always lived in a black community, would "like to test his skills against whites." House is not unlike Clifford Warren, who trained at a predominantly black medical school in the 1950s and who received his earlier education in black schools. Warren also wanted to test his knowledge and skills in the white world because of his lingering doubts about his competence: "I just wanted to test my knowledge as a physician in an all-white medical school. How did I know they weren't teaching me better medicine than at Meharry? I didn't know it as a young person, but I know now that I would have gotten a better education at a black institution." When he performed better than his white colleagues as an intern in an all-white hospital, he was reassured about his black education. Competing successfully against "the toughest odds" provides individuals with a sense of competence and self-efficacy. That competence is related to self-knowledge.

Having Self-Knowledge

To have knowledge of oneself is to assess realistically the strengths and limitations of one's ability to achieve goals. Yvonne Walker-Taylor's father advised her, "Never underestimate yourself and never overestimate yourself." She feels there are ways to judge that. "You should be able to evaluate yourself. If you are a big healthy girl, you are not going to be a ballet dancer. If you are not good in mathematics, you are not going to be an engineer. I've been poor in mathematics [laughs], so I never aspired to become a mathematician. But the things you are good at, know that you are good at them and do them well."

Graham Boston accepts challenges only when he feels he will be "good at them" and "will do them well." He remarked, "I tend to be cautious about the challenges I accept. I try to do things I think I can make happen. I am not a big risk taker. I am a slight risk taker. Now, what I do is work hard and plan it out and get in good shape, so when I start the task, I'll have the feeling I am going to make it." Self-assessment of one's skills has a major impact on the ability to influence others. It is important, therefore, to understand the strengths and weaknesses of leadership styles that affect success. Are you primarily an entrepreneur, a manager, or a team player? Are you an expressive leader (inspire and motivate others) or an instrumental leader (task oriented)? Are you a brilliant creator, financier, motivator, organizer, or promoter?

Benson Robinson, a successful entrepreneur, attributed his success to the way he manages his employees, who are motivated to produce. "My management style has a lot to do with success. I make a point to say, 'Nobody works *for* me; everybody works *with* me.'" Benson, like countless others, also stresses that it is important to like what you are doing. His effective leadership style is product oriented and people oriented. Joshua Smith, also an entrepreneur, agreed that this is an effective management strategy. It is his reason for allowing employees to own about 25 percent of his company's stock. As stockholders, they have a vested interest in the company's success.

Like Benson, Joshua is not only an entrepreneur but also a good manager. Still, he likes to surround himself with people who can challenge him. "It is a part of being able to accept one's strengths and weaknesses." Both of these men have a hiring policy that is more merit oriented than patronage oriented.

If one lives in an oppressive society, it is particularly essential to have knowledge of one's assets and limitations. Therefore, commissioner Michael Lomax copes with the limitations emanating from oppression by being a political change agent. "I've come to understand where my strengths and deficiencies are and where my racial identity affects that and where it doesn't," remarked Lomax. Self-knowledge helps him to negotiate the system, but an ability to assess the environment is also required.

Assessing the Environment

Assessing the environment incorporates the rhythm of timing. For example, many of the Talented One Hundred were born during a time period when major changes were taking place in black-white relations. Like Earnest Ross, they sensed the direction of the racial winds and prepared themselves to take advantage of forthcoming opportunities: "I was born at a time period when I could afford an education. I was born in a period where black-white relations were beginning to open doors, and if you were fast enough, you could run through the crack."

For Ned McMillian, timing involves a sense of "when to hold 'em and when to fold 'em," an old gambler's analogy.

It means where to be, when to talk, when to shut up, and what to say. The interpretation is based on what I know about you. Somebody might call me a nigger tomorrow, and I might hit him upside the head. You might call me a nigger the next day and I might not say anything. It's knowing that and trying to understand the psychology of the country, especially those in the ruling class. Timing is also knowing when to act politically.

Jefferson Barnes, a sociologist, acknowledged,

I am regarded in some circles as political; that is, I carefully assess the political situation before I act and will tend to pursue a line of interest which I think I can win that doesn't override my being black. Some of my colleagues know I get along with the chancellor. They say, "He is able to bring equipment into his department. Hey, wait a minute. That isn't the way it is supposed to be." They don't say and he is a nigger, too. They don't say that. But they say, "How come? How does he get to be buddy with the chancellor?"

Assessing the environment involves understanding and evaluating the motives of individual actors in a variety of social settings. Elizabeth Wright strongly believes it is important to have a bird's-eye view of the social setting. "As a leader, you have to understand what you are dealing with. Why are individuals asking you to do certain things? Why are they coming to you? You have to keep your antennas out. People will use you as much as you will allow them to use you. Sometimes it's all right to be used, but know that you are being used. Don't let people use you in a negative way." Frank Russo, a health commissioner, "does not want to be used in a negative way" by his staff.

Being unpredictable is one way of maintaining control in a predominantly white environment. My deputy knows some of the time she can make decisions for me. But on crucial issues, she tracks me down. I don't care if I am on an airplane to the moon. She does not want the responsibility of trying to figure out things. Never get yourself in a position where your second person is in command, particularly if they are white. Do not place yourself in a position where you are so matter-of-fact—so predictable—that they can almost do things for you without having your input.

Assessing one's environment means taking advantage of untapped opportunities and challenges. Walter Calvin, a director of a foundation, creates opportunities by using his position in the corporate world to gain status as a power broker in the black community. He dispenses corporate funds to various organizations in the community. Yet he also uses his clout in the black community to gain leverage in the corporation. Veronica Pepper, who is in her fifties, said she opens up herself for things to come along: "I see everything as an opportunity. I embrace it and try to do it." While other faculty complain about the lack of resources for professional development and research at his predominantly black college, Tefe Fusi, an African ethnomusicologist, "embraces opportunities by writing, lecturing, and touring during the summer." He views continuous education as a way to climb the ladder. In his culture, personal success is seen as collective success; his failure is seen as a community failure. As an immigrant in America, he believes that he sees as well as seizes opportunities where African Americans do not. "With black Americans, there is a feeling if you put a seed in the soil, it will grow. I have a feeling some think the seed grows by itself, and all they have to do is reap the harvest," asserted Tefe.

William Ofodile's cross-cultural research on minority immigrants, such as Africans and West Indians, and native minorities supports Fusi's claim that they do well in this country. Since they voluntarily come to this country, they have better expectations for educational and economic opportunities. Thus, "immigrants tend to ignore or rationalize discrimination by saying if you come to my country, you can expect to be discriminated against" says Ofodile. "In my culture, if you are discriminated against, you can cite a proverb which says, as a stranger in a foreign land, you don't expect to be treated like at home. The same thing can be said of Africans and West Indians. Thus, race is less debilitating for immigrants in this country. When black Americans go to Africa, they also tend to do well."

Jefferson Barnes agrees with William Ofodile that racial discrimination is less debilitating for Africans and West Indians.

Blacks from the Caribbean and Africa are much more likely to handle racism with psychological agility than blacks from the U.S. I find the Caribbean-born black comes at the world with such a strong equilibrium and strong sense of self that the white man doesn't bother him too much. American blacks are a peculiar phenomenon. They have spent a lot of time in this country and have got it [coping with racism] wrong. I think American blacks are victimized, and victimized in a very important way by white people. They tend to do one of two things. Look around and say I think this world is an unjust place. The way you handle it is by seeing the world in terms of only connections—who you know—power, privilege, and money. And the other version is the world is a just place; and if you work hard and persevere, and if you compromise, you'll get to the top. In general, blacks in this country make one of these mistakes. Either they see it as meritocracy, or they see it as a game. It is who you know, the "old boy network," suggesting you don't have to be good or competent. That is such a trick bag at such an intricate level that African blacks and Caribbean blacks don't get into. I see a central problem with blacks handling racism. When they experience racism, as I said to you, they will experience it. It is inevitable. Their way of handling it is to say, you see, it is racism and it explains what happens to me, or they'll say that wasn't racism. What happened was not racism at all because I was competent or because I was incompetent. It is either good or bad. They don't see the textured nuances in which racism penetrates and interweaves into their lives and can't be separated in a simple binary fashion and be called it was or wasn't racism, or better yet, it was partly competence and partly racism.

Assessing the environment means understanding the rules of the game. Leo Aramis believes when you are a part of a minority group, "you have to understand the rules of the game for functioning in a racist society." He is critical of black professionals who complain of isolation and rejection by white colleagues. They "cry about how hard it is to deal and function in society the way it is." He feels blacks "overplay the stresses and strains" of racism. Placing the past "stresses and strains" in a historical perspective, Leo chides black professionals, saying,

> Wait a minute! They used to lynch our asses for eyeballing. They would cut out our hearts and throw us in the waters, just for mouthing back. Suddenly, we are going to talk about the stresses and strains of being in a corporate setting and white folks don't like us and are going to impede our progress. What in the hell do you expect? I think that's the whole thing about knowing your history and knowing where you come from. You'll have young folks who'll say this is not fair. Who told you it was supposed to be easy? It's not easy. No one said it was supposed to be easy. There was a lot more stress and strain on our forebears who were lynched, shot, beat up, and misused. That was serious strain, and we are not going through that.

Leo implies if blacks understand the nature of a racist society, they don't aspire to be accepted by whites.

> I think a big problem of the 1960s is that a lot of us felt if we went to the right school, worked real hard, did all the proper things, drank the right kind of wine, read the right kind of books, and learned to play tennis and golf, we'll wake up one morning and be white. That is never going to happen, and as long as that's not going to happen, we have to realize that, understand it, and deal with it. I just work at my job. I don't have any need for acceptance and fulfillment there, because I don't expect it. If I get it, that's nice and extra. That's frosting on the cake, but the cake is my own knowledge of myself and what I deal with to sustain me. The cake is fine without the frosting.

Judge Roscoe Champion understands how these rules of the game operate within the legal system. There are blacks who are critical of some of his decisions, claiming sometimes "whites have gotten to him." But he knows "there are certain parameters" within the system. "I can go to the left; however, if I go too far, I'll be removed. And blacks won't even have a black judge on the bench to be lenient at the same time we are trying to make the system responsive to our needs," said Champion. Warner Babbitt cautions that blacks who play by the rules of "corporate Uncle Tomism," that is, "laughing at jokes, trying to impress the supervisor, always being on hand, carrying the supervisor's coat, and making sure the CEO is happy," must understand the "rules of the game."

You have some people who have gotten good at corporate Uncle Tomism, but they have not done the dual thing of making their mark as a real producer and bottom-line contributor in the organization. So they are given the ceremonial things to do and not really brought into the real work like their white colleagues. So it has worked to their disadvantage. There are a few blacks who have managed to use the cloaking mechanism and shocked white folks about what they could produce, and so they keep demanding to be rewarded for what they do. Understanding the rules of the game gives the oppressed insights into the oppressor. These insights can be used as knowledge for personal and social action.

Gaining Knowledge for Personal and Social Action

"One thing that gives black folks a leg up on white folks is we know us, we know them, and they only know them," asserted Leo Aramis. Jonathan Mobutu agreed and has used knowledge gained from being a token black to be more effective as a change agent.

> Serving on different committees allows me to understand the governance of the institution and how it functions. When I sit on a search committee, I know how the politics of the search is going to be conducted. They are going to have a black and a woman on the committee to show there was consideration for blacks and women candidates. They are going to bring in the affirmative action officer to talk about affirmative action. I don't go in with any expectation that they are going to hire a black officer. I am going in with the expectation to learn something about how the institution functions, so I can later use it to the advantage of black people. So that's how I approach committee assignments; I don't accept them as an indication of how I am appreciated. It is a source of knowledge about how to change the institution.

Bernie Roberts also has used his knowledge as a social researcher to change social policy and to reinforce a positive identity in blacks. His research on the black family has affected so many lives. "Black people were believing what white people were saying about them. They were developing a defeatist attitude and didn't aspire. I believe in knowledge for action. Many researchers don't see the impact of somebody using what they do. It is not where I am in the status order, but what I do for others that makes a difference," asserted Roberts.

Sometimes, knowledge is derived from painful lessons that one incorporates into a positive strategy for action. When Jonathan Walden, a thirty-nine-year-old charismatic minister, ran for public office and was defeated, he incorporated his defeat into a positive lesson that will help him with any future bids for a public office. He ran on a Republican ticket, but, he said, "the party did not do all it could to make me a winner. I learned to deal with them. I never let the experience get me down and get me to the point where I can't function. I try to learn from it and try to figure out how to do it differently."

Walden ran an unsuccessful race, but after losing, he was still interested in "figuring out how to do it differently" and deciding whether he should engage in another immediate political battle or wait until a more opportune time in the future. This process requires individuals to prioritize battles. To fight every battle requires an expenditure of energy. The Talented One Hundred have learned to pick and choose their racial battles.

Prioritizing Battles

"Don't pick unnecessary fights. Don't fight just to be fighting. Have some goals in mind. In the process, pace yourself. Don't become bitter and hostile. Fight in a loving way," said Jack B. Lane. Prioritizing battles involves not only how you choose to fight battles but also the timing. Timothy Brownlee knows that the key to his survival as a public administrator is "knowing when to hold them and when to fold them. Timing is really the key, and you need to have a sense of it. As a public official, you never give up your total heart. You never lay your heart out there. If you do, someone is going to step on it. You have to be impersonal."

When Judge Roscoe Champion became the first black judge in his county, he "knew when to hold them and when to fold them." There were serious racial charges leveled against the court. Judge Champion wanted reforms; however, he decided not to take on the battle immediately after assuming office, but waited until he felt he would have an impact.

> Before I went on the court, there were reports that judges were not advising defendants. I never went in and said I believed what those people said, and that you are wrong and the bar association castigated you. I proved to them I was competent. They accepted me. I went back to the problem; I didn't fault them. I said let's make sure we are right. Let's have a record of it to protect us against unfair criticisms. You don't have to say you're racist or it was racist inspired, but it becomes obvious.

Picking and choosing battles and deciding when to wage them is time consuming. It is, therefore, not surprising that so many of the Talented One Hundred ignore, deny, or fail to recall racist incidents. To dwell on these incidents would render them dysfunctional, thus impeding reaching their goals. Nevertheless, when some battles become too much to fight, it is important to have options. According to Ned McMillian, "To be successful, you have to set goals and go after them, but always have an alternative position. Don't keep beating a steel wall if you can't get through it. If you can't go over it, go around it. If you can't get under it, then come back and get another start." Even though McMillian has a successful medical practice and is a professor of medicine, he is working on a PhD in gerontology.

Creating Options

The Talented One Hundred believe in having options. In addition to their primary professions, 50 percent have a secondary profession and 9 percent have a third profession. When I interviewed Diane Earlinger in 1987, she was completing an MBA, even though she had an MD and was successful in her position as an administrator at a federal agency. Having alternatives is a successful coping strategy. The following vignettes illustrate how important this is to the success of the black elite:

"I believe you should be multifaceted and you should do lots of things. You shouldn't be saddled with just one thing to do. I am interested in designing and completing a doctorate in finance or business administration," said Timothy Brownlee, a successful public official.

"When the chairman denied my promotion, even though the dean recommended it, I went on to the next objective. I have never been one to rely on a single occupation or objective," said William Long, a fifty-two-year-old professor in the school of architecture and urban planning at a large university. He has a photography studio and owns real estate.

"As a journalist, I develop employment on the outside. You have to broaden your audience outside the newspaper and use that reputation to go elsewhere or to enhance your reputation in the organization," remarked Warner Babbitt.

One can have options within one's profession, too. "I never rely on more than 10 percent of my business from one contractor. So if there are cutbacks, the company will not fold," stated Joshua Smith. Thomas B. Thomas, a director of marketing for a major company, stated,

I am in a career that gauges everything based on performance—very little of it is personality or whether you get along with people. If I were in administration, I would have to be a nice, personable person. I chose to be in a setting where I would be paid in direct proportion to my value in the marketplace. So, when the company says this is what the objective is, I blow the objective clean out of the wall. When I walk in there and talk about something, I get listened to. If I didn't have any numbers, any dollars, nobody would listen. Some companies are market driven and are strong on performance. Others are not market driven and people work on a salary. Blacks have to select a company that is market driven to give them leverage in the company.

Having options became the major motivating drive for forty-three-year-old Frank Russo. In fact, he claims it was his "guiding light" after his encounter with a racist incident during his childhood in a small southern town in the 1950s.

When I was about ten years of age, I remember how my father and other elderly black men had to respond in the presence of white people. It used to bother me so much. I remember when I was thirteen years old, I got into a fight with a white teenager, the son of a prominent doctor in town, at a packing company where I worked. The white teenager was a supervisor, giving instructions to sixty-year-old

black males. It was driving me up the wall, the way he was doing it. It was humili-
ating for me to watch black men I said "Yes Sir" to and respected having to lower
themselves to a thirteen- or fourteen-year-old white supervisor. It was during that
time I made the decision that I wasn't going to be in a similar position. That was
my guiding light.

Frank Russo is a health administrator and he also practices medicine part-
time and is employed part-time as an administrator in a county agency.

A couple of years ago, the division director called me at home and told me I had to
quit my part-time job, because there was a conflict in regulations with the job I had.
They knew I had that job when I took this one. What bothered me the most was that
I was on my way to work that Friday night, and he told me I couldn't go. I didn't go,
but reflected on it all night. I said to myself [voice rising] too long and too hard have
I worked to be in the same position as my daddy, except that I am at a different level.

"I am going to tell you now and tell you later," said Frank Russo to the director, "I just bought a new car and a house. But one thing you need to understand is that I am not trapped. I have certain standards and certain options and
if you try to bring certain things on me, I'll walk away from here."

I took another job after checking the rules and regulations for possible violations.
I must establish the difference between my father and myself. I must have options,
and my father had none, and that's what I am all about. I've gotten very anxious
and upset when my options [were] limited. If you walk in here today and tell me I
don't have a job, it will set me back a little while, but because of my other options,
my family will still have all the basic things. I'll have to send my Jaguar back, but
I'll get a Toyota. In six months, I'll have the Jaguar back.

It is important for the black elite to be economically independent. Many of
the Talented One Hundred own businesses or plan to have one in the future.
Like Jonathan Walden, they feel that an "independent economic base is a critical viable option."

It allows you to speak out against racism. For me the church is that independent
base of operation. It allows me to more freely express my convictions. However, it
doesn't make much difference to me what's the setting. I will speak what I believe
is right, and I'll suffer the consequences. But I refuse to allow anyone to seal my
speech or to stifle in any way the expressions of my convictions.

But unless you have options, Jonathan Walden cautioned, don't burn your
bridges. He maintained, "I never move on without having something to move
to. I've always had enough good sense not to burn my bridge before getting to
the other side. I may burn it behind me, but not before I get to the other side."
While some individuals burn bridges behind them, others want to build bridges
between the races.

Building Bridges

Clarence Pinkney said that the way he copes as a corporate manager is by "bridging the gap between the powerful and the powerless." Some blacks feel they can best assist other blacks by building bridges between the races and by working within mainstream organizations rather than through separate black groups. It is the view of Veronica Pepper, president of a predominantly white professional association in the behavioral sciences, that "blacks should remain part of mainstream organizations. They should challenge the system to make it what it is. Blacks give over ownership to other people. They see someone else in control, but don't see themselves as part of that system."

Being a bridge builder has helped Veronica Pepper to successfully achieve her goals in serving blacks.

> I've always been involved with helping blacks, particularly children. One reason why I've been so successful in my organizational effort is that I've done less gesturing and polarizing and more problem solving. I know what my objectives are, but I always think there is a confluence of interests. I always tried to speak to the interest of the people I serve—staff and others—who are going to try to bring about changes that will ultimately help black constituents.

Sharla Frances, a chief administrator, agreed, saying, "Being in a mixed setting allows me to influence social policies. It is very hard to influence social policies from a predominantly minority view. You have to understand other people's needs and wants in order to be effective." Jack B. Lane sees merit in this position. But it is also the influence of his participation in the civil rights movement under Martin Luther King Jr. that continues to motivate him to "preach about the building of the beloved community. . . . I go to meetings and try to deal with people on a level [where] they are," said Jack. He attends prayer breakfasts with white public officials, one of the few black members of this elected body to do so. "I don't have any ill feelings or malice toward anyone, whether they oppose me or say all manner of things about me. I just don't have it. I don't have time for it. This is what the movement taught us. You don't have time for ill feelings, to hate, or to hold grudges. You don't have the energy for that. You have to go with the business of trying to make the society better."

While Lane is interested in "building a beloved community," others want to build individual bridges as a crossover to their personal acceptance and professional success. Bonhart Wheeler, a college professor in his fifties at a predominantly black university, adopts the mannerism of middle-class whites, which he feels creates greater acceptance and comfort.

> I find myself in situations where people tend not to relate to me as they relate to other blacks, because of the way I carry myself. People accept me because I don't have many of the mannerisms of blacks. Many whites have not been exposed to blacks who speak well, are composed, have self-worth, and cannot be drawn into

an altercation. When I see it, I rather enjoy it. I see people who never related to a person in such a way tend to change.

While Wheeler enjoys being accepted personally by whites, Dira Ridley thinks it is professionally expedient to establish bridges of comfortableness with colleagues.

If I really want to succeed in this world, which is a predominantly white world, with the power and money, I must be technically competent. But I must also make these individuals comfortable with me as a person. I can be the most brilliant individual in the world, and they know that, but I am going nowhere unless there is a gut-level feeling that I am okay. How do you get their gut feelings to say that you are okay? Does it mean you have to change as a person? The answer is, "Not necessarily, as long as you are not radical."

You'll find among scientists that they are very similar people in their thought processes. Their economic backgrounds might vary. But they are very close in what they like, if they've been exposed to it. Exposure is the key thing. First, I have to get them to feel comfortable with me—gut feelings—and that isn't as hard as you might think, because our economic status is going to be similar. We can drink Perrier water, if you are exposed to it. So you begin to expose yourself to things they like and their lifestyles. But at the same time, it is not becoming like them. You want to maintain your identity. I am black, a Southerner, and my parents are not educated.

Sometimes establishing bridges of comfortableness is merely a gesture of one's humanity to others. When David Benton, an artist, is not treated cordially by whites, before reacting to their slights, he said, "I will say, 'Good Morning' to a surly waitress. I will do human kinds of things and then get the service, or I will speak directly to the person about my mistreatment or speak to others who can do something about it. If I were in a public place, I would demand the service to which I am entitled."

Since the black elite walk between two worlds, they find it is expedient to establish bridges of comfortableness with whites. But they also find it may be necessary to use their biculturality, as Jonathan Mobutu and Thomas B. Thomas do, in coping with racism.

Using Biculturality as a Weapon against Racism

Jonathan Mobutu asserted,

When I am on a committee, a lot of the perspective I bring to bear is bicultural. Black students need someone with whom to identify. I try to show how black colleges have helped students to achieve. I also use my influence in terms of black repertoire. At a place like my university, if you have a certain style of communication, the message can be lost. One of the things you do is raise your tone and start speaking in an urban cadence and in an excitable way to get their attention. For example, resorting to linguistic patterns, saying "Hey man, let's be real!" "Are you serious?" or "Give me a break!" That is out of the usual repertoire. If I sit up and start staring, that projects another image of the bad nigger. So that will defuse any hostility that will come across. So you use that to control the situation in which you find yourself.

Thomas Kochman, in *Black and White Styles in Conflict*, supports the idea that different cultural patterns and styles of communication by blacks are often interpreted by whites as aggressive behavior.[12] But to defuse a racist situation, Thomas B. Thomas finds it is necessary to "lapse into an ethnic bag." Listen to Thomas "signify" on his colleague by putting him in the "dozens."

One day we were sitting in a roundtable discussion and someone asked for a drink of something. This Mormon guy said, "You can use my cup as long as you don't nigger lip it." So immediately I made my presence known. I said, "Why don't you bring things out front? What is nigger lipping it?" He stammered, "You know what that is, don't you?" "Why would I know what a derogatory term like that means?" I said, "I want you to demonstrate the technique you call nigger lipping," I said, "Go ahead. You're so smart. Go ahead." When he is backed into a corner, he takes a cup and sticks his bottom lip out and says, "That's what I am talking about." Then I said, "It looks just like something your mother would do, but it would not be with a cup." [Laughs] He was beet red.

COLLECTIVE MODES OF COPING ON THE JOB

Though the black elite have developed several individual modes of coping on the job, they believe that it is important, as Leo Aramis noted, to keep one's center by maintaining contact with other blacks. Bruce P. Dohrenwend and Barbara S. Dohrenwend, in *Social Status and Psychological Disorders: A Causal Inquiry*, stated that the impact of race and class as major stressors can be reduced by mediating factors, both external and internal.[13] The internal constraints refer to abilities, drives, values, and beliefs. External constraints are the social support network, that is, family, friends, and social clubs. While there are conceptual limitations of studies on social support, other researchers have stressed their mediating effects on stress.[14] Having a strong support network acts as a stress buffer in reducing the impact of social isolation.

Networking

In response to social isolation in predominantly white environments, networks of professional organizations have sprung up around the country to meet the needs of the black elite, from artists to zoologists. The black professional understands there is more power in collectivity than in individuality.

The black artist in the United States, for instance, is "stereotyped and kept at the periphery of the art world," because of "exclusionism disguised as artistic judgment" and "outmoded definitions of black art."[15] An *ART News* survey of thirty-eight artists, dealers, collectors, art historians, and museum curators "reveals unanimity on one point: the art world is not widely informed about the scope and quality of visual art now being produced by Black Americans."[16] Hence, black artists are organizing locally and nationally to change their plight. Aretha Shield exemplifies this trend:

> I am a member of a black artist group. I joined the group because I feel that it is important to take a stand in my community as a visible working artist. I was working in the community, but no one knew what I did. Now that I've joined [the group], more people are aware of my talents. I think sometimes the black artist has more power working collectively than individually. We held an exhibition of black artists' works at a national museum. Individually, we could not have had a show. Under the title black, you can get more doors open rather than just being a black individual, because museums want a black show. But they are reluctant to feature an individual black artist as an American artist.

Jonathan Mobutu has found that organizing black faculty and staff at his university is an effective "strategy in dealing with racism," creating "centers of power." However, when black professionals organize on the job, it might be necessary to use informal networks and go "underground," said Stephanie Tahara. "When you make a strong statement by being visible, you can become a target. You tip whites off to what they need to do. So one of the things you can do is not make a strong visible statement but a strong invisible statement. So you strategize at somebody's house—you are taking care of business, and they don't know whom to pick on."

While organizational networks have flourished among black professionals in predominantly white settings, some have emerged as primarily social networks. Teresa Hale meets weekly with a black women's group to combat alienation and isolation. Her mixed professional memberships are for professional networking, growth, and development. Many black professional organizations in actuality, however, serve dual needs. While observing an annual meeting of the Congressional Black Caucus, Diane Earlinger was able to understand, for the first time, why there was so much gesturing and posturing among black organizations, and why there were so few concrete innovative strategies for achieving goals: There are too many unmet psychological needs. Robert Woodson, chairman of the Council for a Black Economic Agenda, who studies issues of economic, tax, and trade policies and their effects on the black community, understands Diane Earlinger's concerns. Said Woodson, "Many of our politicians are lazy. They don't read or take the time to study. They would rather get up and talk about 'It ain't the man, it's the plan. It ain't the rap, it's the map.' If you got rhyming clichés, you can get over with a black audience. [Laughs] We like being entertained; we don't like being informed." Perhaps, since so many black elite who work in isolation have unmet psychological and social needs, these organizations serve as a latent function for their ego enhancement and self-validation.

A parallel criticism is often leveled against the black church, that is, the emphasis on spiritual fulfillment versus social activism and collective empowerment.

Unlike most black ministers, who emphasize spiritualism, Joseph Lowery exemplifies ministers who fuse spiritualism with activism. He knows that a sense of personal efficacy is related to group efficacy. Individuals' racial identity, class identity, personal identity, support system, and worldview influence "what people choose to do as a group, how much effort they put into it, and their staying power when group effort fails to produce results."[17] Hence, under Lowery's leadership, the aim of SCLC is to improve the black community through organizing at every level to bring economic, moral, and political pressure in the public and private sector.

Although black leaders have a similar goal—to empower the black community—there are different strategies for achieving this end. Robert Woodson, a former resident fellow at the American Enterprise Institute and a Republican, stresses self-help and economic development through organizing low-income people in the black community. He is critical of the traditional civil rights leaders and their tactics, claiming they do not benefit the poor. Joseph Lowery disagreed:

> I reject completely Reagan's niggers who talk about self-help as though we never helped ourselves and as though government has no responsibility. Government is largely responsible for our predicament, and it has a responsibility to deal with it. And furthermore, government has the resources to deal with it. The private sector never moves until government provides the leadership.
>
> Nobody has ever claimed marching was a total answer, even in the sixties. Marching was just one dramatic way of calling attention to the problem or forcing people to deal with the problem. And don't overlook the fact of giving yourself a good feeling that at least you started doing something about it. It is better than throwing a brick or better than sitting in a corner feeling sorry for yourself and letting anger turn inwardly. We'll never stop marching; we will always keep moving onward, bringing more pressure and trying to effect more change. But somehow, young people need to discover a wheel, and they got to find totally new ways of resolving our problems.
>
> There are no new methods. The methods are as old as the problem is. The methods are economic, moral, and political pressure. You do it in coalescence in some instances, and you do it in black power movements in others.

Mentoring

Leo Aramis believes that the black elite need to "train their replacements" as another strategy to insure blacks' progress. One way to accomplish this goal is through mentoring, said Elizabeth Wright, who is particularly interested in helping young women. "I feel strongly that you have a responsibility to help others achieve through mentoring. I got to where I am because there were many people who helped me. We need to have someone to answer the questions for mentees in order to get them at a higher level earlier." Ned McMillian believes this way, too, and has "started a program on minority recruitment and training in medicine," while John Lamont, a scientist, is involved in a program to recruit and mentor science students.

COLLECTIVE AND PERSONAL STYLES OF
COPING OFF THE JOB

Thomas Kochman notes that the behavioral, emotional, and verbal styles of the two races, white and black, are in conflict.[18] Despite economic status, it is likely that blacks more readily choose nontraditional modes of coping, such as religion and humor, while whites are more likely to choose more traditional modes of coping, such as psychological counseling.

The Talented One Hundred have developed effective external ways of coping off the job—they maintain close contact with the black community through familial, friendship, and social networks. They have also developed effective *internal* ways of relieving their stress through exercise, hobbies, music, meditation, and prayer. The black elite come from diverse backgrounds. If they grew up in the segregated South, for instance, they may feel more comfortable maintaining a black social network. This pattern was typical for most of the Talented One Hundred. Only a few individuals stated they felt closer to whites, having lived and worked in predominantly white settings all of their lives. Most said they felt isolated in white environs, and maintained contact with other blacks as a buffer against alienation, isolation, and stress.

When Frank Russo was a junior in college in the South, he had a summer job with the Interior Department in a town in Ohio where there were no blacks.

> I didn't realize the impact it had on me until one weekend. I went to my supervisor and told him I just had to get away from there and go to the next town and spend the weekend. I had to see somebody black. I went to a little town—Cambridge, Ohio. I was walking down the street and saw a black family sitting on the porch, and I stopped to talk with them. This experience allowed me to reflect on blackness and whiteness and how important it is to be around black people. I learned there was a type of conversation I missed. It was evident when I saw an old black lady down by the creek fishing; I could talk to her about my mother's church meetings or frying fish. It didn't matter that we talked, just being in her presence was enough.

Jack B. Lane feels strongly that "it is important for a token black to be anchored in knowing where he or she comes from and not losing contact with family, black social organizations, or institutions and their own blackness. You have to be anchored in yourself, knowing that you are here in this position only for a season, but you do what you can to make a contribution. Be true to yourself. Be true to your people. Be true to the legacy and heritage. You got to reach back and do something."

Joseph Lowery thinks it becomes increasingly difficult for blacks who live and work in a predominantly white setting to "be true to the legacy and heritage and to reach back and do something. I think it is more difficult for a person who is isolated in the workplace and lives in a white community. If he is isolated in the workplace and bought a house in black suburbia, he is also cut off from working, poor blacks, especially if he is not involved in the church. With a few exceptions, the black church is heterogeneous [and] pluralistic, and if you are not active in the black church, you can be far off from poor blacks."

However, Lowery noted, "little by little I see them easing back into social activities and into relationships they are sorry were destroyed in the black community. . . . I had a couple who returned to my church who, for almost four years, had belonged to a white church in the suburbs where they live. They want their kids in Sunday school, which will be their major contact with other black kids."

The black church serves many functions. It is not only a place to find spiritual fulfillment and to relieve stress from social isolation by connecting with other blacks but also the traditional center for political and social activities. In the late 1980s, however, there appeared to be a shift in political and social leadership from the sacred to the secular sector. Lowery sees this trend as a temporary phenomenon. He thinks the black church is crucial as a support base and as a place for making politicians accountable to the black community.

> We are going to realize that there was a temporary shift from the black church to black politics, and now we are shifting back, because we realize two things: (1) Politicians have to get their support from the church/community, and (2) if we don't learn to hold black politicians accountable, they'll learn to become as corrupt as white politicians. We have to keep black politicians accountable and in close touch [with the black community]. We cannot let them substitute chamber of commerce meetings for prayer meetings, nor can we let them substitute cocktails for community. We have to keep them close to where the source is. We can't let them just run back when they get in trouble or need to be elected.

While the black church offers a refuge from the stresses of the workplace, it is also important to have a strong support network of family and friends. "You need an external base you can count on. Unfortunately, blacks in the corporate world have very few they can count on in the organization," noted Kelly Smith. Thomas B. Thomas advised token blacks who work in predominantly white settings to separate their professional and personal lives. "People have to separate the workplace from everything else. It is a place where you go to perform a task. When the task is over, your life starts all over again. If you try to incorporate your professional life with your personal life, and people don't accept you, then you are bent out of shape. Your performance will be poor. So if you separate your professional and social life, you won't have that problem of being isolated."

Jeanette Gear, a judge, agreed. "You have to always be on guard in the workplace, whether white or black, because you are not certain about anything. You don't know if you'll have a job tomorrow. In the corporation, everyone is trying to get to the top. It is very difficult to relax at work. You need to find a group where you can relax and hang loose."

The Black Party: Stress Reducer

For many blacks who live between two worlds, the black party becomes the place to "hang loose." Like the black church, the black party is viewed as a stress reducer, while the white party is seen as a place for professional and business networking. Having grown up in a black community, Warner Babbitt had to rearrange his thinking about parties when he started working in a white world.

> Basically, I thought you go to a party to have fun. I never thought you went to a party to make business contacts. I realized you don't go to a white party to have fun. You go to a party to be seen, make contacts, and get ahead. So parties among whites are seen as business opportunities. In the environment in which I grew up, they were basically seen as social opportunities or a chance to have a good time. You have to rearrange your thinking, and that takes some doing.

For Jonathan Mobutu, who lives and works in a predominantly white setting, a black party becomes a welcome relief from isolation and stress.

> We live in a college town, where there are not any traditional black radio stations. What comes across the air is European music. There are a variety of social outlets that my white neighbors are comfortable with, such as receptions and get-togethers that are sterile in format. Whereas, in the background I've come from, there is a lot of noise, joking, and music that comes out of the black experience. We try to re-create some semblance of that by having regular card parties among black males or house parties among the professional black faculty and staff where we can act the way we want to.
>
> In many of those parties, it is still politically appropriate to invite white people to come, because you want to maintain a useful relationship with your neighbors—so you invite them to come. They'll only stay for a while, and then we start to get down. Take, for instance, when we had a surprise birthday party for my wife, the neighbors were all invited, but they left after a couple of hours. Then we were able to have more of a traditional black party. This is a typical pattern. I think whites leave parties earlier. It is almost a ritual for them. For us, it is a stress reducer, a sense of fellowship, and interaction that we can't get on a normal basis. For them, it is a regular pattern at predominantly white institutions. You go to receptions all the time. The white party is just another formal ritual. Theirs is not a true friendship or camaraderie that drives professional blacks to get together. For us, it is an experience to reenergize and to re-create the black experience. There is also a performance mode to how parties are held in the black experience. You are able to get down and act in ways that you wouldn't if you were in your formal role in a professional setting. You would not find that in the white parties I attend where people have middle-level ranks or above.

Male and Female Coping Styles

While the black party is a stress reducer for both black men and women, Mobutu senses there is a distinct difference in the way they cope with stress off the job.

It seems easier for black males to get together. We have luncheon meetings every couple of weeks, where we just shoot the shit and talk the stuff. We call it the committee, and it has no major function. There is a group of us who play bid whist every three weeks or so. We talk stuff, drink beer and wine. We also compare notes about what's going on; we maintain an informal political network. We have a group of us who play racquetball to get rid of some of that tension.

The women at the university where Mobutu teaches, on the other hand, do not appear to have similar outlets for their stresses. The diverse marital statuses of women at his college seem to affect their chances of socializing, because of the varying degrees of responsibility. In addition to their professional duties, women still have the primary responsibility of child rearing and housekeeping. Perhaps this is one reason why the black women in my population expressed greater isolation than the black men. The married women of the Talented One Hundred were more likely to become involved in their families as a means of coping with work-related stress. Single women used work as a way of coping. Both also found other outlets for coping with stress. Like Mobutu and his male friends, Elizabeth Wright, a college administrator, and her female friends "get a jug of wine and get together at a single girlfriend's house to play Scrabble and discuss consultant work until the wee hours in the morning."

While males and females may have different social modes of coping on the job, they both have developed effective internal mechanisms for relieving stress. When Sharla Frances, a chief administrator for a major city, is "frustrated," she is likely to find herself walking in the woods or in a museum. "I like to be thoughtful, but share it with someone, so I share it with the artists through their works. I want to know what they are thinking and feeling." Having this "continuity snaps me out of a downfall. When I don't have it, I am hysterical," Frances said, laughing. Others relieve stress through exercise, hobbies, humor, music, meditation, and prayer. No more than 2 percent of the Talented One Hundred said they used alcohol in excess. And many indicated without my probing that they never used alcohol or drugs as a way of coping. But some individuals said they ate excessively, while others used humor to cope.

The Role of Humor

Humor is a common way to reduce stress. Many blacks have historically used humor to deal with the contradictions inherent in oppression. Roscoe Champion tries to "laugh at things."

I amuse myself about racial incidents. I just returned with a delegate from another part of the world. On this trip, there were black and white people. Oddly enough, when the three black people were talking, the white people who were part of the delegation would think something was going on. It's like we can't get together. When I go to a social function and blacks fail to acknowledge other blacks in the presence of whites, I find that amusing. It's like they are saying white people are watching, and you can't say anything.

The Role of Spirituality

I found a strong spiritual orientation expressed through prayer or meditation among the Talented One Hundred, which helped them to reduce stress and to keep moving. When I discussed my research for this book with Charles V. Willie, a sociologist, he said, "I've been in the storm so long, give me a little time to pray." Prayer also helped Yvonne Walker-Taylor to cope with the bishop of Wilberforce University.

> It has been a matter of tenacity and a spiritual belief in God that helped me to cope. Religion is an outlet for my stress. It is the root of my being. It is the one thing that holds me up. I think a strong, spiritual background gives you that strong impetus and added confidence in self. So you got to believe somebody is with you, and humans aren't. They'll turn on you. But there's only one thing that will never fail you, and that's God. The stronger you believe, the easier it is to understand what's going on around us, and you can cope with the bad times.

Jonathan Walden's strong spiritual orientation also helps to sustain him in the fight against oppression.

> It is not God's will for us to be oppressed, though it might be His permissive will. If He is all-powerful, as we believe, He has the power to change the course of history anytime He chooses. Therefore, you flow with the way the world was created and use your belief in Him and His desire for you to move beyond your circumstances. Let no one tell you what to do [but God].

When Tefe Fusi, a Catholic, feels alienated in this country, he knows he is never alone because he retains his African spirituality.

> In the African worldview, everyone has access to the spiritual world. I've been through enough rituals to accept that fact and to believe in it, despite the fact that I am Catholic. So I rely very heavily on the belief that I am never alone, and that is also the main reason why people think I am arrogant. I have self-confidence that I am never alone, so I ignore things. It is not intentional. If something is going to happen to me, it is predestined to happen. So I derive my spiritual strength from that more than Catholicism. I believe strongly in the spiritual world and feel decisions will not materialize until that time.

When fifty-nine-year-old Lee Watson's "heart began to skip a beat" she returned to her strong Baptist upbringing. Lee humorously recalled,

> Oh, my God! I've done all the planning and all this work and I built my retirement home and have accumulated all these assets. I plan to retire, and now I am going to die. We've always said religion is a black man's opiate. I got down on my knees and prayed. "Lord, show me the way—you surely can't treat me like this. You are supposed to be a just God and here I am at the end of my life and I've stacked up all these rewards for myself and now I am going to die of a heart attack." I was okay, but just under stress. Now, when I feel stressful, I go through relaxation and deep breathing.

Joseph Lowery cautioned that blacks have to develop a "liberation lifestyle" free of stress and grounded on strong spiritual beliefs to help them cope with racism in this society.

> I have developed a liberation lifestyle. I do what I can, and what I can't do, I don't worry about—you incorporate that in your life. I believe God has called me to do things, and I see my ministry in perspective. I've learned not to change things I can't and not to worry about what I can't change. Leave it in God's hands. If I can't get to it, I hope the Lord will.
>
> The liberation lifestyle is based on what I say is the admonition of the 1980s and 1990s, and that is, we must not fall victim to assaults from without or to our faults from within. A liberation lifestyle will make us free at last—not after death, but right now. The lifestyle is based on a thorough understanding of who we are, and that's spiritual. We are sons and daughters of God. We are sacred human beings with sacred personalities, infinite worth, and made in the image of God. Beyond that, we are not only the sons and daughters of God, but we are the sons and daughters of Mary McLeod Bethune, Frederick Douglass, Martin Luther King Jr., Charlotte Hawkins Brown, and that gives us another strength, resource, and understanding beyond ourselves. So when we live that way, it frees us from self-hate, and we are free at last. We know who we are. We know the people who are trying to abuse us or assault us are ignorant and need our education. They are lost, and they need our salvation. Hence, that frees us from hate. . . . It [liberation lifestyle] ain't judicial or legislative; it ain't computers; it ain't science; it ain't high tech; it's spiritual, and we got to begin there.

Lowery's liberation lifestyle is a positive concept that can elevate blacks to a newfound sense of collectivity and clarity of identity. It is evident from the literature and from the views of the Talented One Hundred that stress can be meliorated if blacks are grounded in an Afrocentric orientation. Social isolation is less likely to occur when one maintains a strong race orientation and a weak class orientation, when one is culturally and structurally segregated in a dominant society, when one has supportive black networks and linkages with the black community, and when one has effective internal coping resources and responses. Conversely, social isolation, greater stress, and lack of identity clarity are more likely to occur when one maintains a strong class orientation and a weak race orientation, when one is more culturally and structurally integrated into the dominant society, when one lacks supportive black networks and linkages with the black community, and when one lacks effective internal coping resources and responses.

SUMMARY

This chapter addresses how the black elite manage the negative emotional impact of racism. While some individuals are proactive, others are reactive. Individuals who are proactive incorporate racism as a major impediment in their lives, but they accept some responsibility for overcoming it. Individuals who are reactive accept only self-blame for the negative emotional stress resulting from race, or they blame only the system. The Talented One Hundred have developed a proactive posture toward racism. They use a variety of personal and collective modes of coping on and off the job to mediate the negative stress of race, along with class, to assist them in continuing as successful actors in reaching their goals. The literature, as well as the collective experience of the Talented One Hundred, has shown that by maintaining a supportive network of family, friends, and peers, black individuals can reduce social isolation in white settings.

In the next chapter, I move beyond the color line to envision the black elite as important players on the global stage.

NOTES

1. Bruce P. Dohrenwend and Barbara S. Dohrenwend, *Social Status and Psychological Disorder: A Causal Inquiry* (New York: Wiley, 1969), 133.

2. Robert Davis, "A Demographic Analysis of Suicide," in Lawrence Gary, ed., *Black Men* (Beverly Hills, CA: Sage, 1981), 179–195.

3. Robert Staples, *Black Masculinity* (San Francisco: Black Scholar Press, 1982), 32.

4. Delores P. Aldridge, "Black Female Suicide: Is the Excitement Justified?" in LaFrances Rodgers Rose, ed., *The Black Woman* (Beverly Hills, CA: Sage, 1980). Also see Lawrence E. Gary, "Health Status," in Gary, ed., *Black Men*, 47–71; Frederick D. Harper, "Alcohol Use and Abuse," in Gary, ed., *Black Men*, 169–177; Frederick D. Harper and Marvin Dawkins, "Alcohol Abuse in the Black Community," *Black Scholar*, April 1977, 23–31. Also see

5. Lois Benjamin and James B. Stewart, "Race, Illness Orientation, and Worldview as Linkages in Welfare Dependency," *Mimeo*, 1986.

6. Diane R. Brown and Verna M. Keith, eds., *In and Out of Our Right Minds: The Mental Health of African American Women* (New York: Columbia University Press, 2003). See also *Report of the Secretary's Task Force on Black and Minority Health* (Washington, DC: U.S. Department of Health and Human Services, 1985); Ronald M. Andersen, Ross M. Mullner, and Llewellyn J. Cornelius, "Black-White Differences in Health Status: Methods or Substance?" *Milbank Quarterly*, 65, suppl. 1 (1987), 72–99; Kenneth G. Manton, Clifford H. Patrick, and Katrina W. Johnson, "Health Differentials between Blacks and Whites: Recent Trends in Mortality and Morbidity," *Milbank Quarterly*, 65, suppl. 1 (1987), 129–197; Harold W. Neighbors, "Improving the Mental Health of Black Americans: Lessons from the Community Mental Health Movement," *The Milbank Quarterly*, 65, suppl. 2 (1987), 348–380.

7. Bebe Moore Campbell, "To Be Black, Gifted, and Alone," *Savvy*, Dec. 1984, 68.

8. Campbell, "Alone," 68.

9. Albert Bandura, "Self-Efficacy Mechanism in Human Agency," *American Psychologist*, 37 (1982), 122.

10. Lois Benjamin and James B. Stewart, "The Self-Concept of Black and White Women: The Influences upon Its Formation of Welfare Dependency, Work Effort, Family Networks, and Illnesses," *American Journal of Economics and Sociology*, 48, no. 2 (April 1989), 165–175; see also Benjamin and Stewart, "Race."

11. Rosabeth Moss Kanter, *Men and Women of the Corporation* (New York: Basic Books, 1977), 214.

12. Thomas Kochman, *Black and White Styles in Conflict* (Chicago: University of Chicago Press, 1981).

13. Dohrenwend and Dohrenwend, *Social Status*.

14. See James H. Geer, Gerald C. Davidson, and Robert T. Catchel, "Reduction of Stress in Humans through Nonveridical Perceived Control of Aversive Stimulation," *Journal of Personality and Social Psychology*, 16 (1970), 731–738; James W. Pennebaker, M. Audrey Burnam, Marc A. Schaeffer, and David C. Harper, "Lack of Control as a Determinant of Perceived Physical Symptoms," *Journal of Abnormal Psychology*, 35 (1977), 167–174; Murray P. Naditch, Margaret A. Gargan, and Laurie B. Michael, "Denial, Anxiety, Locus of Control, and the Discrepancy between Aspirations and Achievements as Components of Depression," *Journal of Abnormal Psychology*, 84 (1975), 1–9; Jerry Suls and Brian Muller, "Life Changes and Psychological Distress: The Role of Perceived Control and Desirability," *Journal of Applied Social Behavior*, 11 (1981), 379–389; Melvin Seeman and Teresa Seeman, "Health Behavior and Personal Autonomy: A Longitudinal Study of the Sense of Control in Illness," *Journal of Health and Social Behavior*, 24 (1983), 144–160.

15. Patricia Failing, "Black Artists Today: A Case of Exclusion," *ART News*, March 1989, 124.

16. Failing, "Black Artists," 124.

17. Bandura, "Self-Efficacy Mechanism," 143.

18. Kochman, *Black and White Styles in Conflict*.

8

BEYOND THE COLOR LINE: AN ALTERNATIVE VISION

"What does Jesse Jackson want? What does Jackson really want?" Over and over, that question has been asked during the presidential campaign, as if there were a mystery shrouded in the answer.

But there is no hidden agenda, no secret ambition, no private deal. The agenda from the beginning has been peace, justice, and jobs. The ambition has been to unite our constituency. The deal has been to capture the nation's imagination and find common ground for change. . . . People have crossed ancient lines of race, religion, and region to come together. They may be black or white or brown, but however different their numerators, the denominator is the same.[1]

Jesse Jackson articulated and raised the aspirations of African Americans. He also captured the imagination of factory workers, farmers, housewives, the unemployed, Chicanos, Native Americans, and the liberal, educated segment of the population to find "common ground for change" in the 1988 presidential campaign. Friends and foes of Jesse Jackson cannot deny the influence of his simple messages, "Down with dope, up with hope! We don't need workfare, we need fair share!" His antidrug message, along with his economic violence and pro-worker populist themes, affected the direction of the Democratic Party and the presidential election of 1988. In addition, Jackson's concern for the self-determination of Third-World nations and global oppression has inspired a new vision of this nation and of oppressed peoples of the world.

Often, it is the oppressed elite who live between two or more social worlds but have transcended both, who lead the way to a new social order. Martin Luther King Jr., the slain civil rights leader who inspired Jesse Jackson, is another example of the black elite who pointed the way to a different social order.

The civil rights movement motivated other disenfranchised groups, such as white women, Asians, Hispanics, the Gray Panthers, and gays. "They have gotten great benefits from the movement," said Michael Lomax. The student movement in China, suppressed by the government, is an example of its global inspiration.

Instead of expending negative energy on the impact of oppression, leaders like Jackson and King use their duality as a positive source of energy to fuel the creative process leading to social change. Their dual consciousness has given them a special way of viewing the world and special insight into understanding the larger socioeconomic processes of society. Too often, the creative process arising from the double-consciousness has been de-emphasized because many believe that the conflicts arising in the black elite living between two worlds require an expenditure of negative energy.

The personal and collective energies that the Talented One Hundred expend daily in dealing with racism can more effectively be utilized in their professional and personal development. John Hope Franklin, black historian, reminded us that these wasted energies are "desperately needed to solve the major problems of peace and survival" in the world.[2] Having a dual consciousness "takes part of your validity," said Johnson Longworth, an artist. "We've got to have double values, and that's schizophrenic. In school, you have no courses in double values and no courses in justifiable schizophrenia. It's the tragic reality of being black in America, and nobody wants to hear your story."

Michael Lomax agreed with Johnson Longworth that the double-consciousness is "a source of conflict." It is not, however, solely a tragic reality for Lomax. He thinks conflict can be creative.

> It [double-consciousness] can be both conflicted and creative. It can be a source of conflict if you don't recognize it; you are pulled in two different directions. We ought to be in conflict, because we are in an inherently conflicted situation. What we have to do is acknowledge it and guard how and why it is pulling us. If we do that, we can't stop these inherently conflicted situations from recurring, but we can use them and negotiate them in ways which are positive. It really is for me a matter of perspective. The situation doesn't change, but how I see it changes.

Even when the double-consciousness is a "tragic reality," Michael Lomax searches for a larger meaning in this reality. He poignantly reflected,

> Maybe what we should recognize is that the conflict we feel as blacks in a white society is really a symbol of the conflict the individual has in contemporary society. It is a world in which conflict exists. It is one symbol, one element of it. While it does alienate us as individuals, it is that conflict and also that requirement to find peace with that conflict that binds us together. If I don't find that in it, I am going to go crazy with it. I got to find my own mechanism for balancing conflict with the need for harmony, individually and collectively.

When Lomax, as a black elite, views his duality as a creative stimulus, he has the potential for positive social action. W. E. B. Du Bois, in his formulation of the "Talented Tenth," also envisioned the role of this educated elite as "global citizen." This global citizen, he noted, would be an important change agent in transforming the larger social structure culturally, educationally, and politically.[3]

As an international citizen, this new man or woman of color understands racial oppression in a broader context. Having traveled extensively, the Talented One Hundred have experienced their linkage with other blacks throughout the diaspora and are working to end global racism and human oppression.

GLOBAL RACISM AND HUMAN OPPRESSION: THE BLACK ELITE AS A CHANGE AGENT

Living outside the United States gave Laverne Townson, a bank manager in Nigeria, a different perspective. She began to understand the linkage of global racism and economic oppression of blacks throughout the diaspora and also the role of the United States media in stemming the flow of positive information about Third-World countries.

> I think more globally about the problems of the Third World. In Nigeria, there is a need to project an image of Africa over colonial masters, and there is a view of South Africa and the United States as imperialist countries. You get a different perspective on the news. I have a better sense of how things operate in the United States being on the outside and looking back. The United States is more inward looking. It doesn't care about other countries, particularly the Third World. Once you are outside the United States, there is a whole new world out there. You get an idea of what is happening in Africa, Europe, and other parts of the world. In the United States, the news you get is that the United States is the center of the universe.

Others have also begun to "think more globally about problems of the Third World." They have started to link their destiny with that of peoples of African descent throughout the diaspora. When one travels around the world, it is an inescapable observation that there is a correlation between color and social and economic oppression. The darker a group's skin color, the more likely it is that the group occupies a lower position in the social order. Yet, this observation is rarely articulated by leaders of African descent. They ignore the fact that one of the most significant "consequences of colonialism was its creation of races and racism through weakening the relevance of other human distinctions."[4] Yet ethnic distinctions are real and remain strong, impeding a global and racial consciousness. These distinctions are fertile ground for former colonial powers to exploit—dividing and conquering peoples of African descent as well as other Third-World people. This divide and conquer mentality is manifested in the United States in the tension between the black middle class and the underclass.

Globally, this divide and conquer mentality is salient in the tension between African Americans and West Indians, and African Americans and Africans.

Black ethnic groups are treated differently by whites in various countries, depending on their status as native born, immigrant, or visitor—or as Aretha Shield said, "Whether it's your black or my black." If the group or individual who receives favorable treatment does not understand that the individualization of racial experience is a part of a global pattern, then a vision for the development of a global racial consciousness—so necessary for changing the conditions of racial oppression—is merely a distant dream.

My Black or Yours?: The Development of a Global Racial Consciousness

In the early seventies, Aretha Shield, a thirty-seven-year-old, fair-skinned African American artist, was studying in England. One day while Aretha was working on an art project, she said a white female invaded her workspace, treating her discourteously. "When I opened my mouth, she found out I was a black American. Apologizing, she said, 'I thought you were West Indian.' I was accepted because I was not their black."

Teresa Hale, a fifty-four-year-old African American psychologist, identified with Aretha Shield's experience. She spent three years in Paris, France, in the late 1950s, where she was treated differently from the native people of color— the Algerians. She recalled, "My one-to-one experiences were positive. . . . [But] France was at war with Algeria, and dark-skinned people could at times be indiscriminately rounded up and jailed—mistakes to be ironed out later. As a foreigner, it was the first time I ever felt American."

Walter Calvin, also an African American, was not only glad to "feel American" but to be an American and an honorary white in South Africa. Being American perhaps saved his life. Calvin, a senior vice president for external affairs for a multinational corporation, has traveled thousands of miles from the rural South to South Africa, but his racial tracks are still the same. Listen to his story.

> I shall never forget an incident I had in South Africa. A white colleague and I were out driving one morning. The traffic was heavy, so we decided to walk the streets of Johannesburg, South Africa. We went across an area which was a university jogging track. After jogging for about fifteen minutes on the track, I suddenly heard catcalls and very foul language. I wondered about whom they were talking and at whom they were hollering. I looked up and about ten Afrikaners were jeering and sneering at me. I did not realize at the moment that particular university was an exclusive all-white Afrikaner university; therefore, no blacks were allowed to do anything on campus unless they had a special pass—let alone jog on the track. One thought ran through my mind while jogging—you learned in the South that you don't run from white people; you don't let them know your fears. You may have them, but you don't show them. I didn't show them. I kept jogging until I finished.

When I finished my exercise, I walked straight up the steps and passed this crowd of Afrikaners. I spoke impeccable English, and then they realized I was black American, which made it all right for me to jog on this track. Had I been a black South African [voice rising], they would have been perfectly in their rights to do whatever they chose to do, including detaining me and beating me until the police came. The police would have done serious harm to me.

He related another incident that occurred while he was on business in South Africa:

When I took a black South African couple from Soweto to dinner in Johannesburg, the maitre d' of the restaurant said, "You can come in, but your friends cannot eat here." And of course, we left. Again, it showed that even as a black American, I am considered in that instance as an honorary white. But my black South African friends, who are identical to me in terms of color, physical makeup, and everything, because of their language differences and birthright, weren't able to be seated with me. Discrimination against my brothers is discrimination against me.

Calvin correctly concluded that "racism is not peculiar to the United States; it is an international phenomenon." Tefe Fusi, an African ethnomusicologist, also discovered the international "race track." He candidly admitted that prior to coming to this country in the 1970s, he got negative information from whites in his country about African Americans.

I got the message constantly from whites before coming here that "your own people over in America do not want you." When I was at home, I associated a lot with white, educated Americans. And all they would tell you about black people is negative stuff. Blacks are lazy and don't want to work. All blacks do is wreck their own communities, rape white women, and steal. This is the kind of image that is created for you. So they told me what to avoid and what not to in America. I was told to go to a white church. I also had a white host family.

Like Fusi, black Americans learn very early from their geography and history classes and from the media in this country the negative concept of Africa as a backward continent. Those who grew up with the Tarzan and Jane movies were firmly grounded in the erroneous notions that Africans swung from trees, lived in grass huts in the jungle, and grunted because they were too ignorant to speak a language. Most black Americans, until recently, were ashamed to identify with Africans. (The recent name change, from black to African American, is a symbolic gesture of this new identification with Africa.) Not knowing that black Americans had learned negative stereotypes about Africans, Fusi was baffled upon his arrival in this country when blacks did not extend open arms. After reflecting on this puzzlement, he recalled that black Americans—particularly fair-skinned ones, whom he referred to as "disappointed white folks"—who came to his country were reluctant to associate with Africans. Fusi began associating with more African Americans. "Then," he said, "I began to see myself in the role of an African American. My consciousness was heightened. By associating with some responsible people from the black community and discussing problems, [I] began to change my whole concept about the black experience in the United States."

On the other hand, William Ofodile, prior to coming to the United States from Africa in the 1960s, had a favorable view of African Americans that was influenced by an uncle who was a missionary. He said,

> I was curious why there was not more mixing between blacks and whites. I asked in my white church why there were mostly white and mostly black churches. The janitor in my church was black, so I would talk with him. He took me to his church. I found differences and would go and spend Sunday afternoon with blacks. I found out Africans did not associate with African Americans, and I began to look into the reason why. The mostly white host families arranged different affairs for them. Africans had strong stereotyped ideas about black Americans, and black Americans had [stereotypes about Africans]. I was involved in both worlds. I think it occurred because of the sheltering of Africans by white host families. This is how I developed my research interest in this area.

When Prince Albert, a sixty-one-year-old British-educated West Indian artist, came to the United States in the 1960s, he, too, was welcomed by whites, but felt distant from African Americans. Prior to coming to this country, he had, like Fusi, heard many stereotyped notions about African Americans.

> The propaganda had been so heavy against blacks in the United States, I was completely undermined into thinking no blacks were capable of the English usage and kinds of expressions of philosophical thinking, until I read James Baldwin and heard M. L. King's speeches. So while in my thirties, I read James Baldwin; this event gave me self-confidence and made me overcome my respect for Europeans and their propaganda.

From my own observation, Africans and West Indians appear to hold more positive views toward one another. While Prince Albert's views about African Americans were negative before he learned about their achievements, he did not have these attitudes toward Africans. His identification with Africa and other Third-World people emerged from another important event in his life.

> The event which most influenced my life was World War II. I remember when Italy invaded Ethiopia, a member of the League of Arabs, but no one did anything. There was a newspaper clipping which showed the Pope of Rome blessing the Italian troops who were boarding ships about to go into slaughtering of the Ethiopians. My father told me it was because they were black. Shortly after, I was amazed to see the world go to war because of the Poles. It made me think that things were divided that way against blacks. During the latter [part] of World War II, when the world died for freedom, where did the French get the guns in six months to kill

Vietnamese? The Belgians were in the Congo, and the Dutch [were] in Indonesia, killing Third-World people.

These examples illustrate how the global pattern of racism manifests itself. In giving preferential treatment to immigrants and visitors of African descent over native-born blacks and those from former colonies, Western colonial powers individualize a group's experiences, creating divisions. These divisions, along with negative stereotyping and real ethnic and political distinctions, make it difficult for people of African descent to see their global interests as linked along racial lines. Alur Nod, African president of an international organization, who marched with Martin Luther King Jr. in the South and who dined in Atlanta's restaurants before African Americans did in the early 1960s, is working to bring about an international perspective. He said,

> We Africans and black Americans don't know one another. We need to know more about one another and to get together to do things. We have a very long way to accomplish the goal to develop our own societies. Blacks, whether it's Africans or black Americans, beg for [their] rights or [their] own destiny. We should put our money into the black community to do things for ourselves. We don't always have to say we consume billions of dollars. We need to say we have to produce for our consumption. Black entrepreneurs are not likely to go to England or Italy to do business because of racism. The only place they have to go is the Caribbean or Africa. We also have to educate our children to be constructive and to learn about their history and culture, like the Jews. The Jews train their kids in the synagogue. Jewish boys grow up knowing they will always be pro-Jew, for their survival. We have to do the same thing. Our people have died in Mississippi, South Africa, and everywhere.

Whether in Alabama or South Africa, blacks have begun to recognize their common linkage. They are interested in addressing global racism in the international arena, and they are concerned about global inequities in wealth and human rights, political oppression, and imperialism in the foreign policies and practices of the United States and other countries. Perhaps the black experience "helps us to better understand the lot of the Hindu lower caste in India or the black in South Africa," said John Daniels, a corporate executive.

Global travels have also allowed blacks to see firsthand the disparity in wealth between rich and poor. Wherever they have traveled, the Talented One Hundred have been struck by the social oppression of others—Catholics in Belfast, Northern Ireland; Jews and Christians in Russia; Palestinians in Israel; and blacks in South Africa. Traveling outside this country has given them a broader perspective and understanding of issues. This was summed up by Leo Aramis, a journalist, whom I interviewed in my office at Central State University in Wilberforce, Ohio, in 1987.

> It gave me a perspective that's necessary. If there is a riot in your office right now, folks on the first floor would say there is a riot on the second floor. Folks in administration

would say Wesley Hall. Wilberforce would say Central State University. Columbus would say a riot in Wilberforce. And California would say a riot in Ohio. But folks in Europe would say that there is a riot in America. It is a perspective that is really important. We don't have it, but we need to get it.

Having gained an international perspective, the Talented One Hundred are clamoring to be heard on issues at home and abroad, such as economic justice, human oppression, and human rights.

THE BLACK ELITE AS LIBERATORS

Martin Buber, existential philosopher, has stated that one who is to be the liberator "has to be introduced into the stronghold of the alien." Freedom movements seek "a kind of liberation which cannot be brought about by anyone who grew up as a slave, nor yet by anyone who is not connected with the slaves; but only by one of the latter who has been brought up in the midst of the aliens and has received an education equipping him with all their wisdom and powers."[5] Living between two social worlds has given the black elite insights into their social existence that transcend the ordinary consciousness. Instead of viewing themselves as marginal people of color within the context of the American society, they see themselves within the larger, global context where people of color are the majority. They have the opportunity, therefore, to become world citizens and lead the way to an alternative social order. The black elite's experiences have not been so restrictive that they cannot fantasize about a new vision or "see their duality as a creative process and as part of the human condition," remarked John Daniels. He understands his duality "in terms of the human experience—the laughter, tragedy, love, and all the rest." This "laughter, tragedy, and love" are what Joseph Lowery referred to as "dark joy," a term coined by Lerone Bennett, author of *Before the Mayflower*. It is this "dark joy" that helps "blacks make it in this world and better understand the lot of others," asserted Lowery.

> I don't think white folks got the joy of the struggle we have. They don't have the blessing of soul and experience. They can't pass on to the world the "dark joy" that has characterized the black experience. We are sad; yet we are happy. It's what the white folks couldn't understand about the black family. I don't know whether you read in the newspaper where I made a statement about Mayor Andrew Young calling Alice Bond.[6] He was reflecting a sensitivity that black officials have to bring to public office.
>
> We were shut out so long that they didn't care what happened to us until blacks came into office. All black officials should have a sensitivity to their constituency, which should far surpass what white people have, because we know what it means to be down yonder in the valley where you couldn't hear nobody pray. We've been excluded, so we know how important it is to be included. We have been uncared for, so we know how important it is to be caring. So we bring a perspective, a feel-

ing, and an experience nobody else has. Who else can feel like that? White folks can't even sing spirituals because they don't know what they are talking about. How can they sing "Swing Low, Sweet Chariot, Coming for to Carry Me Home"? [He sings it.] How are they going to sing that? How are they going to sing, "I Got Shoes"? When the slaves sang that, they didn't have shoes. But they knew they were children of God, and all God's children have shoes. They were defiant; they were forgiving. They were joyful, sad, and that is what I mean by "dark joy." There is a sadness about our experience that we've overcome because of joy. Our hope is a part of that joy. Our struggle is a part of that joy. Our love for each other is a part of that joy. That is why we have to turn *to* each other and not on one another. We are doing too much turning on each other.

Having experienced this "dark joy" and using it creatively, some of the Talented One Hundred are stepping onto the global stage as collective actors for oppressed peoples of the world. They view their Afrocentric perspective on humanity as an important counterbalance to the Eurocentric perspective, which de-emphasizes human concerns and needs. Not incorporating an Afrocentric perspective into domestic and foreign policy has been one of the high costs of racism for whites in America. They have failed to benefit from cultural diversity.

In our multiracial and multiethnic society, we tend to focus on the divisiveness in diversity rather than on the strengths. This is a point that Michael Lomax so eloquently reiterated:

We've spent a lot of time in this country divided by race, ethnic group, and class. We are hostile toward one another. We've done a better job than some other multiracial societies. Japan has a sense of unity because of one race, and they work together to knock our socks off. This country has to find strength in its diversity. We are never going to be a homogeneous nation, and so we must have room for that diversity and pull together as one nation. If we do that, we will have different attitudes toward dropouts and teenage pregnancies as lost resources. . . . We need to focus on being an inclusive rather than an exclusive nation.

In not recognizing strength in diversity, as Michael Lomax pointed out, this society fails to recognize the full potential of groups who can contribute to improving the quality of life for all Americans. Whites and others who promote racial oppression or other forms of social oppression also deny themselves "the full range of choices, experiences, and resources that could be theirs."[7] The Afrocentric perspective offers a rich tradition from which to view the world. Its holistic approach to health and life is the East's gift to the West. The Afrocentric holistic approach to medicine, for instance, is changing Western medical practices, which are based on the separation of mind and body. Thus, diverse cultural and social interaction can be beneficial for the development of society.

In a world that is increasingly global, where noncolored people are in the minority, cultural diversity is functional. White racism is particularly narcissistic because it promotes isolation from all peoples of color. It also inhibits intellectual

growth among whites and other people by promoting contempt, fear, and ignorance of other racial and ethnic groups. Hence, racism distorts the views of
whites and does not allow them to reconcile their own economic, political, and
social interests and needs with the needs and interests of all people.

The value orientations of this society promote democracy and equality as well
as racism. But democracy and equality are incompatible with racism. This leads
to a distorted reality for whites, resulting in moral ambivalence and a social
blindness that dulls the senses. When the senses are dulled to racial oppression,
one looks but does not see. One tastes but does not savor. One touches but does
not feel; hears, but does not understand. A good example was Lee Atwater,
chairman of the Republican National Committee and President George Bush's
campaign manager of 1988, who heard and played black blues but did not understand the rhythm of black people or dance in step with their tune.

After the presidential election, Lee Atwater was appointed to the board of
trustees of Howard University, a predominantly black university in Washington
DC. The students protested his appointment. He resigned, appearing slighted
by their rebuke. In his first meeting with the student protesters, he told these
bright, young students how much he liked rhythm and blues. Like the plantation slave master, he expected that their pent-up frustrations would be released
on the academic plantation by "playing them a tune." He thought students
would forget to ask his position on such issues as affirmative action, the exten-
sion of the voting rights act, and the African National Congress. He thought
they would forget the issue of Willie Horton. Horton, a black and a convicted
murderer, was furloughed from a Massachusetts prison while serving a life sentence. He traveled from Massachusetts to Maryland and assaulted a white couple in their home, raping the woman. As the campaign manager for Bush, then
vice president of the United States, Lee Atwater used Willie Horton as a campaign issue to galvanize whites. This issue played to the worst fears of whites—
black crime and black male supersexuality deflowering white womanhood.

Thus, when the senses are dulled because of moral blindness, "whites become
untrue to themselves and untrue to the world,"[8] writes Robert Terry, a white author who studies the negative impact of racism on white people. They start operating as inauthentic persons in inauthentic organizations.[9] For Terry, "racism leads
to a false consciousness or an ungrounded solution. Either one forces us to live in
an illusionary world that is dangerous to others and to ourselves. Our supposed
strength defeats us. Our supposed wisdom becomes our ignorance and leads us to
judgments that negate our short- and long-term self-interest."[10] He concludes that
the negative impact of racism on whites clouds their "capacity to make accurate
judgments. . . . We [white people] cannot be with and for ourselves or each other
if we do not know who we are and what we are about. Thus racism forces us into
inauthenticity and denies humanity to ourselves and those we touch."[11]

If whites are to achieve authenticity, they must start thinking about the
meaning of their whiteness, accept responsibility for their whiteness, and act to
bring about solutions to the resulting moral ambivalence and social blindness.

SUMMARY

The U.S. Constitution starts out "We, the people," but this document did not include black males or females or white females, among others. Now, in the dawn of the twenty-first century, when the changing winds of human liberation have swept across the global village, from Eastern Europe to South Africa, "We, the people" can choose to translate this cornerstone of democracy into an authentic reality that includes black, brown, red, and yellow males and females. "We, the people" can also choose to continue with inauthentic institutions that lead to alienation of the oppressed. But both alienation and inauthenticity lead to dehumanization of the oppressor and the oppressed.

There is a way out of this quagmire. The new global man and woman of color want to define a new America and a new world for the twenty-first century. Michael Lomax and Jesse Jackson remind us that "We, the people," which must include males and females of all races, have an opportunity to create a new social order. "It is an opportunity for all of us," said Lomax, "to rethink our relationship, to debate, and to struggle" with the dehumanization of racism. We can choose, Jackson stressed, to "cross ancient lines of race . . . to find common ground" for social change, or we can continue to allow the color line, as Langston Hughes noted in his poem "Dream Deferred," "to fester like a sore" and to "sag like a heavy load" on the nation until it explodes. No generation of blacks has a choice to allow the nation to continue to sag or to explode. Each must continue to carry the torch through the night, lighting the way to the dawn of a new day. Only through collective power can we make America and the world ours in the twenty-first century.

The new man and woman of color want to move beyond race and become actors in the international arena. As global citizens, the Talented One Hundred recognize a common linkage with blacks throughout the African diaspora. Hence, they address the issues of apartheid and global human oppression. They also address the issues of nuclear disarmament and defense. A dominant Afrocentric perspective emerges that emphasizes human needs over military defense, and peace and justice over war. When an Afrocentric perspective is excluded because of racism, there is a high cost to whites. They fail to benefit from cultural diversity, and they suffer from a distortion of reality, which leads to their inauthenticity and dehumanization.

NOTES

1. Jesse Jackson, "What We've Won," *Mother Jones*, July–Aug. 1988, 22.

2. John Hope Franklin, ed., *Color and Race* (Boston: Beacon Press), x.

3. Rutledge M. Dennis, "Du Bois and the Role of the Educated Elite," *Journal of Negro Education*, 46, no. 4 (Fall 1977), 388–402.

4. Robert Blauner, *Racial Oppression in America* (New York: Harper and Row, 1972), 115.

5. Charles Vert Willie, *Race, Ethnicity, and Socioeconomic Status: A Theoretical Analysis of Their Interrelationship* (Dix Hills, NY: General Hall, 1983), 253–254.

6. The ex-wife of Julian Bond, the former Georgia state senator and civil rights activist, whose marital dispute received national attention in 1987.

7. Joyce A. Ladner and Walter W. Stafford, "Defusing Race: Developments Since the Kerner Report," in Benjamin P. Bowser and Raymond G. Hunt, eds., *Impacts of Racism on White Americans* (Beverly Hills, CA: Sage, 1981), 71–78.

8. Robert W. Terry, "The Negative Impact on White Values," in Bowser and Hunt, eds., *Impacts of Racism* (Beverly Hills, CA: Sage, 1981), 134.

9. Terry, "Negative Impact," 120.

10. Terry, "Negative Impact," 134.

11. Terry, "Negative Impact," 149.

9

THE COLOR LINE IN THE TWENTY-FIRST CENTURY: GENERATIONAL DIFFERENCES

Since numerous exemplary visionaries of the Talented One Hundred, along with countless other like-minded individuals of the civil rights era, used their marginality as a positive source of change to pave the way for the blurring of the color line in the twenty-first century, what, if anything, is new in the stories the post–civil rights generations tell? If the stories have changed, how do they differ from those of the civil rights generation? What social factors have contributed to these changes? What are the implications of these changes?

In listening to the stories of the Talented Thirty,[1] this chapter begins to answer those questions. In doing so, it explores the larger issues of generational and class divide and shows how the text of post–civil rights generations' narratives differs from that of the civil rights generation in worldview and values. Some striking contrasts in the new generations' accounts include a lack of awareness and understanding of the racial struggle and racial lessons, an increasing belief in the myth of meritocracy, a greater naïveté about racism, and an increasing psychic conflict in their personal and group racial identity. A bevy of social factors underlie these shifting perspectives, such as the desegregation of social institutions in the dominant society, alterations in black communities and in black institutional and organizational affiliations and networks, and changes in the economy and technology, as well as the rise of globalization. An overwhelming acceptance of the ideology of integration as opposed to desegregation by middle-class blacks in the civil rights era is a key reason for the shift in the new stories of younger generations.[2]

Kevin Powell, the thirty-eight-year-old critically acclaimed writer, lecturer, and activist, speaks to this issue, while capturing other generational changes.

He is a part of the civil rights movement's harvest of struggle, one that not only yielded bountiful crops of opportunity, but also produced a new generation, which is more disconnected from its cultural and historical roots as a result of racial integration. Until his social awakening and transformation as a student at Rutgers University, he, too, felt little connection. For most of his formative years, he was educated in a racially mixed setting, and at the age of thirteen, he and his hard-working mother, who was employed as a domestic, moved from their rat- and roach-infested tenement to a white neighborhood. Powell's mother, who had completed only grade school in rural South Carolina before moving to New York, was so inspired by the civil rights movement, like myriads of others of her generation, because it had enlarged her vision so that she wanted to make a better life for her son by moving to a white neighborhood. Leaving behind what Powell called being "trapped in a concrete box," she believed her son could obtain a better education and be better protected from the world of poverty and violence. But for Powell, integration had its flip side.

> Although I think moving to the white neighborhood certainly exacerbated my black self-hatred, on the flip side, moving to that white neighborhood saved my life. Thank God, when I got to Rutgers, I got to work on the spiritual end of it, because living in that all-white neighborhood had damaged me. That's something we have to deal with when we talk about success according to your sanity and your spirit. Like many black parents coming out of the civil rights era into the 1970s, my mother believed that the best institutions for her black child would be the ones where white children went to school. You knew that white folks went to places where we had previously been banned from being a part. And understand that we wanted equal access just like all the others.

On the fiftieth anniversary of *Brown v. Board of Education*, several public intellectuals and scholars, such as Derrick Bell, in *Silent Covenants*, Charles Ogletree Jr., in *All Deliberate Speed*, and Sheryll Cashin, in *The Failure of Integration*, ruminated about the unfulfilled promises of integration.[3] Kevin Powell reflected on its meaning, as well, and concluded from some of the participants in the case that "it wasn't about us trying to get into their schools; we just wanted to have quality textbooks. I think somewhere during the civil rights movement, they got turned around into white folks' schools and white folks' institutions. Everything that they did, their education was better than ours. And so I think a lot of people, including my mother, began to believe that." As a result of the devaluation of blackness, he was disconnected from his cultural roots. Powell, an A student in his white high school, knew he wanted to become a writer, but he admitted, "I didn't know a single black writer existed until I got to college. I didn't know about Malcolm X, Marcus Garvey, Sojourner Truth, and Phyllis Wheatley. No one! All I learned about was Crispus Attucks and George Washington Carver. I believe I heard about Dr. King. I knew that black folks were slaves. But I didn't know that black people lived in the Caribbean. I didn't know about Africa. And that's the flip side."

When Powell lectures at college campuses across the country, he observes a similar pattern of disconnection from cultural roots. He hears and sees the heavy psychological and sociological costs of being isolated in predominantly white milieus and the consequences of internalizing the dominant culture's standards, values, and ways of seeing the world.

I come in contact with a lot of students who have attended majority white schools, or elite private schools, the finest boarding schools in the country, and I can't tell you the level of self-hatred and low self-esteem that I encounter from people who come from middle-class and upwardly mobile black backgrounds. And I grew up in that. I am a light brown–skinned black man and I was deeply self-hating. If you were a black girl who grew up when I was a black boy, who was darker than me, you were not attractive to me. If you had a certain texture of hair, your hair was ugly to me. So in spite of the "success" of going to the right school, we were actually charading with a whole class of black people who had no connection with our communities from the past, had no connection to the history, had no connection to our span of excellence and legacy. Really, in some cases, they believed that some of the stuff we were doing, we had gotten on our own, without any kind of struggle. I feel that this black middle class is the most disconnected we've ever had, dating back to slavery. I think blacks should be able to live wherever they want to live, you should marry who you want to marry, you should send your children to any school you want to send them to, but there is a great disservice done if you don't teach your children, whether they are poor black folks, middle-class black folks, or wealthy black folks, about the rich legacy that we come from. That's got to be the foundation.

For Powell, the imminent danger inherent in not having this foundation is a growing class divide in black communities.

Not only do you develop a black elite, you develop a disconnected black elite, whose whole worldview is just the Hamptons or Martha's Vineyard and also cannot understand why the folks in the projects resent them. They can't understand why some poor black folks think the middle-class black folks act white or talk white. What has happened is a disconnect because of integration. During segregation, when blacks lived in the same community, it didn't matter if you were a middle-class black or a poor black, you saw possibilities from your block that if you had a daddy in your house, someone in the community had a father. If you had a teacher, a doctor, or a lawyer in your house or if you knew someone in a profession, you knew that you could be that. You saw that education was a community experience, so it was not unusual to see someone who might be a grown person in a classroom with someone who might be a child or a teenager. But that has been lost and, as a result, there's this incredible divide that's greater than it has ever been in our community. And a lot of it goes back to the civil rights era and us confusing integration with desegregation. Those are two totally different things.

In confusing integration with desegregation, many blacks of the post–civil rights generations have little or no connection to their ancestral heritage and their history of triumphs and traumas because too many elders did not tell the story. But Powell knows it is essential for a people's sense of humanity. "I don't care what race of people you are; I don't care what ethnic group you are; I don't care what religion you are or your sexual orientation, every group of people needs to be able to bring their history to the table and say, 'This is why I deserve to be at the table of humanity.' A lot of black people in America today don't know what they will be bringing to the table other than soul food."

No doubt, Powell would agree with Elie Weisel, the great philosopher and Holocaust survivor, who said, "Anyone who has lived through tragedy must tell the story." Americans of African descent have lived through their own holocaust of slavery and segregation, so we, too, must tell the story. For in doing so, it becomes the living repository of distilled experiences in the life of a people, which creates unity of purpose and identity, keeps traditions alive, and maintains continuity between generations. Twenty years have come to pass since I first listened to the poignant accounts of the black elite who had come of age during the civil rights movement, or who, until that social revolution, had spent their lives behind iron gates of de jure and de facto segregation. In telling their narratives, they wove a collective tapestry of tales of dark joy, spun by the hands of slavery and segregation and buttressed by the history of resistance and resilience. But, their stories, as Kevin Powell so eloquently summarized, are being missed, en masse, by the generations of the post–civil rights era.

A myriad of social upheavals within black communities might explain, in part, why the story is being missed. Increasingly, social mechanisms for transmitting traditional black culture and values within the community are being lost. First, the familial structure has altered since the 1960s. Parenting of children is more by singular person with less involvement and support of extended family and community. This decline in marriage among blacks is connected to shifts in the economic structure of the larger society, such as deindustrialization, the shift in jobs from urban communities to the suburbs, from the Rustbelt to the Sunbelt, from the United States of America to the globalization of America's economy.[4] With the loss in jobs, particularly among working-class black males, marriage becomes less attractive in the familial formation.

Second, desegregation of major institutions in the dominant society and in black communities, particularly the educational system, is a challenge to transmitting black cultural heritage, let alone validating stories of struggle. Too often, in fact, the culture of people of color is devalued and negated by the system. Since the teaching profession is primarily white and female, 90 percent and 79 percent, respectively,[5] students are taught from a Eurocentric perspective that stresses an individualistic, meritocratic ethos. During segregation, blacks had a plethora of role models to transmit the cultural heritage and traditional values to students in whom they had a vested interest, whereas now only 6 percent of public school teachers are African Americans.[6] Other factors such as the rise of globalization and information technology and the influence of peers and media have undermined the generational connection.

Unarguably, such historical discontinuity is critical, especially since increasing numbers of the most privileged African Americans, the segment of black communities from which future leadership is likely to emanate, are not hearing their foremothers' and forefathers' narrative of struggle. Along with post–civil rights individuals being disconnected from the story of struggle, their shifting worldview has contributed to the generational gap. Their generations' multifarious faces of racism have changed to a more subtle manifestation, as well, and so, as Powell asserts, these post–civil rights individuals are seeing the world more through rose-colored glasses, which inhibits the development of a consciousness of the collective. In addition, their different way of viewing the world and their lack of consciousness of the collective have also increased the class divide. These key themes emerged as salient issues when I interviewed thirty high-achieving professionals in 2004, including Kevin Powell, five decades after the Supreme Court decision of 1954, four decades after the passage of the Civil Rights Act of 1964, four decades after Fannie Lou Hamer and the Mississippi Democratic Freedom Party demanded to be seated at the Democratic National Convention in 1964, and more than a decade after apartheid ended in South Africa.

So much has changed since those events. We have seen, for example, a rapidly expanding black middle class in the last three decades of the past century; by 2001, 1.2 million black families or 14 percent had annual incomes of over eighty thousand dollars, which is 50 percent more than in 1990 and ten times more than in 1970. In fact, the number of affluent black families with annual incomes of more than eighty thousand dollars is increasing more rapidly than among whites.[7] For participants of this study, personal income was requested, and the annual median income was over one hundred thousand dollars.

Likewise, blacks entered a world of work not previously traveled. Black bodies that were once traded as commodities on Wall Street are now traders, working as analysts, asset managers, and investment bankers. They are buying seats on the New York Stock Exchange and are CEOs of some of the nation's leading financial firms and investment banks. Two billionaires have appeared on *Forbes*'s Fortune 500 List, and a substantial number of entrepreneurs and entertainers— athletes, actors, and rappers—are millionaires. Increasingly, blacks are also appointed to high places in the public sector, serving in the post–civil rights era as Supreme Court justice, secretary of state, national security advisor, Joint Chiefs of Staff, secretary of commerce, secretary of education, secretary of labor, surgeon general, and general campaign manager for the Democratic Party. They are being elected in record numbers to Congress and to state and local politics. Blacks are also astronauts, astrophysicists, biomedical and computer engineers, CEOs of small and medium businesses, civil rights activists, doctors, diplomats, educators, engineers, judges, lawyers, pharmacists, and physical therapists, as well as those new fields that have become available during the last three decades. Similarly, many of the parallel institutions that existed in the black segregated market now cater to a broader one. Adding to this positive outlook, black home ownership rates, an important source of wealth, increased from 42.9 percent in 1989 to 48.1 percent in 2003.[8] During the past twenty years, the number of African Americans enrolled in higher education also doubled, and the high school completion rate surged from 68 percent to 76 percent.[9] Clearly, African Americans represent the most formally educated people of African descent throughout the diaspora.

For those talented individuals who were born or grew up after the civil rights movement, with all its attendant seismic shifts and global sociopolitical and economic changes, it is important to begin seeking answers to these major questions: What is the story of struggle and its missing links? What role does the story of struggle play in the formation of the post–civil rights generations' racial awareness, racial consciousness, and response to racism? How do post–civil rights generations perceive, experience, interpret, and negotiate the continuing significance of race and racism in the twenty-first century? In what ways do the black elite of the post–civil rights generations differ from the black elite of the civil rights generation? In what ways are they similar? Is the gulf widening between the classes? How is gender negotiated in a racist society and between the sexes? How do race, class, and gender intersect in the post–civil rights era? Perhaps the voices of the Talented Thirty can offer some insights.

THE MISSING LINK

Far too many storymakers and observers of the civil rights era are not re-creating or passing on to the next generation their embedded collective memories. Whether by intimate or familiar acquaintance, they are not transmitting their knowledge of the reign of terror visited upon blacks by the KKK, the lynch mobs, and the police, who stalked across the back woodlands of the rural South and into its streets, intimidating and spreading fear by beating, maiming, and lynching. It was a shared understanding of the generations who grew up in the segregated South that every white man, woman, and child had personal and collective power over the lives of blacks. Housed in their subterranean recesses are untold memories of mandated laws that forced them to watch movies in the balcony of theaters; to sit in the back of buses and trains; to cool their thirst from separate water fountains; to use separate toilets, swimming pools, parks, and stadiums; to attend inferior segregated schools; to be refused the courtesy of services in restaurants, hospitals, hotels, and funeral parlors; and to be denied the right to vote. From the cradle to the grave, in every nook and cranny of the sociopolitical and economic sphere, the fabric of their lives was defined by the color line. But their stories, even those passed down by grandparents and great-grandparents that reached beyond segregation to touch the hands of slavery, are not being transmitted.

When the civil rights movement challenged the color line, many storymakers and observers of that generation, who put their lives on the line or who stood on the sideline, chose not to pass on their remembrance of atrocities that sometimes accompanied the marches, pickets, boycotts, sit-ins, and freedom rides. The collective struggle of resistance during that era resulted triumphantly in the Civil Rights Act of 1964, which covered virtually all corners of segregation in America's life—both de jure and de facto; the Voting Rights Act of 1965; the Fair Housing Act of 1968; and the United States Supreme Court decision of 1967, which struck down laws against interracial marriage. It is crucial, therefore, for storymakers to tell our narrative of struggle and success to show how it is inextricably linked to the benefits and privileges enjoyed by today's post–civil rights generations. In linking the narrative of struggle to a post–civil rights generation, the storytellers must engage in a process of truth telling and meaning making, which connects the generations to sociological realities of race and racism in America. And, at this point in history, one sociological reality is that, even in our racially and culturally diverse twenty-first-century America, racism is still a permanent and significant feature of this society. Though it is immutable, its manifestations are always changing. A corollary sociological reality is that a racial hierarchy exists in America, as well as globally, and peoples of African descent are at the bottom. Since racism is the system of structures and ideologies for inequality between dominant and dominated racial groups, storytellers must interpret for each generation that group mobility results from collective action, not individual achievement. And that although money, power, and prestige ease the color line, they do not erase it. Hence, the struggle of African American people must be a continuous one, because the hard-earned rights, benefits, and privileges people fought and died for during the civil rights movement can be taken away by those who have the power. Clearly, each generation must, therefore, remain vigilant, employing whatever strategies and tactics appropriate to the sociological realities of its times, both external and internal to its communities.

Out of African Americans' story of struggle and resistance has come unity of purpose, identity, and a set of traditions. Forming that set of traditions, as numerous social scientists like Joyce Ladner have noted, is an oppositional worldview, core values, and a lifestyle to sustain a people's spirit, survival, and resilience. Ladner, in *The Ties That Bind*, discussed, for example, four important principles that formed the worldview in the more homogeneous black community in which the civil rights movement emerged. The first principle, "Identity determines power," implies the importance of knowing yourself, and that self-identity is integrally linked to group identity. The second principle, "We did not raise ourselves alone," reinforces the importance of extended family and community in the parenting process. The third principle, "We are making the future together," emphasizes the importance of collective effort in individual and group upward mobility. The fourth principle, "The past is prologue," suggests the importance of knowing and remembering your history.[10] Out of this way of seeing the world, Ladner noted the following timeless core values emerged that have created communal cohesion and generational bonds: "Remember where you came from," "Trust in the Lord," "Respect is a two-way street," "Don't make excuses," "Do an honest day's work," "Make a way out of no way," "Keep the can-do spirit," "Every child can learn," "Stand tall," and "Your word is your bond."[11]

These traditional core values, emanating out of the black experience of struggle, have been the sustaining force undergirding the black community's resistance and resilience, which is the story that must be told to each new generation. Although each generation adds its own layer of tradition or subtracts from it, truth telling is essential to the genre of struggle in America. For individuals who were born or who came of age after the civil rights movement, to a large extent, the personal and collective stories of struggle of the civil rights generation, including triumphs and traumas, have not been systematically and accurately re-created. While adding, embracing, and passing on the triumphs of the struggle, the civil rights generation, the collective pioneers who first swam in the mainstream, subtracted the trauma from the story. Kevin Powell has observed this phenomenon, as well.

> What I've noticed in traveling in middle-class circles, there seems to be a lot of inhibitions and fears about expressing ourselves in a certain way. And I think part of that, with middle-class black folks, came out of us trying to shield our children from some of the memories that we have, like "I can't talk about this," "I don't want them to go through what I went through." We don't create spaces in our communities as professional black folks. But we can and should talk about our historical traumas, in a way that is not only about relaying the story, but also about healing. And as a result, we have these children, who, when they get to college, are completely disconnected from black students on the college campus, especially if they go to a white college. They also go to the other extreme where they become these superradical blacks who all of a sudden, like the children of white parents, hate their parents, and consider them Uncle Toms and Aunt Jemimas. So they want to reject everything that they have ever experienced because they don't feel it is an authentic black experience. And you'll find these types of black kids all of a sudden embracing the ghetto-centric aspects of black life as if that is the only authentic black experience. I ask them what their parents did or did not teach them when they were growing up.

Perhaps desiring to protect their children from the harsh realities of racism, and for many, the realities of their own humble beginnings, the civil rights generation abstracted important values from the struggle and transmitted them to their children, but without providing a context for their ideals. But the consequences for their omission, their induced collective amnesia, and their conspiracy of silence are the loosening of ties that connect generations to the sociological realities of the continuing significance of race and racism in America and the timeless traditions for resisting.

The post–civil rights generations have rewritten the storyline, sometimes deleting shared, cherished traditions and sometimes turning them upside down, because they have no personal connection to the movement and because too few of their elders have shared and interpreted their stories. In *Children of the Movement*, John Blake indicated that some participants of the civil rights movement did not pass their stories on to their offspring.[12] Hence, keeping black heritage alive is a long, steep climb, and with the vast social changes that have occurred during the past thirty-five years, it becomes even more difficult. For post–civil rights individuals, more fragmented families and communities frame their world.

Kevin Powell understands the different realities of his generation and those of his grandmother and mother.

> There are different expectations, standards, and values. There's a sense of community and common struggle, a pride in having your NAACP membership card that just doesn't exist today. That's a disconnect from where we came from. My grandmother was the anchor of the family. She was the one who said, "Y'all gotta come down South. Don't forget where you came from." My mother and her sisters moved up North, but they brought that with them—their black Southern ways. And it was passed on to me. Now what I've seen with a lot of my peers, and folks who are younger than me, sometimes, it was their grandparents who were born down South and their parents were born in the North, so that would be a disconnect. You have to have a mother who is from the South, so literally it is like I was raised a Southerner. It was less of a disconnect. So when I got to college and I read Zora Neale Hurston's *Their Eyes Were Watching God*, I was like, wow, that's my family. All the traditions, which people call superstitions, we call them Africanisms. And that's what happens to a lot of us who moved north to Chicago, New York, or West Los Angeles; we had the breaking of those value systems. It does something when you don't have that family unit intact where you can get those stories from your elders.

Hence, when the elders ask, "What is happening to this generation?" Powell says the larger question is, "What is the context that we are putting young people in today?" Their world is contextualized by the influence of mass media in an increasingly commodified and globalized information and consumption society, where the influence of peers is often greater than that of parents. Hip-hop is, for example, the "dominant youth culture on the planet, and there is the commodification of young people of hip-hop and the glorification of the worst attributes of ghetto life by the media," says Powell. Although he understands the music is misogynistic, "it is not any more sexist than other forms of American culture." At the same time, he acknowledges that it is currently the more explicit form. Hip-hop music became the canvas for black youths to express their feelings in the 1980s. Powell feels that "The hip-hop generation made something out of nothing, but it adopted patriarchal standards. If you want to have a conversation about patriarchy, sexism, and homophobia, that ain't just hip-hop. That was here before hip-hop got on the scene." In fact, he maintains that "hip-hop was an act of recognition, on some level, that while the Civil Rights movement had altered America and opened up some doors for a smidgen of the community, the vast majority of us were cemented in the ghettos of America."[13] Young people's chances of being exposed to such glorification of the negative aspects of this genre have increased. As Powell stated, "When I was growing up, we had four or five TV channels. Now there are five hundred. When I was growing up, the TV went off around twelve o'clock. The TV is now on 24/7. When I was growing up, we had programs like RIF, *Reading is Fundamental*. You can't find that now. When I was growing up, you had to take all kinds of classes, and you had to take physical education. You know what is these kids' physical education? It is PlayStation or Game Boy."

Olu Brown, a twenty-six-year-old associate minister of the more than six-thousand-member Cascade United Methodist Church in Atlanta, Georgia, knows that living in a consumer-oriented, information technological society has its upside because of the "level of intelligence and information that is now available to younger generations. You've got kids who are in elementary school who have their own personal computer. I remember when we did a term paper, the teacher made us go to the library to look up information using the Dewey Decimal System and the card catalog. Now, you can get on a computer in any library and pull up the card catalog. The mounds of information that are available place our young people so far ahead of our older generations."

But for Brown, there is an ironic downside in this cultural lag.

> Although the information is there and a lot of our kids are more informed than older generations, they don't have the wisdom or the moral conscience to balance it out. We don't have the strength of the struggle. We don't have the wisdom of the past, so consequently a lot of our young people are full of information, but they don't know what to do with the information.
>
> They're full of potential, but they give in too easily because they have never had to struggle for anything. They've been given everything. Consequently, they develop this attitude that says it's mine, I deserve it, and you can't take it from me. But they don't realize that the reason why they have so many things is because somebody died just a few years ago, so that they can have the advantages that they have today.

With greater contact with whites, along with other racial and ethnic groups, African Americans have adopted the more individualistic and materialistic worldview and values of the dominant group, which are often in conflict. As Brown suggests,

> The dilemma is oftentimes the values and the culture of America conflict with the values and culture of being an African American. In capitalist America you can step on anybody's back to achieve what you want to achieve, and you can charge as much as you want to charge as long as someone is crazy enough to buy it. You can become wealthy and buy a car worth five hundred thousand dollars, and drive past

a man with a sign that says, "I'll work for food," and still feel good about yourself. But my blackness says, "The way we made it yesterday is together, and the way we are going to make it today is together, and the only way we can make it together is for somebody to sacrifice for somebody else," which is in direct conflict with capitalism, which is in direct conflict with my American attitude.

Like Brown, Dwayne Ashley, thirty-five-year-old president and CEO of the Thurgood Marshall Fund, observed, "People are about 'How can I play the game and get ahead?' in corporate America." He encountered this conflict after leaving Wiley College, an HBCU, to matriculate at University of Pennsylvania for his graduate studies. Traditionally, black institutions have stressed the history and heritage of African American people and the need to give back to the community. "At Wiley, we did not get the Machiavellian package. No one ever talked about the kind of games that people would play on you in life, the things we were going to have to deal with as we moved out into the workforce. No matter how smart you were, people might beat you at cheating and doing some of the Machiavellian things that people do in corporate America every day to get ahead." Although he feels the values he received at Wiley and from growing up in his black community were excellent and grounded him ethically, Ashley believes, "We also have to teach young people about the games that are going to be played on them so that they don't [compromise] their own values and at least they can recognize the games that are being played. Because if you don't, you may be eaten up alive out there before you even get in the game."

In addition to the adoption of the ethos of the dominant culture, the influence of mass media and the increase in technology, the post–civil rights generations' world is also framed by a more subtle and covert racism, rather than the more overt walls of prejudice and racism of the past, making it more difficult to identify and interpret its many manifestations. Kevin Powell has memories of overt acts of racism during his elementary school days at PS 38 in New Jersey, but he knows his experience is still several shades different from that of the civil rights generation.

During those years, there was a group of white boys called *Bones*. Bones used to beat on niggers every second. They would throw rocks at the black kids. You had these kinds of memories, but the memories that the older ones of the civil rights generation had were very different. They saw "Colored Only" every single day of their life. They saw "For Whites Only" every single day of their life. You felt like Richard Wright felt in *Black Boy* every single day of your life. Say the wrong thing, or look at a white person the wrong way, you could end up dead. In some ways, we grew up with kind of like rose-colored glasses.

Both Brown and Powell, as observers of youth culture, would no doubt concur that the rewritten script of black traditions, as previously described by Joyce Ladner, embraces a worldview that is an alternative to that of their elders. "Identity determines personal power," minimizes group identity, and maximizes self-identity. "We did not raise ourselves alone" has moved closer to "I succeeded by my own merits." "We are making the future together" is shifting more toward "I am making this future by myself." "The past is pro-logue" is changing to the present rather than reeling backward to move for-ward. The larger question becomes how do these shifting worldviews impact values and personal and collective ways of negotiating the racial struggle? How do they interconnect with class and gender? For answers, we turn to the Talented Thirty.

A GENERATIONAL DIVIDE

Although the members of the Talented Thirty have rewritten their narrative script, they retain many traditional themes but with a different spin. The im-portance of spirituality is, for example, essential to their personal identity; twenty-seven individuals expressed a strong religious and spiritual orientation, but, unlike the Talented One Hundred of the civil rights generation, they do not view it as an agent of social change. A strong work ethic is also important, but these individuals are more concerned with the quality of the workplace and the quality of their lives, balancing work with more quality time for family, friends, and themselves. Hence, if a job proves unsatisfactory or there are greater opportunities, they are more willing to seek other employment or use their talents in an entrepreneurial role. From the vantage point of Christie M. Boyd, the thirty-seven-year-old tenured professor of pharmacy at a major pub-lic university in the Southwest, she thinks this is the case with her friends.

> My generation has different standards. If we are not happy, we will not stay in jobs; we will move laterally or horizontally, but we don't stay. It is more of our overall habit of not compromising our work and mental health just to keep the job. In pre-vious generations, I think they were still opening doors for us, setting new stan-dards, and had more of a commitment to the race. We have a commitment, too, and we appreciate and understand history. We know we are a couple of generations removed from the struggle, but we know we are part of the struggle, and we still feel part of the race, but our standards are different. Blacks in the prior generation might work in recruitment and nobody would ever know what they are doing. My generation would demand more. We want the establishment to know that we are doing it. We still have the idea of succeeding and we are still conscious of the fact that whatever we do, whites extrapolate that behavior as representative of all blacks. But our generation is less likely to care about what white people think.

Marie Long, the thirty-four-year-old vice president for constituency relations for AT&T, suggests maybe differences do exist in the work ethic of generations. "I think my parents' generation believed, 'I had to work hard to get this posi-tion, and so everyone else should have to work hard, too.' We are realizing that white people are not working this hard to get these positions, so why should we? We should help others like everybody else does. Networking, 'who do you know,' and recommendations are the easiest ways to get from A to B. We don't need to make everybody go through some hurdles that are unnecessary and that other people aren't doing."

While the work ethic is still strong among the Talented Thirty, some feel it is eroding among younger cohorts. Valerie Waller, the thirty-nine-year-old vice president of marketing and public relations for the Museum of Science and Industry in Chicago, came from a privileged background. Her father, a retired professor of political science, and her late mother, a college administrator, instilled in her the important values of hard work and education; hence, she has difficulty relating to many young people because they have little respect for the work ethic and authority.

> A perfect example is a young woman I know who is twenty-seven years old. She has a degree and works in the information technology world, and she has a visceral reaction to the person who is the CEO of the company asking her for help, because she says he walks by her every day and does not say hello. She said, 'He can wait and be on the bottom of my list. I'm going to do all the other calls before I get to him.' She does not understand the concept of authority and seniority and that he can have you fired today if you didn't show up in his office when he said he needed your help. I don't understand them not understanding the principles of authority and hierarchy in the traditional way that society has operated and, in fact, doing things to visibly defy that idea.

Likewise, Dwayne Ashley believes that the work ethic is different for younger blacks. Along with being well connected, as Maria Long suggested, Ashley feels hard work and striving for excellence are ways of managing racism, a racial lesson that appears to be losing ground.

> We hire a lot of young people, and what I see is there is not a full understanding that you've got to be better than [whites] to really ensure that our opportunity is going to be there. And I think these kids take for granted the importance of your credibility in terms of coming to work on time and following through on assignments and making sure you get them done on schedule. There just doesn't seem to be a real commitment to the kinds of things that were ingrained in us that your word is your bond. If you commit to doing something, your credibility and your bond are all that you have, so you got to make sure you do that because people are going to use a number of things to eliminate you because you are African American. Today kids think they have all sorts of opportunities, so "I can put this down and go to something else. I don't have to do that if I don't want to."

Like Waller and Ashley, Boyd, born and reared in a small town of Louisiana, grew up appreciating the value of hard work, the importance of education, and the essence of resourcefulness instilled by her father, a construction worker and owner of a horse training business, and her mother, an elementary school cafe-teria worker. But in her observation and interaction with younger African Americans who are entering corporate America, she thinks, "even though they aren't totally removed from the race, they feel more entitled." Although Boyd's father completed high school, her mother did not; yet they expected her to at-tend college and found a way to pay for her education at a private black insti-tution. Thus, she does not feel entitled to it. "See, we were still happy, proud, and blessed to get an education. 'Well, you teach me. I shouldn't have to do a whole lot to learn. I pay your salary,' is what younger people say. They ac-knowledge less honor at being educated. In a way, that is good. They are say-ing, this is a part of what we do. Then again, it is bad, because I don't know if they have that sort of emotional commitment. You ask some of these kids about the struggle, and they will say, 'What you talking about?'"

Ashley, thirty-five years old, concurred with Boyd:

> The kids that were born in the seventies and eighties really don't know a lot about people who made all the contributions in the 1950s in the civil rights movement, like Thurgood Marshall, John Lewis, and Elaine Jones of the NAACP Legal De-fense Fund. They don't realize that had it not been for people like that, they would not be enjoying many of the opportunities that they enjoy today. They take it for granted. We got to make sure that the kids get exposed to history because as we have a more integrated environment and kids go to predominantly white high schools now, they don't have the strong community base that I had when I was growing up, where it was taught and reminded to us every day by our parents be-cause they had to struggle so hard to get the opportunities they had. They wanted to make sure we understood the blood, the sweat, and the tears that had been paid for us to have those opportunities. I am not sure that the kids in the new generation are getting that same kind of fire and brimstone about opportunities they have.

Another traditional value of "making a way out of no way" is a striking exam-ple of how the traditional value system has been rewritten among post–civil rights generations, including the Talented Thirty. Since so many do not have collective memories of the struggle or a sense of history, as Boyd and Ashley noted, they feel a sense of entitlement or unearned privileges.

Olu Brown, a twenty-six-year-old, is very aware of this sense of entitlement in his generation.

> If I have been given everything all of my life, and all of a sudden I'm grown and I step into the real world, then I also think I am entitled. One thing I tell young peo-ple is particularly true in America, nothing is for free and somebody can give you something all day, but you know you are going to have to pay a price for it. And so parents do our children a disservice giving them everything, because it sets up a paradigm in our heads that says Mama, Daddy, and Grandma gave me everything and I didn't have to do anything and I still made that grade. And everybody else is going to do it. When they get into the world, the world slaps them in the face. Be-

cause if you get something, you are going to have to work for it, and a lot of us are not prepared because we think we deserve it.

Olu Brown was born and reared in a black community in Lufkin, Texas, but was educated in mostly white schools from K through 12. After high school, he attended Jarvis Christian College, an HBCU, and did his advanced studies at the International Theological Seminary, a black seminary, in Atlanta, Georgia, for his Master of Divinity degree. Growing up, he lived with his mother, a teacher with a master's in education, in a community that he described as having the "culture of a village." In this village there were relatives from the extended family—grandmothers, great-aunts and uncles, cousins, and his mentor, Mr. George, who was born in 1899. In this kinship network, he was taught the importance of family, friendship, honesty, and hard work and the values of caring and serving others who are less privileged. From his grandmother, Brown heard her stories of racism and of life during the Depression. Although Brown's parents were divorced, his mother, who participated in the civil rights movement, taught him about the struggle, and his father, a Presbyterian minister with a master of divinity degree, taught his son about the struggle through his Afrocentric sermons and by introducing him to books. In listening to the wisdom of his ancestors and understanding the history of black struggle, Brown does not feel entitled nor does he feel the disconnection between generations. But he attributes the sense of entitlement many individuals of his generation feel to a lack of historical perspective, and he feels the only way to reestablish that connection between generations is to teach our history of struggle. But Brown, who is married and expects to have his own children, is not certain how to do it.

> It's difficult to say how we teach it. I believe it was taught to my mother and her mother because it was right in your face all the time. But since African Americans have made progress, you hear people say my parents' generation was easier on me because they didn't want me to have to struggle the way they struggled. And I believe part of this is the reason a lot of parents have given kids things with no requirements. So I think what I have to do, and what other individuals my age have to do, is to begin to teach our children the struggle of our foreparents, the struggle of slavery. And even before slavery.

Speaking as a young minister who has embraced a new paradigm of worship for the generation between twenty and forty, the cohort which forms the new leadership of his church, Brown advocates "returning to the biblical examples of blacks where the Africans of Ethiopia were seen as strong warriors, and to talk about the historical context of what my Old Testament teacher would say, a lot of the Bible took place in Northeastern Africa. We need to talk about where we came from, and we came from these great kings and queens before we came to America and were enslaved. We need to talk about how even though we have some sense of freedom, the struggle still continues. And so I believe we have to remind them of who they are and where they've come from and where they can go. And a lot of our young people today think they've arrived."

P. Diddy and Magic Johnson, along with many other rappers and athletes, have arrived to become successful entrepreneurs; as Brown points out, most have not.

> We have rappers who think they've arrived because someone is paying them a few million dollars a year. But the greater issue is, if you don't produce your own stuff, if you don't make your own stuff, and if you don't get your own stuff, then you are not the one who is making the money. The main person is at Sony, Capitol Records, or Arista Records; those are the people who are making the money. You take the same thing for athletics. You can play football all you want, you can be a Michael Jordan all you want, but if somebody can afford to pay you forty million dollars a year and your teammates thirty million dollars a year, imagine what they're making. They need to not only make more money, but also learn to make good decisions and to own something.

Brown is disturbed about the lack of coping skills and resiliency of his generation, particularly among young black males.

> One of the things that I said about African American boys is that it is very unlikely that you will ever hear an African American boy say "I'm sorry." Because in our raising and upbringing, something happened to this level of accountability; so if you are a young African American boy, you blame everything on everybody else except to say it's my fault. We have to teach our young boys, in particular, that when you make a mistake you say "I made a mistake." When you mess up, you say, "I messed up," and you need to say it and not somebody else. And so what has happened to our younger generation because they have never had the pressure to succeed, the pressure to get a job, the pressure to have to go to school and then go to work at night so you can stay in school, the pressure of having to use the colored water fountain, the pressure of having to wait until you get home to use the bathroom, then there's no strength in our courage, there's no strength in our ability to say I'm going to press on. Now you have young people who have never been through the battles of life, have never had to struggle for anything, and so their moral compasses are weak, their self-esteem is weak, and the second they are challenged with a difficult situation, they give up. They can't say, "I know the last time I went through a struggle it was hard, but I made it and I'm going to make it this time." To relate to the issue of entitlement, if I have been given everything all of my life, and all of a sudden I'm grown and I step into the real world, then I also think I am entitled.

Leonard Pitts, the forty-six-year-old Pulitzer Prize winner and national syndicated columnist for the *Miami Herald*, is among the oldest of the Talented Thirty, and no doubt he would be of the same mind regarding this sense of entitlement of post–civil rights generations as Olu Brown, who is twenty years younger. In Pitts's household, all the family members grew up or were born after the civil rights movement. Yet he can see a generational divide in worldview between himself and his five children. He thinks they have a different worldview of success. In his generation, it meant succeeding in the mainstream and overcoming racial obstacles; excuses were not acceptable. Now, he says, for black middle-class children, this is not a goal. They want to become rap stars. Moreover, they use racism as an excuse for not trying.

Pitts was born in Orange County, California. He grew up in a predominantly black neighborhood in Los Angeles, where he was educated for the most part during elementary school, with the exception of one mixed school, in a milieu of exclusively black students. In junior high school, the student body was mixed and the faculty predominantly white, while in high school, the student body was mostly black and the teachers were mixed. After high school, at age fifteen, he matriculated at the University of Southern California, where he received his degree in English. His education far surpassed that of his parents: His father, who had a sixth-grade education, worked as a janitor, and his mother, who had a seventh-grade education, worked as a domestic. His regal, Southern-bred mother, his extended family, and circle of friends had a major influence on his life and helped to shape his values of excellence and his strong work ethic.

> I really wanted to have my mother on my side. She had a belief that made you bigger than the belief you had in yourself. She was a person who saw you as being at a certain level, then saw you as better before you ever saw yourself as better. And you know, on those tight budgets, she would spare no expense to help me. Mom got me my first typewriter in 1967. You know she was going to do what she could for that "budding writer," although she couldn't afford it. She was always in your corner. That made you strive harder to make her proud of you.

In his circle of friends and mentors, he thinks of Nathaniel Davis. "We called him our cousin. He would sneak out and bring us trays from the Ponderosa when my dad died; he was like a big brother in a lot of ways. There was the librarian at the high school, who played an important part in my life. And Mr. Barbee got me my first subscription to a writer's magazine. It really meant a lot to me to have this magazine, which was so helpful to me, and then to have this man who was not even related to me to go in his pocket and pay for the subscription." Pitts had the support of teachers, which, unlike the Talented One Hundred, was rarely mentioned as a source of influence among the Talented Thirty.

> Mr. Jenkins, my tenth-grade English teacher, influenced me, and Ms. Harrison, my old sixth-grade teacher, who is white, saw something in me that she liked. I saw her about two years ago, some thirty years since I was her student, and she was telling my wife how wonderful I was. Then, there were the older people in the church that I grew up in. One of the things about my children is that they don't have anyone

watching them as they grow up. I think it is important, because my mother always had high expectations for me, and one of the things that happens, when people have high expectations for you, is you kill yourself trying to live up to what they think you are. You may not think you're that, but they think you're that and you say, "I'm not going to let them down." And all these older folks at church were like echoes of my mother. There's always the knowledge that if I didn't live up to what they expected, how disappointing it would be. That was very powerful. My kids don't have anything like that.

While being uprooted from his moorings of familial and friendship networks has been beneficial for his career, Pitts thinks,

By the same token, I realize that there are things that my children didn't get that I did. They were not raised around a network of aunts and uncles. I think it benefits you to be answerable to a lot of folks. I'll be very frank with you. I think my kids are spoiled. And I think they, like a lot of middle-class black kids, want to identify with the hood or inner city, and to be like those brought up on the street. There are five computers in my house, there are televisions all over the house, and the two that are interested in music have keyboards. They have all of this stuff. And for those of us who are blacks and grew up in more modest circumstances, the thing we wanted to do was to give our children the advantages that we didn't have. So I don't have any regrets about all that they have and providing things on that level. But by the same token, my kids don't really appreciate all that they have, nor where their parents came from to get them. They have not a clue.

Pitts is not sure about how to close the generational gap or how to teach his children to appreciate all that they have or where their parents came from.

I have taken my kids back to Los Angeles where I grew up. The nineteen-year-old in 1992, about twelve years ago, was seven or eight. And I'm driving down the street showing him this is where I lived, this is where I did this or that, and he says, "This is where you're from?" And I said, "Yes." And he says, "Well, why is it so dirty?" And I don't know if I can make that connection. I tried. Maybe kids don't always see the result of what you're doing. Maybe they will come back later and say something that shows that they understand. But I don't really think they get it. And I don't try to tell them that I never missed a meal, or went hungry. I knew that there were things that I didn't have. I didn't go to the McDonald's, because I thought that was something that rich folks did. You had to be rich and preferably white to go to McDonald's. But I didn't have McDonald's money and so maybe they can't appreciate that. Maybe they just can't. But I wish they could. I don't want them to go into the world as spoiled as I perceive them to be. That's the part that really troubles me—this sense of entitlement. I guess you see it in white kids, too. I hate to make it a racial thing, but it's more troubling to me when it's black kids, because they—my kids—are one generation removed from neighborhoods that they could not survive in. And I tell them you could not survive where I grew up because you are used to one thing and to a certain standard of living. There are things that you would not be able to have. And I don't think they appreciate that.

And the thing you get from where I was raised is not necessarily physical toughness but mental toughness, which I don't think a lot of kids today have. It's just
missing. If you get out of my neighborhood, it's going to kill you or make you tough.

Like Pitts, Sheila V. Williams, the forty-four-year-old president of the National Association of Minority Automobile Dealers (NAMAD), would probably
concur about the lack of mental toughness of her generation's children and
their sense of entitlement.
For parents who are not passing on traditional values and race lessons, she says,

> I think we have to seriously assess what our kids are doing and design safety nets to
> allow them to achieve goals. I think we have to be tougher on our kids than anyone
> else could ever be. We make clear our expectations of our children from working to
> the way they maintain their environment. We have very clear expectations about how
> they address elders, how they assist elders. It's just very, very clear to them what is
> and what is not allowed. When you look back on some of the biggest successes in the
> world, Frederick Douglass, Jesse Jackson, Kweisi Mfume, these African Americans
> came out of lesser-privileged environments but they are rich in guidance, respect,
> and history. Some wonder if we should have focused more on equal as opposed to
> separate. I would not be inclined to disagree with that. Yes, we are integrated now,
> but I don't know that we are faring any better because of integration.

Unlike Pitts, Williams, who is also married with three children, does not feel
that she is spoiling her children. Instead, she has initiated a plan to reinforce
the traditional values of resiliency and resistance. While growing up in a cohe-
sive black community in Nashville, Tennessee, she learned from her father, a
dialysis technician and a union representative who "fought for the underdog,"
and her mother, a housewife, a value system that encompassed respect for elders, compassion, service to others, planning, and hard work. She thinks, "This
generation is lost with respect to being taught to revere and respect their elders and to bestow respect and kindness on strangers." Hence, she feels it is her
duty to teach her children the history, lessons, and values that have made her
and her foreparents resourceful. "One of the things I do for my kids, and I don't
think people do it as much as they should, is work hard. We don't have to because we have the ability to have somebody come in and do whatever we have
to do for us. But we don't do that because we don't think it is good for our kids."
Far too many black professionals that she knows undermine their children's
work ethic and absolve themselves of responsibility and control for parenting.

> They have maids. The kids don't have to do anything. I hear stories from my peers
> and my kids' peers' parents that they can't get their kids to get up. What do you
> mean you can't get them to get up? They can't get kids to keep their room clean.
> What do you mean that you can't get them to do it? I have a motto. Our job is to
> make our kids not need us. We want them to want us. When my kids are twenty-
> four or twenty-five, I want them to make important decisions. It's okay if they say,

"Let's call Mom and Dad and see what they say." They have the judgment. But I don't want them to need us. I don't want them to call us and say, "My life is about to be cut out, would you please . . . ." Instead, I want my kids to be able to call me and say, "Hey, we want to take the grandbabies to Greece so they can experience another culture." I don't want to have to give my kids twenty-five thousand dollars to make a down payment on a home. I don't want to have to go somewhere and bail my children out of jail. So that's why I am trying to give them the tools to be able to survive in every arena of life. And that's not just doing well on your SAT, it is also knowing how to keep a house clean.

Williams, an attorney who graduated from Harvard Law School, thinks "Jane Crow, Esq. is still alive and kicking," and it impacts blacks at every socioeconomic level. Consequently, she wants to prepare her children for living in a society constrained by race and to teach them about giving back to the community. Her activist father, as well as a childhood event that shaped her worldview, influenced her consciousness of the collective. Williams and her sister, who grew up in the post–civil rights era, were the first to integrate their elementary school. The painful days of that experience are etched in her memories: "As we walked to school, it was amazing that there would be grown people lined up along the sidewalk who would taunt us and throw things at us. . . . I have tried hard to understand what would make grown people do that willingly. I think that whole experience has influenced my view about how to create win-win situations around diversity." In her position as the president of NAMAD, she fights for parity in the automotive industry to increase the representation of minority dealerships. And whatever her children's profession, she wants them to also fight for parity.

Olu Brown, Leonard Pitts, and Sheila V. Williams identified a paradigmatic shift in components of the traditional value system, such as the self-reliance, resourcefulness, respect, and compassion that formed the bedrock of resiliency in the African American struggle. As noted previously, they are being lost because of greater contact with the dominant culture, greater fragmentation of black communities, and major socioeconomic and technological changes.[14]

Perhaps the mental toughness is missing not only for Leonard Pitts's children and the children of Sheila Williams's peers but also for millions of others because parents forget to tell their family stories and to teach their kids about black history. Forgetting is sometimes a way to minimize the trauma of unpleasant racial memories, and unless an archeologist unearths these memories, stories remain buried deep in the souls and bones of black folk. Allen and Gail Jones, husband and wife, know this can happen. While their parents taught both Allen, forty, and Gail, forty-one, the cornerstone of traditional values of honesty, spirituality and religiosity, education, and hard work, and the importance of independence, ownership and entrepreneurship, saving and investing, they did not provide the context from which these traditional values emerged as a source of black resistance and resiliency. Hence, Allen and Gail Jones, having no preserved recollections of the civil rights movement or any stories of struggle from their parents or grandparents, would probably assume their value system is typical of upper-middle-class Americans. Owners of a successful chain of seven physical therapy centers in the Hampton Roads area of Virginia, Allen and Gail live with their four children in a comfortable, upper-middle-class, mostly white community. Their two oldest children, boys who are nine and six, attend a private, predominantly white academy. Allen said of his older son, "He just meshes right in." His son does not look at color, Allen says, "They're just people." But he remembered, at an earlier age, his younger son, who was learning his colors, said, "Dad, you're the darkest one in the family. Then there is Allen [his older brother], and there's Mommy. Mommy is the lightest." Although he was indicating some color consciousness, it may suggest, as well, an awareness of race and racism. But they do not talk about racism to their children. Although the Joneses make sure their children interact with other blacks through their Episcopal church and through their familial, friendship, and organizational networks, they believe also that it is important to teach their children about black history, particularly the successes of African Americans. Gail said, "There are a lot of things that blacks have done in history, and black kids have no idea that they have accomplished these things. They automatically assume that a white person invented everything." Allen, the CEO of Dominion Physical Therapy, started out with one employee and now employs forty-eight people. He serves on several prominent corporate and civic boards and committees throughout the Hampton Roads area, and he believes, too, "that you have to know where you came from to know where you are going."

Allen Jones Jr., who was born in Greenville, Mississippi, and moved, at seven, with his parents and four siblings to Hartford, Connecticut, before the family settled in Southington, Connecticut, has his goals set and feels he knows where he is going in life. But, until his interview for this book, he had little knowledge of his family history, except that his parents, who stressed the significance of autonomy and entrepreneurship, owned a store in Mississippi before moving to Connecticut for better economic opportunities. As Allen and Gail listened, I asked the questions, and his father, Allen Jones Sr., a retired steel work manager, with whom we spoke via speaker telephone, filled in the missing links.

For the first time, Allen heard about his father's experience with racism and the reason Allen Jones Sr. left Greenville, Mississippi, his place of birth, and moved with his young family to Connecticut for a better racial climate and greater economic opportunities.

When asked if he had ever discussed racism with his children, or the incident of being fired from the job for using the white bathroom in Mississippi, he answered, "No, I never discussed it in detail. I probably spoke of it just in passing. I never talked to them about racism, because I didn't want the negative seed planted in their heads. Hopefully, they would learn about racism going to school. I told them the difference between black and white, and there is none, when it comes to a person, but I never wanted them to feel that they were less than any white person. I taught them that. I didn't teach the negative side of it, I taught the positive side." Not wanting to share the hardship of struggle with his children, Allen's father extracted from the struggle the important values of independence and working for yourself as a means of resisting white domination, which he transmitted to his children. But the keystone of Allen Jr.'s entrepreneurial spirit reaches back to his grandfather, an independent farmer, who owned land in Mississippi. According to Allen Jones Sr., he did not have any racial experiences because he was "semi-independent." Allen learned that his great-grandfather had owned the land that he divided between his siblings and his children. "And we made our living off the land," Allen Jones Sr. said. He remembers his father's race lessons: "My father taught me that I was just as good as any other man. And to always think that and to treat the white man with respect and to demand that he treated me with respect. My grandfather died when I was five years old. But he taught my father that he was just as good as any other man."

Allen Jones Sr. said,

> I taught my children always to get a good education, and once you get a good education, no one can take it away from you. And after you get that education, be a businessperson and not work for somebody else, but have someone else working for you, because if you are working for someone else, you're always limited to that paycheck that they give you. And if you have your own business, there is no limit to what you can do. You can always expand; you can always do better if you have the knowledge and the expertise. If you have that aggressiveness about you, you can always better yourself.

I inquired about Allen Jr.'s mother's side; he learned from his father that his mother's family had been independent farmers. "When the civil rights movement began, her parents housed some Freedom Riders." When asked if his wife ever told her children about her parents housing the civil rights workers, Allen's father responded, "I don't recall. I don't think so because that's one thing we just didn't talk about, the negative things that we had experienced in our lives." As the interview with his father concluded, Allen stated, "Now you know more about my family history than I do." Gail's late father had left her unidentified photos and mementos of him and others, documenting that he was involved in the civil rights movement. She wanted to begin her search to fill in the missing links. For the first time, Allen and Gail Jones understood, perhaps at the visceral level, the meaning of passing the stories of not only the triumphs of blacks but also the traumas.

One function of transmitting stories of struggle is to reproduce a consciousness of the collective that is so necessary for individual and group mobility. As Sheila V. Williams stated, "We were expected to make this world a better place than we found it." But Williams is cognizant that the struggles of the past are difficult for post–civil rights generations to relate to. "Just as I never had to ride on the back of the bus, these kids never grew up understanding those real differences of people of color and Caucasians. And I think that has manifested itself with them trying to put their arms around what is their responsibility in terms of making a difference. I grew up knowing it was my responsibility to support the NAACP. That was a real entity in my home. And I don't think that that is necessarily the case today." The post–civil rights generation is struggling with their social responsibility because they have embraced the meritocratic ideals and underlying assumptions of the dominant culture about success, work, and personal responsibility.

R. Fenimore Fisher's experience underscores Williams's point. When Fisher, thirty, was interviewed in May 2004, he was executive director of Rainbow/PUSH Wall Street, and he left there to become the director of African American markets at Wal-Mart. He stated, "After seven years of working with the Rainbow/PUSH Coalition, I felt it was time to move on to something new. I will always value and support the work of the organization. My respect and appreciation to Rev. Jackson is limitless." In his position at Rainbow/PUSH Wall Street, an economic empowerment initiative established by Jesse Jackson, he can bear witness to the consequences of those who forget or who do not know their personal or collective history, particularly the role of civil rights organizations, like the Rainbow/PUSH Coalition, whose "mission is the protection, enhancement and gaining of civil rights for underserved citizens." He worked five years for Rainbow/PUSH Wall Street, starting immediately after law school as an intern. He rose rapidly through the ranks to become the executive director of the organization. But despite the tremendous opportunities he had working at the organization, his friends didn't understand his work or felt they could not do civil rights work, because it was not their definition of success. For Fenimore, success is maintaining a leadership position, whether in the public, private, or nonprofit sector, while balancing personal time, family, and friends. If he can combine those aspects of his life, he says, "Money is secondary." Some friends see it differently.

> I've got a circle of friends that recognizes, appreciates, and sees the value of the work of civil rights organizations, but it could never be the type of work that they could do.
>
> What is ingrained in them, I think, is success means working for a white corporation. Success equates to high six-figure salaries. Success to them is not necessarily measured in the power that they have in their position. Success to them is equated to how much money you have in your account, how much your home is worth, and what car you are able to purchase. Despite the fact that I have been exposed to opportunities that people working in corporations for thirty years have never been exposed to, the fact that I have the ability to go with or without Rev. Jackson to testify before Senate committees or state legislatures, which is a tremendous amount of power to have, my circle of friends thinks this doesn't necessarily equate to success.

Interestingly, of the Talented Thirty, eleven individuals viewed success in terms of material acquisition; thirteen identified success as a melding of material acquisitions and service to others; five saw success as primarily service to others; and one individual thought of success as a life journey or as a spiritual process. A solely materialistic notion of success can operate in ways that impede the development of a consciousness of the collective, turning the American dream into a racial nightmare.

Fisher has counseled and advised many complainants who filed discrimination grievances, finding some of the individuals who do not see the value of civil rights organizations most troubling, especially since they have internalized the myth of meritocracy.

> I find this a lot in those who come to us for assistance in the final hours. They have set their careers going to Ivy League schools, and they have all the right connections for achieving success and then feeling that they don't need a Rev. Jackson [Founder of Rainbow/PUSH] or Kweisi Mfume [former president of the NAACP] or Julian Bond [chair of the NAACP] or Marc Morial [president of the Urban League]. They think that they have gotten where they are by their own work and dedication and that they have been promoted and achieved success based on their own merit, and race has nothing to do with it. And then they get downsized, or they get blocked for a promotion that they have been wanting. They start to be phased out emotionally. They're not fired but it's a very adversarial workforce for them, and to have these people who have denied the importance and significance of our advocacy organization, who have developed rather conservative political views of democracy. So you can be Republican, or you can be conservative, but it's one thing to be those things, and another thing to forget our history, as well as to wear cultural blinders when it comes to what we are going through presently. So that group is the most troubling for me. I would say among the middle class and upper-middle class, that group constitutes about 40 or 50 percent. It's a strong number. You'll find among some of the wealthiest black families very conservative viewpoints and attitudes that distance them from the traditional advocates and leaders. What's been successful to them is wealth. There's nothing wrong with that, but again if you are truly a person that lives in reality, you can't achieve those things and take out the context of what we've gone through and continue to go through in this country. People tend to, as Rev. Jackson always says, think of the civil rights era as back in those old days. He continues to preach that those old days are these days.

Fisher, born and reared in Opelousas, Louisiana, has never encountered blatant racism. Yet he is adamant that a need exists for civil rights organizations because the struggle continues but in a different way.

> Our organization, and Rev. Jackson, basically equates the civil rights movement to a freedom symphony. The first stage was to end slavery. The second and third stages [were] seeing an end to segregation and securing the right to vote. We see the fourth stage of this freedom symphony as economic empowerment through access to capital and technology for all of America's underserved and underrepre-

sented people. Our office was established basically to try and secure business opportunities for women and minority-owned business enterprises, to monitor the diversity of board placement—when I say board placement, I mean board member placement in corporate America to monitor and track the procurement spent for diverse spenders, as well as employment discrimination allegations.

Though Fisher has not faced blatant racism, he understands its subtle manifestations and wants to fight it on whatever level. It was the reason he went to work for Rainbow/PUSH Wall Street. As an attorney who graduated from Ohio Northern University Law School, he decided to work for Rainbow/PUSH Coalition for two reasons. First, his late father supported Jesse Jackson's presidential bid in 1984 and worked in his campaign in Louisiana. More importantly, after law school, he could not secure an internship on Wall Street. "I was looking for internships and wanted to work for some of the major firms in New York. I sent out hundreds of letters, but I got no response. And although there are various things that go into selecting individuals, one of the things that the Wall Street Project was promoting was trying to take down the walls around Wall Street and remove the cultural blinders. And so that was the message that was very appealing to me because I was being blocked out of the privileged walls of Wall Street."

Fisher, who was educated from grade school through law school in predominantly white milieus, grew up in privileged surroundings. Despite his opportunities, his parents taught him "not to take any privileges or benefits for granted because at any time they can be taken away from you by a majority of individuals who cannot stand you based upon the color of your skin." So his father, an administrator in the school system of Opelousas, and his mother, an educator, taught him to fight and stand up for his beliefs, not only for himself but also on behalf of others. During his undergraduate days at Louisiana State University, he encountered an incident of subtle racism and he stood up for his beliefs. This event was etched in his memory, and it crafted the way he copes with racism. As student director of minority affairs, he was responsible for organizing the Martin Luther King Jr. celebration. He met with the head of the student union, in what he perceived as a positive meeting, to select a space and obtain a phone in the student center. He stated,

The next morning, I got a call from the administrative director of minority affairs for LSU—an African American woman. She said, "Ryan, I need to talk to you. I got a call from the dean of students and he said he had gotten a call from the head of the student union, saying that you had gone there to have a meeting." I said, "Oh, yeah, it was a great meeting. We're going to have our cubicle set up and phones turned on to do the outreach for the students to get them to come to the MLK celebration." She then went on to tell me, "Well, you know sometimes here things take a bit of time, and it's not good to stir up too much, and you do have the African American Cultural Center, which you could utilize for space." And I said,

"Well, they have their own offices set up and each organization is entitled to office space in the student union." She said, "The dean of students called me and it's just going to be an issue and sometimes we just need to not make waves." Keep in mind my parents instilling in me, "you got to fight," "don't take anything for granted," "you got to be the best." They didn't raise me to be accepting of any form of discrimination whether it was subtle or direct. I got off the phone with her and then I took some time to think through it, and basically what I did was resign from that role of directing the MLK activities and told her that I did not want to be a part of a system that would not allow me the same benefits and advantages that it did to the other white organizations on campus. And for a lot of years I battled with that internally as to whether or not that was the right decision.

Fisher has wrapped his arms around racism and wants to fight it at every level. He knows that in the post–civil rights era his experience with racism is different from that of previous generations. The experience of racism is not only different for him and for individuals of his generation, but the way in which they perceive, interpret, and respond to it is different, as well. To illustrate, he cites this incident that occurred during his formative years when his mother and grandmother picked him up at an airport. The way he perceives, interprets, and responds to racism is similar to the way his mother does, but very different from his grandmother's way. As an only child, his family afforded him many privileges, and one was to equip him for travel to destinations around the country. He recalled an incident when he was nine that indicates the generational response to the color line.

I returned from a trip, and my mother and grandmother came to pick me up. And my mom chose not to go into the parking garage, so she just parked at the front of the airport. As she was waiting for me, a police officer advised her to move her vehicle. He was the traditional Southern good old boy police officer. She said, "Yes, I know." I think she had even pulled out and driven around the airport. I came out and we were putting our luggage in the car, and the police officer saw that we were getting ready to leave, but I guess he wanted to stress his authority and came up and yelled at my mother. "Ma'am, I told you that you needed to move this car right now. Get outta here, gal." I think he might have made the mistake of saying "gal." And my mother, not being one to hold her tongue, started to argue with him. My grandmother, who is sitting in the car, started pleading with my mother to get in the car, don't cause any trouble, and do as he says. And so, my mother, after saying what she wanted to say to the officer, got in the car and my grandmother just proceeded to chastise her. I saw the mother-daughter role between the two of them as my grandmother chastised her. "When the law is upset with you, you should not say anything. Just be quiet." My mother said, "No, I'm not going to do that." We were leaving. My grandmother's experience with discrimination has come out of the self-preservation-survival sort of background, where you don't challenge white authority, because white authority can beat you: White authority can kill you. That was her experience. My mother, growing up in the civil rights era, experienced challenges, fighting for your rights and standing up for yourself. The generation that exists between my mother's generation—the kids that grew up in the 1970s and went to college in the early 1980s—have a sense of ambivalence as to our appreciation of what discrimination was and still is in this country. That generation probably has more depth to their understanding of the civil rights movement and the continuing struggle than my generation, because they were the immediate beneficiaries after my parents, but still experienced that time that I never experienced. When you ask me to list incidents where I had been discriminated [against], I almost felt bad because I didn't have a blatant story to tell. I think probably given the sheltering that my family did with me and the resources we had, I was probably protected from that. I think the generation that I am talking about still remembers, and regardless whether your family lived in whatever neighborhood, you still could be picked up at any time off the road by the cops.

Fisher does not believe racism has declined; rather its manifestations have changed. Still he recognizes it in whatever garment it's cloaked.

I don't think racism is on the decline. I think that the tools used and the strategies used to empower racism have changed. The overt tools of brutality and violence to implement racism will never again, I hope, exist in this country. The tools that are used now are much more calculated in terms of people being set up for investigation while there may be no incidence of malfeasance. You look at what happened to Mayor Street in Philadelphia. Look at what happened to Kofi Anon at the UN. His office was bugged. Those kinds of tactics are much more calculating than what we saw traditionally. It did exist back then, but they didn't have to be used so skillfully, because you always had the ability overtly to disenfranchise people by beating them down. But now the way racism is implemented, as people's lives are elevated to a certain level, you just know that at any place or time you can be shot down by a cleverly placed wiretap or a cleverly placed investigator. You look at also the tools now that are used to keep our race at the bottom level of employment and at the bottom level of economic wealth, and you still have issues of redlining, or financial services companies not locating in our neighborhood because they don't issue business to us. Or if they issue business to us, it's the issue of the length of quality product or the issue of lending loans to us at subprime rates. If you look at financial services, you see predatory lending still in existence. You see our Congress hesitates even to define what predatory lending is. You see within the automotive financing area, issues such as markup. Regardless of our credit rating, the dealers or the finance arms of automotive companies charge African Americans three to five additional percentage points, not based upon credit rating, but based upon our race. This means that on a car loan, we pay two thousand dollars or three thousand dollars more than white people pay. So when you look at answering in terms of this racism, is it on the decline? No! But the tools used in racism are much more hidden today where we, as a people, don't realize that we pay more for less, live under stress, and die earlier, because there is an economic imprisonment of our race. And that's the new racism. It's always been the racism for us, but that's the one that is now at the pivotal point of power.

Fisher says the post–civil rights generation cannot recognize the more subtle form of racism. This new form of systematic, institutionally and ideologically embedded racial inequality is what Lawrence D. Bobo refers to as laissez-faire racism.[15] Thomas M. Shapiro, in *The Hidden Cost of Being African American*, using two hundred in-depth interviews and national survey data with ten thousand families, documents how racial inequality in assets is transmitted across generations by subtle discriminatory policies.[16] Citing additional examples of this new racism, including lending practices in housing, Fisher wants to be the bellwether for individuals in his generation and raise their level of awareness.

> [Blacks] cannot recognize it. But they would, if they just took a little bit of time to review the interest rates they are paying on their cars and their homes, to review the amount of time to get state resources delivered to their communities, and if they live in predominantly black communities, they have to deal with redlining. "With my credit, I can't get any kind of loan, so let me just go ahead and take what the bank is giving me, so I can get my four-thousand-square-foot house," without realizing that you could have shopped around and at least you could have gotten a lower interest rate. You're being taken advantage of because they understand your mentality of "Oh, you're so happy to get this loan." If they took the time to realize that at work, you have been invited to do all the research on this project. But when it comes to meeting with the CEO, your white boss says, "We won't need you this time." Until my generation starts realizing all of these instances are not isolated incidences, but are a part of the new version of racism, we're going to keep missing it. It's going to keep going over our heads. The dirty form of racism truly is what is keeping us from achieving the greatest form of success, and truly Dr. King's dream for us was equality, in my opinion.

Is Fenimore Fisher's understanding of racism typical of the way post–civil rights generations perceive, experience, interpret, and respond to it? Let us turn to the Talented Thirty for clues.

Looking through Rose-Colored Glasses: Responses to Racism

Racism, as defined in the prologue and summarized here, is a system of power and ideology of racial domination or exploitation that incorporates beliefs in a particular race's biological and cultural inferiority, and hence employs such beliefs to justify and impose differential and unequal treatment for that group. Do the black elite of post–civil rights generations see racism, which embodies both institutional and attitudinal components, through rose-colored glasses, as Kevin Powell suggests? Do they speak a different language of race than their elders do? Do they see racism through a broader lens, which embraces both institutional and attitudinal aspects, or do they look through a narrow lens, which incorporates only prejudicial attitudes and individual or group discriminatory acts directed toward nondominant racial or ethnic groups? As noted in the prologue, the expanded version that emerged during the black power movement in the late 1960s emphasizes, on the one hand, the racist policies and practices that are built into the fabric of society, as well as the prejudiced belief system used to justify and prescribe unequal treatment. On the other hand, prejudice refers to unfavorable feelings and beliefs directed toward any person or group based upon a set of assumed characteristics and faulty generalizations, while discrimination is action meant to harm nondominant racial and ethnic groups. In "Talking Past Each Other: Black and White Languages of Race," Robert Blauner suggests that blacks and whites see race and racism differently. Looking at racial change from the 1960s to the 1990s, he concluded that blacks see racism as alive and well and central to American society, whereas whites view it as peripheral, except on collective public moments, such as the O. J. Simpson trial. Excluding the more race-conscious extremist, Blauner posits that "Whites see racism largely as a thing of the past," laid to rest by the civil rights movement. Moreover, whites tend to think of racism in more personal terms, while blacks are more likely to view it in more impersonal terms, incorporating the institutional aspect as part of their racial worldview.[17]

> They [Whites] defined it in terms of segregation and lynching, explicit White supremacist beliefs, or double standards in hiring, promotion, and admissions to colleges or other institutions. Except for affirmative action, which seemed the most blatant expression of such double standards, they were positively impressed by racial change. Many saw the relaxed and comfortable relations between Whites and Blacks as the heart of the matter. More crucial to Blacks, on the other hand, were the underlying structures of power and position that continued to provide them with unequal portions of economic opportunity and other possibilities for the good life. . . . Whites are more likely than Blacks to view racism as a personal issue. Both sensitive to their own possible culpability (if only unconsciously) and angry at the use of the concept of racism by angry minorities, they do not differentiate well between the racism of social structures and the accusation that they as participants in that structure are personally racist. The new meanings make sense to Blacks, who live such experiences in their bones.[18]

Born and reared in the boiling cauldron of overt racism, the African Americans that Blauner interviewed over three generations, from the 1960s to the 1990s, certainly lived such experiences in their bones. And so did the Talented One Hundred whom the reader met in the previous chapters. But does racism fill the marrow of the Talented Thirty's bones? For most, the answer is a resounding no—at least, not in the way the Talented One Hundred experienced it. Of the Talented Thirty, four could not recall or recognize ever experiencing discrimination, while eleven identified only one experience; and even when some suspected a racist episode, they were hesitant to use the label. In general, like the Talented One Hundred, the Talented Thirty felt racism has not disappeared; rather it has become more subtle in its manifestations and therefore more difficult to pinpoint, particularly as it interlocks with gender and class. On the contrary, the generations have strikingly different experiences and perspectives on racism. Eighteen of the Talented Thirty incorporated a larger definition of racism, while twelve employed the prejudice-discrimination model. Through the expanded lens of Lisa Boykins and the narrow focus of Robert

Traynham, the camera is angled to capture their polar perspectives of racism and the sociocultural factors and events that shaped their social and racial consciousness, attitudes, values, and worldview.

Lisa Boykins

Lisa Boykins, an entertainment attorney for Paramount Pictures, is the director of business, pictures and television, where she negotiates and drafts contracts to distribute Paramount pictures and movies to cable networks. From her vantage point, "Racism has permeated this country's history, and while we have overcome in a lot of ways, we still have a long way to go. Race and racism are still a part of American culture, and so ingrained in the American ethos, but it is more sophisticated than it was years ago."

For Boykins, her deeper understanding of racism came during her college days at the University of Notre Dame, where she had some of the most meaningful defining moments in her life. There she met excellent professors who would influence her life course, particularly about civil rights and social justice and about how to use her knowledge as an instrument of social change. One such professor, a Latino, who was involved with minority groups and who taught courses on minorities in politics, organized a conference on civil rights at the campus. He introduced her to Derrick Bell, the first African American tenured professor in the Harvard Law School and the author of the classic *Faces at the Bottom of the Well: The Permanence of Racism*. Bell, who later resigned his tenured post at Harvard in protest over racist practices and policies, influenced Boykins to consider a career in law. She would eventually study law under him at New York University, where her understanding of racism was enlarged. When asked if she thought racism would ever disappear, she responded, "I guess I am an optimist, but I would say in time," and her voice trailed off, and she remembered the words of her professor.

Derrick Bell has written this book, *Faces at the Bottom of the Well*, and I think that the person that most influences my views in the wider society would be Derrick Bell. And he is right on point when he says that racism is a permanent fixture in American society and why that is true. It doesn't mean that we can't succeed in a lot of different ways. You can succeed in spite of racism. There is the idea that we now live in a color-blind society in which you can transcend race. I think there are a few people who try to transcend race, like Michael Jordan, Oprah Winfrey, and Michael Jackson, but they had their moments where they might be reminded, "You may be a millionaire but you're still black." Even Oprah has talked about times when she has gone shopping with her jeans and the baseball cap and they didn't recognize her. She was knocking on the door of a store where they have to buzz you in and the person inside wouldn't buzz her in. Or the times when Tiger Woods won the golf match and one of the players remarked, "I don't think they serve collard greens and fried chicken at the victory dinner." Notwithstanding their great achievements and their great success, even people at that level have these moments where they encounter racism, and I'm sure that it has to have a great sting.

Lisa Boykins, who defines her political persuasion as progressive liberal, believes that for others to have opportunities, affirmative action is still necessary. She is concerned about the drop in black enrollment as a result of cutbacks in affirmative action. At the University of California, Berkeley, for example, the media have reported widely that black admissions dropped by 30 percent for the fall's freshman class of 2004. Out of an expected freshman class of 3,821, only 98 black students had registered by the spring of 2004. Thus, Boykins is more typical of members of the Talented Thirty who feel affirmative action is necessary for racial progress in education and in the workplace, although eight individuals felt it needed to be reformed.

> To say that we don't need affirmative action today is to deny the permanency of racism, the legacy of racism. I think that we don't live in a color-blind society, and I believe in affirmative action. And I think it gives meaningful opportunities to people who may, in some instances, not have had access. I especially am a proponent of affirmative action in the area of higher education. In the last few years, the attacks on affirmative action have really had an impact on African Americans who are matriculating in colleges and universities around the country. If I wanted to put my finger on the one thing in my view that would make such a big difference, access to education is so clearly the answer. If you don't have the opportunity to go to college, you won't have the opportunity to go to professional school. You won't have the same opportunities for jobs and income; that's going to hurt you in your opportunity to send your kids to college. It's just so cyclical. And for people not to realize that how we're going to make a difference is to give young people of the primary and secondary level better public education but, also, to make it possible for those kids to go to college. We are really on a downward spiral. We're going backwards in terms of the rate of our membership increasing.

Whereas the Talented One Hundred identified the issue of race and racism as the most important problem facing the country, Boykins, like the Talented Thirty, thinks, "The most important issue facing the black community now is educational opportunities. You know that a legacy of the *Brown v. Board of Education* decision's unfulfilled promise for public schools in urban settings has really declined as a result of white flight and lack of resources, and so you have a de facto school system once again. It's sad to say, but I doubt that President Clinton would have sent his daughter to the public school system in Washington DC. Jimmy Carter didn't either. If George Bush's kids had been high school age, I'm sure he wouldn't have either. Insofar as the public school system in the nation's capital, no person who has the means to do something different would send their kids to those schools, and that's where our kids are."

She offers a litany of problems interrelated to the lack of quality education, such as poverty, teenage pregnancy, crime, and the high rate of incarceration.

"Those issues that plague our communities really need to be addressed. But for me, it all goes back to the opportunity to achieve an education."

Though Boykins does not wear the banner of race woman across her sleeves, generally, she knows, as described above, institutional or attitudinal racism when she sees and experiences it.

> You can always look back and wonder did people treat you differently? Did something happen that scarred you for life? Well, there certainly have been times when I had an awareness of being black, notwithstanding the things that I have achieved that would rightfully give me a place at the table. But people sometimes seem to feel that they have encountered me somewhere, that I was a secretary, not a lawyer. I worked at this Wall Street law firm, with a couple hundred lawyers, and they had main offices in Washington, London, and Tokyo. It was really an international law firm. And out of all the offices around the world, there were only three black women. And there were times when I was in the Washington office, and periodically, I would have occasions to go to the New York office for meetings. I would wear a suit and have my briefcase. I would look professional, and I remember one time I was in the hallway chatting with a partner, and there was an associate from the New York office, and the partner introduced me and then walked away. As I was chatting with the associate, he said, "So are you a legal assistant in the Washington office?" Now, why would he think that? Why would I travel up from Washington with this partner to this meeting that we had just come out of? Why did he not initially think that I was a lawyer? In the minds of these people at the law firm, the company is not going to hire you as a lawyer, so you must be a legal assistant. And so those are the moments when you are reminded that this wasn't thirty years ago. I graduated from law school in 1995 and I worked at this law firm from 1995 to 2000, and these are the experiences we are talking about in the twenty-first century. Currently, you look around and realize the reason people have this perception is because there are so few of us. So I guess, in his mind, this image that he has is reinforced, and the reality is that there are not a lot of women of color who are in law firms or who work on Wall Street. So at the same time, while I was taken aback from that, I can understand why the assumption was made.

Boykins handles such encounters with aplomb. "I have learned enough in my life that you have to pick your battles. You can't make a firm case out of everything. But when the moment comes along when someone genuinely does or says something that's offensive, that from your personal dignity standpoint you can't let go, and then you say something in response. But in those types of situations where people inadvertently are making assumptions about who they think you are, you correct them and then you move on." Working in the entertainment industry, she is acutely aware that such distorted images of black women and men are institutionalized and reinforced in Hollywood.

> I am most concerned about the images that Hollywood projects. Look at the black movies: They are just riddled with stereotypes, and you can say the same thing about a lot of the black music that is out there. You look at the images and the

videos, and the message of the music. When hip-hop first came out in the seventies, I recall that the message in the music was positive and uplifting. It was about the people's experiences and how they survived and persevered. It was also about parties and things. Now, the message in the music denigrates people, especially black women. We can't have it said that it is just society that is propagating all this negative imagery out there, although in a lot of ways they are benefiting from it financially. We also have to look at the role we play in being the mouthpiece. We are the ones that are rapping, we are the ones in the movies that are projecting these stereotypical images, we are the ones that are buying the tickets, and we are the ones buying the CDs. I know it's a lot more complicated than what I am saying right now, but I think it's just a cause for some introspection about what role are we playing in our subjugation and in reinforcing these negative stereotypes. I think that Hollywood is for whatever is going to make money. The only color they care about is green. So if they have the perception that this is the only type of black movies that black people are going to want to go see, we'll have crossover to appeal to white audiences. And movies that have serious themes or deal frankly with race issues or depict black people in a different light, if they generally perceive that white America and black America would not embrace those kinds of movies or those kinds of images or that those kinds of movies would not be successful, then why make them?

Although she is not in a position to counteract those images, Boykins knows African Americans who are producers and creators of films and CDs. She thinks:

They will do what they can within reason. You are working somewhat within the system. I guess there are two ways to handle it. You can be an outsider protesting and raising hell, but with no power to really change things, or you can figure out a way to work within the system and try to make a difference with the projects and the people you come in contact with. And I think the people I know, the blacks who are development executives and who have some influence in what goes on television, they try to afford opportunities to black people where they can, and they try to do things in as positive a way as they can. But it's so much bigger than that, in terms of who has the say-so, and what the public embraces.

For Lisa Boykins, success is not only achieving your personal goals, but having a "commitment to social justice, a commitment to working in the community, a commitment to giving back something, a commitment to helping inspire young people and to making a difference in the lives of those who come after you." Her actions match her ideology. For instance, at the Maya Angelou Charter School, an alternative high school in Washington DC for students involved with the juvenile justice system, she was a volunteer, teaching the course Civil Rights at the Crossroads and mentoring students, some of whom who later went on to college. She understands that her accomplishments and opportunities are connected to a larger personal sacrifice and collective struggle of family and other foremothers and forefathers. Her graduation from New York University was symbolic of such an epiphanic moment.

Shaping of Consciousness   On the day Lisa Boykins graduated from law school, she was not paying homage to nor musing about the likes of such pioneer black women lawyers as Charlotte E. Ray, Isadora Letcher, and Ollie Mae Cooper, on whose backs she had stood. Rather, she was thinking of and showing reverence for her grandmother, born in 1916 just fifty-three years after the Emancipation Proclamation, who was there to witness a pivotal milestone in the life of her granddaughter.

> My grandmother came to my law school graduation, and I couldn't help but imagine that when my grandmother was my age, which would have been in the early forties, black women weren't even admitted to law school, and even if you could get a degree from somewhere else, where would you practice? You know, in some states, blacks weren't even allowed to be on juries. They weren't able to vote in the South. It just was something for me to consider the world of changes that she had seen in her lifetime. She could never imagine going to law school, or imagine a world where black women would be professionals and have the careers that they do today. We still have a long way to go, but for me, when I think of what it was like for her, it makes me realize what a proud moment that was and for me to accomplish something that she could never have accomplished when she was my age.

Boykins's portrayal of her grandmother's segregated world in the early 1940s, at age twenty-six, stood in sharp contrast to her multicultural and racially mixed world of 1995. Her grandmother could not have attended an integrated school in rural South Carolina or have matriculated at the then white male University of Notre Dame. It is unlikely that Boykins's grandmother would have traveled abroad to earn a master's degree in international policy and diplomacy in France, worked for the United States Embassy in France and for George Herbert Walker Bush when he attended the G7 Economic Summit there in 1989, or obtained a law degree from a premier, predominantly white university. And, if her grandmother could have earned a law degree, after her schooling, she could not have worked as a lawyer on Wall Street at an international law firm in a profession that, according to the 2000 census, still has only 1.9 percent black females and 2.0 percent black males. Though this was not the world of Boykins's grandmother's young adulthood, she, who had "no fancy education" and worked at "odds and ends jobs," could bear witness to the world of seismic shifts in the color line and gender line of three generations during the twentieth century.

Boykins, who was born in Philadelphia, Pennsylvania, to a nurse who graduated from the University of Pennsylvania and an engineer who graduated from Cheyney State University, was reared by her grandparents in the nearby predominantly white suburb of Ardmore until she was thirteen years old. After four decades, her grandparents returned to South Carolina, where the remainder of Lisa Boykins's formative years took place in a community of black professionals. Boykins's grandparents—and especially her hat-and-gloved, refined,

Southern, church-going grandmother, who had a strong spiritual orientation and work ethic, as well as a value system of communal sharing—had a strong influence on her. From their stories, she understands that had it not been for her grandparents' sacrifices, and those of others like them, these opportunities "would never have come along. And today, people my age, or a decade younger, see it as commonplace that you are able to go to college and get jobs with prestigious companies. They recognize that there are a lot of people in that position, but it is pretty much a given that people are going to college, and that's what privilege means to them for the last thirty or forty years. You see even the notion of higher education and professional school is now an expectation among the black middle class. It is not like, 'Gee, I wonder if my kids are going to go to college.' It is assumed."

With a deeper understanding of the permanency of racism, Lisa Boykins, a progressive liberal, does not assume that education is a given for the middle class, as evident with the decline in the participation of African Americans in the University of California system resulting from the demise of affirmative action. She is unlike Robert Traynham, a conservative Republican, in terms of her views on education and affirmative action. But her understanding of and experiences with racism have shaped the way she sees issues impacting the black community. The same is true for Robert Traynham, so let us now turn the lens toward him.

Robert L. Traynham

Robert Traynham, the deputy chief of staff and director of communications for the Senate Republican Conference at the U.S. Capitol, has not lived with racism in his bones and, in fact, from his perspective, it has not brushed the outer layer of his skin. At twenty-nine years old, Traynham, the highest-ranking African American Republican staffer on Capitol Hill in 2004, stated, "I don't believe I was ever discriminated against in anything." A high achiever, his life has been on the fast track since seventeen. As a seventeen-year-old college freshman, he was introduced to public service when his English professor at Cheyney State University in Pennsylvania, an HBCU, challenged the class to write a letter to President Bill Clinton, noting that the best one would be sent to the White House. His letter was chosen, so in the summer of 1993, he was assigned to the Office of Presidential Advancement and became the youngest staff member ever to work full-time at the White House. There he acquired a taste for politics, but his taste buds were more conservative than the Democratic administration where he interned, so he joined the Republican Party and he never looked back. He had several additional internships while in college, one of which was an appointment to work at the Capitol for a U.S. representative in Congress. Before his current position, he held dual positions for Senator Rick Santorum, both as press secretary for the senator's 2000 Republican reelection campaign in Pennsylvania and for his senatorial office at the

U.S. Capitol in Washington DC. He has served as a special assistant to the 1996 Republican National Convention and worked for the Republican National Committee. In addition, Traynham served as political director for Black America's Political Action Committee, an organization whose mission is to elect black conservatives to national office. He is a member of and senior fellow at the Center for New Black Leadership. Traynham said that since the retirement of former Congressman J. C. Watts in 2002, "By default, I am the highest-ranking black Republican official on Capitol Hill. Because of the leadership staff, it elevates me above the hirelings. And so, by default, a lot of people call me the shadow congressman because I am not elected, but because of the position that I hold, and some of the activities that I do." Given his illustrious career track, one would assume that his life chances have not been constrained by racism, which he perceives and interprets through a narrow lens, and, at times in the sociological lexicon, he confusingly conjoins racism with the concept of classism.

> Because society is changing, I think the very definition of racism is changing. I think what you see now is not necessarily the Jim Crow racism of the fifties and sixties in the South. I think what you see now is common to the high-tech racism. I mean if you do not know how to control a mouse, this is racism now. If you do not know the terminology of the stock market, this is racism now. If you are not on the side of winning terrorism, it's just a new kind of racism out there—racism we have never seen before. If you don't have, in my opinion, access to a laptop, if you don't have, especially in Washington DC, access to the right social or academic credentials, you're looked down upon. And I think there are people that are in place that will make sure that you don't have what they have. And this is, in my opinion, the new racism of the twenty-first century. In other words, what I am trying to say is that I personally believe that there isn't racism between blacks and whites anymore, but I do believe there is racism based on class and based on social standing.

Since racism in the larger sociological framework incorporates a dominant and nondominant group power relation, nondominant racial or ethnic groups can be prejudiced but not racist, because they are constrained by the actions, the influences, or the perceived wishes of the members of the dominant group.

But, Traynham thinks, "There is racism with black on black; I think there is racism with white on white. Again, it's based on class. If you don't have a certain car or you don't live in a certain neighborhood, whatever the case may be, there are preconceived notions out there that you are not of the same status [as] another individual." When asked if he felt blacks in the United States could oppress whites, he said, "Of course I think that can be the case. I think maybe in a predominantly black neighborhood that could happen. But I don't think that's widespread, because I don't think that's inherent in black individuals' makeup." Traynham defines racism as "the power to oppress another race" and "the unique ability to have the resources in order to keep another race down." Traynham said, "I do believe that's happening, but again, in my opinion, the definition of racism—rather the practice of racism—is finished." The self-described eternal optimist is conflicted about the end of racism. He has hope that racism will end, but even he has misgivings. "If you believe in Machiavelli's *The Prince*, if you're a realist, I think you can make the argument that racism will always be here. Now, I think it's a constant battle if you are trying to suppress racism, in trying to deal with it. But I do not believe that we will live in a society [where] racism will never occur. However, it is my hope and my desire that we continue to move in a direction that will completely eliminate racism. But I think we are a long, long way from that."

Perhaps it was Traynham's desire to move in a direction that he felt would completely eliminate racism when he defended and redefined the remarks that Senator Trent Lott of Mississippi made in December 2002. At the one hundredth birthday party for Senator Strom Thurmond of South Carolina, who in 1948 ran an overtly racist campaign for president on the States' Right Party ticket, Lott remarked, "I want to say this about my state. When Strom Thurmond ran for president, we voted for him. We're proud of it. And if the rest of the country had followed our lead, we wouldn't have had all these problems over all these years either." Although Lott represents the state with the largest percentage of African American citizens in the United States, Traynham thought it was prudent to give him a pass.

> A couple of senators came up to me and said, "Robert, what do you think about this? How do you feel about this? I need to know how you feel because it will help me convey my thoughts." And I told the senators exactly what I thought about Senator Lott, which was that he was a very kind, decent individual, who unfortunately made a statement that he obviously regrets. But I do think that he is a good person, who unfortunately got a little carried away. And so, at that moment, I was almost like a counselor to these two senators, telling them exactly how I felt and assuring them that it's OK. It's OK to talk to me; it's OK to talk about these things. You know, we are all human. Again, it just created a comfort level with Republican senators, which, frankly, I don't think others had at that time.

Traynham cites three additional examples to show that he has not given racism a free pass and that he recognizes at some level it is sustained by the institutionalized policies and practices in law, education, and healthcare.

> There was an amendment on the floor of the United Stated Senate, which basically said that individuals who are incarcerated should not be allowed to vote again once they get out of prison. That disproportionately affects people of color. And I remember vividly, talking to several U.S. senators who said they agreed that people who are incarcerated should not be able to vote. I remember speaking to a lot of senators and saying, as a person of color, I take issue with that. These individuals have served their time; we need to unshackle them. We need to be able to give them the resources in order to be a good productive citizen. I personally lobbied

four or five senators to change their vote to allow these individuals—in my personal opinion, African Americans who were incarcerated—to be allowed to vote. And that amendment passed. And I was very proud of that. I was very proud that in a small way I was able to make a difference.

In another example, a letter came across my desk, basically saying that Congressman J. C. Watts would be hosting a black college summit, the first annual and the first ever, basically inviting all the black college presidents for a series of meetings to talk about policies and about how the federal government could help. A good friend of mine in Congressman Watts's office called me and said, "You know, Robert, we can't get any other Republicans involved." I personally called my friends in Republican offices saying this is the right thing for you to do. You need to have your boss there, and your boss needs to speak to these college presidents. Well, that was about four years ago, and I need to tell you that we are on our Fifth Annual HBCU Summit. The record of attendance has been phenomenal for Republicans. We had about 115 representatives of HBCU colleges from all over the country, and we had a record 60 Republicans, both from the House and Senate sides, to show up to meet with these college presidents and to talk about issues that are important to them. I like to think again that I had a small say in that. Because we are showing these folks that there is another side to the Republican Party, albeit a small one.

In his third example, he speaks to issues of healthcare.

One of the things that I have done is to raise the awareness of the black press and the Republicans with the Bush administration about this disease [AIDS] and inform them how deadly this disease is and how disproportionately it affects black Americans. I have been very fortunate to represent the Senate Republican conflict, which involves some senators going to Africa and learning specifically about the disease of AIDS and trying to find a cure. And as a result of that, we were able to assist in writing the global AIDS bill. So again, in little things like that, we try to raise awareness with the Republican senators. And I think it has gone a long way.

According to the Joint Center for Political Studies, African Americans remain Democratic in their partisan identification, 80 percent to 12.6 percent Republican, and in their behavior, 90 percent to 8 percent Republican. Younger blacks are more likely to vote Republican.[19] Of the Talented Thirty, fifteen identified with and voted for the Democratic Party in the 2000 presidential election, four voted Republican, and eleven declared themselves as independent but voted mostly for the Democratic ticket. In the 2004 presidential election, 11 percent of blacks voted for the Republican party. Though African Americans make up a small percentage of those voting Republican, Traynham strongly feels that not only should blacks be represented in both parties, but even more importantly, "Blacks should have a voice. Blacks should have a say at the table where discussions are being held on issues that are important and that reflect African Americans. Unfortunately, there aren't a lot of people at the table when it comes to speaking on behalf of blacks on the Republican side.

And that's why I have a very unique, a very sacred duty and certainly a calling, if you will, to be able to sit at the table and say, 'Listen guys, have you thought about it this way? Or you might want to say it this way. Or perhaps, one of the things you may want to do is to go down this road instead of that road.'"

And for this self-described compassionate, conservative Republican, raising the level of awareness of public policymakers means building a larger base of conservative black leadership to promote an alternative empowerment paradigm for African Americans. It is his reason for joining the Center for New Black Leadership.

> With no disrespect for our forefathers and foremothers, theirs is an old way of thinking, that the way we have done things in the past is the way we should do things in the future. And I am speaking specifically of Democratic candidates in terms of supporting the Democratic Party, and I am speaking specifically of the UNCF [United Negro College Fund], the NAACP, and the Urban League. First, I say that those organizations are vital and important in our society. However, there is nothing wrong with taking a fresh look, of turning the page, of trying to think outside the box. For the past twenty years, we have had a singular way of thinking that the way to solve social ill problems is to pour more money into the problem. I disagree with that. I think perhaps the approach should be that money is part of the solution, but it's not the entire solution. What about trying something different? What about instead of forcing people to stay on welfare by giving them more money if they have more kids, what about perhaps putting a work requirement in there? By doing so, you are also telling them that before we put you to work, we are going to retrain and educate you so that you will have the tools if you go out into society. What about instead of just literally putting kids through an educational system that just fails them, what about testing them and identifying those with learning disabilities early, so they can be corrected? You know, President Bush said something that was very powerful. He said, "We must end the self-bigotry of low expectations." And I could not agree with him more because for all too long, we have literally led the black society to think that the only way we can get them through the system is to push them through. But what do you have? You have a society where a large number of black Americans who are graduating are illiterate. You have a lot of individuals who are graduating from inner city high schools who cannot put a sentence together. We have a lot of black individuals who, unfortunately, believe in the status quo as opposed to thinking outside the box. We have new black leaders who say let's think outside the box. Let's try something that may be new and innovative, but let's try it. It may be good. So I'm all about change. And I'm all about helping my black people all over the world, but I am not about stagnant work. And I think that's what the Center for New Black Leadership is all about.

What policies does Traynham want to enact to help black people all over the world? If implemented, will they help blacks or will they harm blacks by reinforcing, as some critics like Kevin Powell would say, the existing embedded racist policies and practices?

When I tell people that I am for accountability in school, that I am for No Child Left Behind, the president's educational goal, when I tell people that I don't necessarily believe in some aspects of handouts and making people grovel and wallow, that challenges people's thinking. When I go out and say that there is a limited role for government, it challenges people's thinking. When I am just being me, and that is being a strong Republican, and a strong supporter of this president, that, in itself, pushes people's buttons. It's our approach to the education problems, it's our approach to defense spending, it's our approach to campaign financing, and it's our approach to the very thinking, the very being of the world of government. It's our approach to the environment; it's our approach to how you approach things when it comes to African American subjects. You know some people would say there's still a need for affirmative action. I agree with that. However, I would like to think that we should start thinking out of the box here and start saying should we retool some type of affirmative action.

Traynham thinks one way to retool affirmative action is by eliminating quotas. "I don't necessarily believe that Harvard University, or frankly, Cheyney University, needs X number of blacks or to enroll X amounts of whites. I don't need quotas. I don't think that's the right approach. I think that the approach should be that every single person should be given the same opportunity to apply to Cheyney University and to Harvard University." But he cautioned that it is important to remain sympathetic to some segments of society, particularly those in the rural and urban communities who have not had his privileges or those of more affluent persons.

As adamantly as Traynham opposes quotas, he is equally swayed to support President George W. Bush's defense policy on terrorism, despite its disproportionate impact on people of color. "The war on terrorism is obviously something that is needed. It is unfortunate that we have to wage this war in Iraq, but I do believe that Saddam Hussein had weapons of mass destruction. I believe that this is a war that is needed, and, frankly, I do believe that the world is a much safer place because we are in Iraq. And I do believe that we are more safe here because we have created the Department of Homeland Security, and we have strengthened our airline security, because now we have a system in place where we can track down killers and get rid of them. I believe that we are winning the war." But even the president who declared war in Iraq has said that the war in Iraq is not winnable.

Viewing his personal success as interconnected with his collective success, he thinks of himself "as a foot soldier, as someone who is still climbing the mountain, as someone that even though I have a lot of things to be thankful for, the work is still not finished. I will not rest until more black Americans are elected to Congress; I will not rest until I see more black Americans in the Republican Party; and I will not rest until I see more black Americans on television, not necessarily in the back of the camera, but in the front of the camera. There is still so much more work to be done, but I really consider myself to be an activist in that regard."

Shaping of Consciousness   Robert Traynham was born in Philadelphia, but his early formative years, including his church and schooling from K through 12, were spent in Yeadon, Pennsylvania, a predominantly white suburb of "God-fearing Americans who paid their taxes and mowed their lawns." His hard-working parents were the second black family to move to his neighborhood's block. They, too, were "God-fearing Americans who paid their taxes and mowed their lawns." His father, an electrical engineer for the U.S. Postal Service, completed high school, and his mother, a secretary at Cheyney State University, is currently pursuing her bachelor's degree there. His parents taught him the importance of being the best that you can be, of spirituality and religion, and of having a strong work ethic. The hallmark of his family values was having a good education and striving for excellence.

> When I was growing up, my grandparents' house was always filled with limited editions of black inspirational photographs or paintings that they bought over the years. And I remember one time asking her, "Grandma, why do you buy all this art? Do you just like it?" And she said, "Yes, I love the art. However, I know that I am giving to a good cause." And I asked her a couple of years later, "What did you mean by that?" And she said, "Well, keep in mind that when we buy this art to beautify our home, I am also buying because I know that I am giving to a good cause." And she would point to a painting and say, "See that painting there? It cost a thousand dollars, but five hundred dollars of that went to the Negro College Fund so that you, and others like you, can go to college and be able to set your goal to whatever you want." And I remember being in the car with my grandmother. And I said, "Grandma, what if I grow up to be a trash man?" And I expected her to say, "You're not going to be a trash man. You're going to college and you're going to be a doctor, or a lawyer." And I remember her looking over at me at the stoplight and she said, "Boy, if you want to be a trash man, I want you to be sure that you clean up all that trash and that you be the best trash man you can be. I don't care who you are. I don't care what you do. I want you to be the best, whether it's a trash man, a crossing guard, a chef, or bus driver, I want you to get awards and be recognized for what you do."

Not only did his family stress excellence for self-identity but also incorporated it as a part of his dual racial socialization. "I think my mother and my grandmother always instilled in me to be cognizant of the fact that you always have to be a little better, you always have to be a little more on guard, and you always have to be just a little bit more prepared than your colleagues." Inspired by his family values, the high-achieving Traynham is the first in his immediate family to go to college and the first one in his family to get a college degree, a BA in political science from Cheyney State University of Pennsylvania. He chose Cheyney because it is the oldest HBCU (Wilberforce University in Ohio also claims that distinction) and because it is a convenient distance from Washington, where he could have an up-close view of government. He also earned a master of arts degree in political communications from George Mason University.

His passion for politics might have been ignited in his home. Although his father, a conservative Democrat, and his mother, a Republican, voted, Traynham does not recall them ever discussing politics. But he does remember the daily ritual of watching the evening news with his father. Even at eight, Traynham says he was intrigued by how government works and remembers asking his father sophisticated questions, such as why President Reagan was just cutting taxes. Wherever the seed was planted, he believes that through politics he has found the road to helping and empowering others. His lesson in giving back to the community came from those who helped him along the way.

> Let me just say that I was helped along the way. My grandparents and my parents struggled to put me through college. They bent over backwards and made sure that I had the resources that I needed to make sure that I could be a good-quality student. And I will never forget that as long as I live. And also, I had my extended family—my aunts, my uncles, and cousins, and other individuals who pitched in. I remember vividly a cousin of mine giving me fifty dollars to help me pay for my bus fare that month. And so I never ever forget that in order for me to run this marathon, I had dozens and dozens of people around me who helped me to walk. So if there is anything I can do to reach out and help other people, I feel that it is my calling. And I feel that there is an obligation given to me because of the position I currently hold. And I never forget the individuals I call family who are still living in poverty and are still struggling to make ends meet.

He will not forget because his parents always taught him to remember where he came from. He remembers especially the admonition of his grandmother, who migrated from the South to the North: "Remember, no matter how far you go in life, that you are always a gifted and talented African American." He says his grandmother is "a living, breathing inspiration. This is a woman who grew up in the segregated South; this is a woman who saw the ugly head of racism; this is a woman who literally was denied some of the very opportunities that I currently have and enjoy. So it's bittersweet. The sweet part is that I have been able to accomplish a lot. The bitter part is that I had to do it on the backs of my grandparents, your parents, and other folks who were denied the opportunities, and they really fought and died so that I could be the best that I could be and that I could be in the Republican Party."

Traynham and his counterpart of young, affluent conservative African Americans would have their share of critics standing ready to refute their interpretation of racism and their social policies as detrimental to the collective interest of blacks' progress. R. Fenimore Fisher, whom we met earlier, feels this way. But first he agrees with Traynham that he should strive to be the best that he can be. And he would respectfully agree that emerging young black conservatives like Robert Traynham are entitled to their own viewpoint and their right to join together, because, he says, "We do need an eagerness among younger blacks to take leadership positions, and I feel that it is very important to respect the viewpoints under consideration. However, the foundation of the viewpoint, I strongly disagree. We cannot get anywhere in terms of advancement personally or professionally without a keen understanding of your history. And to discount our history as old guard and passé is really, in my viewpoint, one of the most misguided steps that you can make concerning our development." Fisher believes younger African Americans like Traynham "are going to start finding out what corporate America is about." And moreover, they have not "even begun to understand what a shift in political power means in terms of the impact it can have on an entire race of people." With time and experience, Fisher predicts that such individuals "will come to a circle to find out that the civil rights era is not passé, and the leadership of that era is not old guard and irrelevant."

Fisher expressed frustration with conservatives who come to Rainbow/PUSH Wall Street in their final hour of despair and complain about racism, so he feels that persons such as Traynham "will see that taking a segregationist opinion and separating [themselves] from our history is going to be detrimental to [them] in the end and detrimental to [their] personal development and growth. You can't go through this world and achieve all you can achieve by wearing a set of blinders. You have got to look at the world objectively, and if you look at the world through rose-shaded glasses, you are not going to be able to be an effective competitor in this world. And I'm not saying that conservative viewpoints on fiscal spending are wrong, because I probably agree with it personally. But if you are also going to discount the fact that racism still exists in this country, and you are going to try and say that we are on an even keel, then you are very misguided."

Pamela Price

Pamela Price, thirty-eight years old, admitted to having some misguided notions about racism until she faced the color line. The politically conservative businesswoman heard others say, "It's a white man's world. I began to see face to face what that saying really means." When Price, the inventor of the Ding Stopper, a device to protect cars from minor dings, wanted to develop a partnership with some major corporations—such as General Motors, Ford, Chrysler and Wal-Mart—to produce and market her product, she "was constantly told no over and over. I even remember going into my local Wal-Mart store to speak with a representative, and I was told, 'Oh, this is ugly. This isn't going to work. Nobody wants to buy this.'" Price was not discouraged and forged ahead to work with a company in China to produce her invention. And she uses infomercials to sell her product in the metropolitan area of Washington DC. The invention has received some national exposure, so she is planning to market the product nationally and internationally. Price is candid enough to confess that she did not understand the need for civil rights organizations, like Rainbow/PUSH, until she faced discrimination. "I look back and I see Jesse Jackson fighting for blacks, and now I can really appreciate what they are trying to do, whereas before, I think I really took these rights for granted. Now I comprehend what the struggle is all about. It's a real thing."

For others who think African Americans are on an even keel, Fisher, a Democrat who is a fiscal conservative with a liberal view toward social policies, suggests taking another look because the struggle is a "real thing."

> If you look at the fact that when the White House issued its brief in support of ending affirmative action admissions quotas at the University of Michigan on Dr. King's birthday, the public face that they put [on] in terms of introducing that brief supporting the ending of affirmative action was Dr. Condoleeza Rice. It sends out a profound message to all Americans as to where we are in terms of our civil rights. The White House did not have to issue any kind of position. Actually, to some extent, it was a political rift for them to take such a public position to ending affirmative action. But because of the mentality that exists in this era of strong conservatism, they issued it. And so people who are living in a world of "you know, there's no discrimination, and these rights will always be there and never taken away" should also reconsider that they are a part of a party that is reflective of its identity. I am not a promoter for the Democratic Party, because we need to also share with the Democrats that we don't want to be taken for granted and that our concerns and issues are addressed, such as being able to pay for college education for our children. In order to send our kids to the schools that we want to, we need to make sure that we are members of parties that are supporting our issues, whether that's Democratic or Republican.

Dwayne Ashley, the thirty-five-year-old president and CEO of the Thurgood Marshall Foundation, is neither Democrat nor Republican; he is an Independent with a moderate stance, and he voted Republican in the 2000 election. But he knows the struggle is a "real thing." Like Fisher, he is concerned about jobs and economic and political stability, and, in his experience, civil rights organizations, like the NAACP, are not passé. He thinks it is "very dangerous when you have a country that has shifted to one party controlling the Senate, the House, and the executive branch of the government," and, he adds, "the judicial branch because the country shifts to just one opinion. I am concerned about that as a black American." Despite the fact he supported this political shift, he is acutely aware of the threat of racism.

Growing up in a predominantly black neighborhood of Houston, Texas, he heard stories from his father, who was manager of a research laboratory, and his mother, who owned and operated a nightclub, that heightened his awareness about race and racism. But until Ashley, who attended mixed schools from K through 12, had his encounter with racism, at age twenty-one, he did not fully understand his parents' race lessons.

> I had a direct experience with discrimination in racial profiling. In my senior year when I was about to take my last final examination and graduate from Wiley College in Marshall, Texas, I drove to the local hamburger place, and my car stalled on

me at a red light. As the car stalled, a car pulled up behind me. It finally started and I proceeded to move on through the light when it changed and lights started flashing. I pulled my car over, and I was getting out of the car, wondering why I was being stopped. A white gentleman gets out of the car and says, "Put your hands on the car." Now mind you I was a senior in college, graduating *cum laude* and had been a campus leader and never been in any trouble with the law. Another white gentleman in the car told me to be quiet because I was, of course, asking, what have I done and why are you stopping me? I went to get my insurance papers, and he said, "No, get back over here." He would not allow me to get the insurance papers, and I proceeded to say, "You are violating my civil rights." Of course, this other gentleman was saying to me, "Quiet." It turned out that I ended up being arrested and there were about ten phony charges made up against me. I had to spend a night in jail. I made two phone calls that night. I called my mother to let my parents know, and I called the president of the local NAACP chapter. I was a member of the NAACP, a student organization at Wiley. She got involved, and it turned out that the sheriff of the town had this reputation for harassing black males. She got all the charges dropped and I was released on my own recognizance the next day.

In 2004, Ashley said, "I opened up this newspaper and learned that there had been a national class action suit filed against this sheriff for racial discrimination, going back years and years—all these people came forward to admit similar stories like what had happened to me. So coming out of college, I understood that racism was alive and well and that it was going to be something that I was going to have to deal with the rest of my life. And that incident, I think, instilled in me to do the kind of work that I do."

Through the Thurgood Marshall Scholarship Fund, a nonprofit organization, designed to serve public black colleges and universities, Dwayne Ashley raises money for scholarships and programmatic and capacity-building support for these institutions. In doing so, he works hard to fight racism in corporate recruitment and in obtaining corporate and governmental funding so public black colleges "can get their just due in higher education." Ashley says, "Racists don't want to recruit at black colleges. They do a lot of business with black people. In fact, it's a large percentage of our business, but they don't recruit there. The people who are holding these executive-level jobs at these companies, and I see the numbers, try to do business with us because they are interested in trying to address the issue of diversity because they can't find a diverse candidate. I know that we are graduating seven thousand students each year with baccalaureate degrees, and yet I hear consistently that we can't find candidates."

When he sends out direct mail requesting funds, it never fails that he gets overtly racist mail saying, "I'm not going to give to the Nigger colleges." But he is more aware of the subtle impact of corporate giving. "There [was] $212 billion given in 2001 to charity. Of that $212 billion, $39 billion went to higher education, and .09 percent of that went to HBCUs. That is shameful. We make up 13 percent of the American population in this country. Yet, we don't even get a full percent of charitable giving in this country."

When Ashley was a graduate student, majoring in government association at the University of Pennsylvania, he learned his political savoir faire and the rules of the game for corporate America by employing strategy and political influence. "Our schools are located in twenty-two states and the District of Columbia, and we have senators in all those states, we have congressmen in all those states, and, of course, the governors. There are corporations that do business in those states and we are holding those officials accountable to ensure that our schools get their just due and that our organization gets what we deserve. If they are not accountable, they are going to see it in the vote that is made against them in elections."

Like Fisher, Ashley understands both direct and indirect racism; yet he finds that loads of young people that he hires, those individuals born in the 1970s and 1980s, do not have a full understanding of the subtleties of racism. In fact, they don't believe it exists. In speaking to youths across the nation, Yasmin Shiraz, a thirty-four-year-old author, lecturer, and entrepreneur who grew up in a predominantly white suburb in Delaware, has also met numerous young adults who have never experienced racism, or who do not think racism exists and who believe blacks are on an even keel in this society. She opined,

> You can experience racism for so long that you almost become numb to it. I think it's a denial piece. We want to be accepted, and the existence of racism means that we can't have acceptance. Who wants to think that the way we were born is not going to allow someone to accept us? So I think that people say that they never have experienced racism because when they did, they thought it was something else, maybe that person was in a bad mood today. And they go through all of these little denials and reflections because they do not accept what has happened. I believe there are people who really in their heart believe they never experienced it. But I also believe that if you are black and you live in America, you are going to experience it at some point. You may call it another name, you may call it the person had a personality conflict, or you may call it the person had a bad day. But the reality is, I am hard pressed to believe that an African American can live in America his or her entire life and not experience racism.

When it comes to racism, Shiraz has a perennial third eye, particularly in her performance before a white audience.

> Instead of blacks just getting up and going to do what we need to do, we are often thinking about how it's going to be for us. For example, I did a presentation at my daughter's school for those who have an interest in becoming a writer. I did it because I wanted [whites] to know that they are the ones seeing all those negative images of blacks on television, and in no way my daughter is like that. We are always cognizant of the images that are out there about us as African Americans. We can never just be, there is always something looming overhead. This duality personally exists when I am taking my daughter to school. If I go to her school in shorts and a baseball cap, [whites] wonder about whether I am unemployed. So it's all about what image am I fighting today? In dealing with racism on a personal level and a

professional level, I always try to be as professional as I can be at all times. When I am in front of a white audience, I don't know if I jump a little higher. I don't know if I am more animated or more passionate in my speech. But I know that I have to fight the stereotype that they carry about black people. And when I am in a black audience, I am always going to put my best foot forward, but I do not feel that climate where I am confronting a stereotype. Persons who are in denial of ever having experienced racism also make an extra charge. When they are around whites, they might say, "Oh, I'm just excited today," or "Oh, I just wanted to do my best." They see through the third eye, but it's still denial.

Shiraz, who is married with two children, is aware that her seven-year-old daughter is also developing a third eye for racial inequality. She and her husband live with their children in a predominantly white upper-middle-class neighborhood in northern Virginia. She avoided discussing the subject of race with their precocious daughter, who, at four, commented to her mother, "Mom, I see a lot of women who are white with brown babies, but I don't see a lot of women who are brown with white babies." At seven, she suggested to her mother that some racial issues might exist on the playground. In reporting the conversation, the mother noted that her daughter has a couple of white girls who claimed to be her good friend, and one says that she is her best friend. However, when she wants to play a game, she may be told that she can't play the game that day, or once they start playing, she is always last, or when they are playing tag, and the other girl gets caught, she will say, "I quit if you won't let me play." Shiraz's daughter said, "You know, Mom, whenever my black friends play the game, we stick to the rules. There is nothing about quitting or changing the game." In discussing the incident with her husband, his response was, "We don't want to put race in it. We don't want to make it a black and white issue right now." Shiraz stated wryly, "That may be true, but I know by my daughter's own admission, and maybe by her other black friends, that she never talks about such issues. When she talks about being treated badly, it is always with a white classmate." The day will come when she must give her daughter the race lesson, but she is not looking forward to doing so. "The thought that I have to tell my daughter that the way that she was born, the fact that her skin is brown, people are going to judge her and not like her. That's no picnic for parents to have to tell their kids. I know that at some point that's what I will have to do. No one wants to think that their very being is under attack." To maintain control and independence over one's destiny, Shiraz, the founder of a magazine and publishing company, advocates black entrepreneurship.

EXPERIENCING BLATANT RACISM

Whether it is the educational setting or the world of work, members of the Talented Thirty operate in less hostile and more multiracial and multicultural milieus.

Unlike the Talented One Hundred, who confronted overt racism sometimes daily, the Talented Thirty do not. They interact comfortably, as previously mentioned, in diverse settings, where most have personal friends and close acquaintances who are white, as well as other people of color. But as Kevin Powell reminds us, "We live in a multiracial society that was founded on the notion of white supremacy in this country, and white supremacy is still real in this society." Still when it occurs, they are taken aback.

Leke Adeyiga, twenty-seven-year-old computer software engineer for an international corporation, has encountered racial profiling while driving, and he has seen white women grab their purses when he is walking through the mall with friends. And despite the fact that he was an honor student in college and both of his parents have PhDs, his white peers at the University of Virginia thought of him as an affirmative action case. In addition, when he dresses down at work on Fridays, people in his building stare at him or eye him suspiciously. While these occurrences are annoying, it is more upsetting to have his intelligence questioned and his integrity impugned. "I was taking a computer class my second year in college and I had a professor ask, 'Do you think you can do this?' We were asked to solve a problem and you had to adhere to codes. Now you can do codes several different ways, but the rules remain the same. The majority of the class solved it the exact same way, except for two of us who did it in a very unique way. And he made a comment on my paper, 'Did you actually solve this problem? Did you cheat off such and such?' Of course, I stayed after class and asked him about it. And he said, 'Well, you guys solved it in the same way and I just can't hardly believe that you didn't cheat off of him.' It turned out that I was sitting in the front of the class on the left side and this other guy was sitting directly in the opposite corner."

Sometimes, when he is in the company of his white friends, they see him as different and they feel comfortable making racist remarks. "At one of the basketball games people were making remarks right in front of me about people on the other team. And I said, 'Why are you saying things like that right in front of me?' They asked, 'Why are you getting offended? We're not talking about you.' And I'm like, 'You're not talking about me?' And they say, 'No, you're different.'"

Sometimes when blacks are similar in manner, lifestyle, or class, or closer in physical appearance, whites are generally more accepting of them. Other times, whites might not know the racial identity. When Debra White, vice president of technology at Hampton University, worked as a marketing representative at IBM, one of her colleagues assumed she was white and made a racial slur about blacks. When she confronted the woman to indicate that she was black, she was surprised and embarrassed.

Emily Pitts, forty-four, is the first black woman to become general partner at Edward Jones Investment Company. In an industry that has a scarcity of blacks, she has experienced her share of subtle racism, such as a lack of support when she worked for Merrill Lynch and Dean Witter. At Charles Schwab, her situation improved, and she obtained her Series 7 and Series 8 licenses. When she started work at Edward Jones as an investment representative, her experience within the company was unbelievably positive and supportive, as she described it. The blatant racism came from clients, of which she has a litany of examples.

> I had one fellow who walked into the office and shook my hand and asked if I was Emily, and he said, "Oh, you're black!" And I held my hands up like I was looking at the back of my hands and I said, "I know." And that's the way I probably have ducked racial issues, by keeping them light-hearted. There's no need for me to get defensive. I just go back to my upbringing, always treat other people kindly. When I took over the office of Edward Jones, I was called to introduce myself. The gentleman on the phone did not know that I was black. He knew about the black guy who was in the office before and quickly told me, "People told me about doing business with black people. That guy didn't even call me." And I just said, "Well, Sir, I really don't think it had anything to do with his race. As a matter of fact, he sat down with me and made sure I was as familiar with your account as I was with all the other clients. And the main reason I was calling you was to see when I could come by and meet you and your wife." "Oh, come any time," he said. So I called him the next day and asked if I could come by and he said, "Sure, come on by." When I got to his house, it was a Kodak moment. He [and his wife] sat there and literally their mouths were hanging wide open, because he had said all of those things. But I never even acknowledged that. Their mouths were hanging open and they were like, "You don't sound like you're from the South." And so I went on and explained to them that I was from Chattanooga, which is South, but north of Atlanta. They explained to me that they had black friends, and that they had worked at the [M. L.] King Center. One guy called me back when I was at Charles Schwab and said, "Wait a minute, you sound like you're educated. I have to tell my friend about you," like I was a species from outer space. And he just couldn't get over the fact that I could talk and knew what I was talking about. When I walked in the office, he said, "How did you get in here?" And I said, "Pardon?" And he said, "I know you walked through the door, but how did you get in here? They don't allow [black] people in this business."

Indra Thomas, a thirty-five-year-old opera singer, is allowed in the opera business, but she is limited to certain roles. Although she has performed a wide repertoire at such places as Carnegie Hall and Lincoln Center and with the New York Philharmonic, Atlanta Symphony, Boston Symphony, and Boston Pops, when she debuts with the Metropolitan Opera House and other opera houses, she is confined to the roles of Aida, Carmen, and Cleopatra.

Is it racism? While blatant racism is difficult to miss, the more subtle or covert manifestations may be overlooked or not readily labeled as such by the Talented Thirty. Marie Long, thirty-four-year-old vice president for constituency relations for AT&T, was educated in private, majority white schools and was "part of white culture" from kindergarten to law school. Although she interacted well with whites, she knew that she was not white. She thinks, however, whites are more comfortable interacting with educated, affluent blacks. "There is a level of comfort where white people will sit there and say, 'Oh, you are not like the black people that I know.'" Still, when she feels slighted or when she wonders why her office is not as nice as someone else's, she questions, "Is it because I'm black? Is it because I'm a woman? Is it because I'm younger? You never know what is the threatening piece."

Christopher Robinson, thirty-seven-year-old director of diversity marketing for General Motors, can identify racism when it is sometimes more direct, such as once being called a supernigger by his white boss or when racial profiling occurs. At other times, Robinson, who lives in an affluent community in Michigan, is conflicted, feeling it may be related to class.

> My wife's car was pulled over in our neighborhood, and she was questioned for no reason. So I absolutely know that racism is alive. Again, I think people change when they know who you are, what your resume says. People suddenly are more accepting because you are more like them. But the minute someone thinks you have less education and less status, you're not as acceptable. And I am not sure that is a racial thing. I think whites would have the same perception of the person if he were a Caucasian with similar background. The difference is they might be given the benefit of the doubt beforehand. You automatically come in as an African American of color, wearing who you are, and you have to prove what you are or who you are not in the eyes of these people. A Caucasian person is already admitted into the club. It's just a matter of can they stay there, once their status is revealed.

Keith Baker, forty-four-year-old Endowed University Professor of Physics at Hampton University and researcher at the Jefferson Laboratory in Virginia, knows that he has to continue to prove himself in the eyes of whites, despite having impeccable credentials in physics from MIT as undergraduate and MS and PhD degrees from Stanford University. In his laboratory, he is not interested in studying the composition of the social universe and trying to figure out if race matters. Rather, he is interested in bringing new understanding to our physical universe by studying dark energy and dark matter. But Baker lives in a social world, where the dark matter and dark energy of racism are not always understood. Take, for example, the reaction of his supervisor, when Baker headed an ambitious experimental research project at the Jefferson Laboratory in Newport News, Virginia.

> This experiment was large and very expensive to run. It included over ninety different people from many different countries, so the leader has the ultimate responsibility for making sure that the experiment gets done. That was an important event in my life. The person who was the head of the physics division at the time when I was a young assistant professor told me, "I think you're in over your head. I think you are trying to build these chambers and these wire detectors which are so very

expensive and very hard to build, and I think you ought to do something else." To paraphrase, he was saying, I think you're in over your head, I think you should sit down and take a smaller bite and build up some credentials and then jump on something like this because you can risk failure. So anyway, after we had done the experiment, I got the data analyzed, and had the first paper published in a really prestigious journal. So just to get back at him, I took it to him and plopped it on his desk and said, "OK, now here you go, see, I proved you wrong." And he said, "Yes, I knew it all the time." So what you take from that is that's what you tell young scientists. Tell them what they can't do and they will kill themselves trying to prove you wrong and everybody is happy. He got a good experiment done; I got a really good experiment done, so we sat around and laughed about it. He's a great guy and he and I laugh all the time now about it. Is it just a tactic to get a young, eager, hungry scientist to succeed by lighting a fire under them? I once thought that was racism, but in looking back now, I think he was just trying to motivate me and challenge me.

Baker's story has an interesting parallel to that of his great-grandfather, an unschooled mathematical genius, who, during the dark days of segregation, found whites threatened by his superior intelligence because it negated their belief in black inferiority. "My mother said that even before education was common among African Americans as it is now, my great-grandfather was able to do mathematics better than even some of the more educated whites. In fact, they used to come and try to trick him. They would give him math problems to stump him, because, you know, you can't have a black man better than whites at doing math. And he would work problems different ways, saying I can work it this way or that way. This happened on several occasions."

Even the cautious scientist, who relies on empirical evidence, must sometimes call racism by its name. Baker discussed an incident with a colleague, whom he presently regards as a friend but during earlier times competed against at Jefferson Laboratory.

I saw this white guy in the hall running, screaming, and cursing. I could tell it was about me. He accused me of things and I accused him of things. Anyway, at the time, I said, "I'm not taking this crap any more." So I went to the physics leader and I said, "You're going to do something about this white dude, or else, because I refuse to let him [do that to] me." First of all, African Americans are not allowed to do this. If I were to [do that], I would get fired. And even if I wind up punching this white dude, I'm going to have to do some jail time, and he probably won't. So at the time the assistant looked at me and said, "I cannot believe you said that." He couldn't understand how I thought there was a difference between the way he was treated as a white male and the way I was treated as a black male. And I told him black guys can't go through the hallways yelling and screaming and they sure can't hit. This is not the way the world is set up. I thought there was racial bias. Looking back now, there was some bias, but I was more sensitive to being an African American than I should have been.

Lee Jones, associate dean for academic affairs and instruction at the College of Education at Florida State University, would tell Baker "that black men's existence is political. Most black men are overlooked by a lot of opportunities because of their mere threat. I think our whole makeup is imbued with a perception that black men are angry, there's a perception that we are dominant, and that our goal is to overthrow and to overtake. Those perceptions are not spoken; those are unspoken perceptions. I know they're there because in quiet and intimate settings with white colleagues, they share that. But that's not something for people to know about."

SELECTED EXAMPLES OF INSTITUTIONALIZED RACISM

Racism in Science

Fifty-year-old Keith Jackson is president of the National Black Physics Society and Associate Director of the Center for X-Ray Optics at Lawrence Laboratory in Berkeley, California. He is the oldest of the Talented Thirty, so as the civil rights movement was winding down, he was coming of age in America. Therefore, he says, "I had the advantage of clarity." Jackson understands the many ways of racism, including the practices that have a harmful impact on blacks even though the community-prescribed norms guiding those actions have been established with no intent to harm. Keith Jackson, who received his PhD in physics, would probably tell Keith Baker that he was not being too sensitive and that having his work or abilities second-guessed stemmed from a widespread belief in the presumed incompetence of blacks by the dominant group. Sometimes it may be a subconscious reaction to reinforce that belief. Jackson thinks of a brilliant, young African American physicist who has received a lot of criticisms because he was "trying to revolutionize theoretical science. 'How dare he!' It is like Isaac Newton, who tried to squash the servant guy who had invented calculus. Well, basically that's what happened to [him]." Similarly, the community of scientists does not want to recognize the contributions of physics programs at HBCUs such as Florida A & M University, Hampton University, or Howard University. Jackson discussed some common problems that black physicists face in the United States. First, he notes the challenges of producing scientists that exist along the pipelines, beginning from K through 12. He cites this example to capture the issue. "Someone from the education department brought up some kids and took them to one of our facilities. At the end of it, these guys who like to have these little surveys asked them to describe what a scientist was, and one kid wrote down that it looked like a British guy with a beard. The problem is that any child that came here and looked at the staff would see immediately that there is no place for him."

Second, if they make it through the pipeline to graduate school, Jackson says, "The problem in graduate school is not in the course work but the research. And that's where most African Americans have the most difficulty—finding a research sponsor. You know, nobody can force somebody to take you on. That's when people would start to falter."

Third, a support system is crucial in the production of scientists. When he was at Stanford, Jackson, like Baker, had a strong network of supportive people. After supportive white and black faculty left or died, in 2004, Jackson said, Stanford had no black graduate students in physics. The attitude is, "'Well we're going to try to recruit African Americans from just the big schools like MIT, Harvard, and places like that. And we don't care if we don't have but one a year.' So once you get to the point where there is no support group, people can get really isolated. And that's where we had the situation that even though people were the valedictorians of their class at Stanford, they couldn't find a major professor to work with them."

Fourth, when black scientists graduate, they have difficulty obtaining a post-doctoral post, which is now a necessary requirement for a faculty appointment and other employment. "We have a number of young physicists who have just gotten their degrees from big schools. And they need to get post-doctoral appointments. And those appointments in the U.S. are targeted toward foreign nationals. Henceforth, there are very few African Americans with post-doctoral appointments, so they fall out of the pipeline. There are fewer than five African American post-doctoral candidates that have appointments in our country. Without a post-doctoral appointment, you can't get a faculty position at a major university. That means death."

Fifth, Jackson thinks it sets up a comparative disadvantage for his young colleagues in the society he heads. But he is not sure if they see it, understand it, or just accept it: "It is just a simple logical analysis. They know you have X number of jobs in the United States, and Y number of jobs in the European Union, and they are equal; that means $X = Y$. If you are scientist A, which is white, you have access to two X jobs, and if you are scientist B, which is African American, you really have access to only one X job. And that's what you have, a two-to-one comparative disadvantage." In two openings at Lawrence Laboratory for a post-doctoral program, Jackson said, three black male candidates responded. "One guy graduated from Howard University, one graduated from Stanford University, and one another place. And neither one of the positions was slated for U.S. citizens only. But all three of the applications got lost. And no action was taken. Oh, yes, the third application was a bogus one—one I submitted, with name, so I could track it. And when I pointed this out, I got, 'Oh, it got lost.' You know it's always made to look like the people applying for employment didn't follow through. And I said, 'I know one followed through because that was me.' Then it calls for an investigation."

Sixth, Jackson points out that inequality occurs in research funding. While Jackson does not have a personal problem with funding, because the chemical companies support his projects, he stated,

I don't know of any African American scientists that can get funds from the Department of Energy. Historically, the Department of Energy has basically funded diversity and the national laboratories through what is now called the Office of Science. The Office of Science sends eight hundred million dollars a year to colleges and universities and they fund the national laboratories. And there is not a single African American that works in the office. And they have been able to almost completely not fund any African American projects. If you look at the Office of Science funding, it has been decreasing since 1995 when Hazel O'Leary was there. At that point there was a peak of about sixty million dollars. This year it is at twelve million dollars. My colleagues in physics are very intimidated by them—the younger people and some of the older people—because they don't understand how the office is structured. The office lies. They might say we only support people who are Nobel Prize winners. Okay. Now after those eight people get two billion dollars a year, take two billion dollars and divide it by eight, and see what you get for support. All the major initiatives in physics are there, but if you look at their twenty-year plan, we are invisible. They had no intentions of making any inclusion of the African American community. And I constantly remind them of the law of the United States of America. You can't do that with your April 15 money. And if you want to continue to get your level of support, you had better start worrying about the aspirations of your own people and not those people in Europe and other places. It is significant that the only federal agency that didn't contribute anything to funding our society was the Office of Science, which is the largest [funding source] of physics projects in the nation. We put together a proposal for the meeting and submitted it to the National Science Foundation and some other offices, including the Office of Science. The other sources reviewed it favorably. The Office of Science failed to send it out for review. I called Patricia Beamer because I had to submit another proposal, and I told her we had done that in September. And the Office of Science chose not to send it out for review. We received excellent reviews from all the others. By the way, even if you send something out for review it puts you under no obligation to fund it. So they were under no risk, but the point would be that if you send something out for review and it gets rave reviews, then you have to fund it. And I think they wanted to be able to say, "You people weren't serious. You didn't do this. You didn't do that." But the point was the proposal was all right and they chose not to send it out for review. The person who made that decision is somebody who is a not even a physicist. He has no contact in the African American community.

Racism in Building and Construction

John Sibley Butler, in *Entrepreneurship and Self-Help among Black Americans*, notes how African Americans have historically created prosperity and mobility in America through education and the creation of their own business enterprises behind the walls of segregation.[20] H. J. Russell is such an example. Michael Russell, thirty-eight-year-old CEO of H. J. Russell and Company in Atlanta, Georgia, heads the organization started over fifty years ago by his father, the man who helped to finance the civil rights movement. It is the nation's largest minority-owned construction and real estate firm, which grossed $303 million in 2003, and it is number eight on *Black Enterprise*'s list of top black businesses. Over the decades H. J. Russell and Company has shaped the contour of Atlanta with its list of major contracts for large projects that includes the

Georgia Dome, Philips Arena, Turner Field, Coca-Cola headquarters, Harts-field-Jackson International Airport's main terminal, the Atlanta City Hall Complex, and the Georgia World Congress Center. The company employs approximately 650 people, and about 60 to 70 percent are African Americans. Although his company is diverse, Russell thinks black men and women have a better chance to assume a leadership role in his organization than with white corporations. Moreover, he stated, "We take a lot of pride that many African Americans are allowed to raise their families in a very comfortable way through being a part of the H. J. Russell and Company's family." The company's central office is in Atlanta, but there are offices in Dallas, Chicago, Chattanooga, Phoenix, and New York City. "We do projects pretty much all over the eastern United States. We have been fairly active in many urban areas," said Russell.

> We've been able to make payroll. A lot of companies can't say that. That's always a positive thing. In the big scheme of companies, we are a good medium company with a good reputation, but we have a tremendous opportunity for growth and to take the company to a whole other level in the future. I see particularly in our real estate development area tremendous opportunity for continuing growth in our construction business, and continuing to grow people and grow our expertise will allow us to do bigger and better things over the years. And I think we are improving our infrastructure and processes, and once you do that, it allows you to continue to grow the business. And I think we are doing that and will continue to move in that direction.

When his father, Herman Russell, started his business, he faced greater challenges than his son, Michael Russell, who operates in more diverse milieus. Despite the company's solid reputation in the community, challenges still exist. "We have to be better than our colleagues in the majority community with what we do; we have less room for error. I feel that there is still a network that, though not impossible for us to tap into, we have to work harder to tap into it. I say all of that, but at the same time, I am very optimistic that if you are a company that has a good reputation like ours and you continue to perform at a high level consistently, you can continue to grow and your people can continue to prosper."

Stereotypes still abound about the competence of people in black businesses, even in those successful companies like H. J. Russell. "I think you can have a client that will not allow me or my firm the opportunity to build something for them because they just don't have the confidence that an African American owned or managed firm can really deliver. So therefore, I see one of my colleagues get a project that I can't get because (1) that confidence is there; and (2) we don't have the personal relationship because I'm not running in the same circles as this individual. So what I am saying is that you just have to work through it. You can't let that be your excuse. If you work harder and continue on, you're going to find some clients who will recognize the value you do bring, and you have to be able to take advantage of those opportunities when they present themselves." Russell thinks that entrepreneurship "is one powerful method to empower African Americans. It always helps when you have businesses that can help control your own destiny and not only yourself, but in the case of our business, we employ a lot of African Americans."

Gregory Bernard Levette, thirty-four-year-old architect, general contractor, and owner of an architectural firm, has faced racism on a personal level, but, like Michael Russell, he understands some issues are part of the structural foundation of the building and construction industry, for example, obtaining major contacts and securing financial backing from lending institutions. Levette, who started his company three years ago, is the third generation of entrepreneurs in his family. "The problems that we have are getting the larger projects, except on joint ventures. It is very rare when we are given the project alone. Whites feel that we don't have the experience to do it alone, but we do, or they feel that we don't have the resources to operate a project that large. But many of us do." Levette, who lives and works in the metropolitan Atlanta area, cites this example. "Here in Dekalb County, we have the second largest and wealthiest African American community in the country. A new hospital is being built there. It is a sixty-million-dollar construction project, which was awarded to a large white company out of Birmingham, Alabama. And we have very large and capable black companies, and I just don't understand why they weren't given the opportunity to do this or, at least, to be a part of a joint venture." Although the hospital is in a black community, the board, which has a white majority, made the decision to award the contract to a white firm. Levette says, "I think that's true across the board. Next to this hospital, there is a high school going up. This high school is a forty-million-dollar building, and it is being built by the largest white company in Atlanta." He questioned that decision as well, and wondered why the major company did not have a joint-venture partnership with one of the larger black contractors. He indicated that many of the companies had grown their business and gotten their foot in the door by participating in school projects with this company.

Levette pointed out another problem in getting contracts. "In getting a contract, you must have bonds in order to carry a contract like this. You are dealing with a forty-million-dollar project, and one of the other setbacks that black construction companies have is being able to carry a bonding capacity. Like I say, it goes on your credit, and these companies have excellent credit but feel these bonding companies, who will give white construction companies up to fifty million dollars, will only insure black companies up to twenty million dollars bonding capacity." Still another issue for the real estate developer is securing loans from banks. He and his wife are about to begin their first residential development, and initially they had this problem.

Finally, he has observed that the building projects that white contractors put in black communities are inferior in quality compared to those in white communities, so he is interested in changing that inequity. More importantly, he is interested in closing the inequality in the black community.

THE GROWING CLASS DIVIDE IN BLACK AMERICA

While there has been a system of stratification within the black community since slavery,[21] by all objective indicators, this divide is growing since the late 1960s. According to data based on the U.S. census, between 1968 and 1995, the poorest black household lost ground. In 1968, the wealthiest blacks earned $60,782, compared to the $10,624 for the poorest blacks; in 1995, the former earned $84,744 compared to the latter's $10,200. Additionally, according to the Economic Policy Institute, in the downturn of the economy from 2000 to 2002, the annual real income for black workers dropped. One-fifth of blacks were poor in 2000, 30.4 percent of black workers earned poverty-level wages, and the pension coverage and employer-provided health insurance of black workers eroded.[22] Moreover, the enrollment of black men in U.S. colleges has declined, and an astounding percentage of young black males are warehoused in prison. Additionally, the black infant mortality rate has increased, while black life expectancy has decreased.

During the mid-to-late 1980s, when I interviewed members of the Talented One Hundred, numerous individuals expressed reservations about the growing class gap, often noting that as the black middle class moves farther up the ladder of success, poor blacks have fallen farther down its rungs. The previous generation of the Talented One Hundred had expressed concern that transmission of the traditional value orientation of collective effort and uplift would be lost on their children and themselves in this newly desegregated America. Hence, collective racial progress would be thwarted. But were their concerns justified?

Seemingly, the gap between the haves and the have-nots is not only widening economically and spatially but psychologically and sociologically. Robert Traynham believes the black class divide is increasing in his generation.

I think there's some truth to that. Take, for example, there are some areas around the country where upper-middle-class and rich blacks vacation. And the reason why they vacation there is because it's a beautiful place. But, another reason they vacation there is because they are around "their own."

I have a number of friends that are currently experiencing that [divide]. I tell them I feel that I have an obligation, as a black American and mainly as a friend, to tell them that they are becoming lost in translation with their blackness. And I do see that occasionally. And it's a reminder to me to never, never, ever lose that. A couple of months ago, a good friend of mine and I were hungry, and I said to him, "Let's go down to the soul food restaurant for lunch, I haven't been there in years, but I am in the mood today for some grits and some stuff." He has a PhD and is thirty-two years old. He looked at me and said, "No, we won't be going there." And I said, "Okay, are you not in the mood for that? What would you like to have?" "Well," he said, "let's just go somewhere a little more hoity-toity." I just looked at him, and I said, "What do you mean by that?" And he said, "I just don't want to be around those folks." And I told him that that was one of the reasons I wanted to go there. I not only wanted that kind of food, I wanted to see those kinds of folks. I need to be around my people. But he said, "No, we won't be going there." And I called him on it. I said, "That is very, very sad when you don't feel comfortable being around your own people." I said, "I am telling you as a friend and because I love you, that you are wrong. And you need to become much more in tune with your insecurity and deal with it." That is insecurity at its worst, because you are afraid to deal with your blackness and insecure about blackness as a whole.

Traynham's musing on the class divide in the black community is not a new phenomenon. The Talented Thirty also think the class gap is widening, particularly among post–civil rights generations. Twenty-five of the Talented Thirty indicated that blacks they knew, as well as the black elite in general, in their perception, were more concerned about self-interest than assisting the masses of blacks. Jacqueline M. Moore, in *Leading the Race: The Transformation of the Black Elite in the Nation's Capitol, 1880–1920*, revealed how the black upper class distanced itself from the masses but altered its ideologies and strategies toward them when the racial climate changed. In the post-Reconstruction era, as the color line harden in the late nineteenth and early twentieth centuries, the upper-class blacks realized that assimilation into the dominant white culture was unlikely, and their collective status "was inextricably tied to that of the entire race."[23] Hence, the children of the old black elite adopted the ideology of racial solidarity and worked to promote racial uplift. This new elite "became less an aristocracy and more of a class of people trained in their responsibilities as leaders of their race."[24] In Julia Winch's *Philadelphia's Black Elite*, she portrayed the conflict the black elite felt in their responsibility toward the masses. While they viewed themselves as connected to the black masses, they also felt apart from them, because their interests did not always coincide.[25] More contemporary studies, such as Mary Patillo-McCoy's *Black Picket Fences*, continue to show both allegiances across class lines as well as schisms.[26]

Given the emerging ideology of meritocracy and the greater naïveté about the presence of racism among post–civil rights generations, classism in African American communities is on the rise. This class divide, along with the clash of culture and of generations, was evident in the reactions to the controversial remarks by Bill Cosby, the educator and comedian, who castigated blacks who don't take responsibility for their economic status, teach their kids poor speaking habits, and blame police for their incarcerations. Cosby's remarks were made at a Constitution Hall event in Washington DC in May 2004 commemorating the fiftieth anniversary of the *Brown v. Board of Education* decision that paved the way for integrated schools.

Cosby said of African Americans who are unwilling to take responsibility for their economic status, "Ladies and gentlemen, the lower economic people are not holding up their end in this deal. These people are not parenting. They are buying things for kids—$500 sneakers for what? And won't spend $200 for 'Hooked on Phonics.'" In chiding the language pattern of poor blacks, Cosby remarked, "They're standing on the corner and they can't speak English. I can't even talk the way these people talk. 'Why you ain't,' 'Where you is.' And I blamed the kid until I heard the mother talk. And then I heard the father talk. . . . Everybody knows it's important to speak English except these knuckleheads. . . . You can't be a doctor with that kind of crap coming out of your mouth!" And for those who blame police for their incarceration, he asserted, "These [imprisoned blacks] are not political criminals. These are people going around stealing Coca-Cola. People getting shot in the back of the head over a piece of pound cake and then we run out and we are outraged, [saying] 'The cops shouldn't have shot him.' What the hell was he doing with the pound cake in his hand?"

In response to the controversy, Kevin Powell had this to say. "We know that Bill Cosby comes from a working-class background in [Philadelphia]. We know that he struggled to make his name as an athlete first and, then, most prominently as a comedian. In the 1970s, when I was growing up as a working-class black child, two things connected me to Bill Cosby—his cartoon, *Fat Albert*, which was rooted in working-class life, and the film that he did with Sidney Poitier, which was also rooted in working-class black life."

When I heard his comments, the issue wasn't whether he was right or wrong, but that they were only targeted at poor black people. As someone who is middle class, and does very well financially and careerwise, to me the dysfunctions he was describing and attributing to poor black people, I have seen across the board in middle-class black folks, as well. I have seen the lack of love for themselves, the low self-esteem, their failure to create any kind of community and to hold up their part of the bargain. I think it's wrong to just point the finger; it's wrong, it's classist, it's elitist to just say, "These people." You might say to me, "Well, he has a right to say it. He's Bill Cosby. He's a multimillionaire. He gives millions of dollars to colleges and things like that." I don't disagree with what he has done, but there's something wrong with privilege if you don't have a sense of humanity to go with that privilege. There's nothing wrong with challenging black people if you are going to do two other Cs before you get to the word challenge: (1) You got to contextualize it; (2) there has got to be a little compassion, and then you challenge. Dr. Cosby, who has a doctorate in education, must know what the educational system is like in this country's public schools. I live in the inner city where kids who graduate out of here are functionally illiterate. I go to prisons all the time and I'm here to tell you that the youngsters I talk to in prisons, only after they got into the prison system did they realize the education they had been robbed of. So that's the issue. It's a whole lot of middle-class and wealthy black folks who feel the same way, that these poor black people are just bringing us down.

As Olu Brown surveys his community in Atlanta, Georgia, and reflects upon the class divide, he thinks,

There is no difference between a rich black man and a rich white man. In some circumstances, both of them seem to forget who they are, but not across the board. I see elitism in the black race of "I made it and so you can make it too." And it's

sad that exists. If you look at the wealthiest black families, at best, they are probably two generations wealthy. They can have some crazy kids tomorrow who can
blow all of their money. Now you look at the Kennedys. Their wealth goes back
generations, so that their kids can mess up a generation or two and still have
money. Even the wealthiest of the blacks have not succeeded to the point that they
can look down on the poorest because we haven't been rich that long and we
haven't been educated that long. There are folks who have PhDs whose grandparents never made it out of elementary and high school. So we really haven't made
it so far that we can stick our noses up at our own people.

Similarly, Bernard Levette knows people who reject the notion of racial solidarity with poor blacks, as well as those who are conflicted about their creed
and deed.

I have had friends say no one helped them to get where they are. They didn't have
help from their parents, or they had to pay for college on their own or "I got a
scholarship and I got it based on my good grades, so why should I be obligated to
help someone else when no one helped me?" I have heard that from numerous associates and even friends. Often I hear people preach that they are pro-black this
or pro-black that and they want to help someone better themselves, but when it actually comes down to it, they are nowhere to be found. They don't want to give of
their time, especially to young people to encourage them to do well.

Emily Pitts, general partner at Edward Jones, sees eye-to-eye with Levette
in acknowledging that many black professionals she knows think only of their
self-interest, although she suggests that it may be situational because of the nature of the financial industry.

I think there are very few who are genuinely concerned about others. I think it's
not about being against others, but their concern is with helping themselves. The
reason I can speak for the ones I know is because they are mostly in the same industry that I am. It's every man for himself. That's just the nature of the business.
They are not necessarily in the position to help others, because they are brokers,
and they have to make it for themselves. Nobody is responsible for one's success
but oneself. Now if I take that same bunch of people and put them in a different
environment, I think they would be more sensitive to helping others.

William Lyne, along with other scholars, suggests that the bonds between the
black elite and poor blacks have been so frayed that the increasing number of
high-profile leaders and elected officials rarely represent the interests of poor
blacks.[27]
Dwayne Ashley deems this to be the case.

As you move up the ladder of success, financially and economically, the more the
gap develops between you and the community. That gap is filled with those persons from our race who are middle class. That's a small percentage of us, and I
think that most people would identify with that. They can't always understand

some of the challenges that people face on a day-to-day basis, like the poverty issues. Many of us never experienced the dire levels of poverty that past generations
have seen. Many in [the post–civil rights] generations were born into black middle-
class lives, where they didn't ever experience any of those issues. They haven't seen
family members of that generation who are poor.

Are the children of the civil rights generation, such as Ashley, likely to identify
more with (that is, feel closer to) the white middle class or more with working-
class and poor blacks in terms of values, behaviors, and attitudes? Of the twenty-
nine individuals to whom this question was posed, fourteen identified with
whites, seven identified some values and lifestyles that made them feel closer to
both the white middle class and black working class, eight identified with the
working class, and only one person identified with poor blacks. Interestingly,
Kevin Powell was that individual.

I am like Langston Hughes. It is where I come from. My mama and my whole family are Geechies. I did a speech in Missouri for the Missouri Black Caucus. After
it was over, they asked me where I wanted to go. And I told them I wanted to go
to the hood, where there were juke joints. I like to be where regular folks are, with
no airs, and no shame in how loud they talk, or how hard they laugh, how much
they may cry or get angry. There are no inhibitions whatsoever. Now, do I like the
finer things of life? Absolutely, I like nice restaurants, nice hotels, and I like to
travel. But at the end of the day, I still see the world with working-class eyes, and
at the end of the day I can't claim to be successful or part of any elite group like
the Talented Tenth if I can't bring all of my homeboys or homegirls with me.

Members of the Talented Thirty who came from a working-class background
were also more likely to identify with or feel closer to that class. But when Ashley responded to the question, he stated, "I would say closer to middle-class
whites. Well, I think that my values, based upon the way that my family raised
us, are much more aligned with mainstream America. I think the challenges that
we are faced with economically, that is, many families in our community, I don't
directly identify with some of those challenges. I am more aligned economically
with middle-class whites." This question produced a myriad of conflicted responses among the Talented Thirty who came primarily from lower-middle-class
to middle-class backgrounds, unlike the Talented One Hundred, a significant
number of whom came from the working-class backgrounds and rarely identified with whites. Moreover, they were more likely to have, as Dwayne Ashley
mentioned, relatives who were inextricably linked to poverty. Hence, individuals of the civil rights generation were more likely to see those they knew personally as having a commitment to help lift as they climbed the ladder. Do the
Talented Thirty feel similarly or differently? The data suggest a mixed picture.
Jameka Whitten, a twenty-eight-year-old project manager for the African
American segment at Bank of America, believes, "You have a social responsibility to your community, and however you define that community is up to the in-

dividual. To me, it means that I am going to mentor teenagers, talk to children, and give back when I can." Her consciousness of the collective was shaped by a brief bout with homelessness during her formative years, and her friends then were different from her current circle of acquaintances and friends from more af-fluent social backgrounds. "I did not grow up in a very wealthy household. I won't say I was impoverished, but I was exposed to a different side. So I can appreciate things, and I can appreciate people not being given all of the opportunities and not being able to take advantage of them. If you never had to do without, then you don't understand why you need to help others." Whitten has observed that when privileged blacks of her generation do assist others, it is similar to mission-aries entering a foreign territory.

> I have seen that even with my college friends. I was on the lower end of the eco-nomic spectrum at Northwestern. And the interesting thing seemed to be that everyone was going to go into Chicago and work with the underprivileged pro-grams. It was as if the [children] were the "other." I saw myself as just hanging out with the kids to share and to teach. Those children were the same as me only in a different place. Those [students] who were in the same boat that I was, they treated the children the same as I did.

Journalist Debra J. Dickenson, in *The End of Blackness*, noted that many children of wealthy blacks have no connection with poor black communities, so to reconnect their children to the "hood," she alludes to black camps, where parents pay to have their children spend time in urban communities to get in touch with their blackness.[28]

To Give or Not to Give

While group mobility and individual mobility are intertwined for some of the Talented Thirty, for others they are not. Lisa Boykins is one who does not make such a distinction. It is her belief that "To whom much is given, much is expected."

> We all, as human beings, have some obligation to give back in some way, and I'm not saying that you have to work in the soup kitchens. But people give back by con-tributing money and time, and some people find other unique ways to make a dif-ference. I do think that those blacks who have the opportunity to go to college, to go to graduate school, to be professional, or to achieve at least what society defines as success should be able to do something to help black people, whether they are young black people, people who are your peers, or some way to give something back. But again, that's a very individual decision, and I certainly don't condemn those who don't see any obligation, or feel that just because they're black, they have to go out and save the world. I think it's just a way to appreciate your success even more and to feel better about it when you do something or that we have an obligation to leave the world a little bit better than we found it, so that our being here has made some kind of a difference.

Boykins knows so many committed black professionals who care deeply about issues that impact less fortunate people of color, such as social justice issues and access to education. "I think that there're very many lifelong committed people. There are some professional people whose attitude is 'Hey, I got mine and you get yours. I don't owe any particular obligation to anyone else. I had to work hard for mine. So don't blame me if you don't have any opportunities.'"

Leke Adeyiga, like others of the Talented Thirty, feels that being a role model is one way of giving back.

> You do have some responsibility to give back in a way by being a positive person— almost a role model. At the same time, I don't believe that anyone should be given a handout. Nothing should be given for free, and everyone eventually is going to have to find his own way. The only person who is going to look out for you is you. Sometimes, it feels like black people feel that they are entitled to something. That's not necessarily true. I don't believe anybody is really entitled to anything. You have to go out and get what you want. You're going to have to put in your work and then you can get a scholarship at most institutions, but if you don't put in the work, if you don't study and make the grades, you're not going to be there too long. You may get a job for many reasons, but if you can't do the job, you're going to be gone. I can't appreciate the apathy when people feel they are entitled to something.

Christopher Robinson posits that "people give in their own ways. Everyone has different motivations and different ways to satisfy their lives, and to many people giving back is part of that. But I have a hard time believing that all African Americans desire to give back to their communities. We are living great lives and being positive role models out in the community. I believe that is giving back. One important aspect of that is to have both parents raise your family and provide an atmosphere that is loving and kind and to teach the kids what is important, so when they grow up, they can be contributing members to the community and not pulling it down."

Although some African Americans of her generation are not as willing to assist the less privileged, Whitten has observed that they are more disposed to share with those who have similar cultural capital. "There is a lot of networking going on between blacks. I'll tell you what happened when I came to the [Bank of America]. I was in graduate school, so I came into the bank doing contract work. I was sitting in the background watching everyone, and they were looking at me with a jaundiced eye. It wasn't until people found out what school I went to [Northwestern University] that they started networking and being a little bit more open and invited me to [functions], which actually helped me get the position I am in now." If she had been a secretary, she indicated, "My colleagues would not have likely assisted me. It wasn't until I let it slip where I went to school that things changed a bit."

Ways of Giving Back

Besides being a role model, through the institution of higher education, Debra White, Lee Jones, and Damario Solomon-Simmons have found ways to
close the class divide. After working at IBM for over fifteen years, Debra
White, vice provost for technology at Hampton University, says, "We all want
to feel that a contribution is being made," so she has found a way to give back
by sharing her technological skills and talents with Hampton University, a
prestigious HBCU. Under her leadership in the field of technology, the institution has been listed among the one hundred most wired campuses by Yahoo,
and according to a 2003 survey conducted by the *Princeton Review*, it was
listed number six among the most connected campuses in the country. Says
White,

> I can't describe it, but that very first graduation I attended, I sat there and looked
> at all those beautiful black faces and I knew that I had made a contribution to their
> lives, and it was a tremendous feeling. We can never feel that we have arrived, be-
> cause the students need to know that when they leave this institution they need to
> feel that they are leaving a university that is second to none. That's what I strive for.
> And when I interview people for a job, if they don't have that passion for young
> people, then they are not ready to carry on the mission of this institution. So it's
> very, very important to me to be at a historically black institution. I have never be-
> fore been in one; I was always in an environment where I was made to feel that I
> had to work four times harder just to get to stage one.

Lee Jones, associate dean for academic affairs and instruction at Florida State
University, strongly adheres to the notion that black professors play a critical role
as scholar activist and community builders. The mission of his national organization, Brothers of the Academy, is to link gown and town. Likewise, Damario
Solomon-Simmons, a twenty-seven-year-old assistant professor of law at the University of Oklahoma, established the African American student-athlete network,
a mentoring program, while in law school. Its purpose is to maintain a communal
bond and establish an academic, athletic, political, cultural, and social support
system for student athletes of African American descent.

Yasmin Shiraz is the founder and publisher of *Mad Rhythms*, a hip-hop magazine, and author of *The Blueprint for My Girls*. She uses her insights and entrepreneurial skills to motivate college students to become entrepreneurs.
Moreover, through her speaking tours, she assists and motivates young, poor urban black females to navigate through the difficult terrain of coming of age in
America. She uses rap and rhythm and blues stars as a way to connect with
young females, always being careful to point out that the process of becoming
successful requires hard work, intelligent decision making, and being personally
responsible. "I often use education and good decision making in helping a young
person understand how their favorite celebrities handle their life," says Shiraz.

Olu Brown says the essence of his "ministry is to individuals who are poor." Yet, his "ministry would also go to middle-class individuals across the color lines." His ministerial plan includes a partnership with various institutions and organizations in black communities.

> I believe that I have been called to rebuild communities and lives therein. This is how I differ from a lot of my peers. I believe that my calling is to bring together the gap between megachurches and megaghettos. We have megachurches right in the heart of some of the worst black communities. It seems to me that if I can grow a church, which means to me growth economically and in membership, and the people who are drawn to me are suffering, I haven't built a good ministry. It seems I have raped my community economically. I want to build communities. How is it that the church can form joint relationships between entrepreneurs, developers, constructors, the academic community, realtors, private investors, and existing communities? How can the church rebuild a community and create a cycle of wealth and a cycle of ownership for the generation behind us to buy, so that we can maintain what we do today? We have to move outside our churches and rebuild, not so that churches can become wealthy landlords, but [so] that the church can reinvest in retail strips and housing properties, so that we can rebuild our areas.

In closing the class divide, Brown admits his dilemma in choosing a type of community in which he would like to purchase home, because he feels it, too, makes a political statement. "If I am going to help people in the struggle, I need to live in the struggle, and to live outside the community, people would somehow dilute what I say or what I feel and how much certain individuals would allow me to help them. Because I can understand that they would say, 'Look, you're trying to change where we are, but you're not living where we are.' I struggle with that in myself right now, so my wife and I have decided to buy a house in a community where we would live in the struggle."

Like Olu Brown, Kevin Powell feels, "My life calling is to be a servant for the people. Money, fame, personal achievement, and all that mean very little to me when pain and suffering is still real on this planet. I am interested in the powerless becoming powerful. That's what I'm about. I'm a leader. I am clear about that now. And I don't mean that in an arrogant way; as the ministers say, you just know what your calling is," says Kevin Powell. One of his current callings is galvanizing thousands of black men, women, and youths across the country to confront sexism in black communities through his State of Black Men Tour. These consciousness-raising town hall meetings and workshops are held in black churches around the nation to deconstruct black manhood away from patriarchy and violence as manifested in the hip-hop generation and the older generation. As a leader, Powell wants to bridge the gap of race, class, and gender, as well as the generational divide in this nation.

NOTES

1. Using a purposive sample, I interviewed thirty high-achieving black men and women, mostly by telephone, in 2004. They are referred to collectively as the Talented Thirty. These individuals represent diverse occupations and regions of the country. The interviews lasted approximately one and one-half hours each. All individuals gave me permission to use their names except one. This change contrasts sharply with previous interviewees, the Talented One Hundred, most of whom used assumed names. Since so few of the Talented One Hundred were employed at that time in high-status positions, they feared some reprisal for speaking so candidly.

2. See Charles Pete T. Banner, *The Fruits of Integration: The Black Middle Class Ideology and Culture, 1960–1990* (Jackson: University Press of Mississippi, 1994).

3. For discussion of the issues of integration and desegregation, see Sheryll Cashin, *The Failure of Integration: How Race and Class Undermine America's Dream* (New York: Perseus Publishing, 2004); Derrick Bell, *Silent Covenants: Brown v. Board of Education and the Unfulfilled Hopes for Racial Reform* (Oxford: Oxford University Press, 2004); Charles Ogletree Jr., *All Deliberate Speed: Reflections on the First Half-Century of Brown v. Board of Education* (New York: Norton and Company, 2004).

4. Andrew Billingsley, *Climbing Jacob's Ladder: The Enduring Legacy of African American Families* (New York: Simon and Schuster, 1993). Also see M. Belinda Tucker and Claudia Mitchell-Kernan, eds., *The Decline in Marriage among African Americans* (New York: Russell Sage Foundation, 1995); Robert B. Hill, *The Struggles of African American Families: Twenty-five Years Later* (Lanham, MD: University Press of America, 1999). For discussion of changes in the black family see Lois Benjamin, *Three Black Generations at the Crossroads: Community, Culture, and Consciousness* (Chicago: Burnham Press, 2000).

5. PSEA, Leadership for Public Education, "Status of the American Public School Teacher," http://www.HeyTeach.org/ht (accessed August 28, 2004).

6. PSEA, "Status," 2.

7. John J. Macionis, *Sociology* (Upper Saddle River, NJ: Pearson Prentice-Hall, 2005), 277.

8. Facts & Figures, "Minorities," *State of Working America 2004/2005*, Washington Economic Policy, 2, www.epinet.org (accessed September 14, 2004).

9. William B. Harvey, *Minorities in Higher Education, The Twentieth Annual Status Report, 2002/2003*, Washington, DC: American Council on Education, 3.

10. Joyce Ladner, *The Ties That Bind: Timeless Values for African American Families* (New York: John Wiley and Sons, 1998).

11. Ladner, *Ties*. For discussion of changing black values, see Benjamin, *Three Black Generations*; Robert B. Hill, *Strengths of Black Families*; Andrew Billingsley, *Climbing Jacob's Ladder*; Harriette Pipes McAdoo, *Black Families* (Thousand Oaks, CA: Sage, 1997).

12. John Blake, *Children of the Movement* (Chicago: Lawrence Hill Books, 2004).

13. Kevin Powell, *Who's Gonna Take the Weight?: Manhood, Race, and Power in America* (New York: Three River Press, 2003).

14. See Benjamin, *Three Black Generations*.

15. Lawrence D. Bobo, "Racial Attitudes and Relations at the Close of the Twentieth Century," in Neil Smelser, William Julius Wilson, and Faith Mitchell, eds., *In America: Racial Trends and Their Consequences*. Vol. I. (Washington, DC: National Academy

Press, 2001). See also Eduardo Bonilla-Silva, *White Supremacy and Racism in the Post–Civil Rights Era* (New York: Lynne Rienner, 2001).

16. Thomas M. Shapiro, *The Hidden Cost of Being African American: How Wealth Perpetuates Inequality* (Oxford: Oxford University Press, 2004).

17. Robert Blauner, "Talking Past Each Other: Black and White Languages of Race," *American Prospects*, no. 10 (Summer 1992): 57–58.

18. Blauner, "Talking," 58.

19. David A. Bositis, *Blacks and the 2004 Republican National Convention* (Joint Center for Political and Economic Studies, Washington, DC: 2004).

20. John Sibley Butler, *Entrepreneurship and Self-Help Among Black Americans: A Reconsideration of Race and Economics* (New York: State University of New York Press, 1991).

21. See James E. Blackwell, *The Black Community: Diversity and Unity* (New York: Harper and Row, 1985); Henry Louis Gates Jr., *America Behind the Color Line* (New York: Time-Warner, 2004).

22. Facts and Figures, "Minorities," *State of Working America, 2004–2005*, Washington Economic Policy, 2, www.epinet.org (accessed September 15, 2004); see also Gates, *America Behind the Color Line*.

23. Jacqueline M. Moore, *Leading the Race: The Transformation of the Black Elite in the Nation's Capitol, 1820–1920.* (Charlottesville and London: University Press of Virginia, 1999).

24. Moore, *Leading*, 214.

25. Julia Winch, *Philadelphia's Black Elite: Activism, Accommodation, and the Struggle for Autonomy, 1787–1848* (Philadelphia: Temple University Press, 1988).

26. Mary Patillo-McCoy, *Black Picket Fences: Privilege and Peril among the Black Middle Class* (Chicago: University of Chicago Press, 1999).

27. William Lyne, "No Accident: From Black Power to Black Box Office," *African American Review,* 34, no. 1 (2000).

28. Debra J. Dickinson, *The End of Blackness: Returning the Souls of Black Folk to Their Rightful Owners* (New York: Pantheon Books, 2004).

SUMMARY

Over one hundred years ago at the dawn of the twentieth century, W. E. B. Du Bois forewarned, as previously noted, that "the problem of the twentieth century is the problem of the color line." During the latter part of the twentieth century, William Julius Wilson's book, *The Declining Significance of Race*, fueled the academic and public debate that class was becoming more important than race in affecting the life chances of the day-to-day existence of African Americans. But other scholars refuted that assertion, maintaining that the face of race and racism is still significant in shaping the life experiences of people of African descent. Though mutable in its manifestations, racism is still a permanent feature of this society.

Wilson was writing at the time when the civil rights movement, along with the public policy priority of equal opportunity, had given numerous blacks a foothold on the ladder of success. Hence, by all objective indicators, blacks were moving economically, socially, and politically into mainstream America in unprecedented numbers. Despite stories of their objective achievements, the black elite had untold accounts of the subjective side of success in their encounters with covert and overt racism. My study focused on what it meant to be a marginal black elite living between two worlds of class and race in the post–civil rights era in the twilight of the twentieth century. Through the personal lived portraits of one hundred of the most privileged African Americans, referred to as the Talented One Hundred, this work documented that, in spite of their educational and economic accomplishments, race emerged as a central theme in their lives. Although the color line is eased, no matter how much wealth, power, and prestige the Talented One Hundred have, it is not erased.

The black professionals of the civil rights generation who came of age in the overly racist cauldron of America understood the ethos of collective struggle as essential for group mobility.

In the new chapter, "The Color Line in the Twenty-First Century: Generational Differences," the Talented Thirty, members of the generations who were born or came of age in a multiracial and multiethnic milieu of the post–civil rights era, do not fully grasp the depth of racism in this country. As a result of integration, the trepidations that previous generations of the Talented One Hundred had about the loss of racial identity, heritage, and history in their children are more observable in the generations of the Talented Thirty. They appear to be developing more of a class orientation than a racial orientation. Not having a collective memory of the racial struggle for civil rights in the sixties or the context for understanding it, they have developed a greater naïveté about racism and have accepted the dominant group's myth of meritocracy. Moreover, along with the previous generation's failure to tell the story of the struggle of resistance and resiliency, the changing black familial and communal structure and the economic and global changes that affect all segments of society have impacted the formation of a collective consciousness in blacks. In general, the post–civil rights generations' values are centered more in the dominant cultural values of materialism and economic success than the ethos of collective effort and uplift. Their worldview and values negate the strong racial consciousness that is necessary for group progress. It is evident in the widening economic, social, and spatial gap between the have-nots and post–civil rights generations; the gap between generations; and the gap between genders. Hence, the post–civil rights generations experience even more psychic conflict than the civil rights generations. If racism, though mutable in its forms, is a permanent feature of this society, what do these expanding gaps mean for the future group mobility of the race? Unless a mechanism is put in place to teach our history and lessons of struggle to the next generation, the issue of the twenty-first century is not only the color line, but the dividing lines of class, gender, and generation within black America.

SELECTED BIBLIOGRAPHY

Adams, Kathrynn. "Aspects of Social Context as Determinants of Black Women's Resistance to Challenge." *Journal of Social Issues*, 39, no. 3 (1983): 69–78.

Adorno, T. W., et al. *The Authoritarian Personality*. New York: Harper, 1950.

Aldridge, Delores P. "Black Females: Is the Excitement Enough?" In LaFrances Rodgers-Rose, ed., *The Black Woman*. Beverly Hills, CA: Sage, 1980.

———. *Focusing: Black Male-Female Relationship*, 2nd ed. Chicago: Third World Press, 1995.

Aldridge, Delores P., and Willa Hemmons, "The Structural Components of Violence in Black Male-Female Relationships." *Journal of Human Behavior in the Social Environment*, 4, no. 4 (2001): 209–226.

Alsop, Ronald. "Middle-Class Blacks Worry about Slipping, Still Face Racial Bias." *Wall Street Journal*, November 3, 1980.

Andrews, Gavin C., Christopher Tennant, Daphne M. Hewson, and George E. Vaillant. "Life Event Stress, Social Support, Coping Style, and Risk of Psychological Impairment." *Journal of Nervous and Mental Disease*, 166 (1978): 297–316.

Armah, Ayi Kwei. "Fanon: The Awakener." *Negro Digest*, October 1969.

Asaanti, Molefi Kemet. *The Afrocentric Idea*. Philadelphia: Temple University Press, 1987.

———. *Afocentricity and Knowledge*. Trenton: African World Press, 1990.

Askenasy, Alexander R., Bruce P. Dohrenwend, and Barbara S. Dohrenwend. "Some Effects of Social Class and Ethnic Group Membership on Judgments of the Magnitude of Stressful Life Events: A Research Note." *Journal of Health and Social Behavior*, 18 (1977): 432–439.

Azibo, Daudi Ajani Ya. "Perceived Attractiveness and the Black Personality." *Western Journal of Black Studies*, 7, no. 4 (1983): 229–238.

Back, Kurt, and Ida Harper Simpson. "The Dilemma of the Negro Professional." *Journal of Social Issues*, 20 (1964): 60–71.

Bandura, Albert. "Self-Efficacy Mechanism in Human Agency." *American Psychologist*, 37 (1982): 122–147.

Banner, Charles Pete T. *The Fruits of Integration: The Black Middle Class Ideology and Culture, 1960–1990*. Jackson: University of Mississippi Press, 1994.

Bell, Derrick. *Silent Covenants: Brown v. Board of Education and the Unfulfilled Hopes for Racial Reform*. Oxford: Oxford University Press, 2004.

Bell, Michael J. *The World from Brown's Lounge: An Ethnography of Black Middle-Class Play*. Urbana: University of Illinois Press, 1983.

Benjamin, Lois. "Black Women Achievers: An Isolated Elite." *Sociological Inquiry*, 52 (1982): 141–151.

———. *Three Black Generations at the Crossroads: Community, Culture, and Consciousness*. Chicago: Burnham Press, 2000.

Billingsley, Andrew. *Black Families in White America*. Englewood Cliffs, NJ: Prentice-Hall, 1968.

———. *Climbing Jacob's Ladder: The Enduring Legacy of African American Families*. New York: Simon and Schuster, 1993.

Birmingham, Stephen. *Certain People: America's Black Elite*. Boston: Little, Brown, 1977.

"Black Plight, Race or Class?" *New York Times Magazine*, June 27, 1980.

Blackwell, James. *The Black Community: Diversity and Unity*. New York: Harper and Row, 1985.

———. *Mainstreaming Outsiders: The Production of Black Professionals*. Dix Hills, NY: General Hall, 1981.

Blackwell, James, and Philip Hart. *Cities, Suburbs, and Blacks*. Dix Hills, NY: General Hall, 1982.

Blake, John. *Children of the Movement*. Chicago: Lawrence Hill Books, 2004.

Blauner, Robert. *Black Lives, White Lives: Three Decades of Race Relations in America*. Berkeley: University of California Press, 1989.

———. *Racial Oppression in America*. New York: Harper and Row, 1972.

———. "Talking Past Each Other: Black and White Languages of Race." *American Prospects*, no. 10 (Summer 1992): 55–64.

Bobo, Lawrence D. "Racial Attitudes and Relations at the Close of the Twentieth Century." In Neil Smelser, William Julius Wilson, and Faithe Mitchell, eds., *In America: Racial Trends and Their Consequences*, Vol. 2. Washington, DC: National Academy Press, 2001.

Bonilla-Silva, Eduardo. *White Supremacy and Racism in the Post–Civil Rights Era*. New York: Lynne Rienner, 2001.

Bositis, David A. *Blacks and the 2004 Republican National Convention*. Washington, DC: Joint Center for Political and Economic Studies, 2004.

Bowser, Benjamin P., and Raymond G. Hunt, eds. *Impacts of Racism on White Americans*. Beverly Hills, CA: Sage, 1981.

Brashler, William. "The Black Middle Class: Making It." *New York Times Magazine*, December 3, 1978.

Brown, Diane R., and Verna M. Keith, eds. *In and Out of Our Right Minds: The Mental Health of African American Women*. New York: Columbia University Press, 2003.

Bulhan, Hussein Abdilahi. *Frantz Fanon and the Psychology of Oppression*. New York: Plenum Press, 1985.

Butler, John Sibley. *Entrepreneurship and Self-Help among Black Americans: A Reconsideration of Race and Economics*. New York: State University of New York Press, 1991.

Campbell, Bebe Moore. "To Be Black, Gifted, and Alone." *Savvy*, December 1984: 67–74.

Cannon, Mildred S., and Ben Z. Locke. "Being Black Is Detrimental to One's Mental Health: Myth or Reality?" *Phylon*, 38 (1977): 408–428.

Carmichael, Stokeley, and Charles V. Hamilton. *Black Power: The Politics of Liberation*. New York: Vintage Books, 1967.

Cashin, Sheryll. *The Failure of Integration: How Race and Class Undermine America's Dream*. New York: Perseus Publishing, 2004.

Cheatham, Harold E., and James B. Stewart, eds. *Black Families: Interdisciplinary Perspectives*. New Brunswick, NJ: Transaction, 1990.

Chimenzie, Amuzie. "Theories of Black Culture." *Western Journal of Black Studies*, 7 (1983): 216–228.

Cobb, Sidney. "Social Support as a Moderator of Life Stress." *Psychosomatic Medicine*, 38 (1976): 300–314.

Cole, Johnnetta Betsch, and Beverly Guy Sheftall. *Gender Talk: The Struggle for Women's Equality in African American Communities*. New York: Ballantine Books, 2003.

Coles, Robert. *Children of Crisis*. New York: Dell, 1967.

Collins, Sharon. "The Making of the Black Middle Class." *Social Problems*, 30, no. 4 (1983): 370–382.

Collins, Sharon M. *Black Corporate Executives: The Making and Breaking of a Black Middle Class*. Philadelphia: Temple University, 1997.

Comer, James P. *Beyond Black and White*. New York: Quadrangle Books, 1972.

Cones-Edwards. Alice F., and Jeanne Spurlock, eds. *Black Families in Crisis: The Middle Class*. New York: Brunner/Mazel, 1988.

Cortz, Dan. "The Negro Middle Class." *Fortune*, November 1966.

Cose, Ellis. *The Rage of a Privileged Class*. New York: HarperCollins, 1993.

Cross, William E., Jr. "Black Family and Black Identity: A Literature Review." *Western Journal of Black Studies*, 2 (1978): 111–124.

Cruse, Harold. *The Crisis of the Negro Intellectual*. New York: William Morrow, 1967.

Dates, Jannette L., and William Barlow, eds. *Split Image: African Americans in the Mass Media*. Washington, DC: Howard University Press, 1990.

Davis, Allison, and John Dollard. *Children of Bondage*. Washington, DC: American Council on Education, 1940.

Davis, Angela Y. *Women, Race, and Class*. New York: Vintage Books, 1983.

Davis, George, and Glegg Watson. *Black Life in Corporate America: Swimming in the Mainstream*. Garden City, NY: Anchor Doubleday, 1982.

Davis, Robert. "A Demographic Analysis of Suicide." In Lawrence Gary, ed., *Black Men*. Beverly Hills, CA: Sage, 1981.

Delaney, Paul. "Middle-Class Gains Create Tension in Black Community." *New York Times*, February 28, 1978.

Dennis, Ruth E. "Social Stress and Mortality among Non-White Males." *Phylon*, 38 (1977): 315–328.

Dickinson, Debra J. *The End of Blackness: Returning the Souls of Black Folk to Their Rightful Owners*. New York: Pantheon Books, 2004.

Dohrenwend, Barbara S., and Bruce P. Dohrenwend. "Class and Race as Related Sources of Stress." In S. Levine and N. A. Storch, eds., *Social Stress*. Chicago: University of Chicago Press, 1970.

Dohrenwend, Bruce P. "The Social-Psychological Nature of Stress: A Framework of Causal Inquiry." *Journal of Abnormal Psychology*, 62 (1961): 294–302.

Dohrenwend, Bruce P., and Barbara S. Dohrenwend. *Social Status and Psychological Disorder: A Causal Inquiry*. New York: Wiley, 1969.

Dovidio, John F., and Samuel L. Gaertner, eds. *Prejudice, Discrimination, and Racism*. Orlando, FL: Academic Press, 1986.

Du Bois, W. E. B. *The Souls of Black Folk*. New York: Fawcett, 1961.

———. "The Talented Tenth: Memorial Address." *The Boule Journal*, 15 (1948): 3–13.

Eaton, William E. "Life Events, Social Supports and Psychiatric Symptoms: A Re-Analysis of the New Haven Data." *Journal of Health and Social Behavior*, 19 (1978): 230–234.

Edwards, Audrey S., and Craig K. Polite, *Children of the Dream: The Psychology of Black Success*. New York: Doubleday, 1992.

Eisenberg, Bernard. "Kelly Miller: The Negro Leader as a Marginal Man." *Journal of Negro History*, 45 (1960): 182–197.

Elam, Julia C., ed. *Blacks on White Campuses: Proceedings of a Special NAFEO Seminar*. Lanham, MD: University Press of America, 1983.

Ellison, Ralph. *Invisible Man*. New York: New American Library, 1952.

Ensel, W. M. "Social Support, Stressful Life Events, and Illness: A Model and Empirical Test." *Journal of Health and Social Behavior*, 20 (1979): 108–119.

Essed, Philomena. *Understanding Everyday Racism*. Newberry Park, CA: Sage, 1991.

Facts and Figures, "Minorities," *State of Working America*, 2004–2005. www.epinet.org (accessed September 1, 2004).

Fanon, Frantz. *Black Skin, White Masks*. New York: Grove Press, 1967.

Farley, Reynolds. *Blacks and Whites: Narrowing the Gap?* Cambridge, MA: Harvard University Press, 1984.

Feagin, Joe R., and Clairece Booher Feagin. *Discrimination American Style: Institutional Racism and Sexism*, 2nd ed. Melbourne, FL: Robert E. Krieger, 1986.

Feagin, Joe R., and Melvin P. Sikes. *Living with Racism: The Black Middle-Class Experience*. Boston: Beacon Press, 1994.

Featherman, David L., and Robert M. Hauser. *Opportunity and Change*. New York: Academic Press, 1978.

Fernandez, John P. *Black Managers in White Corporations*. New York: Wiley, 1975.

———. *Racism and Sexism in Corporate Life*. Lexington, MA: D.C. Heath, 1981.

Fleming, Jacqueline. *Blacks in College*. San Francisco: Jossey-Bass, 1984.

Fogel, Robert W., and Stanley L. Engerman. *Time on the Cross: The Economics of American Negro Slavery*. 2 vols. Boston: Little, Brown, 1974.

Franklin, Clyde W., II. *Men and Society*. Chicago: Nelson-Hall, 1988.

———. *The Changing Definition of Masculinity*. New York: Plenum Press, 1984.

Franklin, John Hope, ed. *Color and Race*. Boston: Beacon Press, 1968.

Frazier, E. Franklin. *Black Bourgeoisie*. New York: Free Press, 1957.

———. *The Negro Church in America*, 5th ed. New York: Schocken Books, 1964.

———. *The Negro Family in Chicago*. Chicago: University of Chicago Press, 1932.

———. *The Negro Family in the United States*. Chicago: University of Chicago Press, 1939.

Freeman, Richard B. "Decline of Labor Market Discrimination and Economic Analysis." *American Economic Review*, 63 (1973): 280–286.

———. *Black Elite: The New Market for Highly Educated Black Americans*. New York: McGraw-Hill, 1976.

Fullwood, Sam, III. *Waking from the Dream: My Life in the Black Middle Class*. New York: Doubleday, 1996.

Gary, Lawrence, ed. *Black Men*. Beverly Hills, CA: Sage, 1981.

Gates, Henry Louis, Jr. *America behind the Color Line*. New York: Time-Warner, 2004.

Glaser, Barney G., and Anselm L. Strauss. *The Discovery of Grounded Theory*. Chicago: Aldine, 1967.

Glazer, Nathan. *Affirmative Discrimination: Ethnic Inequality and Public Policy*. New York: Basic Books, 1975.

Graham, Lawrence Otis. *Our Kind of People*. New York: HarperCollins, 1999.

Grier, William H., and Price M. Cobbs. *Black Rage*. New York: Basic Books, 1968.

Gurin, Patricia, and Edgar Epps. *Black Consciousness, Identity, and Achievement*. New York: Wiley, 1975.

Hare, Nathan. *Black Anglo-Saxons*. London: Macmillan, 1970.

Harper, Frederick D., and Marvin P. Dawkins, "Alcohol Abuse in the Black Community." *The Black Scholar*, April 1977, 23–31.

Harvey, William R. *Minorities in Higher Education, The Twelfth Annual Status Report, 2002–2003*. Washington, DC: American Council on Education.

Henry, Charles P. "Ebony Elite: America's Most Influential Blacks." *Phylon*, 42 (June 1981): 120–132.

Hernton, Calvin C. *Sex and Racism in America*. New York: Grove Press, 1965.

Hill, Robert B. *Economic Policies and Black Progress: Myths and Realities*. Washington, DC: National Urban League, 1981.

———. *The Strengths of Black Families*. New York: Emerson Hall, 1972.

———. *The Struggles of African American Families: Twenty-five Years Later*. Lanham, MD: University Press of America, 1999.

Hochschild, Adam. *The Mirror at Midnight: A South African Journey*. New York: Viking Penguin, 1990.

Hooks, Bell. *Ain't I a Woman?* Boston: South End Press, 1981.

Hoose, Phillip M. *Necessities: Racial Barriers in American Sports*. New York: Random House, 1989.

Hopson, Darlene Powell, and Derek S. Hopson. *Different and Wonderful: Raising Black Children in a Race-Conscious Society*. New York: Prentice-Hall, 1990.

Hughes, Everett. "Dilemmas and Contradictions of Status." In Lewis Coser and Bernard Rosenberg, eds. *Sociological Theory*. New York: Macmillan, 1976.

Jeffries and Associates. *Facts about Blacks*. Los Angeles, 1982–1983.

Johnson, James Weldon. *The Autobiography of an Ex–Coloured Man*. New York: Knopf, 1912.

Jones, Edward W. "Black Managers: The Dream Deferred." *Harvard Business Review* (May–June 1986): 84–93.

Jones, James. *Prejudice and Racism*. Reading, PA: Addison-Wesley, 1972.

Kanter, Rosabeth Moss. *Men and Women of the Corporation*. New York: Basic Books, 1977.

Kardiner, Abram, and Lionel Ovesey. *The Mark of Oppression*. Cleveland, OH: World, 1962.

Kilson, Martin. "Black Bourgeoisie Revisited." *Dissent*, Winter 1983, 85–96.

King, Michael. "Ambition on Trial." *Black Enterprise*, February 1990, 132–138.

Kochman, Thomas. *Black and White Styles in Conflict*. Chicago: University of Chicago Press, 1981.

Lacayo, Richard. "Between Two Worlds." *Time*, March 13, 1989, 58–68.

Ladner, Joyce. *The Ties That Bind: Timeless Values for African American Families*. New York: John Wiley and Sons, Inc., 1998.

Landry, Bart. *The New Black Middle Class*. Berkeley: University of California Press, 1987.

LaRocco, James M., James S. House, and John R. P. French, Jr. "Social Support, Occupational Stress and Health." *Journal of Health and Social Behavior*, 21 (1980): 202–218.

Lawrence-Lightfoot, Sara. *I've Known Rivers: Lives of Loss and Liberation*. Reading: MA: Addison-Wesley Publishers, 1994.

Lazear, Edward. "The Narrowing of Black-White Wage Differentials Is Illusory." *American Economic Review*, 69 (1979): 553–564.

Lyne, William. "No Accident: From Black Power to Black Box Office." *African American Review*, 34, no. 1 (2000): 39–59.

Macionis, John J. *Sociology*. Upper Saddle River, NJ: Pearson Prentice-Hall, 2005.

Mann, Coramae Richey, and Lance H. Selva. "The Sexualization of Racism: The Black as Rapist and White Justice." *Western Journal of Black Studies*, 3, no. 3 (Fall 1979): 168–177.

Marable, Manning. "Beyond the Race-Class Dilemma." *The Nation*, April 11, 1981, 417–436.

———. "Reaganism, Racism and Reaction: Black Political Realignment in the 1980s." *The Black Scholar*, 13, no. 6 (Fall 1982): 2–15.

Martin, Michael T., and Howard Cohen. "Race and Class Consciousness: A Critique of the Marxist Concept of Race Relations." *Western Journal of Black Studies*, 4, no. 2 (1980): 84–91.

McAdoo, Harriette P. *Black Families*. Beverly Hills, CA: Sage, 1981.

———. "Black Kinship." *Psychology Today*, May 1979.

———. "Factors Related to Stability in Upwardly Mobile Black Families." *Journal of Marriage and the Family*, 40 (1978): 761–776.

McAllister, Bill. "The Plight of Young Men in America." *Washington Post, National Weekly Bulletin*, February 12–18, 1990, 6.

McBride, David, and Monroe H. Little. "The Afro American Elite, 1930–1940: A Historical and Statistical Profile." *Phylon*, 42 (June 1981): 105–119.

Memmi, Albert. *The Colonizer and the Colonized*. Boston: Beacon Press, 1967.

Mills, C. Wright. The Sociological Imagination. New York: Oxford University, 1959.

Moore, Jacqueline M. *Leading the Race: The Transformation of the Black Elite to the Nation's Capitol, 1820–1920*. Charlottesville and London: University Press of Virginia, 1999.

Moss, Alfred A., Jr. *The American Negro Academy: Voice of the Talented Tenth*. Baton Rouge: Louisiana State University Press, 1981.

Moss, James A. "Brashler's Black Middle Class: A Rebuttal." *The Crisis*, 86, no. 7 (August–September 1979): 307–310.

Moynihan, Daniel Patrick. "The Schism in Black America." *Public Interest*, 27 (Spring 1972): 3–24.

Myrdal, Gunnar. *An American Dilemma: The Negro Problem and Modern Democracy*. New York: Harper, 1944.

Nobles, W. W. "African Root and American Fruit: The Black Family." *Journal of Social and Behavioral Sciences*, 20 (1974): 52–63.

Ogletree, Charles, Jr. *All Deliberate Speed: Reflections on the First Half-Century of Brown v. Board of Education*. New York: Norton and Company, 2004.

Onwubu, Chukwuemeka. "The Intellectual Foundations of Racism." *Western Journal of Black Studies*, 3 (1979): 157–167.

Park, Robert Ezra. *Race and Culture*. New York: Free Press, 1950.

Patillo-McCoy, Mary. *Black Picket Fences: Privilege and Peril Among the Black Middle Class*. Chicago: University of Chicago Press, 1999.

Phinney, Jean S., and Mary Jane Rotheram, eds. *Children's Ethnic Socialization: Pluralism and Development*. Newbury Park, CA: Sage, 1987.

Pinderhughes, Elaine. "Afro American Families and the Victim System." In M. Mc-Goldrich, J. K. Pearce, and J. Giordano, eds., *Ethnicity and Family Therapy*. New York: Guilford Press, 1982.

Pinkney, Alphonso. *The Myth of Black Progress*. Cambridge: Cambridge University Press, 1984.

Pitt-Rivers, Julian. "Race, Color, and Class in Central America and the Andes." In John Hope Franklin, ed., *Color and Race*. Boston: Beacon Press, 1968, 264–281.

Piven, Frances Fox, and Richard A. Cloward. *Regulating the Poor*. New York: Pantheon Books, 1971.

Pomer, Marshall I. "Labor Market Structure, Intragenerational Mobility, and Discrimination: Black Male Advancement out of Low-Paying Occupations, 1962–1973." *American Sociological Review*, 51 (1986): 650–659.

Porter, Judith R., and Robert E. Washington. "Black Identity and Self-Esteem: A Review of Studies of Black Self-Concept, 1968–1978." In Alex Inkeles, James Coleman, and Ralph H. Turner, eds. *Annual Review of Sociology*, 15 (1979): 53–74.

Powell, Kevin. *Who's Gonna Take the Weight?: Manhood, Race, and Power in America*. New York: Three River Press, 2003.

PSEA. Hey Teach.org. Leadership for Public Education. "Status of the American Public School Teacher." www.heyteach.org/ht.teacher-state.com (accessed August 28, 2004).

Reddy, Maureen T. *Crossing the Color Line: Race, Parenting, and Culture*. New Brunswick, NJ: Rutgers University Press, 1994.

Reed, Adolph, Jr. *Class Notes: Posing as Politics and Other Thoughts on the American Scene*. New York: The New Press, 2000.

Reich, Michael. *Racial Inequality: A Political-Economic Analysis*. Princeton, NJ: Princeton University Press, 1981.

Robinson, Randall. *The Debt: What America Owes to Blacks*. New York: Dutton, 2000.

Rosenberg, M., and R. Simmons. *Black and White Self-Esteem: The Urban School Child*. Washington, DC: American Sociological Association, 1971.

Rosenthal, Robert, and Lenore Jacobson. "Teacher Expectations for the Disadvantaged." *Scientific American*, 218 (April 1968): 19–23.

Sampson, William A., and Vera Milam. "The Intraracial Attitudes of the Black Middle Class: Have They Changed?" *Social Problems*, 23 (1975): 153–165.

Seeman, Melvin. "On the Meaning of Alienation." *American Sociological Review*, 24 (1959): 784–790.

Seeman, Melvin, and Teresa Seeman. "Health Behavior and Personal Autonomy: A Longitudinal Study of the Sense of Control in Illness." *Journal of Health and Social Behavior*, 24 (1983): 144–160.

Seyle, Hans. "Stress and Disease." *Science*, 122 (1955): 625–631.

———. *The Stress of Life*. New York: McGraw-Hill, 1956.

Shapiro, Thomas M. *The Hidden Cost of Being African American: How Wealth Perpetuates Inequality*. Oxford: Oxford University Press, 2004.

Shimkin, Demitri B., Edith M. Shimkin, and Dennis A. Frate. *The Extended Family in Black Societies*. Chicago: Aldine, 1978.

Singley, Bernestine, ed. *When Race Becomes Real*. Chicago: Lawrence Hill Books, 2002.

Snyder, Mark. "Self-fulfilling Stereotypes." *Psychology Today*, July 1982, 60–68.

Stack, Carol. *All Our Kin: Strategies for Survival in a Black Community*. New York: Harper and Row, 1974.

Staples, Robert. "The Black Family Revisited: A Review and a Preview." *Journal of Social and Behavioral Sciences*, 20 (1974): 65–78.

Stember, Charles Herbert. *Sexual Racism: The Emotional Barrier to an Integrated Society*. New York: Elsevier, 1976.

Stewart, James B. "Psychic Duality of Afro Americans in the Novels of W. E. B. Du Bois." *Phylon*, 44 (1983): 93–107.

Stonequist, Everett V. *The Marginal Man: A Study in Personality and Culture Conflict*. New York: Russell and Russell, 1961.

Tatum, Beverly Daniel. *Life in Isolation: Black Families Living in a Predominantly White Community*. Doctoral Dissertation, University of Michigan, 1984.

Taylor, Robert Joseph, James S. Jackson, and Linda M. Chatters, eds. *Family Life in Black America*. Thousand Oaks, CA: Sage, 1997.

Thompson, Daniel C. *A Black Elite*. Westport, CT: Greenwood Press, 1986.

Thornton, Jeannye. "The Quiet Power of America's Black Elite." *U.S. News and World Report*, April 6, 1981.

Tucker, M. Belinda, and Claudia Mitchell-Kernan, eds. *The Decline in Marriage among African Americans*. New York: Russell Sage Foundation, 1995.

Valentine, Charles A. *Culture and Poverty: Critique and Counter-Proposals*. Chicago: University of Chicago Press, 1968.

Watley, William D. *Roots of Resistance: The Nonviolent Ethic of Martin Luther King, Jr.* Valley Forge, PA: Judson Press, 1985.

Wattenberg, Ben J., and Richard M. Scammon. "Black Progress and Liberal Rhetoric." *Commentary*, 55 (1973): 35–44.

Weiss, Leonard, and Jeffery Williamson. "Black Education, Earnings and Interregional Migration: Some New Evidence." *American Economic Review*, 62 (1972): 372–383.

Welch, Finis. "Black-White Differences in Return to Schooling." *American Economic Review*, 63 (1973): 893–907.

Wideman, John Edgar. *Brothers and Keepers*. New York: Holt, Rinehart and Winston, 1984.

Wilkins, Roger. *A Man's Life, An Autobiography*. New York: Simon and Schuster, 1982.

Williams, Melvin D. *The Black Experience in Middle-Class America: Social Hierarchy and Behavioral Biology*. Lewiston, NY: The Edwin Mellon Press, 2001.

Williams, Robin M., Jr. *American Society: A Sociological Interpretation*, 3rd ed. New York: Knopf, 1970.

Willie, Charles Vert. *Caste and Class Controversy*. Dix Hills, NY: General Hall, 1979.

———. *Five Black Scholars: An Analysis of Family Life, Education and Career*. Lanham, MD: University Press of America, 1986.

———. *A New Look at Black Families*. Dix Hills, NY: General Hall, 1981.

Wilson, William Julius. *The Declining Significance of Race*. Chicago: University of Chicago Press, 1978.

———. *Power, Racism and Privilege*. New York: Macmillan, 1973.

———. *The Truly Disadvantaged: The Inner City, the Underclass, and Public Policy*. Chicago: University of Chicago Press, 1987.

Winch, Julia. *Philadelphia's Black Elite: Activism, Accommodation, and the Struggle for Autonomy, 1787–1848*. Philadelphia: Temple University Press, 1988.

Woodward, Michael D. "Ideological Response to Alterations in the Structure of Oppression: Reverse Discrimination, the Current Racial Ideology in the U.S." *Western Journal of Black Studies*, 6, no. 3 (1982): 166–173.

Wright, Richard. "The Ethics of Living Jim Crow: An Autobiographical Sketch." In Abraham Chapman, ed., *Black Voices*. New York: New American Library, 1968.

INDEX

Adeyiga, Leke, 272, 287
affirmative action: ending quotas in, 268;
  and racial progress in education and
  jobs, 255; retooling of, 264;
  retrenchment in commitment to, 84;
  and U. S. Supreme Court, 33; and
  veto of 1990 Civil Rights Bill, 33
African Methodist Episcopal Church,
  176–77
Afrocentric perspectives: amelioration of
  blacks in the, 209; balancing concerns
  of, 128; blacks' biculturalism, 13; as a
  buffer to racism, 78; cultural diversity
  and whites in, 221; rejection of, 124;
  sounds and elements of music in, 118
Aida, 273
AIDS, 262
Akpan, Kufra (pseudonym), 146
Akron, Ohio, 167
Albany State College, 181
Albert, Prince (pseudonym), 11, 218
Aldridge, Delores, 184n4
Allen, Lisa (pseudonym), 73, 111–12
American Council on Education, 173n26
American Federation of Musicians, 25
*American Journal of Economics and
  Sociology*, 121

American Sociological Association, xiii
Anderson, Marian, 153
Angelou, Maya, 183
Annan, Kofi, 251
Antioch Baptist Church, xxii
Aramis, Leo (pseudonym), 15, 25, 53, 58,
  66, 94–95, 133, 152, 194–95, 219
ART News, 201–02
Ashley, Dwayne, 235, 237, 268–70, 284–85
Atlanta, Georgia, 121, 234, 239, 278
Atlanta Journal-Constitution, 70–71
Atlanta Symphony, 173
Attucks, Crispus, 226
Atwater, Lee, 222
Aunt Jemima, 160n2, 232

Babbitt, Warner (pseudonym), 20, 38, 68,
  92–93, 150, 194, 206
Baker, Keith, 274–76
Baldwin, James, xiv, 120
Bandura, Albert, 186n10
Bank of America, 285, 287
Barnes, Jefferson (pseudonym), 7, 18–19,
  26, 29, 56, 70, 109, 192–94
Basie, Count, 25
Beatrice International Corporation, 97
Bell, Derrick, 226n3, 254

ABOUT THE AUTHOR

Lois Benjamin is Endowed University Professor of Sociology at Hampton University. She is the author of *The Black Elite: Facing the Color Line in the Twilight of the Twentieth Century*; *Three Black Generations at the Crossroads: Community, Culture, and Consciousness*; and *Dreaming No Small Dreams: William R. Harvey's Visionary Leadership*, and editor of *Black Women in the Academy: Promises and Perils*, among other works.